Alexander Winchell

Reconciliation of Science and Religion

Alexander Winchell

Reconciliation of Science and Religion

ISBN/EAN: 9783337035853

Printed in Europe, USA, Canada, Australia, Japan

Cover: Foto ©Lupo / pixelio.de

More available books at **www.hansebooks.com**

RECONCILIATION

OF

SCIENCE AND RELIGION.

By ALEXANDER WINCHELL, LL.D.,
AUTHOR OF "SKETCHES OF CREATION," "THE DOCTRINE OF EVOLUTION," ETC.

NEW YORK:
HARPER & BROTHERS, PUBLISHERS,

PREFACE.

WHAT are the natural relations between science and religion? This is a question in which the public has recently manifested a profound interest. On this question a layman and scientific teacher here ventures to offer some thoughts. The discussions in which they are embodied aim to reach some of the ground-principles on which the propositions of science and religion alike rest. They enunciate a substantial basis of harmony and mutual helpfulness, and disclose a promised synthesis of deepest scientific conviction and simplest religious faith.

The author has written as he felt profoundly moved to write. He has made a record of honest and earnest convictions; and he flatters himself that his record nowhere betrays the spirit of a partisan.

The thoughts here presented, though lying generally beyond the peculiar domain of natural science, have mingled themselves, by a spontaneous interplay of the psychic powers, with the dry details and lofty generalizations of strict science. They have been to the author a source of enjoyment, consolation, and assurance; and he hopes they may serve to ballast the faith of others who have less opportunity for reflection, but who must, nevertheless, if they think at all, grapple with the inevitable and irrepressible questions which arise concerning the validity of their religious beliefs.

The author has always entertained an unshaken conviction of the unity of all truth; and the right of all our faculties to activity within limits prescribed or sanctioned by reason. He holds that reason is the only criterion of truth, and must even arbitrate the claims of an assumed divine revelation. He holds that the religious faculties are not cognitive, but must be served by the cognitive faculties; and that, while religion is spontaneous, its grounds may be subjected to a rational authentication. He holds that though history has shown that ecclesiastical systems unavoidably incorporate more or less of secular beliefs, such beliefs are not thereby rendered sacred or essentially religious, and ought to be modified or rejected according to improved knowledge. He holds that the religious sentiments are co-ordinate with the knowing faculties, and demand from intellect the concession of a free field for exercise; and that the phenomena of their activity, in the history of our race, afford the data for an inductive philosophy of religion. He holds that systems of science and religion approved alike by rational tests must be found in complete harmony; and that the so-called conflict between science and religion is partly fictitious, and partly a conflict between science and religious or ecclesiastical systems; while the conflict with these systems reduces itself to a collision between the effete science which they embody and the results of more advanced science.

The author likewise maintains that natural science, while affording the data from which philosophy may reason to Deity, does not, in its proper character, reach a theistic issue; and that, as a corollary, exclusive physicists and biologists incur the danger of overlooking the importance of supramaterial and transcendental verities. He composes himself, nevertheless, in the conviction that no scientist, however exclusive, can possibly reach a firm datum which is not on one of the many lines of ratiocinative thought converging toward Deity and supramaterial realities. He holds that this position is confirmed by the bearing of the profoundest results of recent science and the declarations of its votaries.

In these and other dominant ideas pervading the various

papers assembled in this volume is the disclosure of their essential unity and continuity. In reference to the much mooted scientific question of the derivative origin of species, the reader will detect indications of a growing faith. A certain class of proofs has been accumulating at a rapid rate; and the author's present conviction is that the doctrine of the derivation of species should be accepted; and that the most tenable theory of the causes, instrumentalities, and conditions of this derivation is that propounded, in 1868, by Professor Edward D. Cope.

These papers do not represent the author's conception of a complete and systematic discussion of the relations of science and religion. They are rather separate outcroppings of the results of much study and reflection, which have correlated and consolidated themselves in the author's mind in a broad underlying system of which no opportunity has presented itself, as yet, for a fuller exposition.

In the hope that the reasonings here presented may prove helpful to young persons engaged in the serious work of fashioning a system of belief; corrective or strengthening to those whose beliefs are matured; and admonitory to such as have left their beliefs to the control of circumstance—to student, theologian, and scientist—to all thoughtful persons, this essay toward a good understanding between religion and science is cordially and respectfully submitted.

THE AUTHOR.

ANN ARBOR, MICHIGAN, *March*, 1877.

CONTENTS.

THE INTERACTION OF THE RELIGIOUS AND THE INTELLECTUAL FACULTIES.

	PAGE
I. NECESSARY RELATIONS OF THE RELIGIOUS AND THE INTELLECTUAL FACULTIES	17
The Religious Nature of Man	19
Rise and Progress of Scientific Thought	26
Results of the Interaction of these Forces	36
II. INTERACTION OF THE RELIGIOUS AND THE INTELLECTUAL FACULTIES IN ORIENTAL AND GRECIAN PSYCHIC HISTORY	41
Laws of the Interaction of Faith and Intellect	42
Egyptian Psychic History	46
Chinese Psychic History	48
Indian Psychic History	51
Grecian Psychic History	55
III. INTERACTION OF THE RELIGIOUS AND THE INTELLECTUAL FACULTIES IN CHRISTIAN PSYCHIC HISTORY	66
First Psychic Cycle	66
Second Psychic Cycle	72
Third Psychic Cycle	74
Fourth Psychic Cycle	82

SCIENCE AND PHILOSOPHY IN RELIGION.

IV. THE DOCTRINE OF CAUSALITY	87
1. Original Causation	87
The Notion of Causality	93
Implications of the Notion of Causality	101
V. THE DOCTRINE OF CAUSALITY—*Continued*	120
2. Causal Intermediation	120
Relation of Matter and Force	120
Philosophy of Cause applied to Science	134

	PAGE
VI. THE DOCTRINE OF INTENTIONALITY	150
Correlation in general	151
Homology	156
Fundamental Types of Animals	159
The Vertebrate Type	161
Membral Homologies of Vertebrates	166
Cosmical Homologies	174
VII. REASON FOR THE FAITH	178
Causes of Skepticism	179
I. The Necessity of some Religion is upon us	184
II. Constructive or Deductive Theistic Belief	191
III. Deductions from the Theistic Proposition	199
IV. The Christian Scriptures answer to these Deductions	203
V. Our Reasonable Duty	205
VIII. THE CONFLICTS OF FAITH	207
The Human Powers engaged	208
The Reconciliation	222
IX. THOUGHTS ON CAUSALITY, WITH REFERENCES TO PHASES OF RECENT SCIENCE	231
X. IS GOD COGNIZABLE BY REASON?	266
The Achievements of Greek Philosophy	271
Forms of Theistic Proof	292
XI. GOD IN THE WORLD	304

GLIMPSES OF THE EVIDENCE, À POSTERIORI.

XII. GOD AND RELIGION IN NATURE.—ILLUSTRATIONS OF INTENTIONALITY AND OF OTHER BIBLICAL TEACHING	333
I. Manifestations of Power in Creation	333
II. Manifestations of Intelligence in Creation	337
III. Manifestations of Beneficence in Creation	342
IV. The Unity of Creation	347
V. The Religious Nature of Man	351
VI. Genesis and Geology	356
VII. The Mosaic Deluge	363
VIII. Man in the Light of Geology	368
IX. The Finiteness of the Existing Order of Things	373
X. The Bible in the Light of Nature	379
INDEX	385

ANALYSES.

I.

NECESSARY RELATIONS OF INTELLECT AND FAITH.

Rights on both sides of the existing conflict, 18.—The controversy one of long duration, 18.—Two imperishable forces antagonizing each other, 19.—Religious characteristics innate in man. Proofs, 19-20.—The significance of a power native to humanity, 20-21.—Generalizations from religious phenomena, 21-22.—What is the religious nature? Answer, 22.—Contrasted with the cognitive powers, 22-23.—What is conscience? Answer, 24.—It is not a knowing faculty, 24.—Sway of the religious feelings in the life of man, 26.—Incipient antagonism of the knowing faculties, 26.—Continued aggressions of the knowing faculties, 27.—Fidelity of religious faith to its objects, 27.—Science seeks only truth—true divinity, 28.—Faith accepts what science offers as true, and hallows it, 28.—Faith tends to conservatism; science to progress; hence strife, 29.—Distinction betweeen pure religious faith and its accessories, 29.—The progress of science reforms the accessories, 30.—Alternating ascendency of faith and intellect, 32.—Explanation of the chronic conflict, 32.—Religion necessary to the welfare of science, 33.—Antagonism a universal law in nature, 34.—Faith finds an avowed enemy in the depraved heart of man, 35.—The antagonism of faith and intellect beneficent, 36.—It has purified the religious system, 36.—The constant and the variable factor in religion, 37.—Historical development of the religious system, 37-39.—Imperishability of religion, 39.

II.

ORIENTAL AND GRECIAN PSYCHIC HISTORY.

Periodicity in the dominance of faith and intellect, 41.—Laws of the interaction of faith and intellect, 42-43.—Psychic cycles, 44.—Orbits of faith and intellect, 44.—Psychic epicycles, 45.—Overlapping of phases, 46.—Bifurcation in cyclic movements, 46.—EGYPTIAN PSYCHIC HISTORY: *First Psychic Cycle,* embracing the era of Memphis, 46; *Second Psychic Cycle,* embracing the period of the later monuments, 47; *Third Psychic Cycle* dates from Alexander's conquest, 48; *Fourth Psychic Cycle,* from the conquest by the Arabians, 48.—CHINESE PSYCHIC HISTORY: *First Psychic Cycle* precedes Confucius, 48; *Second Psychic Cycle,* from Confucius to the overthrow of Taoism, 49; *Third Psychic Cycle*, from Wen-ti to the introduction of Buddhism, 49; *Fourth Psychic Cycle*, extending to the present, 50.—INDIAN PSYCHIC HISTORY: *First Psychic Cycle*, Brahmanism, 51; *Second Psychic Cycle*, the Zoroastrian revolt, 52; Return to early simplicity and purity, 52; *Third Psychic Cycle*, the Buddhistic schism, 53; Advancing ceremonialism, 54; Psychic movements among the Hebrews, 55.—GRECIAN PSYCHIC HISTORY: *First Psychic Cycle*, Homeric, 55. *Second Psychic Cycle*, Religious Phase, the Ionics and Pythagoreans, 56; Intellectual Phase, embracing the Eleatics, Atomists, and Sophists, 57-60. *Third Psychic Cycle*, Religious Phase, Socratic, 61; the Eleatics, Hedonists, and Platonists, 61–62; Intellectual Phase, Aristotelians, 63; Stoics, 64; Epicureans, 64-65; Skeptics, 65.

III.

CHRISTIAN PSYCHIC HISTORY.

First Psychic Cycle: Religious Phase, Eclecticism, 66; the New Academy, 66-67; Alexandrian-Jewish learning, 67; Neo-Pythagoreanism, 68; Pythagorizing and Eclectic Platonists, 68; the advent of Christ, 69. Intellectual Phase, the Latin Skeptics, 69; Neo-Platonism, Alexandrian-Roman School, 69-70; Syrian School, 70; Athenian School, 70; Patristicism, 71; Gnosticism, 71.—*Second Psychic Cycle:* Religious Phase, Irenæus, and Tertullian, 72; First Council of Nice, 72. Intellectual reaction in Augustine, 73.—*Third Psychic Cycle:* Scholasticism, 74. Religious Phase, a divorce of philosophy and faith, 74; Erigena, 75; Berengarius, 75; Roscellinus, 75; Abelard, 75; supremacy of ecclesiasticism, 76; influence of Aristotle, 76; Alexander of Hales, Albertus Magnus, Thomas Aquinas, Occam, Pomponatius, 76; Luther and the Reformation, 76-77. Intellectual Phase, Roger Bacon, 78; Eckart, 78; "revival of letters," 78; Saracenic influence, 78; poetry, 79; discovery, 79; science in Italy, 79-80; intellect begins to encroach, 80; Macchiavelli, Montaigne, Hobbes, Descartes, 80; Bayle, Locke, Berkeley, Hartley, and Priestley, 80-81; French philosophy, 81; growing arrogance of intellect, 81-82; culmination in the French Revolution, 82.—*Fourth Psychic Cycle:* Religious Phase, 82; Intellectual Phase dawns with the "Vestiges of Creation," 83; Omens of the future, 83-84; a Synthesis of Thought and Faith, 84.

IV.

ORIGINAL CAUSALITY.

Retrospect, 87-89.—False theories of the origin of religious feeling, 89-90.—Intuition as one origin of the theistic concept, 90.—Extravagances of the "Mystics," 91.—Our notion of cause, 93.—Denial of causation, 93.—Theories of the origin of the idea of causality, 93-94.—Its origin not empirical, 94.—Only one species of cause, 96.—The use of the term "cause" in science, 96.—Aristotelian and Scholastic "causes," 96.—"Secondary" causation, 98.—Implies a first cause, 98.—Notion of primordial causality, 99; *Causation implies the existence of real cause*, 101.—Chance, 101.—Doctrine of the atomists not wholly atheistic, 102.—*Causative reality antecedent to all its effects*, 103-104.—*Causality implies correlative subjectivity and objectivity*, 104.—In creative causality the objectivity is potential, 104.—*The causal efficiency must possess consciousness*, 105.—*There must be a conception of a non-existent effect*, 106.—Limitations of foreknowledge, 106.—*The consciousness of the principle of causality must arise*, 107.—*Necessity of motive*, 107-108.—Final cause in the history of speculation, 108-109.—Modern opinion becoming unanimous in its defense, 110.—Its recognition a necessity of thought, 110.—Limitations of our knowledge of final causes, 112-113.—Inconsequential assertions against final causes: Haeckel, 113-114.—The question of final causes one of "common sense," not of science, 115.—*A contingency or condition may be discerned*, 115.—*The influence of the contingency must be cognized*, 116.—*Desire necessary to exertion of efficiency*, 116.—*Causality implies intention*, 116.—*Causality implies volition*, 117.—Evolution of the concept of personality, 119.

V.

CAUSAL INTERMEDIATION.

Use of the term "cause," 120.—No causality in matter, 120.—Does force inhere in matter? 120.—The theory implies that all motion is a search for equilibrium, 123.—It implies a running-down of the material system, 123.—The inherent efficiency of matter unthinkable, 124.—Cause must be present in time and space, 125.—Delegated force, 125.—Matter viewed as adynamic, 126.—Matter viewed as the vehicle of primordial force, 126.—The theory implies the subsidence of molecular activities, 126.—Matter viewed as the seat of a force momentarily renewed, 126.—Force viewed as the direct effort of Supreme Will, 127.—Objections to doctrine of divine immanence considered, 128.—Matter regarded merely as a manifestation of force, 128.—The attributes of matter inhere in some substance, 128.—Relation of the dynamic theory to pantheism, 130.—Theism not an outcome of science, 131.—Divine immanence compatible with law and order, 132.—Intelligence the best explanation of order, 133.—Relations of science and philosophy, 134.—No induction possible without deduction, 135.—What is implied in mediate causation, 137.—The principle of *congruity*, 138.—The principles of *efficiency* and *conditionality*, 139.—ERRORS IN SCIENTIFIC REASONING: 1. *Subjective mistaken for objective condition, and then mistaken for efficiency*, 140; influence of the "environment," 141.—2. *Subjective condition mistaken for efficiency*, 142; evolution a subjective condition, 143.—3. *Objective condition mistaken for efficiency*, 145; connection of mind and matter, 145; "unconscious cerebration," 145.—4. *Instrumental relation mistaken for cause*, 146; heredity an instrument, not a cause, 147.—5. *Cause arbitrarily assumed*, 148.—" Organized experiences," 148.—Origin of life, 149.

VI.

THE DOCTRINE OF INTENTIONALITY.

Intentionality implied in causality, 150.—And in correlations of plan, 151.—Influence upon the mind of facts of intentionality, 151.—Mechanical correlations, 153.—Modal correlations, 153-154.—Evolution the method of methods, 154.—Homology, 156.—Psychic teleology, 156.—Heredity an instrument of homology, 157.—*Fundamental types in the animal kingdom*, 159.—Persistent in all situations, 159.—In all ages of the world, 161.— *The Vertebrate type considered more particularly*, 161-163.—Modifications of the archetype, 163-164.—Its unfolding in geological time, 164.—Interpretation of the facts, 165.—Centripetal and centrifugal forces in organization, 165.—Theism of the hypothesis of derivation of species, 166.— *Homologies of appendages of vertebrates*, 166-168.—Intelligence the only explanation of correlations between environment and organs, 168.—*Homologies in the limbs of extinct American horses*, 168-169.—Two possible explanations, 170.—Defects in the evidence for derivation, 172-173.— *Homology in the field of cosmical existence*, 174-176.—Continuity of cosmical phenomena, 176.

VII.

REASON FOR THE FAITH.

Reason must be satisfied in accepting revelation, 179.—*Causes of skepticism:* 1. The evil heart, 179; 2. The progress of knowledge, 179; 3. Rash generalizations in the interest of unbelief, 181; 4. Cowardice of believers, 182; 5. Mistaking non-essentials for fundamentals in theology, 183.— The reasons can not be defended, 183.—I. *The necessity of some Religion is upon us*, 184.—The great religions of the world, 185-187.—Inductive generalizations from them, 187.—Religious nature of savages, 188-189.— And of prehistoric peoples, 190.—Religion a universal phenomenon of humanity, 190.—II. *Constructive or Deductive Theistic Belief*, 191.—Primary Beliefs, 191.—They are spontaneous and native, 193.—They are authoritative, 193.—Proofs, in brief, 193-195.—Testimony of Fichte, 195-196.—Résumé of the argument, 196.—Fundamental intuitions of deductive theism: Real Being, 196.—Causality, 197.—Intelligence, 197-198.— Ethicality, 198.—Goodness, 198-199.—Integration of the intuitions, 199. —III. *Deductions from the Theistic Proposition:* Peace and rejoicing, 199-200.—The "unthinkable" and unsearchable known, 200.—Grounds to expect a verbal revelation, 201-203.—Its relations to humanity, 203.— IV. *The Christian Scriptures answer to our Deductions,* 203.—Tinctured to some extent by the imperfections of the human medium, 203.—But still in consonance with the universal system of truth, 204.—V. *Our reasonable Duty*, 205-206.

VIII.

THE CONFLICTS OF FAITH.

The historical controversy, 207-208.—The human powers in action, 208.—The religious sentiment, 208.—Authority of both classes of intuitions, 209.—Their different spheres, 210.—Intellect progressive, religion conservative, 212.—Faith clings fondly to its objects, 212.—Intellect pronounces some of them unreal, 212.—Action and reaction of these forces, 212.—Exemplifications strew the pathway of history, 213.—Protagoras, Aristarchus, Socrates, Christ, 213-214.— The conflict in reality between old science and new, 215.—Periodicity in the interactions, 215.—The conflict in the scholastic ages, 216.—Slavery of intellect, 216.—Two orders of truth supposed, 217.—Rebellion of Luther, 217.—The emergence of intellectual freedom gradual, 218.—Champions of free thought, 218.—The other swing of the pendulum, 218.—Champions of doubt, 218.—Readjustment after the French Revolution, 218-219.— Later strides of intellect, 219.—Doting faith still inclines to hug her idols, 220.—And science is again shaming her for it, 220.—Résumé, 221.—Another renaissance of faith, 221.—The prospect of reconciliation, 221-222.—The Biblical record of creation, 222.—The antiquity of the human race, 223.—Its unity, 223-224.—The origin of species, 224.—The origin of life, 224-225.—Mental physiology, 225-226.—Rights of the religious nature, 227.—Religion not a human enactment, 227.—Religion in schools, 227-228.—The reconciliation to be sought, 229.—An incident from Casalis, 229-230.

IX.

THOUGHTS ON CAUSALITY.

Utterances of Tyndall, Huxley, and Haeckel, 231.—Synopsis of Professor Tyndall's Belfast address, 232.—His "materialism" not atheistic, nor pantheistic, nor antispiritualistic, 237.—He recognizes the rights of the religious nature, 237.—Phenomena and realities, 240.—Science and philosophy defined, 240.—Chance considered as the explanation of an event, 242.—The Lucretian atomic hypothesis, 243.—Increased knowledge discloses mere effect in supposed cause, 243.—Recession of real cause, 244.—Convergence of lines of causation, 245.—Ineradicable belief in primary causation, 245.—Influence of monotheism, 246.—Science does not attain to real causes, 246-247.—Antecedent not necessarily cause, 247.—Inductive and deductive procedures, 248.—Law not efficient, 249.—The law of the "survival of the fittest," 249.—Conditions are not causes, 250-251.—The "environment" only a condition, 251-252.—Consecutiveness not a causal relation, 252.—Principle applied to the hypothesis of derivation of species, 252-254.—"Organically remembered" experiences, 254.—Concomitancy not a causal relation, 255.—"Unconscious cerebration," 255.—

Where is the essential ground of force? 256.—Not in dead matter, 257.—Nor in living matter, 257.—Is force external to matter? 257.—Its seat in supreme intelligent will, 258.—Significance of the position, 258.—Order explained by intelligence, not by its denial, 259.—Force viewed as a "mode of motion," 259-260.—From human will to the all-causative Will, 260.—Different species of force, 261-262.—Analysis of our concept of primary causality, 263-264.

X.

IS GOD COGNIZABLE BY REASON?

Questionings of the age, 267.—All truth belongs to Christianity, 267-268. —Influence of physical surroundings upon human character, 269.—Criticism of various philosophies of religious phenomena, 269-271.—Religion of the ancient Athenians, 271.—I. The idea of God universal, 274.—II. Not an intuition independent of experience, 274.—III. The universe demands a God, 275.—IV. Ideas of the Absolute and Infinite, 276.—Criticism of theories denying the cognoscibility of God by reason, 276.—The Pre-Socratic schools of philosophy, 278.—The Socratic school, 279.—Results of Greek philosophizing, 280.—These appropriated by Christianity, 280.—The preparatory office of Greek philosophy seen: I. *In the field of theistic conceptions*, 282.—1. In weakening the power of polytheism, 282.—2. In formulating the theistic argument, 284.—Forms of the argument, 284.—II. *In the department of ethical ideas*, 286.—III. *In the field of religious sentiment*, 287-289.—Characteristics of Dr. Cocker's work, 290-291.—Modes of theistic proof, 292.—I. The argument from common consent, 292.—II. The argument from direct revelation, 294.—III. The argument from immediate intuition, 294.—IV. The Ætiological argument, 295.—V. The Teleological argument, 296.—VI. The Homological argument, 296. —VII. The Ontological argument, 297.—Ontological concepts, 297-299.—All arguments rest back on the Ontological, 299.—Kant's critique of the theistic proofs, 269.—Possible predicates of the Unknowable, 300.—Are truths necessary to reason, absolute? 300-301.—The direct way of Leibnitz, 302.—The last datum of reason, simple belief, 302-303.—Sacred sanction of the primary beliefs, 303.

XI.

GOD IN THE WORD.

Mistaken method of propagating religious truth, 304-305.—Various grounds of belief, 306.—Beliefs possess various degrees of validity, 307.—Influence of religious feelings on belief, 308.—Men differ in warmth of religious feeling, 308.—Religious belief as begotten by authority, 309.—Different teaching required where the religious predisposition is wanting, 310.—Influence of allegations of conflict between religion and science, 310.

—A painful dilemma, 312.—Character of Dr. Cocker's work, 312-314.—
What is the First Principle of all things? 314.—Cocker's views of time
and space, 315.—A criticism, 316.—Author's view of time and space,
317-318.—Beginning and end of the cosmical order, 319.—The highest
law of the universe a teleological idea, 320.—Parallelism of Genesis and
geology, 320-322.—A criticism, 320-322.—Author's opinion on Gen. i., 2,
321-322.—Theories of the relation of God to the world, 322.—The world
not self-sustaining, 323.—Immanent relation of God to the world, 324.—
God's method with mankind, 325.—Prayer considered from the stand-point
of science, 325-326.—The moral government of the world, 326-328.—
Cocker's view of conscience, 326.—The author's view of conscience, 327.—
General definition of religion, 328.—Freedom of the will, 328.—A speci-
men of successful authorship, 328-329.

XII.

GOD AND RELIGION IN NATURE.

I. MANIFESTATIONS OF POWER IN CREATION, 333.—Power in the uplifting
of mountains, 333.—The strain of the rocks revealed in the quarry, 324.—
The power which molds and moves a planet, 334.—This power the attribute of some *being*, 335.—Vastness of the sun's distance, 336.—Cosmical
power exerted through measureless space, 336.—II. MANIFESTATIONS OF IN-
TELLIGENCE IN CREATION, 337.—Accidental and purposive arrangements contrasted, 337-338.—The hand a purposive arrangement, 338.—Its internal
mechanism consummate, 339.—The plan of anterior appendages, 340-341.
—The reflection of intelligence which is infinite, 342.—III. MANIFESTA-
TIONS OF BENEFICENCE IN CREATION, 342.—The vast and varied utilities of
coal, 342.—All pre-arranged for man while yet in futurity, 343.—Vastness
of the preparations, 344.—The intelligibility of nature a beneficent provision, 345.—Having relations only to man, 346.—Man in his constitution provided with happiness, 346.—IV. THE UNITY OF CREATION, 347.—Vastness
of the empire of gravitation, 348.—Gravitation is will acting according to
method, 348.—Uniformities of the solar system, 348.—Gravity active
among the fixed stars, 349.—Light communicates between them and us,
349.—One substance in earth, and sun, and star, 350.—One common history, 350.—One method, one empire in infinite time as in infinite space,
351.—V. THE RELIGIOUS NATURE OF MAN, 351.—All people devout before
the spectacle of the heavens, 351.—The universal feeling of the divine,
352.—Religious condition of lowest savages, 353.—Religious manifestations of all cultured peoples, 353-354.—The knowledge of God can not
be evaded, 354.—Reason also leads from Nature to God, 354-355.—VI.
"GENESIS" AND GEOLOGY, 356.—Intellectual progress since the date of
King James's translation, 357.—The Biblical account of creation poetical
but truthful, 358.—Some things premised, 358.—Seven successive periods
of geological history, 359-361.—Seven corresponding periods in the sacred

account, 361.—Supplementary note on the particle *eth*, 362.—Note on the interpretation of *yom*, 363.—VII. THE MOSAIC DELUGE, 363.—No geological record of a universal deluge, 363-364.—Extensive emergences of lands in human times, 364.—Geological and traditional evidences of great local deluges, 365.—Chaldean, Chinese, Persian, and Greek traditions, 365-366.—Fijian, American, and Mexican traditions, 366.—Six points of agreement, 367.—The deluge was not universal, 367.—VIII. MAN IN THE LIGHT OF GEOLOGY, 368.—1. He belongs to the last fauna, 367.—2. Man's advent comparatively recent, 369.—Great events within the human period, 369-370.—3. Man's birthplace in the Orient, 370.—Evidence from continental faunas, 371.—Evidence from history and tradition, 371.—4. Man's advent the prophecy of the ages, 372.—5. Man the last term of the organic series, 372-373.—IX. FINITENESS OF THE EXISTING ORDER OF THINGS, 373.— Changes in progress imply a beginning, 374.—And an end, 374.—1. The land wearing out, 374-375.—2. Terrestrial refrigeration impending, 375.—3. Solar refrigeration, 376.—4. Effect of the resisting medium, 377.—The fiery consummation predicted by St. Peter, 378.—X. THE BIBLE IN THE LIGHT OF NATURE, 379.—Résumé, 379-380.—Biblical statements verified by science, 381-382.—The Bible proved truthful must be accepted as a whole, 382.—Antecedent probability of supernatural revelation, 383.—Revelation the recognized response to the want, 383-384.

THE INTERACTION OF THE RELIGIOUS AND THE INTELLECTUAL FACULTIES.

RECONCILIATION

OF

SCIENCE AND RELIGION.

I.

NECESSARY RELATIONS OF THE RELIGIOUS AND THE INTELLECTUAL FACULTIES.

The din of a great controversy sounds in our ears. Men of thought have been summoned to choose their banner, and range themselves upon one side or the other of the line of battle. It is the "conflict" between Religion and Science which has thrown the world into commotion.

It might be expected that I should appear before you in a militant character. I do not. I shall assume the office of a mediator. It may mark a stronger character to love war; but when I see "a house divided against itself," I love peace. I shall be reproached for weakness. We shall hear of somebody "on the fence." Extremists will say I have no opinion, and court the favor of both the combatants. I shall, nevertheless, be brave enough to face *such* dangers; and I shall deliberately incur the risk of *losing* the favor of both combatants by refusing to take sides with either. To be positive is not to be strong; to be dogmatic is not to be brave. To be right is to be both strong and brave. I have a fancy there is some merit in keeping cool while others are excited. It is easier to go with the crowd than to resist it. It pampers our indolence to adopt opinions; but to form opinions is better. Wherever conflict is possible, neither side has all the right, nor all the virtue, nor all the truth. Perpetuated conflict implies imperishable life and vigor on both sides of the line of battle. Conflict imbittered, uncompromising and cruel, implies excited passions and judicial blindness. Conflict arises through a law of existence as broad as society—as broad as nature. Progress is the issue of conflict, in every realm of being. Truth is a structure reared only on the battle-field of contending forces. Conflict is universal. Conflict is beneficent. But progress does not arise out of the extermination of one of the conflicting elements, but out of an arbitration which negatives extravagant claims, brings to light forgotten truths, and settles the contending elements in a temporary equilibrium. The "golden mean" is formed of the genuine metal. . The judicial attitude is not the neutral or apathetic one. I fancy it is regal —honorable to the loftiest intellect—congenial to the purest conscience.

The great "conflict" of our day is between the claims of the religious nature and those of the intellect. On one side is consternation over the supposed encroachments of a hostile science; on the other, exultation over a deliverance from fancied bondage to religious credulity. I shall attempt to show that this consternation is unreasoning and groundless, and this exultation short-sighted and delirious.

Every student of the history of mental activity must have observed that a similar strife has been in existence ever since the dawn of reflective thought. Could we penetrate the prehistoric periods, I am confident it might be traced back to the very cradle of humanity. The religious instincts and the knowing faculties have always regarded each other with jealous eyes. I can not believe that this enduring conflict has no appointed place in the beneficent economy of a superintending Intelligence. I am persuaded it has a profound significance; and it must be that a discovery of it will promote the interests of peace, comity, and truth.

A careful scrutiny of the real forces concerned in this secular controversy shows them to be the religious instincts and perceptions, on the one hand, and the cognitive powers on the other. Each has been resisting the supposed encroachments of the other; and, in resisting, has carried its pretensions beyond its own legitimate territory. I have said that conflict implies a living principle arrayed on each side of the line of battle. I repeat that here are *two living forces*, which must strive in vain to exterminate each other, or even to deprive each other permanently of any of their natural rights. Why, then, are they always at war?

From time immemorial we have heard denials of the religious nature of man. On the one hand, it has been imagined that the importance of Christianity would be aggrandized if it should appear that for all religious knowledge the world is indebted to Jewish and Christian inspiration. It was not perceived that the denial of man's religious intuitions is the extinction of all power of apprehending *any* divine revelation, or becoming the recipient of religious instruction. On the other hand, it has been thought that the importance of Christianity would be diminished if it should appear that no preparation for religious teaching had been made in the plan of human nature. The belief has always been in existence, however, that some form of religious endowment is the characteristic of humanity, in all the conditions of its existence. This belief will be found supported by a great amount and variety of evidence.

1. The *universality of religious belief* and practice among all the peoples of the earth is a fact of the utmost significance. Its importance is enhanced by the fact that it has been combated by the most powerful intellects, and the strength of that array of debasing passions whose interests are alien to all the teachings of religion.

2. The religious nature of man is demonstrated by the prevalence of *vast religious systems*, which have embraced among their adherents four-fifths of all the populations which have ever lived.

3. Man's religious nature is evinced by the fact that nearly all the *poetry* of the world is a clear reflection of it; while all the *philosophy*, either of ancient or modern times, has had for its object to find out the nature of the First Cause, recognized as the centre of all ethical aspirations and the ground of all ethical obligations, or else to unfold the law and order existing in the world as the ordination of the Supreme Will. The collisions between philosophy and religion, either in ancient or modern times, have not involved denials of divine existence and moral relations, but only of a particular mode of relations between God and the world, and between God and man.

4. Man's religious nature is demonstrated by the essentially religious character of certain *observances* among all the savage tribes of the world. It is here that misapprehensions have arisen; but I am prepared to assert, after due examination, that there are not a dozen tribes in existence among whom may not be detected some belief or sentiment of an essentially religious character. It may be very unchristian in its mode of manifestation, but it will be found based on a recognition, more or less clear, of superior creative, controlling existence, to which man owes some sort of allegiance.

5. The existence of a religious nature is indicated by certain *relics of prehistoric times*, which, so far as we can judge, admit of no other than a religious interpretation. Such relics reach back to the remotest epoch of the Stone Age.

I must content myself with indicating these sources of evidence respecting the innate character of our universal religious sentiments. I desire next to remind you of the *significance* of any faculty, sentiment, or susceptibility found to be implanted in the very ground of our being. In the first place, it must be *good*. The whole tenor and purport of Nature's plans teaches that the parts are adjusted for the mutual benefit of each other. In the next place, *it can not be illusory*. There is not an instance in nature of the existence of one correlate and the non-existence of its fellow. The echo implies the real voice. Religious longings imply the reality of their object, as the power of vision implies things visible. Not even are the brutal instincts deceptive. Gratification answers to desire. The insect care which arranges food for offspring still in the egg, and only to be developed months after the death of the mother which arranges it, is no more exempt from deception than humanity's longing for its God, or the individual's cry for divine help. Once establish the innate character of a sentiment, a belief, or intuition, and we trace in it a divine purpose, a divine utterance.

But I dismiss also the discussion of this theme. I have reached convictions, after much study; and my immovable belief has been a source of consolation and calm. I would earnestly commend to every thinker the study of the evidence in support of the existence and authority of innate sentiments, beliefs, and intuitions.

I must pass over, similarly, all discussion of the generalizations induced from the religious phenomena of our race. The following are the grand facts common to the religious faiths of the world:

1. A Supreme Being, the Author of all things in existence.

2. A Revelation of the Supreme Being, either in sensible things or in the intelligence of inspired men.

3. A System of Worship—which is either instinctive and aimless, or intended to propitiate the Deity, and win happiness for the worshiper. This worship consists in the uplifting of devout thoughts, sacrifices, feasts, fasts, prostrations, genuflections, singing, dancing, crossing, and a great number of other practices suited to the intellectual condition of the worshiper.

4. Prayer—the universal cry of humanity in distress.
5. Future existence.
6. Moral responsibility.
7. A system of Future Rewards and Punishments.
8. A Priesthood, charged with the direction of religious ceremonies, and clothed with a special investiture of divine authority and power.

These facts I find to be the constants in the varying faiths of mankind. I will add that two other facts reveal themselves in *most* of the religious systems of the world—both the greater and the less. These are, 1st. A belief in the efficacy of vicarious expiation; 2d. An expectation of a Redeemer. This is hinted in the philosophical writings of Plato and the later Platonists; and was a belief cherished by the Aztecs, as it is by the Pueblos, Mojaves, and various other savage tribes. Faith in a system of divine incarnations, also, is found disseminated through the religions of India, China, Persia, Egypt, and ancient Greece and Rome.

I maintain, from such evidence as I have referred to, that man is endowed with an innate religious nature, which expresses itself universally in a system of outward manifestations. The discussion which I have in view requires that I should point out precisely as possible what this religious nature is. I shall aim to set it in antithesis with the cognitive powers. That their true relations are antithetical is proved by the chronic antagonism which they display.

Should we assert that the religious faculty of man is that which recognizes divine existence, and recognizes religious and moral obligations growing out of human relations to divine existence, we should furnish a current definition, but I think we should fail to discriminate between that which is simply and exclusively ethical and that which falls within the province of the knowing faculties. Recognition implies cognition and reflection. These belong to the other term of the antithesis.

RELIGIOUS FACULTY DEFINED.

Should we assert that the religious faculty is that which *feels* the reality of the divine—the reality of a standard of right, and the duty to conform to it, it might be objected that we relegate religion wholly to the realm of feeling, and thus throw reproach upon its character. Still, I might remind you that a percipient element exists in all feeling, as well as a sensational element in all cognition. When the lowest savage feels a mere sentiment of the supernatural, he has, in truth, a species of cognition of Deity; and when he feels an impulse to refrain from the commission of an atrocious deed, he must possess a perception of the principle of right and the law of duty. Thus, when I speak of the *feeling* of the reality of divine existence, I inclose in the expression that kind and degree of apperception which are implied in all feeling.

This, however, it must be admitted, is not that clear cognition which belongs to the domain of the intellect, which appropriates the facts of the external world, and the inner realm of consciousness; which seizes and interprets the intelligible manifestations of Deity, discusses the ground of moral obligation, and weighs the circumstances which enter into the solution of a moral problem. And yet, so far as I can discern, the *essential nature* of man's religious endowment must be differentiated from this higher cognition. This determination, I think it will appear, exalts the character of religion, exonerates it from a multitude of reproaches, and places it in the position of a controlling or motive power in relation to the intellect. The cognitive faculties bring us into intelligent relations to the cosmos and all knowable existence; the religious faculties prompt to the search after the Author of the cosmos, and the discovery of the relations of visible to invisible existence; they thus reach out beyond the sensible and the fleeting, and through their instrument, intellect, take hold on absolute reality, enduring relations, and future life.

Conscience, which belongs to the group of ethical feelings, is frequently treated as the faculty of moral cognition. Greatly as it would please me to fall in with this idea, I feel compelled to deny to conscience proper the power of discrimination. Discrimination is the judgment that two things cognized are different or incompatible. Now, if cognition and judgment belong to conscience, we must cease throwing the intellectual and the moral powers into different categories. We must admit that power of conscience is measured by strength of intellect. Conscience, I must maintain, is a feeling of the existence of a standard of right, and an accompanying impulse to bring the actions into conformity to the standard. But conscience does not discern that standard. Discernment is an attribute of intellect. Intellect is fallible. Accordingly, the practical standard of one man or one tribe may not be the practical standard of another. But conscience is true to its rule. Whatever is set up as the standard of right, conscience whips its possessor into submission.

We may confuse the subject by speaking of "moral judgments." This expression, however, can only mean a judgment upon a question of right and wrong. If we think conscience pronounces this judgment, we deceive ourselves. The moral criterion is not discovered by conscience, nor cognized by conscience. It is discovered by the reason of humanity, and cognized by the intellect of the individual. We are not to suppose that this deprives us of fixed standards of morality. The voice of humanity gives a consistent utterance. On the fundamental moral and religious questions it never contradicts itself. It is true, that among some of the most degraded tribes, ethical standards are but dimly discerned. Even religious perceptions may be clearer. The conscientious impulse, also, is correspondingly feeble. But Livingstone tells us that among the Hottentots, whose moral perceptions—that is, whose perceptions of the data of moral determinations—were exceedingly perverted, there was still a confession that they really understood the right as white men understood it, and had never entertained different views on those subjects.

It is obvious that conscience, in the restricted sense, acts only in correlation with other powers of the soul. The *reason* of humanity recognizes certain necessary and infallible standards of right and wrong. The *understanding* apprehends relations subsisting between certain acts and these standards, and the *judgment* affirms a compatibility or incompatibility. Now, the conscience, in its essential character, becomes a *wakened sensibility*, inflicting pain in case of an incompatibility, and awaking pleasure if the contemplated act conform to the standard of right recognized in the reason. Now, we may style the whole of this complex operation an act of the conscience; but if so, conscience means, not only a moral sensibility, but also the set of mental activities concerned in the excitement of that sensibility; and then, for the moral sensibility—the only thing which is *sui generis* in the whole series of acts—we have no name whatever. I prefer to restrict the term conscience to the *moral element* of a moral judgment.

Conscience is a constituent of the religious nature of man. There can be no religious nature without a conscience; but conscience in itself does not rise to God. There is a theistic intuition dwelling in the soul, and there are theistic judgments deduced from the myriad phenomena which surround us in nature, and arise within the field of the moral consciousness. It is thus that the being of God stands revealed to us. All men acknowledge it; all men instinctively feel that they stand in relations of dependence and obligation toward that being. This intuition or feeling of God, and this sense of certain relations toward him—this is the essence of the universal religion. Conscience, the companion feeling, prompts to a discharge of duty toward God, as well as toward man. This body of feelings makes up all that is peculiar in the religious nature of man. How infinitely less than a conflict between science and this religion are the narrow contests that have been waged over such dogmas as consubstantiation, the geocentric theory in astronomy, the non-existence of other habitable worlds, the immaculate character of the sun's face, or the scholastic subtleties of homoousianism, homoiousianism, and heterousianism!

The religious feelings sway the life of man with transcendent potency. Until the reflective intellect has been brought into active and continued exercise, they dominate all his judgments and all his acts. The earliest and strongest beliefs of the race are religious ones. The agency of the Unseen Power is recognized in every striking or inexplicable phenomenon; and it is the nature of the religious sentiments to find gratification in every recognition of the presence of their object. An invisible spirit broods in the midnight sky, smiles in the life-inspiring sun, frowns in the dark mountain cliff, or rages in the tempest of lightning and wind.

The development of habits of closer observation and reflection is accompanied by the discovery of certain invariable sequences in the order of physical phenomena. The necessary idea of cause, dwelling in the mind, suggests the existence of a causal relation subsisting between the terms of an invariable sequence. Certain events which, under the influence of the same idea, had been attributed to the direct causation of the Unseen Power, also revealed in the intuitive consciousness, are now accepted as the result of physical causes. This is the first step in the road to science. The very first effort at reasoning upon scientific data, therefore, deprives the religious nature of one of its occasions to recognize the presence of its God. The religious sensibility surrenders this gratification reluctantly and complainingly. It is easy to understand that those individuals in whom intellect is most active, and those in whom the religious sensibility is least susceptible, would be the first to take these infantile steps in science. It is easy to understand that those with intellects less exercised, or religious natures more quickened, would look with a feeling of displeasure, or even of sharp dissent, upon the opinions and consequent practices of their neighbors. The murmur of heresy must have arisen while yet our race was in its Oriental cradle.

But divine causation, thus far, would be removed but one step from visible phenomenon. The soul of man would still recognize divinity in the physical cause occupying the place of invariable antecedent. With the progress of intellect, however, this would be revealed as the invariable sequent of some other physical antecedent; and some of the extraordinary and more striking of nature's phenomena would also be traced to their true physical causes. Religious faith, in the mean time, would cling to its cherished objects; and the strife with progressive and iconoclastic intellect would be perpetuated.

Thus, step by step, religious faith, which casts its hallowing mantle over every object upon which it fixes, finds itself compelled to recede farther and farther into the realm of things and agencies unseen and mysterious; privileged to hug and to venerate only that which abides in the obscurities for the time being unpierced by the rays of science. Its sacred things are torn from it, vulgarized and bandied about from crucible to retort, till the divinity which was in them escapes in gas, or steam, or electricity. It is intelligible that religious faith, which seeks only real divinity, should become jealous of science, which cares only for the reality of divinity. Faith is a blind love, and asks no questions about the worth of its object. Intellect is all eye, and has no heart to be touched by the sorrows of a blighted affection. So Faith recedes, pierced with regrets, suffused with tears, sometimes with stubborn resistance, sometimes after a bitter and prolonged conflict.

But Faith stands true to her God. She never, for a moment, doubts that divinity abides immediately behind the veil. She never falters in her veneration for the things still left to her as revelations of the divine. Disappointed again and again by the substitution of physical causation for her supposed divinity, she feels that divinity certainly exists, and that divinity *must be revealed* in the world. Nor does science seek to strike a blow at this central assurance. Keen as its vision may be, uncompromising as its methods are, its aim is truth; <u>and as no proof has been found of the unreality of the divine,</u> whose image is mirrored in the universal consciousness, the voice of science has never been heard disputing its dominion in the world. On the contrary, philosophy, which builds upon the data disclosed by science, has always started out with the divine existence as its postulate, and has expended its loftiest efforts in seeking for the mode of that existence, and the nature of its relations to man and the world.

In saying this, I hold science and philosophy irresponsible for the indiscretions of some of their devotees. The great calamities of the world have proceeded from the passion or misjudgment of individuals. It must be admitted that individuals from the ranks of science and philosophy, with the perversity and blindness of madmen, have, at intervals, dared to ignore the divinity whose voice, even in their own hearts, they could not silence, and have attempted to rob religious faith completely of its object. Exasperated by the faithful lash of conscience, the *wicked heart* has sometimes driven the intellect to make the rash and fatal declaration that there is no God, no future, no moral tribunal; but the offended and indignant conscience of the nations has rung out its withering reprobation of the blasphemy, and the balance of rights has been momentarily restored.

Religious faith, I have said, hallows and sanctifies all that it can appropriate. This is its nature; this is its excellence. Its essential attitude is to assume the sacredness of divinity clothing every object, every event, every established belief. So far as concerns religious faith in its pure simplicity, every thing exists in direct relation to God. There is no system but religion. There is no knowledge which is not a part of its theology. There is no accepted belief which is not incorporated into its confession. There is nothing secular. Accordingly, when intellect, in the course of time, has attained to certain explanations of physical phenomena, albeit under the perpetual protest of the religious feelings, these feelings, submitting at length, immediately incorporate the new beliefs in the religious creed, and sprinkle the incongruous mass with holy water. Religious faith now discovers, or thinks it discovers, new demonstrations of divine agency in the natural world, and new corroborations of the various articles of its creed.

Meantime science marches onward.[1] It is the law of intellect to accumulate daily something new, and to rise daily to a higher plane of observation. This is the excellence of intellect. Intellect pioneers; intellect piles up her accumulations. Faith conserves and sanctifies what intellect gives her. It is not her office to scrutinize, and assort the true and the false. The disappointment and grief of Faith arise from the unreality and worthlessness of much which she receives from the hands of science. Science is an indefatigable reaper; but how many tares do we find bound up with the wheat! How many exploded theories have left their wrecks along the highway of

---

[1] "Faith is in its nature unchangeable, stationary. Science is in its nature progressive; and eventually a divergence between them, impossible to conceal, must take place. It then becomes the duty of those whose lives have made them familiar with both modes of thought to present modestly, but firmly, their views; to compare the antagonistic pretensions calmly, impartially, philosophically" (Draper, "Conflict of Science and Religion," Preface, p. vii.). But, earlier than Draper, the same ideas were set forth by an English writer of great learning and ability. "Christianity," he says, "being stationary and authoritative, thought progressive and independent, the causes which stimulate the restlessness of the latter interrupt the harmony which ordinarily exists between belief and knowledge, and produce crises, during which religion is re-examined" (Farrar, "A Critical History of Free Thought," p. 12).

time! How many abandoned explanations and beliefs lie scattered by the way-side! These all have been the sacred vessels of religious faith. Every fragment of these exploded systems exhales the perfume of sanctifying incense. Nay, every wreath of incense which has ascended from them—hollow and false as these systems were—has testified to Heaven the fidelity of faith, and proclaimed to man the reality of its object.

Faith has been doomed a hundred times to pluck out the effete constituents of her creed. This is no more true in Christian countries than in those swayed by Pthah, Brahma, Buddha, or Zoroaster, Jove or Mohammed. Faith has never yet been able to refrain from incorporating in her creed current beliefs of an extraneous and necessarily evanescent character. These have embraced contemporary opinions on the institutions of society, on the origin and rights of government, on the figure and age of the earth, on its relation to the heavenly bodies, on the number of planets, and a hundred other subjects which it is the rightful province of science to investigate and determine, but about which faith is wisely created absolutely blind. How often has faith, rasher than the atheism of science, staked the credibility of her entire system upon the truth of an opinion liable to be falsified by the discovery of a fossil bone, or by the color of the solution in a test-tube!([1])

The gravest consequences to the interests of religious faith have arisen from her devotion to effete dogmas of science long

---

([1]) "All religious theories, schemes, and systems," says Tyndall, with a truthfulness which can not be gainsaid, "which embrace notions of cosmogony, or which otherwise reach into the domain of science, must, *in so far as they do this*, submit to the control of science, and relinquish all thought of controlling it" ("Belfast Address," Appletons' ed., p. 94). And, again, "The facts of religious feeling are as certain to me as the facts of physics. But the world, I hold, will have to distinguish between the feeling and its forms, and to vary the latter in accordance with the intellectual condition of the age" (*Ibid.*, Preface, p. xxxiv.).

supposed to be inculcated by texts of revelation. Here the authority of Scripture was added to the sanction of faith's acceptance and adoption; and the struggle to supersede the error was correspondingly stubborn and acrimonious. Interpretations of Scripture long suited to current apprehensions of natural phenomena have been unwisely insisted upon, long after science had rendered her final verdict. The inexpediency of hazarding the credibility of a pretended revelation on the truth of an opinion not demonstrated true, is something which seems to me self-evident; but the Church has had the infatuation to run that hazard in a score of cases where the opinion was not even presumptively true—nay, where it had been already demonstrated untrue—as if she had madly resolved to commit the crime of *felo-de-se*. But yet revelation stands; and religious faith remains as deeply rooted as ever. Could there be a stronger proof of the indestructibility of both? The religious system, invincible to the assaults of its enemies, has withstood equally the suicidal daggers of its friends.

But religious faith, sooner or later, has receded from most of its preposterous claims. Loaded and encumbered as it has been by the *débris* of exploded science or effete philosophy, or stale ecclesiasticism, or conventional dogmas, or absurd ceremonials, or preposterous assumptions, or heathenish superstitions, it has had to undergo many mortifications, many ablutions, many rehabilitations; and it comes now out of the conflicts of the ages unchanged in its fidelity to God and duty, possessed of all the fervor of its youth animating the sturdy strength of its maturity, and clothed in cleaner and purer accessories of investiture than it has ever possessed in all the history of our race.

It appears from a cursory acquaintance with the facts, that faith and science have lived in perpetual strife. Faith has been wont to appropriate whatever has fallen within her reach, and science has declared, from time to time, that certain of her claims were indefensible; and she has been compelled to recede. Now, intellect, in the flush of victory, has pushed its antagonist to the verge of tyranny, and the religious instincts have revolted and regained their rights. Now, in turn, religious faith has maintained an ascendency over human opinion, and has even given laws to science and philosophy. Such an invasion of its dominion the intellect could not long endure. Arising in the majesty of truth and justice, it has asserted its freedom, broken its fetters, and, in turn, made reprisals upon the religious system. The fortunes of the day have oscillated like the swing of a pendulum, or the ebb and flow of the tide. Sometimes the religious system has yielded to slow and steady encroachments, until intellect assumed the airs of arrogance, and loud assertions were sent forth that religion was a superstition, and faith was fed only by fables. Then, from such an extreme of irreligion, the popular mind would swing back with a revulsion, as it had, at other times, from the opposite extreme. All this will be illustrated by a review of the facts of history, which I hope to present in a subsequent lecture.

From our stand-point, it seems to me that these phenomena are explicable without disparagement to the character either of intellect or faith. The conflict exists between the conservatism of faith and the progressiveness of intellect. It is the nature of religion to be invariable, and this central character is transferred to all the accessories of the religious system. Religion is based on the being and attributes of an unchanging Deity, and the dominion of unchanging principles. It implies that its world of surroundings is unchanging, eternal, and divine. It is no reproach to the religious sentiment that it can not discriminate between that which is fixed and true, and that which is fleeting and false. If it had the power to make these discernments, it would be intellect, and not religious sentiment. Intellect is its eye—it needs no other. If intellect proves an unreliable witness to the truth, faith shows its fidelity to its mission by embracing the true and the false with impartial tenderness.

It is the office of intellect to discover the truth, and vouch for it to the other departments of the soul—the religious, the æsthetic, and the pathematic. If intellect sometimes errs in the interpretation of phenomena and the induction of general principles, this is no reproach, since the penetration of the human intellect is finite, and its utterances must be fallible. It still remains loyal to truth. It seeks, also, to retrieve its errors, and, though consecrated by a misled devotion, banish them from existence. The conflict, in truth, exists between new science and the old; and the only concern of faith in the controversy is to prompt the old to resistance.

We may conceive of conditions under which this conflict would never arise. Were the religious nature so constituted as to content itself with appropriating only the central truths of the religious system, science and philosophy, which recognize these, would never attempt to drive faith from its positions. The fact is otherwise, and this reveals the cause of the secular conflict. We can easily understand the reason why the fact is as it is—at least one of the reasons. Were the religious nature content to hold fast simply the *essential facts* of religion, the proud and unmolested intellect, going on from conquest to conquest, would assume a dominating attitude. The ethical perceptions and sentiments, though gifted with an undying vitality, would exert but little influence over the lives of men. This subjugation would be aided by the alliance of the grosser passions of mankind. The name of God would be almost forgotten, and his commandments be quite unheeded. The law of might would assert supremacy among men; civilization would be strangled in its cradle; the means and instruments of intellectual culture would not be created, and the exaltation of man—even of the intellect of man—would be an impossibility. As we understand the moral government under which we live, it contemplates a perpetuated and vivid remembrance of God; a perpetual communion with the spirit of God, and a sensitive respect for the law of God. In view of the intellectual and passional constitution of man's nature, it is needful that the claims of God be frequently and vigorously asserted to accomplish the purpose of his government over us. It is necessary that those claims be made obtrusive and encroaching. Thus the other powers are aroused, and the knowledge of God and his law is kept alive in the soul. Thus, a living, grasping, encroaching, religious consciousness is the condition of intellectual and social advancement.([1]) Thus, even religious superstition and ecclesiastical tyranny, so generally deplored as the mediæval impediments to the march of civilization, may be, in reality, the providential means of conserving the only conditions which render human progress possible.

In the light of these considerations, we shall not contemplate this conflict as a war of extermination. It is only a grand example of progress through antagonism. It is subordinated to the universal economy of God, exemplified in nature, in morals, and in individual experience. There is no excellence which has not had a conflict, no virtue without temptation, no heavenly joy without a taste of earthly sorrow. In nature, the law of antagonism rules everywhere. Attraction contends with repulsion; rarefaction, with condensation; evaporation, with precipitation; centripetal force, with centrifugal force. The whole cosmos is merely a panorama of the phenomena of a transitory conflict between opposites struggling into a state of ultimate rest. The attacks and reprisals of the religious and intellectual forces are but a particular instance of the general law. I prefer to regard these movements simply as the normal action and reaction of moral forces, rather than a case of abnormal warfare. Instead of the *conflict* of religion and science, I should prefer to speak of the interaction of the religious and

---

([1]) "Nations plunged in the abyss of irreligion must necessarily be nations in anarchy" (Draper, "Intellectual Development of Europe," p. 103).

intellectual faculties. I deplore the view that this is a war in which one of the combatants has no rights. I deplore the spirit which seeks to put faith and science in deadly antagonism. This is a weakness of which representatives of both interests must plead guilty. I deplore the spirit which continually represents religion as a superstition; providential care as the reign of arbitrary will, caprice, and disorder; law as excluding providence; and creation as the "carpenter theory" of existence.

Religion has always been compelled to wage a warfare of quite another kind. The passions of men, not satisfied with their legitimate gratification, clamor always for excessive indulgence. This demand is in sharp collision with the law of the religious nature, which, accordingly, offers unceasing resistance. Naturally the repulses of faith at the hands of science have brought cheer to the baser nature of man; and naturally, too, the baser nature has sometimes availed itself of the ascendency of religious faith to bribe the spiritual power to serve its base purposes. But the prostitution of faith is exceptional, and intellect has never had fellowship with the vice which exults in its victories. The final cause of the hostility of religion to vice is easy to discover. Vice not only antagonizes the moral law revealed in the soul, but its influence upon the individual and upon society is fatal to all those ends involved in social and intellectual elevation.

The conflict of religion with the evil passions of men has engendered a special series of oscillations in the fortunes of religion. Relapses from a condition of religious activity have resulted, sometimes, from the steady seductive influence of the baser nature, as well as from the quickened activity of intellect, or its actual encroachments. Then the voice of the reformer would be raised on high, and the universal conscience would cry out in response. These have been occasions for the rapid strengthening of the religious system—sometimes for the establishment of a spiritual tyranny, which, in turn, has provoked intellect to manly resistance. The part which has been performed by each of these antagonists of religious faith will appear as we shall glance over the records of history.

If the sharp interaction of the religious and the intellectual forces is the order of nature and of Providence, it is needful and beneficent. We have nothing to fear from it, and may calmly and confidently contemplate the progress of events and anticipate the issue. There is no need of fear for the interests of religion. All we have to fear is the evil to which human passions may prompt. Ambition, and love of power, and sensuous gratifications, more than zeal for the faith, may nerve the arm which rivets the fetters of an ecclesiastical despotism. Pride of intellect or a vindictive disposition may prompt the representative of science to affect an unconcern about religious questions; to feign a belief that Deity and his purposes must remain unknowable, or even to oppress with ridicule and scorn the character which remains faithful to the religious promptings of human nature. Our solicitude may be usefully turned to the arrest of such encroachments upon the mutual liberties and rights of the parties to this strife.

The results of the interaction of these forces are written upon the pages of the religious history of our race. Whatever may be the beneficent influences of the vital activities of the religious instincts upon the fortunes of intellectual progress, it is apparent that the religious system, under the pruning and restraints of the cognitive faculty, has undergone a gradual advance.([1]) The proposition does not imply a progressive improvement or perfection of the religious nature. This is no

---

([1]) "Disorganization is the temporary result; theological advance the subsequent. Whatever is evil is eliminated in the conflict; whatever is good is retained. Under the overruling of a beneficent Providence, antagonism is made the law of human progress" (Farrar, "A Critical History of Free Thought," p. 12).

truer to the great realities which it represents in an age of civilization than in an age of barbarism. The progress consists in a gradual excision of crudities, excesses, and meaningless accessories. The religious nature is a blind instinct feeling for its object. It is an infant crying in the night for its food. It accepts whatever the intelligence offers as real and true, and consecrates it as the objective revelation of real divinity. The body of accessory beliefs accepted at any particular period, accreted around the central facts of religion, constitute, for the time, the religious system. With the enlargement of the intellectual horizon, the cruder accessories become eliminated. The religious system always consists, therefore, of constants and variables. Progress is incident only to the variable factor. This is the human and finite and imperfect element of religion. The constant factor is an eternal truth, resting on the Rock of Ages. This is the infinite and perfect and unchanging element in religion. The variable factor represents weak, struggling, aspiring humanity; the constant factor, the eternal All-sufficiency. The former is practical or actual religion; the latter is the absolute or ideal religion. The former is the nearest approach which feeble humanity has been able to make toward its perfect standard; the latter is the perfect standard to which humanity aspires.

In the infancy of intellect, the religious system is encumbered by an environment of grossest crudities. Every motion in nature reveals the agency of the supernatural. Every object is the shrine of divinity. Benignant spirits award success in hunting or in war, while sickness and misfortune are the visitations of malignant ones. These are propitiated and appeased by dances, howlings, brutal sacrifices, and sometimes beastly orgies. This is the stage of Fetichism. The next stage in advance may be styled Totemism. The intellectual mists have lifted from the ground, and common things are discerned in their natural relations. But supernaturalism reigns in all the realm above

commonplace. The cataract thunders the power and majesty of the Invisible; the tempest is a paroxysm of divine rage; the foliage of the breezy forest hums the melodies of unseen sprites; and the rippling stream, as it floats the solemn worshiper in his rude canoe, murmurs a spirit lullaby. With the further advance of knowledge, divinity seems retired into the grand and mysterious abodes of nature. The mountains, with their serene and inaccessible summits, are the homes of divinity; or the sky spreads a brazen floor in the court of the celestials, and the stars beam with the radiance of divine intelligence. This may be styled the stage of Shamanism. The system known as Magianism is scarcely more advanced, but its worship recognizes a more limited number of divine abodes or manifestations. The elements permeate and constitute and dominate nature, and are the fittest representatives of the All-powerful and All-pervading. The sun is justly regarded as the great life-giving and controlling agent of the natural world; and fire, its essential characteristic, becomes the representative of the sun and the emblem of the Supreme Efficiency. The Anthropomorphic stage may be the next in advance. The intellect has discovered that thought and purpose are not the attributes of inanimate objects. The Being who plans and executes and ordains in the cosmic realm must possess a nature akin to that which plans and wills in human affairs. The Deity must be an intelligence. Human in his spiritual attributes, the groping intellect could scarcely escape the assignment of human shape and human passions. Higher attainments of reflective thought, however, would reveal the fact that bodily form is the accident of humanity; that it implies limitation and dependence. The Infinite Reason must be incorporeal, without parts and without locality. This is the stage of pure Spiritualism, which we have reached. Its morning rays have illuminated the loftiest peaks of human speculation in ages surprisingly remote, and in nations unexpectedly separate. Yet the difficulty of a purely spiritual conception of God is so great that anthropomorphism has pervaded most of the religious systems of the world, and even taints the purest and best of the present age. We are not casting a taunt at any system of religion in saying that it is adulterated with anthropomorphism. It could not be otherwise. This is the ordination of Heaven, and is pleasing to Heaven; just as the weakness and shapelessness of the embryo are involved in the plan of creation—the very index and condition of progress—the clear promise of coming perfection. In anthropomorphism man confers upon his God the highest attributes and the loftiest character of which he has any conception; and if, on attaining the stage of a pure spiritualism, he retains anthropomorphic and anthropopathic images, symbols, and forms of speech, they serve merely as a scaffolding over which his feeble thought climbs to the lofty and dazzling and adorable truth.

Religious systems have changed, but religion remains as changeless as the being of God. Religious systems have become extinct; but, like the integuments of the chrysalis, they have infolded a *living germ*, the law of whose development implies the casting-off of its effete accessories. The human intellect has marched onward, unconsciously and unintentionally purifying and spiritualizing the religious system; while the religious nature, perfect from the first, has yielded timidly and reluctantly to the processes which have promoted the unpremeditated progress of the religious system. A progress unpremeditated by both of the agencies which have contributed to its realization must be providential. In asserting that intellect has not purposed the advancement of religion, I allude, of course, to the purely secular nature of the search for truth which is the office of intellect. If intellect search for the truth respecting God, or duty, or future life, this manifests no religious character in intellect. The religious nature may appropriate the results reached; it may even prompt intellect, as it often does, to engage in researches which will yield religious fruit;

nay, more, and finally, there is no truth attainable by intellect which is not available to the religious nature; there is no truth which the religious nature can afford to despise; and I venture to utter a proposition which brings us back to the simple, direct, and primitive faith of humanity: there is no truth which is not an immediate reflection and revelation of God.

The service which intellect, under the promptings of religious instinct, can render to the religious system will be indicated in later lectures of this course. In the present lecture I have enunciated general truths relating to the necessary interaction of the religious and the intellectual faculties. These truths may be regarded as deduced from the necessary laws of the human mind; but they must be amply exemplified in the history of the world: and I shall devote the next two lectures to a rapid historical sketch of the so-called "conflicts" of religion and science. I do this not only to present an inductive basis for the generalizations already brought forward, but because these conflicts have been unjustly made a ground of accusation against religion as the foe of science and of the civilization which runs parallel with it.

II.

INTERACTION OF THE RELIGIOUS AND THE INTELLECTUAL FACULTIES IN ORIENTAL AND GRECIAN PSYCHIC HISTORY.

I HAVE attempted to show that the essential natures of the religious and the intellectual forces in man foreordain a species of antagonism; that this perpetual antagonism is not, nevertheless, an abnormal condition, but a grand example of the universal economy of God, who has ordained antagonism as the condition of progress in the natural and the moral worlds. I have deduced from the necessary relation of the ethical and cognitive powers a necessary series of oscillations in the relative dominance of religious and intellectual influences in the lives of men; and have indicated that the exponent of these oscillations has been, as it must be, a series of alternating periods of religious and of intellectual activity and progress. Such alternations, since the antagonizing forces belong to humanity as such, must characterize the history of all nations, all races, and all times.

The present lecture will aim to show that the facts of the religious and intellectual history of the human race illustrate and confirm these deductions, and become, in reality, a broad inductive basis on which these propositions may be rested as valid generalizations. A prolonged and attentive study of the facts which make up the religious and intellectual history of our race has caused my attention to be directed to the following facts subsidiary to the general inductions: 1. Religious faith recedes from its normal condition to one of abnormal subordination, or advances to one of abnormal supremacy. 2. Intellect, from its normal condition, either advances to a haughty dictatorship, or falls into a condition of servitude. 3. These movements of faith and intellect are reciprocal and responsive. 4. The direction of the movement is determined by the initiative: if faith lead in activity, a religious phase succeeds; if intellect take precedence, religious pretensions shrink, and an intellectual phase succeeds. The two phases complete a psychic cycle.

I proceed now to enunciate in advance the general principles induced from a study of the facts of human history.

LAWS OF THE INTERACTION OF FAITH AND INTELLECT.

I. ABNORMAL STATES OF FAITH.

1. The abnormal states of Faith are insensibility, debility, and overactivity.

II. THEIR CAUSES.

2. Moral *insensibility* results from the supremacy of evil passions. This condition is not directly concerned in the interaction of the religious and intellectual faculties.

3. The state of *debility* (disregarding moral causes) results from intellectual encroachments.

4. The state of *overactivity* results from aggrandizements secured through political power, or perhaps, sometimes, through intellectual indolence.

III. RECIPROCAL MOVEMENTS OF FAITH AND INTELLECT.

(a) *Toward the Norm.*

5. From a state of debility, the moral norm is regained by a moral reaction or revulsion arising in the religious nature. The process is a moral *revival*. Concomitantly, intellect returns to a state of soberness and sanity. The basis of the revival is laid in a previous period of intellectual ascendency; but its quickening force is the religious consciousness.

6. From a state of overactivity, the moral norm is reached by a rebellion of the intellect. The result lifts intellect again into a state of normal authority. The process is a *reformation* in the political and the religious system, or, at least, in the latter.

7. The watch-word of a revival or a reformation is "*primitive faith;*" and to the strength and simplicity of the primitive (normal) faith it struggles to return.

(b) *From the Norm.*

8. From the primitive faith follows a divergence. Its simplicity is succeeded, according to what seems a psychical law, by a tendency to complexity, marked by a growing ritualism, sacerdotalism, aggressiveness, intolerance, tyranny.

9. Against these excesses the intellect begins to rebel, and the germs of a new reformation are planted. Meantime, intellect is repressed, and ultimately falls into a state of complete bondage.

10. The new reformation brings back faith to its normal simplicity, and intellect to its normal action.

IV. Résumé.

11. Thus, when Faith takes the initiative in action, starting from the state of simple (monotheistic) faith, we witness the following series of results:

Faith ascendant.. { Faith simple; complex..... } Revolution.
{ Intellect normal; rebellious. }

12. Revolution now throws the initiative upon Intellect, and, starting from the coincident norm of intellect and faith, we witness the following results:

Intellect ascendant.. { Intellect normal; dominant... } Revival.
{ Faith normal; debilitated.... }

Both movements may be thrown into a diagrammatic form, and more clearly illustrated to the eye:

44 PSYCHIC CYCLES.

	Duplex Psychic Cycle.					Duplex Hemicycle.		
	Religious Phase.		Intellectual Phase.			Religious Phase.		
FAITH.	Normal.	Complex.	Normal.	Debilitated.		Normal.	Complex.	
INTELLECT.	Normal.	Rebellious.	Normal.	Dominant.		Normal.	Rebellious.	
	Faith Ascendant.	Reformation.	Thought Ascendant.		Revival.	Faith Ascendant.		Reformation.

The psychical history of our race presents, therefore, a succession of Religious and Intellectual Phases alternating with each other. During the Religious Phase, Faith takes the initiative in action, and is in the ascendant, while Intellect is in the descendent. During the Intellectual Phase, thought takes the initiative, and is in the ascendant, while Faith is in the descendent. The Religious Phase supervenes on a Revival, and is terminated by a Reformation; the Intellectual supervenes on a Reformation, and is terminated by a Revival. On the completion of a cycle, consisting of the two phases, Faith and Intellect stand in the same relative positions as at first.

These movements may be otherwise illustrated. Faith and Intellect move in two equal intersecting orbits, having a common centre. The norm is a plane bisecting the angle formed by the planes of these orbits. The orbit of Faith is alternately above and below the normal plane; and the same is true of the orbit of Intellect. The two orbits intersect each other in the plane of the norm, and we have here two equipotencies. That which occurs when Faith passes its ascending, and Intellect its descending, node is a Revival Equipotence; and that which occurs when Faith passes its descending, and Intellect its ascending, node is a Reformative Equipotence. (See next page.)

This particular example of a deeply rooted tendency to periodicity in the psychic activities of mankind confirms the truth of an adage long extant, that "History repeats itself." The phenomenon is grounded on the psychical identity of the race, and the uniformity of the physical laws under which phenomena are wrought out, which become conditions of psychic activity. Each individual's developmental experience repeats the history of every other individual. Each tribe or civic community, beginning as a child, proceeds, with greater or less rapidity, through a series of educational stages determined by the psychic forces of an unchanging human nature, played upon by the stimuli emanating from the presence and contact of a material environment changeless in its mode of action.

It would not express the whole of the cyclic system to represent these cycles as either the only psychic cycles realized in human history, or as movements sharply isolated and definable.

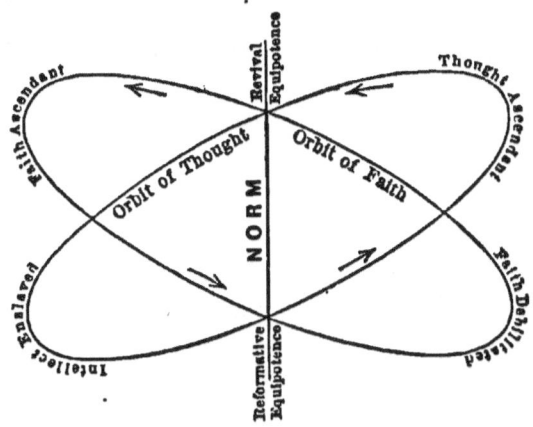

Within the sweep of one cycle have been evolved cycles of less magnitude and salience; and this system of cycles and epicycles has been embraced in grander cycles which represent psychic movements which embrace entire races. Thus the Indo-European race sweeps through three grand psychic cycles, the first ending with the fall of the Persian Empire; the second, with the fall of the Roman Empire of the East; and the third, extending to our own times.

Further, it must be clearly stated that the religious and intellectual phases are seldom quite consecutive. The latter arises before the termination of the Religious Phase. Sometimes it runs for centuries parallel with it, and sometimes even dies out while yet the Religious Phase persists. The partial or complete contemporaneity of the two phases implies a division of the public into a religious section and an intellectual section.

The series of cyclic movements sometimes bifurcates, as in the divergence of the Zoroastrian, and afterward the Buddhist, system, from the Brahmanic. The Brahmanic continues its cyclic development by itself, while the two others, each in turn, begin a series of cyclic evolutions of their own; and all three reach to our own times. A similar phenomenon is seen in the histories of Christianity and Islamism.

These grand movements in the field of psychical history are not obscurely seen in the vicissitudes of the nations of remotest antiquity.

Egyptian Psychic History.

Egyptian history, which, according to respectable authority, stretches back to the remotest date (5004 B.C., according to Manetho; 3623 B.C., according to Bunsen; 2700 B.C., according to Poole), presents a series of vicissitudes which we may group into four Psychic Cycles. The FIRST PSYCHIC CYCLE embraces the first Ten Dynasties. As with the mythic periods of all nations, the earliest, or prereflective, period of Egypt seems to have been characterized by a dominance of the religious nature. This is the first *Religious Phase*. We may regard it as preceding the epoch of the culminating prosperity of Memphis. The *Intellectual Phase* followed, and appears to be well marked; though its remains have but recently been brought to the notice of the world. These monuments, exhumed through the industry and sagacity of M. Mariette, sustained by the enlightened patronage of the Khedive, have been brought together in magnificent collections at Boulak, in Upper Egypt, and at

Cairo. They are described as evincing a degree of artistic and intellectual development superior even to that which is represented in the later and better-known monuments stored in the museums of Paris and Berlin.(¹)

The SECOND PSYCHIC CYCLE embraces the period of these later monuments. The *Religious Phase* covered the period of the formation and prevalence of the ancient religion embodied in the First Book of the Sacred Canon, as described by St. Clement.(²) This, like the most ancient book of the Vedas, consisted of hymns to the gods. The complete Canon contained forty-two books, of which the Second treated of the whole duty of a king's life. The celebrated "Book of the Dead," belonging to the Eleventh Dynasty (2500 B.C.), is supposed to have constituted a part of the Canon. This, nevertheless, must be regarded as a foreshadowing of the next phase, since "it is obviously the product of a matured sacerdotal philosophy—the Apocalypse of Egypt."(³) The "Book of Transmigrations" embodies similar doctrines, and probably belongs to the same stage of development. The *Intellectual Phase* of this Cycle is marked by the appearance of the later books of the Sacred Canon. These seem to have constituted a complete encyclopedia, and well exemplify the universal truth that all learning among primitive peoples is turned over to the custody of religion—priest and philosopher being one. In these books were treatises on astronomy, hieroglyphics, cosmography, geography, topography of Egpyt, and a particular description of the Nile. All this knowledge was represented as derived from Thoth, the first Hermes Trismegistus, by order of the Supreme God. The preparation for this phase began 560 B.C., when Amosis gave permission to Greeks to settle in Egypt. Jews had already

---

(¹) Taylor, "Egypt and Iceland," chaps. ix., x.
(²) Clemens Alexandrinus, "Stromata," book vi., chap. iv.
(³) Moffat, "A Comparative History of Religions," p. 63.

been there since the capture of Jerusalem by Nebuchadnezzar (588 B.C.).

A THIRD PSYCHIC CYCLE of Egyptian history dates from the conquest of Egypt by Alexander (332 B.C.). Though Egypt has never since had an independent existence, and her psychic development may be regarded rather as Greek, Roman, Saracenic, and Turkish, it is interesting to note that we still discern the cyclical movement. The *Religious Phase* of this cycle was clearly exemplified in Alexandrian Judaism and its later displacement by Alexandrian Christianity; while an *Intellectual Phase* is strongly marked by the planting and development of science and theosophy under the Ptolemies.

A FOURTH PSYCHIC CYCLE, beginning with the conquest of Egypt by the Arabians (640 A.D.), presents a *Religious Phase* in the bloody fanaticism of Mohammedanism, bearing down all resistance; and an *Intellectual Phase*, which is dawning like another "Renaissance" under the auspices of the present Egyptian Viceroy—the West discharging the obligations it incurred to the East in the European Revival of Letters.[1]

Chinese Psychic History.

We turn, next, to glance at the psychic history of the Chinese. The FIRST PSYCHIC CYCLE may be taken as extending from the epoch of the oldest records to the period of Confucius. The *Religious Phase* begins with the date of the oldest of the Sacred Writings, said to have been written by Fu-hi, 2800 B.C. This is known as the Yi-king, meaning "Transfor-

---

[1] The light of learning has been reflected reciprocally between the East and the West as between two mirrors. In earliest historic times, Egypt Assyria, and Persia sent the light of learning to Greece. Greece reflected it back to Egypt and Syria as a sequence of the Alexandrian conquests; Syria and Constantinople sent it again into Greece, Italy, and other parts of Europe in the Middle Ages: and now, again, the learning of Europe is seen reflected back upon Egypt, Constantinople, and Syria.

mations." The Second Book, or She-king, consists of chants of a sublime and devotional character, like those of the Rig-Veda. The *Intellectual Phase* grew up with the development of reflection, and was for a long period coincident with a declension of moral and religious earnestness. Literature increased; but the teaching of the Sacred Books was neglected.

The SECOND PSYCHIC CYCLE was introduced by Confucius, who, like other reformers, directed attention to the duties inculcated by the ancient religion. His period was between 551 and 479 B.C. Though Confucius did not return to the spiritualism of the primitive faith, he revived religious interest, and reinstated a respect for the Sacred Books in the hearts of his countrymen. He collected together the fragments of the old canon, and compiled and composed three additional books, which constitute a portion of the Sacred Writings of the Chinese. These books make no assumption of inspiration nor support by miracles; but their authors are regarded as excelling in wisdom and goodness all others of their race. The moral and religious revival introduced by Confucius signalizes the *Religious Phase* of this Cycle. Almost simultaneously arose another teacher, Lao-Tse (604 B.C.), who introduced the religion of the supreme reason. The sum of his recorded instructions is embodied in the Tau-teh-king, the classic of reason and virtue. Lao-Tse, the Schelling of China, planted the germs of a transcendental philosophy, which, with the abatement of the influence exerted by Confucius, gained sufficient strength and acceptance to prompt the head of the dynasty of Ts'in (220–200 B.C.) to *doom the Sacred Books to destruction.* The reign of Taoism marks the *Intellectual Phase* of the Second Cycle.

The THIRD PSYCHIC CYCLE was ushered in by the termination of the dynasty of Ts'in and the reproduction of the Sacred Books under Wen-ti (135 B.C.). A new religious zeal spread through the empire, marking a *Religious Phase.* Of its decline, and the invasion of the *Intellectual Phase*, I have learned nothing very specific. We know, however, that in the year 66 A.D. Buddhism made its advent into China, and awakened the long-slumbering religious sentiments to the demands of a system more spiritual, and more consonant with the simple instincts of the soul, than the degenerate system which had supervened upon the revival under Wen-ti. This event, then, marks the beginning of the *Religious Phase* of the FOURTH PSYCHIC CYCLE in China. The later periods of Buddhist history, as is well known, have been marked by a growing ceremonialism and diminishing spirituality. China has shown signs of an intellectual awakening, and the advent of an *Intellectual Phase*. While the Buddhism of China has reached a degeneracy which forebodes another religious revival, the intellectual aristocracy of the empire, however small their minority numerically, are steadily leading its institutions into the light and learning of advanced civilization.

I have dwelt too briefly on the events of Chinese history to convey a vivid impression of the fluctuations depicted in the spiritual life of the people; but the salient facts pointed out teach us that the cyclic movements are real. The fact arrests the attention of Moffat, who says: "Among the sacred books of antiquity, outside of the Bible, there is no plainer recognition of the supreme authority of one personal God than in the utterances of some of the Chinese monarchs. The progress of natural religion, in China, as elsewhere, has been that of degeneracy, tending to a multiplication of gods, and the assumption of objects of worship from various sources; and then, the separation of the learned from the unlearned by a pantheistic or otherwise godless philosophy."[1]

---

[1] Moffat, "A Comparative History of Religions," p. 179.

Indian Psychic History.

We turn also, briefly, to the psychic history of India. The FIRST PSYCHIC CYCLE is Hindoo, and the dominant religion is Brahmanism. Its *Religious Phase* is stamped by primitive Vedaism, or the religion of the Rig-Veda Sanhitâ, whose epoch is thought to be about 1400 B.C. Max Müller and other Orientalists have made us well acquainted with the pure and exalted devotion which characterizes the Mantras, or Hymns, of the Rig-Veda Sanhitâ. Some of these Hymns are almost worthy to be placed by the side of the loftiest Psalms of David. They illustrate in a most interesting manner the eminently religious characteristics of a primitive people, and, at the same time, the simplicity, beauty, and correctness of their theology. The human mind in India, however, following a law which seems necessary, began to gather about the primitive system a body of rites and complications of a merely external character. However the intelligence failed to discover the significance and propriety of empty forms, the religious nature, as everywhere, manifested a proneness to ceremonials and unessentials. A burdensome ritual grew up, embodied in the books known as the Brahmanas, which are supposed to date back, approximately, to 1000 B.C. In the lapse of time, other books, embodying other or more elaborate directions for the conduct of religion, grew into existence, under the designation of Sutras. These are not later than 600 B.C. At this period, the Brahmanic priests had come into the exercise of a sacerdotal despotism. As it must be, under such circumstances, reflective minds had long felt a more or less outspoken dissent. Though ritualistic tyranny was only checked, not uprooted, and continued yet, through many centuries, an *Intellectual Phase* was setting in. Hindoo speculation was elaborating systems sometimes fanciful, sometimes profound. To this period belongs the monistic theosophy of the Vedanta—the theoretical poetry of the Mimansa. Here, also, belongs the dualistic philosophy of the Sankya, which is attributed to Kapila; and the atomistic philosophy and theistic school of Patangali. These systems mark clearly the phase of thought and growing dissent which always succeeds a period of religious encroachment, even when it does not terminate it by a revolution. In this case, Brahmanic ritualism outlived skeptical philosophy, to awaken successive protests of a more religious kind, to undergo itself a revival incident to the expulsion of an intrusive system, and then to lapse into a baser ritualism than before, which lingers to our times, overlapped distinctly, however, by an awakening of intellect which promises for Hindoostan an era of correct thinking and regenerated religion.

But, in the mean time, superimposed upon the tidal movements of Brahmanic thought, two great cycles have revolved, which stand forth so conspicuously as to constitute the characteristic movements of Indian psychic history. These are, respectively, Zoroastrian and Buddhistic. The first we may regard as marking the SECOND PSYCHIC CYCLE in India. Its religion is that of the Avesta. It signalizes a sharp dissent from the encroaching demands of the Brahmanic system. Though arising long before Brahmanic ritualism had attained its culmination, and, perhaps, before the completion of the Brahmanas, it constitutes a logical and real succession. It was, in its *Religious Phase*, an attempt to return to the simplicity of the primitive monotheistic faith and worship. Its adherents, originally seceders from Brahmanism, increased most rapidly on the north of the Himalayas, and ultimately made Zoroastrianism the State religion of Persia. The vicissitudes of this religion are but a revolution of the wheel of thought. The Gathas of the Yasna, constituting the oldest Book of the Avesta, give expression to the simplest and purest and loftiest devotion. The Vispered, the Second Book of the Avesta, discloses the growth of a liturgical system. The next step shows the inweaving of the threads of speculation. The Third Book of the

Avesta is the Vendidad, which embraces the ethical philosophy of Zoroastrianism. The degeneracy of this religion has never become extreme. Though the religion of the State under such absolute monarchs as Darius (500 B.C.) and Cyrus, it continued to be characterized by a monotheism and purity which still excite our admiration. It was Darius Hystaspes who engraved the famous inscription on the rocks of Behistun, ascribing his successes as a ruler and general to the assistance of the Supreme God—a bold and devout acknowledgment imperishably sculptured on the face of a cliff, high-lifted before the gaze of his own subjects and the populations which should succeed even to the latest time. "A great God is Ahuramazda, who made the earth, who made the heaven, who created men, and provided blessedness for them, who made Darius king, the sole king over many. * * * Through the might of Ahuramazda am I king. * * * Through the grace of Ahuramazda do I rule this kingdom." This is the proclamation of a monarch mightier than David. Cyrus acknowledged the same God;(¹) and Cambyses, the great general, ridiculed the gods and idols of the degenerate Egyptians.

This *Religious Phase* was followed by an *Intellectual* one, not strongly marked, but signalized by the invasion of free thought and the slow corruption of the ancient religion. This, again, was succeeded by the development of Parseeism, which persists feebly to the present day.

Meantime, however, the THIRD PSYCHIC CYCLE of Indian history had begun. Its course has been somewhat parallel and contemporaneous with the later history of Brahmanism and Zoroastrianism. It is a third religious system of Sanskrit-speaking peoples. It is the religion of the Tripitaka. Buddhism may be regarded as the reduplication of the Zoroastrian rebellion against the excesses of Brahmanism. That was a diver-

---

(¹) Ezra i., 2.

gence; this was a schism. The revolt was absolute. It rejected the doctrines, the sacerdotalism, and the whole pantheon of the Brahmanic system, and returned to the simple practices of virtue, abstinence, and religious contemplation. The *Religious Phase* begins with the preaching of Buddha, about 550 B.C. Note, again, the circle of evolutions. The oldest books of the Tripitaka are exclusively religious and ethical. The Vinaya-Pitaka is a body of moral precepts. The Sutra-Pitaka is a collection of the sayings of Buddha. Next, however, follows the Dharma-Pitaka, in which we recognize a growing development of speculative thought. This book consists of dogmatic philosophy, cosmology, and other secular learning. Next, we see Buddhism (250 B.C.) becoming the State religion of India under Asoka. It degenerated, by degrees, into formalism, idolatry, and unreasoning inanities. Then the revolt arose to which I alluded in speaking of Brahmanism; and the latter system, in a regenerated form, replaced Buddhism. The Buddhists were expelled 250 A.D., and spread through China, Tartary, Corea, Japan, Burmah, Siam, and other regions, preaching and propagating their religion with a missionary spirit quite comparable with that which, during the same periods, was spreading Christianity over the Western world. Buddhism in the East, like Christianity in the West, has thus maintained a dominant position in all the countries to which it spread, down to the present day. This dispersion of the adherents of Buddhism through so many countries has kept the system in the perpetuated condition of a rising religion; and it has been vitalized, through so many centuries, by that zeal which is the condition and characteristic of the youth of a religious system. Nevertheless, Buddhism has undergone its destined degeneracy in every country which it has possessed. It has become encumbered with accreted forms and rites; and heresies have riven the body ecclesiastic to its centre. Several general councils have been held for the compilation of sacred books, the suppression of heresies, and the strengthening of the system; but the *Intellectual Phase* is marching on. Its rise may be regarded as signalized by the appearance of the Abidharma, or body of metaphysics; and its march, by the entrance of Western ideas and institutions into the inert mass of Chinese, Japanese, and other Oriental politics.

I shall not occupy you with any detail of the psychic movement among the Hebrews and Assyrians. In reference to the former, it suffices to remind you that the bounds of such movements are disclosed in Biblical history. The Book of Genesis — which stands before us, more properly, as eleven separate compositions — is the surviving monument of the earliest *Religious Phase*. This was the Bible of the Patriarchs. The religion was patriarchal. Intervening between the compilation of the Book of Genesis and the birth of Moses was a decline of faith, and an infusion of the literature and religion of the Egyptians. A *Second Religious Phase* was ushered in with the giving of the "Books of the Law," and endured to the end of prophecy, when another decline set in and occupied the interval to the birth of Christ. At this epoch a *Third Religious Phase* dawned upon the Hebrew nation, and its history began to be merged into the common history of Europe.

These references to the salient epochs of Oriental thought and religious emotion, so brief as almost to fall within the domain of statistics, demonstrate, I think, that the mode of interaction of the religious and intellectual faculties is a reality, in the form in which I have depicted it. But more interesting exemplifications follow.

Grecian Psychic History.

Grecian psychic history is marked by a more luminous line of light than that of any other ancient people. The FIRST PSYCHIC CYCLE is Homeric. The priests and prophets of the *Religious Phase* were such semi-mythical personages as Homer and Hesiod. The theology and cosmology developed in their writings, while revealing, like all primitive faiths, a knowledge of one Supreme Divinity, disclose a bias toward polytheism and gross religious perversions, which indicate that these writers lived in the corrupted decline of an older system, of which we have no records, unless it be in the Orphic Hymns. These, however, though anciently regarded as of older date, embody speculations which mark a more developed stage of thought. I prefer to consider them, with Aristotle, the exponents of a rising spirit of philosophy, which Pherecydes (548 B.C.) brought to a fuller development. It involves speculations of a mystical and pantheistical character, and gives expression to the *Intellectual Phase* of the Homeric Cycle.

Overlapping this was the beginning of the SECOND PSYCHIC CYCLE, whose *Religious Phase* embraced the Ionic and Pythagorean Schools of Philosophy. The Ionic Philosophy was Hylozoism, based on the fundamental principle of the animalization of forms of inorganic matter—not atheistic, nor even materialistic in the offensive sense, for its adherents were engaged in the earnest pursuit after the *One Principle*, which, in their consciousness, was the revelation of God. Thales (640 B.C.) thought the first principle of all things was *Water;* Anaximander (611 B.C.) thought it was το ἄπειρον, the *indefinite*—perhaps the equivalent conception of Chaos, or the condition of absolute homogeneity; Anaximenes (528–524 B.C.) thought he had discovered the first principle in *Air;* while Heraclitus discovered it in *Fire.* The "Fire" of this philosopher, however, was an ethereal element, which he identifies with a pervasive divine spirit or reason, which he conceived as eternal and immanent in the world. The Pythagoreans were charmed by the harmony which they recognized in Creation. *Numbers,* which exactly express the harmony and rhythm of nature, were regarded as the substance, or, at least, the symbols, of that harmony. Pythagoras, their founder, lived 582 B.C. His most conspicuous disciples lived considerably later, and after the rise of other schools of philosophy. Philolaus held that the "world is eternal, and ruled by the ONE who is akin to it, and has supreme might and excellence. The director and ruler of all things is God. He is one and eternal, enduring and unmovable, ever like himself, and different from all things beside him. He encompasses and guards the universe."(¹)

Hicetas, who taught the axial revolution of the earth, and Ecphantus, who taught the same, were still later Pythagoreans; and there was a revival of Pythagoreanism in the century before Christ. It is not needful, however, to reproduce details. I desire only to fix upon the rise of Ionic and Pythagorean philosophy as a real revival of correct religious thought and feeling. I could quote extensively from the fragments of these earnest and devout old philosophers, to prove that they felt the evidence of the One Divine Existence within them; felt the evidence that man and the world proceeded from the Being thus revealed; and earnestly sought, throughout the world, for the subtle essence which might be regarded as constituting that energizing existence. How these early gropings of Grecian speculation reveal the longing, and even the necessity, which the human mind feels for something *sensible* to call its God, or, at least, the shrine of its God! And how such facts, reproduced along the whole historic line of thought, palliate the idolatry and image-worship which have defaced the records of religious sentiment, and so often obscured or eclipsed the divine reality which idols and pictures have symbolized!

But the dawn of a phase of speculation less devout had already passed. The essence of the Eleatic doctrine was the immutability of substance. The earlier Eleatics, who were monistic, maintained the unity of substance; and, in their theistic conceptions, brought themselves into relations to God, almost

---

(¹) Ueberweg, "History of Philosophy," vol. i., p. 49.

as simple and reverential as the Ionics and Pythagoreans; and, in their notions of divine personality, excelled them in clearness. Xenophanes (569 B.C.) combats the anthropomorphism of Homer and Hesiod, and enounces the doctrine of One God.

Εἷς θεὸς ἔν τε θεοῖσι καὶ ἀνθρώποισι μέγιστος.

Parmenides of Elea (499–485 B.C.) founds the doctrine of unity on the conception of being. He was ahead of Hegel in predicating being of thought, for he says,

Τὸ γὰρ αὐτὸ νοεῖν ἐστὶν τε καὶ εἶναι.

Zeno of Elea (490–485 B.C.) marks the emergence of the skepticism which was to swamp all faith. He denied the veracity of sensuous perceptions, denied all motion, and denied all reality of existence. Melissus of Samos put forth the aphorism "Only the One is," disguising under this cover the doctrine of the continuity of substance—a sort of monistic pantheism. Being, with him, is eternal, and will not perish; it is infinite.

The later Eleatics were pluralistic—holding to the distinction of matter and spirit. Empedocles (about 500 B.C.) taught that Earth, Water, Air, and Fire are the four "roots" of things, the moving principles of which are "love" and "hate." He seems to have glimpsed those forces which have emerged in modern science as "attraction" and "repulsion." Anaxagoras of Clazomenæ (about 500 B.C.) opens wide the door for the advance of the Atomists. He maintained that there exists an unlimited number of ultimate elements, which he calls "seeds" (homœomeriæ of Aristotle). These were originally in a state of chaos; but the divine mind (νοῦς), which he holds in antithesis to matter, brought order out of them. All origin and decay are thus a mingling and unmingling.([1]) Organic forms come

---

([1]) We have here the germ of a philosophy of the evolution of the heterogeneous by successive differentiation of the homogeneous.

into existence through the fecundation of the earth by germs previously contained in the air. Anaxagoras has recourse to the divine mind only in the domain of phenomena inexplicable by known causes. For this, Aristotle reproaches him with the suggestion that when his knowledge should have become more extended, the divine mind could be dispensed with altogether. This reminds one of the reputed atheism of Laplace, as distinguished from the theistic astronomers. We see, at least, that the divine immanence recognized by the older philosophers had, in Anaxagoras, shrunk to a remote and occasional relation. This shrinkage of divinity was carried a step farther in the Atomists. Leucippus posited the full and the void as principles of things. The full consists of indivisible primitive particles differing only in form, position, and arrangement. These had no creator, for they existed from eternity. Their orderly arrangements in the world do not result from "love" and "hate," nor through all-ruling mind, but from natural necessity. Democritus (about 460 B.C.) is responsible for the fuller development of a system which has seen its last renaissance in recent times.([1]) He maintained that the atoms were endowed with an eternal motion. He foreshadowed the Cartesian "vortices" and perhaps the "nebular" cosmogony, in conceiving the atoms to generate a vortical movement by the descent of the heavier through the lighter, and attributing the evolution of worlds to such movements. Organized beings were thought to be generated in moist earth.

([1]) While the conception of atomicity enunciated by Professor Tyndall bears a recognized analogy with the theories of Democritus and Bruno, it is not, perhaps, exact to represent the later atomic doctrine as a revival of the older ones. Tyndall's idea of "matter" is unique, and requires new definitions, as he intimates. Indeed, it is doubtful whether his materialism, in spite of the phraseology, is not a view which annuls the distinction between the natural and supernatural by disclosing deductively *an ultimate ground of universal nature which lies quite beyond the domain of nature.*

The progressive and aggressive movement of a daring and profane intellectualism is still further exemplified in the philosophy of the Sophists. They also exhibit a transition from the cosmological speculations of their predecessors to the strictly anthropocentric studies of the Socratic and Platonic schools. They were egotists and rhetoricians—some of them very vain ones. It was one of their phrases that "might makes right." Protagoras, their founder (born about 490 B.C.), is the author of the saying, "man is the measure of all things"—πάντων χρημάτων μέτρον ἄνθρωπος. This was his fundamental theorem. He held, with some modern thinkers, to the relativity of all truth; and even the existence of the gods he announced as a subject so beset with difficulties, that it was impossible to arrive at the fact. In this, however, he undoubtedly refers to the *popular* divinities. Gorgias (483–375 B.C.) went quite over to nihilism. "Nothing exists," he says. "If any thing existed, it would be unknowable; and if any thing existed and were knowable, the knowledge of it could not be communicated to others." Hippias taught that law is the tyrant of men. Prodicus says truly that the men of the earliest time deified whatever was useful to them—bread, as Demeter; wine, as Dionysus; fire, as Hephæstus, etc.; but he falsely employs the fact to prove that all notion of divinity is of human origin. The "Later Sophists" were quite numerous, but need not be cited at length. Critias said, "The belief in the gods was invented by a wise statesman as a means of keeping the people in subjection." Xeniades affirmed that "all is deception; every idea and opinion false; and that whatever comes into being *comes from nothing, and to nothing returns*"—a dogma which shows that the Aristotelian "Ex nihilo nihil fit" is not a necessary datum of thought, as exclusive of the concept of an original creation.

Thus we see demonstrably how the Second Cycle of Grecian thought ended with a precipitation of philosophy into the bottomless gulf of universal skepticism. Before this extremity had been reached, the soul of man had summoned itself to an attitude of oppugnance. The THIRD PSYCHIC CYCLE had begun. Its *Religious Phase* stands forth in the history of thought, adorned with the figure of Socrates—uncouth in exterior, but radiant with beautiful thought. Socrates was born about 471–469 B.C. He went about the streets of scoffing Athens a missionary of the truth of the One God, and perished for his fidelity to that truth. His system is too well known to require exposition. He held, in brief, that the world is governed by a supreme divine Intelligence, and that a special Providence cares for men in this life. The existence of contrivance in nature is proof of a contriving mind. The Megaric, Elian, and Cynic Schools, which succeeded Socrates, were Socratic, with modifications greater or less. Among the Megarics, Euclid united to the ethical principle of Socrates the Eleatic theory of the One, to which alone true being could be ascribed. Diodorus Cronus taught that the necessary is real; and only the real, possible. Among the Cynics, Antisthenes (born 444 B.C.) taught a virtue more rigorous than Socrates. "The essence of virtue," he truly says, "lies in self-control." He accordingly carried self-control to the extent of abstinence from things indifferent, and even a resort to penal self-inflictions. He isolated himself from society and government. Yet, as to the *religious faith* of the people, he held it to be as little binding as their laws. This refers, undoubtedly, to their polytheism. Diogenes of Sinope carried Cynical asceticism to the most repulsive extreme, and became more a "dog" than the brutes which his philosophy satirized. Cynicism, in post-Stoic times, found, also, many adherents among the Romans; but it was rather Socratic in mildness.

The Cyrenaic School marks a strong divergence from Socratic teaching. It is an incident, however, of the Religious Phase inaugurated by Socrates, and constitutes within it a subordinate cycle. The fundamental factor in their philosophy is *pleasure*. It is hence called "Hedonism." Aristippus and his followers, however, maintained that it is wrong to be controlled by pleasure. To the sensuous pleasures Anniceris added the pleasures of sympathy, friendship, gratitude, piety toward parents and fatherland, social intercourse, and the strife after honors. It may be added that, in psychology, Aristippus was a sensationalist; in theology, Theodorus was atheist; and Euhemerus maintained that a belief in the gods began with the veneration of distinguished men. Hedonism was on the high-road to Epicureanism. Plato, however, towered so commandingly over his contemporaries that the full tide of religious philosophy swept on for a hundred years.

Plato, the founder of the "Academy," or, by distinction, the "Old Academy," was born 427 B.C., and wrote thirty-six compositions in fifty-six books. His philosophy centres in the theory of "ideas." The "idea" of Plato is archetypal. The highest idea is the idea of the "good," which is equivalent to God. With Plato, the world is generated; matter is eternal; order was introduced by God; the soul is immortal; the highest good is the greatest possible likeness to God. The "ideas" of Plato have proved as undying as he really believed them. Platonism, after running its first course, was revived, with modifications, in the Middle Academy, and again revived, with restorations, in the New Academy. Once again it was revived by the Neo-Platonists of Alexandria, and mingled itself with the Judaism, and, later, the Christianity which invaded that ancient capital. It found a congenial lodgment in the breasts of many of the early Christian Fathers, and contended with Aristotelianism through all the Scholastic ages; and has actually inspired a school of philosophy in one of the modern English universities. Plato was, *par excellence*, the spiritual theist of antiquity. The proofs of this are accessible to all. Some of his most distinguished followers, of the Old Academy, are Speusippus, who leans pantheistically; Xenocrates (339–314 B.C.), who identifies ideas with numbers; and Heraclides of Pontus, who taught the daily rotation of the earth from west to east, and the immobility of the firmament of the fixed stars.

The middle portion of the fourth century before Christ witnessed the dawn of another *Intellectual Phase*, and a period of increasing secularism, irreligion, skepticism, and speculative reveries. We notice the rise of five lines, or schools, of freethinking. Earliest, and in some respects most orthodox, was the Aristotelian; but almost simultaneously, and still imbued with the theological spirit of Socrates, were the Cyrenaics, whom I have already grouped on the religious side of the boundary, but followed by the Stoics, who, still honoring the teachings of Socrates, were gradually led into peculiarities of principle and practice which assign them to a fitting place on the speculative side of the boundary. On one side of these, however, were the philosophers of the Middle Academy, and, on the other, the Epicureans, for whom history has found a place among the scoffers at religious faith; and, finally, the open Skeptics, the central idea of whose misnamed philosophy was universal doubt. A few comprehensive characterizations must bring us to a dismissal of these philosophies. Arcesilaus (315–241 B.C.) was the founder of the Middle Academy, but Carneades (214–129 B.C.), the skeptic, gave it its character and fame. He declared knowledge to be impossible, and constructed a philosophy of the probable. Aristotle, the Peripatetic (born 384 B.C.), was a monotheist, holding to the eternity of matter and the world, in which the mind of God is expressed in harmonies and in structural relations. God, he teaches, is a spirit, the first principle in the world, existing "not merely as a form immanent in the world, like the order in an army, but also as an absolute, self-existent substance, like the general in an army." Theophrastus, a disciple, leaned toward the doctrine of divine immanence in nature; while Aristotle inclined to a belief in divine transcendence. Eudemus devoted himself to theology. Strato of Lampsacus (288 B.C.) transformed the doctrine of Aristotle into a consistent naturalism. "The formation of the world," he affirmed, "is the result of natural forces." Aristotelianism outcropped in Alexandria, and exerted a powerful influence there for five centuries. During the Scholastic period, the dialectic of Aristotle was the favorite instrument for the defense of doctrines; and, to this day, the founder of the Peripatetic School is reputed the creator of the science of zoölogy, as he was the real inaugurator of the inductive procedure in the search for truth.

The Stoical School was founded by Zeno of Cittium (350–258 B.C.). They held that the working force in the universe is God. The beauty and adaptation of the world can only have come from a thinking mind. They incline to the immanence of the divine force. They discriminated the agreeable and the morally good. In philosophy, they were sensationalists. Physics includes cosmology and theology. Whatever is real is material. Matter and force are the two ultimate principles. The cosmos undergoes periodical destructions and renovations. The human soul is a part of the Deity—a doctrine which reminds us of Orientalism, and one which was singularly persistent through the Middle Ages.

Stoicism was honored with a crowd of disciples. Nearly the oldest of these was Cleanthes, author of the celebrated Hymn to Jupiter. Two hundred years later, it secured a powerful hold upon the Roman mind, and numbered among its adherents the well-known names of Seneca (3–65 A.D.), Lucan (39–65 A.D.), Epictetus, and Marcus Aurelius.

Epicurus (371–270 B.C.) marks a decided antireligious turn of philosophic thought. In natural philosophy he was an Atomist. In psychology, he held perceptions, representations, and feelings to be criteria of truth. In respect to theology, he held it to be useless, as God is an unnecessary explanation of phenomena. Every thing proceeds from natural causes. As nothing can come from non-existence, and nothing which exists

THE PYRRHONISTS. 65

can cease to exist, the atoms of which all things are made, and the space in which they eternally move, have existed from eternity. The soul is material, and composed of fine atoms, and has no existence after death. In ethics, he followed the Cyrenaics, holding happiness to be synonymous with pleasure, and virtue the only sure and possible way to happiness. Standards of ethics are not innate, nor arbitrarily imposed, but are the best judgments of the wise and good as to what is useful to society. Among the numerous adherents of Epicureanism were Apollodorus, author of more than four hundred books; some of the Ptolemies of Alexandria, Phædrus, Lucretius, the author of the poem "De Rerum Naturâ," and Virgil, who sets forth Lucretian views in the Æneid.

The aphelion of philosophic thought was reached again in the Skeptics. Pyrrho of Elis (about 360–270 B.C.), professing to be disgusted with the conflicting and mutually destructive opinions of the philosophers, pretended that all beliefs are a matter of equal indifference; and that every thing depends on human institutions and customs. Timon (325–235 B.C.) considered all the Greek philosophers babblers, except Xenophanes, who had sought for real truth, and Pyrrho, who had found it. Our perceptions and representations of things are neither true nor false, and can therefore not be relied upon.

The Skeptics thus mark the extreme swing of the pendulum of thought. We listen here to the echoes of the same voices which spoke in the philosophy of the Sophists. The Third Cycle was completed by steps parallel with those of the Second Cycle. Socrates and Plato mark its highest religious development, as the Ionics and Pythagoreans had done in the previous Cycle. Thus, also, the Cyrenaics, Stoics, Peripatetics, and the Middle Academy stand collectively for the phase represented in the Eleatics; and the Epicureans answer to the Atomists, as the Skeptics to the Sophists. The Third Psychic Cycle of Grecian history was real and complete.

III.

INTERACTION OF THE RELIGIOUS AND INTELLECTUAL FACULTIES IN CHRISTIAN PSYCHIC HISTORY.

THE Skeptical spirit which completed the Third Psychic Cycle in Greece survived and struggled into a new development in the later skeptics; but even now a revulsion was at hand. Another cycle of Grecian thought had already dawned. This dawn we must regard as the morning rays of the FIRST PSYCHIC CYCLE of Christian history. Its meridian was more than a century in the future. Its *Religious Phase* is manifest in three points of resurgence from the chaos of doubt. First, the Eclectics, of whom, perhaps, Cicero is chief (106–43 B.C.), manifested the initial movement; second, the New Academy brought Platonism back to its pristine spirituality; third, Judaism, working in Alexandria, leavened the Greek philosophy which had found its way thither.

Cicero's Eclecticism consisted in his adhesion to the Skeptical theory of cognition taught by the Middle Academy; his indifference to physics, and his wavering attitude in ethics, between the doctrines of the Stoics and the Peripatetics. He held to the certainty of moral consciousness, and the doctrine of innate ideas, and hence maintained that the *consensus gentium* is a criterion of truth. He is particularly attached, like Socrates, to the belief in Providence and immortality. The Sextians, originating at Rome, were also Eclectic, arising about the epoch of Christ, and holding a position equidistant from Pythagoreanism, Cynicism, and Stoicism.

A somewhat more decided revival was inaugurated by Philo of Larissa, the founder of the New Academy, during the life-time of Cicero. It is sufficient to note that in him the spirit of Plato re-appeared in many of its original lineaments. This affords Draper the opportunity to date the decline of Greek philosophy from the opening of the New Academy. Antiochus of Ascalon, a successor of Philo, betrays already another falling-off, as his teaching approximates that of the Stoics.

The most signal manifestation of the religious revival was discerned upon the southern shore of the Mediterranean. It grew into existence, like most of the great events of history, from an insignificant beginning. Nebuchadnezzar had razed Jerusalem, and a few poor exiles from the captive city had settled in Egypt by permission of the government. By the time of Ptolemy Philadelphus (284–247 B.C.) they had exchanged their native language for the Greek. The occasion thus arose for a Greek version of the Jewish Scriptures. This was undertaken under the patronage of Ptolemy—the principal canonical writings being completed under Ptolemy Euergetes, 247 B.C., and the Hagiographa as late as 136 B.C., and perhaps later. Hebrew literature was thus made accessible in the popular tongue. Ptolemy also received the translators with the highest honors, sometimes entertaining them at his royal table. Under such circumstances, the literature and institutions of the Jews became a favorite and fruitful study; and their excellencies were ingrafted, by degrees, upon the Greek systems extant in Alexandria. Aristobulus (181–145 B.C.) had already written a commentary on the Pentateuch, and dedicated it to Ptolemy Philometer. His faith was a compound of Judaism, Aristotelianism, and Stoicism. He regarded the power of God which dwells in the world as distinguished from his extramundane, absolute existence. The progress of Judaistic theosophy is notable in the Second Book of Maccabees—a mixture of Alexandrian dogmas and Jewish doctrines; in the society of Essenes, who combined, with aspirations after the spirit of prophecy, the abstemiousness of the Cynics and something of the mysticism of the Parsees; in the Therapeutes, who believed in prophecy, magic, celibacy, demons, monasticism, and pre-existence; and, most of all, in Philo the Jew (born about 25 B.C.), whose philosophy was a blending of Platonism and Judaism. Philo was eminently theistic. He aspired after the spirit of prophecy, and maintained that God is accessible by direct intuition. A lower degree of certainty is attainable, he thought, through the æsthetic, or moral, and the teleological view of the world. He rejects the doctrine of the incarnation of the Logos, though he regards the Logos as the instrument through whom God formed the world.

With other signs of the coming revival must be reckoned Neo-Pythagoreanism, which arose in the first century before Christ. Introduced by P. Nigridius Figulus of Alexandria, its best-known adherent was Apollonius of Tyana, who held that the one God must be distinguished from other gods, and that no offerings should be made to him. He is sometimes represented as a miracle-worker and soothsayer, ascetic in his habits, and desirous of introducing reforms in morals and religion. Philostratus has compared him to Jesus.

The Pythagorizing and Eclectic Platonists constitute another link in the series leading toward spiritual light. They renewed and further developed the Platonic doctrine of transcendence, in especial opposition to Stoic Pantheism and Epicurean Naturalism. Their ranks are illustrious with many well-known names. Thrasyllus (died 36 A.D.), the grammarian, and arranger of the Platonic dialogues; Plutarch (50-125 A.D.), who opposed the monism of the Stoics, and postulated two cosmical principles, God and matter; Maximus (146 A.D.), Apuleius (born 126-132 A.D.), and Galen are the names of thinkers groping toward the twilight already shining in their heavens. Celsus, of the same philosophic school, opposed Christianity, and Numenius held to three Gods—the Father, the Son, and the Grandson.

The advent of Christ, and the rapid spread of his teachings, furnish the proof that Christianity was, at length, the form of religious faith for which the world was longing and groping. Now the spirit of religion rose rapidly to its culmination, and its influence was quickly felt in all the civilized countries of the world. What were the doctrines of this new teacher, I need not indicate. He founded a school, humanly speaking, which has flourished with a vigor and persistence with which even the schools of Plato and Aristotle may not be compared; since all their learning has been useful only as the instrument of propagating the learning of the School of Christ.

True it is, nevertheless, that the intellect of man was not permanently satisfied with the simple and normal pretensions of the faith of primitive Christianity. The dawn of the *Intellectual Phase* of this cycle was even now apparent. The outspoken Skeptics of the philosophic world were foremost in opposing all religious belief. Ænesidemus, in the first century after Christ, was the leader of the Latin Skeptics, and he was followed and indorsed by Sextus Empiricus (200 A.D.); while the Roman Favorinus, who lived under Hadrian, made theology, and especially the doctrine of Providence, the object of especial attack. The learned Varro (100 B.C.-28 A.D.), who wrote four hundred and ninety books, regarded the anthropomorphic gods as mere emblems of the forces of matter. Though counted with the Skeptics, his Skepticism was rather opposed to the popular mythology than to the spirit of rising Christianity.

A more conspicuous, if not a more radical, lapse is noticeable in the rise of Neo-Platonism. This was a theosophy which waged a conflict with the increasing power of Christianity.[1] It was the expiring effort of Greek philosophy. It took its stand first in Alexandria. Afterward it broke out in a Syrian

---

[1] This period witnessed the "First Great Crisis" of the Christian faith (Farrar, "History of Free Thought," Lecture II.).

School, and, about the same time, planted itself in Athens. The Alexandrian-Roman School was founded by Ammonius Saccas (175–250 A.D.), who was brought up a Christian. Following him were Origen the Platonist, and Origen the Christian (185–254 A.D.), and Longinus the grammarian. Plotinus (204–269 A.D.) taught at Rome, and brought Neo-Platonic doctrine to a system. He was an ascetic, and eat no flesh. He carried idealism to an extreme. He was not, by any means, an opposer of religion, but rather an erratic and vagarist. He held that "the business of man is to return to God, whom he, as a sensuous being, has estranged from himself. The means by which this return is to be accomplished are virtue, philosophic thought, and, above all, the immediate, ecstatic intuition of God, and the becoming one with him." Porphyry (born 232–'33 A.D.), though holding that the end of philosophizing is the salvation of the soul, and believing in the mysticism of Plotinus, wrote a book against Christianity, opposing especially the divinity of Jesus.

The Syrian School was simply a fanatic theurgy, with an exuberance of religious faith—misguided and superstitious—which makes it a smaller cycle superimposed upon the ascending aspect of the Intellectual Phase, which was now in progress. Jamblichus (died about 330 A.D.) held fully to the polytheistic cultus, and practiced magic and necromancy. Hypatia, the last of this school (415 A.D.), though the teacher of Synesius, the Christian Father, died, herself, in a Christian city, a martyr to polytheism.

In the Athenian School of Neo-Platonism, the theoretical element was again dominant. It was founded by Plutarch, son of Nestorius (350–433); it embraced, among its successive scholarchs, Proclus (born 411), who wrote a book against the Christians, and was expelled by them from Athens; and ended with Damascius, the last teacher of Greek philosophy at Athens. The edict of Justinian closed the Athenian schools in 529 A.D. The teaching of Christianity closed over the chasm as if no void had been produced by the extinction of a system which had reigned in the world for eleven hundred years.

Meantime intellect had begun to assert itself as against the claims of faith, even within the Church itself. The *Intellectual Phase* here was Patristic; and Patristicism was Neo-Platonistic. It represents a *unity* of philosophy and faith. Early in the second century after Christ, Neander tells us, a diminished power and purity of the religious spirit had become apparent. There was a striving after forms and norms—just as we see it in the century succeeding Luther. Ritschl thinks the Catholic Church grew out of this struggle.

But especially did the spirit of speculation grow rife; and Gnosticism was one of its fruits. This was a theosophy—an attempt to advance from Christian faith to Christian knowledge. It philosophized on the relation of Christianity to Judaism and Hellenism. The various objects of religious belief were made personal beings, and a semi-Christian mythology was organized. In the more heterodox branch of Gnostics, we rank Simon Magus; Basilides, who elaborated a system of theosophy; Valentinus (140 A.D.), who prepared an organon; Carpocrates (160 A.D.), who taught a universalistic rationalism; also the Ophites and Perates and the Bardessanes (154–224), who simplified the Gnostic doctrine. In the more orthodox branch, we reckon Flavius Justinus (150 A.D.), the philosophical apologist for Christianity, who held that the idea of God is innate, as well as the most general moral ideas; and with him, the other apologists, Quadratus, Aristides, Melito (170), Bishop of Sardis, who declares Christianity to be a philosophy; Apollonius, Miltiades, Aristo, Tatian (160–170), who reviles Hellenic literature and philosophy; and Athenagoras (176–177), who, like Tyler and Lewis, appeals to Greek poets and philosophers against polytheism, and makes a first attempt at *à priori* proof of the unity of God. Among others concerned in the intellectual movement may be mentioned Hermias (about 225 A.D.), a quasi-eclectic Platonist, but a weak philosopher; Clement of Alexandria, who appropriated what was good in Gnosticism; Origen (185-254), who elaborated the first body of Christian faith; Lactantius, author of "Institutiones Divinæ," and the long list of theologians who engaged in the controversies respecting Monarchianism, Ebionitism, Patripassianism, Sabellianism, and Arianism — terms which are the signs of various heresies respecting the Trinity.

Such progress of free thought, even within the body of the Church itself, prompts us to the anticipation of another tide of religious zeal. The theosophists, orthodox and heterodox, close the FIRST PSYCHIC CYCLE of Christian history.

Irenæus, Tertullian, and the First Council of Nice signalize the *Religious Phase* of the SECOND PSYCHIC CYCLE. Irenæus (140-202), famous as an opponent of the Gnostics, was one of the chief founders of the Catholic Church, whose doctrines had become consolidated about 175 A.D. Jews and Jewish Christians had been expelled from Jerusalem as early as 135 A.D., after the rising under the lead of Bar-Kochba; and now Jewish Christians were joined with ultra-Pauline Antinomians and Gnostics in denunciation for heresy. Tertullian (160-220), the extreme and merciless opponent of heretical thinking, had already prompted ecclesiastical authority to lift its voice. Philosophy had been pronounced by him "the mother of heresies." Jerusalem must be more completely separated from Athens— the Church from the Academy. It was Tertullian who reached the unenviable pinnacle of credulous folly in the saying, *Credo quia absurdum est.* And yet, with all his passionate and blindfold orthodoxy, he maintained that "all which is real is material." Even God and the soul were composed of matter. Tertullian and Tatian went to the greatest extremes in placing faith and philosophy in antagonism with each other.

In full consonance with the dogmatic spirit of Tertullian,

the First Council of Nice, in 325 A.D., established a positive rule of belief; and by a relentless dictum crushed out heresies which argument had not been able to silence. Gregory of Nyssa (331-394) was the first to harness philosophy to the service of establishing the complex of orthodox doctrines. In the doctrine of the divine essence, as distinct from the persons in the Trinity, he anticipates the School-men. With him we associate Cyprian (200-258), Hilarius, the champion of Athanasianism in the West—yet holding to the materiality of the soul; Cassianus, Faustus, Bishop of Regium, and Gennadius, all of like belief; Gregory of Nazianzen, Basil the Great, and Methodius, in whose hands philosophic thought became more enslaved to ecclesiastical dogma.

Before the intellect, however, had been repressed to that state of abject servitude which marks the scholastic ages, we witness a reaction which I note as the *Intellectual Phase* of this cycle. Aurelius Augustine (354-430) was one of the profoundest philosophers, as he was the most eminent theologian, of Christian antiquity; and while it is not necessary to reproduce the detail of his teaching, I deem it safe to adopt St. Augustine as the exponent of a noble and manly movement in the realm of thought. Synesius cut loose from the doctrines of the final destruction of the world and the resurrection of the dead, and inclined to a belief in pre-existence. Numenius, also (about 450 A.D.), believed in pre-existence, and denied the final catastrophe, while on other points he agreed with the Neo-Platonists and Aristotle. Multiplied were the labors, and many the names, of the theologians who appeared upon the field between the years 500 and 800 A.D.—such as Æneas of Gaza, the Neo-Platonic Christian dogmatist; Joannes Philoponus, who pronounced the ideas of Plato the thoughts of God; Joannes Damascenus (700 A.D.), who wrote a system of theology long in use; Boëthius (470-526), the Neo-Platonic Christian; Beda, the Anglo-Saxon (673-735), and, finally, Alcuin (736-804), who founded the "cloister schools," in which were taught the *septem artes ac disciplinæ liberales*.

The SECOND PSYCHIC CYCLE of Christian history here ends, and the THIRD begins. The Third Cycle runs on through the periods of transition to Scholasticism, the full dominion of Scholasticism and the Renaissance, down to the epoch of the French Revolution in 1790. The *Religious Phase* is signalized by the strengthening, and, finally, complete ascendency of ecclesiastical authority in matters of opinion, resisted occasionally by individuals, at the peril of their personal liberty, and even their lives, and provoking three historical revolts—that of the Albigenses, in 1207; that under Wiclif, in 1376; and that led by Luther, who shattered the power of unreasoning tyranny, and opened the way for the rehabilitation of free thought. The *Intellectual Phase* may be regarded as beginning with what is known as the Revival of Letters, quickened by new methods of investigation; rewarded and aggrandized by new discoveries in geography, astronomy, geology, and other sciences; strengthened and rationalized by the promulgation of the great philosophic systems of Bacon, Descartes, Spinoza, Locke, Leibnitz, and Wolf; and, finally, according to the law of progressive assumption and self-aggrandizement, reaching that pitch of haughty domination over the cowed but indestructible religious nature of man which broke forth in the blasphemous and bloody atheism of the "Reign of Terror."

This Religious Phase of Christian history exhibits a marked tendency to a subjective divorce of philosophy and faith, accompanied by an outward subservience of philosophy to faith. Hitherto they had been identical. The religious system had been one which all reason could defend; but, with the adoption of articles of faith more or less extraneous and incongruous, faith and philosophy came more and more frequently into collision. The final establishment of an arbitrary standard of belief left philosophy no field for exercise, except the defense of dogmatic faith. Wherever philosophy and theology came into collision, philosophy must yield to the dictum of the Councils; and obedience was enforced even under pains of imprisonment, torture, and the fagot. But intellect was still forced, by a law of its nature, to discern evidence and draw conclusions. If the judgment were right, how could the conclusion be resisted? The Church was infallible, and how could its edicts be gainsaid? Were there two orders of truth—the one apprehended by reason, the other promulgated by authority and received by faith? This was the despairing conclusion of the thinkers of the Middle Ages. This conviction tacitly runs through all their writings. Philosophy and science, they say, teach thus and so; but they do not reach to the domain of religious truth. By faith we hold to such and such opinions. Such a record has been left behind by Aquinas, Scotus, and Newton. Such recognition of conflict was acted on, but seldom avowed. Pomponatius (1495) openly declared that the Catholic creed should not seek defense from reason—that, in fact, there are two species of truth; and for this he was taken in hand by the Lateran Council.

Erigena (born 800–820 A.D.) first taught that the dicta of the Fathers must be adopted as law; and, though he professes to regard true philosophy as identical with true religion, he betrays the prevailing disposition to leave religion to determine what *is* true philosophy. Toward the close of the eleventh century arose a marked intellectual movement, represented by such names as Berengarius (990–1088), who took rationalistic views of the Lord's-supper; Roscellinus, who was led through Nominalism to Tritheism; and Abelard (1079–1142), who failed in respect for the authority of the Fathers. But the ecclesiastical power was vigilant and ready. Roscellinus was summoned before the Council of Soissons in 1092, and forced to recant; and Abelard was condemned by the Synod of Soissons in 1121, and the Synod of Sens in 1140. The close of the epicycle(¹) was marked by Amalric (died 1206–1207) and his followers, who philosophized somewhat pantheistically. Their doctrines were, however, condemned by the Synod of Paris in 1209, and the Lateran Council of 1215. A ban was also placed on Erigena, and on the physics, and afterward the metaphysics, of Aristotle.

Ecclesiasticism was now installed in supreme power. The dialectic of Aristotle, after serving the ends of the adversaries of the Church for a thousand years, was gradually brought into the service of the Church; but not without many a misgiving, and many a protest. Alexander of Hales (died 1245) set the first conspicuous example. Albertus Magnus (born 1193) remodeled the philosophy of Aristotle to suit the requirements of the Church. Thomas Aquinas (1225–1274) drew out most sharply the antithesis between dogmatic and rational faith. Yet he maintained that the dogmatic faith was simply unapproachable by reason, not contrary to it. Duns Scotus (died 1308), while not affirming the antagonism of reason and faith, goes beyond Aquinas in relegating theological propositions to the category of the unprovable. William of Occam (died 1347), however, lifted his arm against the cherished axiom of the conformity of faith to reason; and, though his works were proscribed by the University of Paris in 1339, the twofold character of truth was generally recognized among Averroists and Alexandrists at the end of the fifteenth century, especially in Northern Italy. Among these, Pomponacci is most conspicuous and worthy. The Lateran Council, nevertheless, in 1512, condemned the distinction between the two orders of truth, and pronounced every thing false which was in conflict with revelation as interpreted by the Church.(²) Luther (1483–1546) broke the pow-

---

(¹) This period is styled by Farrar the Second Great Crisis in the history of Christian Faith (Farrar, "History of Free Thought," Lecture III.).

(²) This claim of the consistency of faith and philosophy, at the same

er of the Romish Church, without fully enfranchising human thought. In his own person, he represents merely a change of masters. "The Sorbonne," he complains, "has propounded the extremely reprehensible doctrine that whatever is demonstrated as true in philosophy must also be accepted as true in theology." Toward philosophy and science Luther manifested a hostility as fierce as had been shown by any of the Scholastics.([1]) Melanchthon (1497–1560) also opposed philosophy at first; but soon discovered that philosophy alone could reduce the new religious movement to an effective system; and Luther, at a later period, acquiesced — convinced perhaps by a reflex action of the free spirit which he had himself evoked, and which was destined to gather strength with the unfolding of the new ideas which now began to fill the world. Of the intolerance of Calvin and other apostles of the Reformation I need not speak; nor of the bitter and despairing contest waged by Romanism with the rising power of science.([2]) The characteristic

---

time that sheer authority pretends to dictate faith and enchain intellect, is evidently equivalent to a confession of conflict between intellect and the faith imposed upon it. This relation of the two great factors in psychic history is, therefore, the reciprocal of that in which intellect, affirming, similarly, a conflict with faith, presumes to prune the creed so far as to trench upon beliefs which are universal and inoppugnable. Between these antipodal states of conflict lie two states in which the combatants observe an armistice. In both, the full authority of reason is recognized; but in one, the authority of the Church is held of equal weight, and hence the system of truth is conceived to be a duality; in the other, the authority of the Church is held to be null when it contravenes the dictates of reason, and the system of truth is conceived as a unity. In the former, the combatants agree to disagree; in the latter, they recognize each other as allies.

([1]) Ueberweg, "History of Philosophy," vol. ii., p. 17. Luther and Melanchthon were both violently hostile to the Copernican system in astronomy. See the references in President White's exhaustive paper on "The Warfare of Science," in *The Popular Science Monthly* for February, 1876, p. 394, and in a later separate issue.

([2]) On this subject see the paper by President White, already cited; as

features of this prolonged Religious Phase gradually fade out as the sun of modern science rises in the heavens; and ecclesiastical authority recedes, at first, to its normal, unaggressive attitude, and then, in turn, crouches beneath the bitter and vindictive revilings of a mad and resurgent spirit of freethinking.

The rise of the *Intellectual Phase* of this cycle may be traced back to the time of Roger Bacon (1214–1294), who "preferred to study nature rather than busy himself in scholastic subtleties." He atoned, however, for his opposition to the spirit of the times by ten years of imprisonment.([1]) Eckart (born after 1250), a chief of the German Mystics, in his independent attitude, was a forerunner of modern science; and, through his ethics, prepared the way for the Reformation. He affirmed that all religious truth lies within the sphere of human reason.

The "revival of letters" was now fairly inaugurated. The new literary movement was largely due to the removal into Italy of learned men from Greece and Constantinople. The Greeks and Arabs had always kept alive an acquaintance with the learning of antiquity. The Eastern Christians and the Mohammedans had long since revolted against the decrees of the early Church; and the latter, especially, had developed an Intellectual Phase to which Europe now became largely indebted. Alkendi (870), Alfarabi (died 950), Avicenna (born 980), and Algazel (born 1059) in the East, and Averroës (1126–1198) in the West, exerted an influence which had now spread over the whole of the civilized world. Averroism, especially, asserted

---

well as Draper, "The Intellectual Development of Europe," and "The Conflict between Religion and Science."

([1]) Roger Bacon was one of the most remarkable intellects which the world has produced. He is far more worthy than his pompous and pampered namesake, of two centuries later, to be regarded as the restorer of the inductive method of scientific investigation. For a full notice of Friar Bacon and his "Opus Majus," see Whewell, "History of the Inductive Sciences," vol. i., p. 512–522.

its presence in much of the philosophy and theology of the world down to a recent period. Numerous contributions to science were also introduced from Arabia. Now, also, occurred a renewal of industrial and commercial activity. Now arose free cities and free citizens. Now a new secular form of culture grew up. "All the natural and moral sentiments proceeding from contact of man with man were brought into prominence in poetry and increased in importance." To these results Dante (1265-1321), Petrarch (1304-1374), and Boccaccio (1313-1375) greatly contributed. A wonderfully increased mental activity next resulted from the invention of the art of printing, in 1440; and then the discovery of America thrilled the civilized world with new ideas, new projects, and new activities. In consonance with the developing spirit of original inquiry, Vives (1492-1540), returning to the ancient method of Aristotle, proclaimed, as Friar Bacon had done, that nature could only be known through direct investigation by way of experiment and observation. To make no further allusion to the revolution endogenous within the field of philosophy and theology, we can not overlook the influence of the external pressure exerted upon the scholastic system by the development of the germs of science which had been planted by Friar Bacon, Vives, Cesalpino (1509-1603), Columbus (1435-1506), and Vanini (1585-1619, burned at the stake for naturalism). Cusanus (1401-1464) had revived the idea of the earth's axial rotation. Copernicus (1473-1543) established the heliocentric theory in astronomy. Kepler (1571-1630) discovered the fundamental laws of planetary motion. Leonardo da Vinci (1452-1519), as Hallam says, "within the compass of a few pages anticipated almost all the discoveries which have been made in science from Galileo to the contemporary geologists." Gassendi (1592-1655), the mediæval Epicurean, is the stepping-stone, in popular estimation, between Lucretius and Tyndall. Telesio (1508-1588) abandoned the disputatious philosophy for the original investigation of nature; and founded at Naples the Academia Telesiana, the prototype of all modern academies of science. Bruno (1548–1600) was another monadist—the prototype of Leibnitz; for his monads were both psychical and material. He suffered, however, for his pantheism; for he rotted several years in the dungeons of the Inquisition, and was finally burned at the stake (1600). Thomas Campanella also (1568–1639) was persecuted and imprisoned thirty years for the heresy of maintaining that we have a twofold revelation of God—Nature and the Bible. The service of Galileo (1564–1641) to modern science needs but mention. Sir David Brewster regards him as possessed of greater merit than Lord Bacon in the establishment of an inductive philosophy; and Biot pronounces Bacon worthless in comparison. Newton (1642–1727) may be regarded the last great light of science preceding the French Revolution.

The independence of the modern philosophic spirit began now to be sensibly felt. Persecutions for opinion's sake had nearly ceased. Macchiavelli (1469) made war on the Church as an obstacle to the unity and freedom of his country. Montaigne (1533–1589), while admitting the necessity of a revelation, attacked Christianity insidiously, and revived the spirit of speculative skepticism. Taurellus (1547–1606) returned to the Platonic attempt to rationalize the doctrines of the Trinity and creation. Hobbes was a strict sensationalist, and a skeptic in philosophy and religion. Descartes (1596–1650) made the fact of thinking his point of departure for the erection of a deductive system — in this, following Augustine, Occam, and Campanella. His doctrines were prohibited by the Synod of Dordrecht in 1656, and his writings were placed in the "Index Librorum Prohibitorum" at Rome in 1663; while in 1671 a royal order forbade the teaching of Cartesianism in the University of Paris. Bayle (1647–1706) employed the early Protestant principle of the contradiction between reason and faith

—always a blind and fatal admission—to expose the absurdities incorporated in the orthodox system. Spinoza (1632–1677) transformed the Cartesian dualism into a pantheism, whose fundamental conception was the unity of substance. Locke (1632–1704), the eminent sensationalist, laid the foundation on which Berkeley (1684–1753) erected his system of universal immaterialism or idealism; while Hartley (1704–1757), on the same basis, reared a system of materialism; and Priestley (1733–1804) accepted this materialism without renouncing the Christian faith. Leibnitz (1646–1716), while professing a moderate orthodoxy, introduced into his monadology principles and assumptions which have rendered service to religious doubters. He had a multitudinous following; but is indebted to Wolf (1679–1754) for the compilation of his system. Lessing (1729–1781) offered a rationalizing interpretation of the Trinity and other Christian doctrines.

The skeptical bent of French philosophy was even more decided than that of English and German thinking. The objective point of attack was the system of received dogmas, and the prevailing tyranny exercised both in Church and State. Fontenelle (1657–1757), by his popular discourses on the Plurality of Worlds, had rooted the new astronomy in the common mind. Voltaire (1694–1778) had been foremost in popularizing the Newtonian doctrines, and had brought the antagonism of the Church (both Catholic and Protestant) to Copernicanism well-nigh to a bitter crisis. Maupertius (1698–1759), by the measurement of a degree of latitude in Lapland, contributed to the prosperity of encroaching science. Montesquieu (1689–1775) lifted up his voice against absolutism equally in Church and State. Rousseau (1712–1778), a materialist and pantheist, would raze all modern systems to the ground, and start the work of reconstruction from a new chaos. Mettrie (1709–1751), the forerunner of Bain and Maudsley, traced all psychical activities to the bodily organization. Condillac (1715

–1780) threw a substructure under this psychology, by surpassing Locke in denominating all knowlege " but transformed sensations." Bonnet (1720–1793) attempted to stand with one foot on the land and one on the sea; but did not succeed to the satisfaction of his generation. Diderot (1713–1784) and D'Alembert, the editors of the "Encyclopédie," were brilliant skeptics—the former pantheistic, the latter revolutionary. Condorcet (1743–1794) preached the gospel of pure reason. Robinet (1735–1820) denied divine personality. Helvetius (1715–1771) founded his ethics on self-love. Buffon (1707–1788) cherished an unavowed belief in Naturalism, and cultivated physiology and psychology in a materialistic sense. Hume (1711–1777) was an empiric and a doubter—denying the possibility of attaining to a knowledge of God's existence or the soul's immortality. D'Holbach (1723–1789) wrote the *chef-d'œuvre* of materialism, embodying every thing which was heterodox in La Mettrie, Condillac, Diderot, and Helvetius. Finally, the fruitage of this luxuriant crop of skepticism ripened, and the world beheld it in the carnage and blasphemy of the Revolution of 1790, which Volney (1757–1820), impenitent to the end, pronounced a just attempt to realize the ideal of the rule of reason.

In this national and civil chaos we reach the end of the Third Psychic Cycle of Christian history, and begin the FOURTH. It will not be necessary to trace the course of the agencies and the agents concerned in the revival of a normal religious faith. Suffice it to say that the religious consciousness of the civilized world manifested a revulsion. The tyranny of undevout reason had passed the limits of endurance. God, as a personal power, was again recognized; pantheism in its protean forms was trampled under righteous feet; Deity and the soul ceased to be monads; thought and volition were no longer the products of exosmose, endosmose, and secretion; earthy slime ceased to generate worms, and the gospel of Lamarck was laid upon the shelf.

The close of the *Religious Phase*, and the beginning of the *Intellectual* one, may perhaps be regarded as marked by the appearance of the anonymous "Vestiges of Creation" (1842); and its march as denoted by the establishment of the geological doctrine of the great age of the world; uniformitarianism and progressive development in the ancient history of the world; the unity of the history of the solar system, and, in its methods, of the entire cosmos; the establishment of the nebular theory; the doctrine of the transmutation and conservation of energy; the unity of the material forces; the theory of the physiological origin of psychic phenomena; the doctrines of heterogenesis, derivation of species, and universal evolution, with or without the exclusion of divine intervention. These, however tenable or untenable some of the theories may be, are the exponents of a recent intellectual movement, which, if we interpret the history of thought correctly, has recurred time and again in the experience of our race; and is destined, like other intellectual phases, to be superseded by the return of a normal trust in the authority of our religious intuitions; a regenerated, a broader and stronger religious faith, and an actual progress toward a standard of absolute truth.

The FIRST PSYCHIC CYCLE of Christian history was characterized by the earnest *search of Thought for a worthy form of Religious Faith*. Its Religious Phase was Apostolicism, and its Intellectual Phase, Heresism. The SECOND PSYCHIC CYCLE was characterized by the *Unity of Thought and Faith*. Its Religious Phase was Tertullianism, and its Intellectual Phase was Augustinism. The THIRD PSYCHIC CYCLE was characterized by the *Servitude of Thought to Faith*. Its Religious Phase was Scholasticism, and its Intellectual Phase was the Renaissance. The FOURTH PSYCHIC CYCLE has been characterized by the *Divorce of Thought from Faith*. Its Religious Phase has been Protestantism, and its Intellectual Phase Naturalism. The next Psychic Cycle, it seems to me, will witness a *Synthesis of Thought and Faith*—a recognition of the fact that it is impossible for reason to find solid ground that is not consecrated ground; that all philosophy and all science belong to religion; that all truth is a revelation of God; that the truths of written revelation, if not intelligible to reason, are nevertheless consonant with reason; and that Divine agency, instead of standing removed from man by infinite intervals of time and space, is, indeed, the true name of those energies which work their myriad phenomena in the natural world around us. This consummation—at once the inspiration of a fervent religion and the prophecy of the loftiest science—is to be the noontide reign of wedded Intellect and Faith, whose morning rays already stream far above our horizon.

SCIENCE AND PHILOSOPHY IN RELIGION.

IV.

THE DOCTRINE OF CAUSALITY.

1. Original Causation.

THE lengthy, and yet synoptical, sketch of the historical interactions of Intellect and Faith presented in the last two lectures was little more than a bald digest of recorded facts. Want of time prohibited, and still prohibits, the utterance of many things calculated to qualify broad statements, to add to the evidence, and strengthen the argument. It would have been gratifying to note more particularly the progress of scientific development in post-scholastic times; the influence of the discovery and settlement of America, and the successful war for independence in the United States; the great influence of maritime discovery—the doubling of the Cape of Good Hope, the discovery of the Pacific Ocean, and the circumnavigation of the globe. It would be gratifying, also, to note the real service which was performed for literature and classical learning, for philosophy and the dialectic art, by the Romish Church during the Middle Ages; to trace the history of mediæval thought among the Nestorians, the Mohammedans, and the Jews; and, while illustrating the laws of the Interaction of the two great forces of humanity, to acknowledge our indebtedness to Eastern influences for the Revival of Letters.[1] It would

---

[1] Some of these topics are treated with great originality by Draper in "The Intellectual Development of Europe." See, also, Whewell, "History of the Inductive Sciences." These two authorities, however, are widely apart in their estimate of the indebtedness of civilization to Arabian thought. But see Hallam, "Literature of Europe," vol. i.

be agreeable, if not highly desirable, to guard myself against misconstruction when, in sketching the progress of religious phases, I have found myself under the necessity of tracing them into ceremonialism and sacerdotalism, sometimes fanaticism, and oftener a rigorous surveillance over the intellect. It might be well for me to guard myself against misinterpretation when, in sketching the progress of an intellectual phase, I have had to bring freethinking, materialism, pantheism or some form of recognized heresy, into an antithesis with religious excesses —as if sound intelligence must necessarily be heretical and anti-religious.

In reference to this, I fall back upon the general propositions enunciated in my first lecture for explanation and defense. Both these forces have the right to existence and free action. It is the law of faith to encroach upon intellect; and the law of intellect to assert its freedom, and even to retaliate. This interaction is an ordination of Heaven, and is beneficent; it is the condition of the approximation of man toward high ideals of religion and knowledge. These two forces must, nevertheless, learn to respect each other; and each must feel that its own welfare is bound up in the tolerance and highest activity of the other. Without intelligence, religion degenerates into a fetichism, which is next to the negation of religion. Without religious faith dwelling and acting in the human heart, society sinks to a level where even intelligence expires in the ruins of public and private morality. There is a system of beneficent correlations and co-operations between Intellect and Faith which all interests urge us to recognize and cherish. There *are* services which intellect is able to render to religious faith, which faith ought to be eager to secure; and, dropping all mediæval fancies or fears in reference to possible contradictions in the system of truth, cheerfully, cordially, and, interestedly accept the complete and indissoluble *unity* of truth, and, as a corollary, the *sacredness* of all truth which God has ordained to exist. On this platform we can bid investigation godspeed, and hail with gratitude every trophy which it brings back to us from the field of the unknown—fearing nothing which reason can prove true, but only that which reason is capable of proving erroneous—assured always that the time will come when all which science can establish will be counted an indispensable auxiliary to a purified and robust faith.

I have not the vanity to think that, after all the earnest endeavor and loyal aspiration which have marked the twenty centuries of reflective thought, I am the first to discover the methods in which the interests of Faith may be subserved by the efforts of Intellect. I venerate the names which shine in the skies which have bent over other generations of men; and after the survey which I have taken of the profound intellectual labors of the hundreds who have gone before, no less earnest and far more able than I, it seems fitting that I should drop the pen, and silence the tongue, and listen reverently to the voices which come up from antiquity; from the cloisters of the Middle Ages; from the retirement of the philosophers whose wisdom has led us out into this light in which we exult, I fear, with less of gratitude than of pride. But I can not rest inactive. The throbs of brain, like the pulsations of the luminiferous ether, can not be stilled. Be it better or worse than others have done, the brain, as long as it lives, must work. May Infinite Wisdom and Goodness open the way to eternal truth!

I have said that faith in God is a living principle in the life of humanity. Whence comes this faith?

I deny, first, that it grows out of a superstitious fear of invisible powers, as taught by Hobbes, Comte, Lubbock, Büchner, and a few others. I deny, in the second place, that it is a feeling descended from an ancient veneration for ancestors, or for the wise and good, as taught by Euhemerus, Burton, and some others. I deny, thirdly, that it is a faith inculcated or enforced by those who peopled Olympus with divinities, to inspire obedience to the laws of society and the State, as Critias, Mutius Scævola, Pyrrho, and others of the ancients asserted. I deny, fourthly, that it is a sentiment derived originally from inspired revelation, propagated by the chosen people of God, and quite unfelt among tribes whom the messages of the Bible have never reached. I hold, with nearly all the philosophers of antiquity, with Spencer and Tyndall and Huxley, and nearly all the leading scientists and thinkers of modern times, that the religious sentiment and belief arise *spontaneously* in the human soul, and are absolutely the characteristic of universal humanity. The grounds for these denials and this affirmation have not received from me a casual attention. It is not my purpose to spread them out in this connection; but reference has been made to them in a former lecture.([1])

How comes this universal theistic conception into existence? My reply is that it comes through two channels: 1st. INTUITION; 2d. DEDUCTION. Intuition alone is almost the only light of lowest savages; but deduction along various brief lines of thought comes to the aid of the mind in the feeblest infancy of reflection, and strengthens its conclusions more and more, as long as reflective thought continues to grow in breadth of grasp and clearness of discernment.

There is no need to hesitate at the announcement of the stupendous and humbling fact that God is revealed directly to human reason. This intuition of God is one of the common data of human intelligence. We find it in us and in all men; like the intuition of the relation subsisting between the whole and the sum of its parts; but it is a tremendous fact, when we pause to think upon its significance. Much could be adduced to sustain the thesis that God reveals himself directly to human consciousness. The very universality of theistic beliefs shows that humanity can not dodge the divine presence; more than

---

([1]) See, also, the Seventh Paper, "Reason for the Faith."

this is the wide-spread belief among philosophers and theologians, that direct communion with God is both possible and normal. I only need refer you to the doctrines of some of the Pythagoreans, and especially the Neo-Pythagoreans; to Socrates;(¹) to Plato and the Platonists, and especially the Neo-Platonists—to Philo the Jew, Plotinus, and Jamblichus; to the Neo-Platonistic Fathers and Schoolmen; to Eckart and the Mystics; to Cusanus, Jacobi, Schleiermacher, Nitzsch; to that Oriental faith in divine communication manifest in Buddha and the Buddhists, and again in Magianism and Parseeism; and, finally, to the doctrine of Jewish and Christian inspiration, and to the pretensions of the founders of nearly all religious systems. It seems to me that the sentiment of the philosophic world is strongly in support of a doctrine which, in recent times, has sunk almost into forgetfulness, if not rejection. But I shall not elaborate the evidences which sustain me in this belief.

(¹) "Pythagoras the Great always applied his mind to prognostication; and Abaris the Hyperborean, and Aristæus the Proconnesian, and Epimenides the Cretan, who came to Sparta, and Zoroaster the Mede, and Empedocles of Agrigentum, and Phormion the Lacedæmonian; Polycrates, too, of Thasus, and Empedotimus of Syracuse; and, in addition to these, Socrates the Athenian, in particular. 'For,' he says in the "Theages," 'I am attended by a supernatural intimation which has been assigned me from a child, by divine appointment. This is a voice which, when it comes, prevents what I am about to do, but exhorts never'" (Plato's "Theages," xi., *ad init.*). Clement proceeds to name many others reputed to be prophets and soothsayers (Clem. Alex., Strom., book i., xxi.). It is not imagined, of course, that the pretense of soothsaying is any evidence of the intuition of Deity; but it seems certain that the wide prevalence of it among both civilized and barbarous peoples may be cited as evidence of opinion respecting the possibility of intercourse with the power of the unseen world. Clement further says: "By reflection and *direct vision*, those among the Greeks who have philosophized accurately see God" (Strom., book i., chap. xix.). The higher religious intuition Clement calls "self-operating wisdom" (Strom., book i., chap. xx.).

The doctrine of the immediate intuition of Deity suffers, at first view, no little disparagement from the fact that so many of its defenders have been carried away by a spirit of credulity or enthusiasm—given to divination, astrology, alchemy, and other mysteries, which, in the history of speculation, are set down as characteristics or accessories of philosophic mysticism. It is proper to bear in mind, nevertheless, that those possessing an unusual development of any mental power are correspondingly liable to fall into a certain class of failings not common to the average mind. An excessively and exclusively logical mind is abnormally slow of conviction under the force of moral evidence. An unusually vivid imagination commits a multitude of sins of which the prosaic individual would be incapable. And yet the logical faculty and the imagination are noble and exalted faculties, not to be reproached for the sins and errors which become possible under a development which may be excessive relatively to the other powers of the mind. Even excessive amiability has its concomitant and consequential failings; and something similar may be said of morbid conscientiousness, extravagant affection, or unbridled benevolence. Yet none of these failings would be used as evidence that the powers from whose overdevelopment they arise are not useful and beneficent; still less that they do not really exist, or that their objects are unrealities. So those in whom the divine intuition is clearest may owe this excellence to auxiliary susceptibilities which make them, in the actual world, the easy victims of credulity and error.

I reply, in the second place, that the universal theistic belief comes into existence through simple processes of deduction. There is more than one highway to the cognition of God, however single and narrow may be the road to heaven. The *concensus gentium*, as Cicero says, is one of the grounds of belief. What all mankind believe must be true. *Vox populi, vox Dei* —I do not mean the voice of the rabble or of the majority—

but the voice of humanity, with no minority dissenting. Such a faith can not be hollow without projecting discord into a world where all else is harmony. But this, also, is a line of thought which I propose to pass by.

Foremost of all, then, the intuition of causality affords the most important datum for supporting a theistic deduction. To the discussion of this thesis I invite your attention.

The word CAUSE is one of the most familiar in the language. Every person believes himself to know what it means, though few persons have reflected with attention on the complete content of this concept, and its relation logically and historically to the cognitive, sensitive, and voluntary powers of the soul. That the idea or notion of causality is a universal datum of human thought all admit, as they must admit; but whether it be a mere acquired belief, or an endogenous and necessary and characteristic power of the soul, is a question upon which entire unanimity has not been reached.

It may illustrate the extravagance and bad logic of speculative skepticism to state that the Middle Academy denied even that causation is a possibility—and thence concluded the invalidity of the notion of causality. A cause is a relation, says Ænesidemus, for it is not to be conceived without that which it causes; but the relation has no existence except in thought. Again, he argues that, in any case, cause and effect must be either synchronous, or else cause or effect must precede. If we suppose them synchronous, it is impossible to determine which is cause. If we suppose effect to precede, an absurdity is at once apparent. If, finally, we suppose cause to precede, this is also an absurdity, since cause is no cause until effect exists; and this results in a synchronism which confounds cause and effect, as under the first supposition. Such reasoning, like Zeno's argument against the possibility of motion, is simply a species of dialectic legerdemain.

The various theories respecting the origin of our notion of

causality may, I think, be reduced to three: 1. That it is Exogenous, or based on data derived from without. Hume says it is habit which leads us to expect certain sequences from given antecedents. Glanville says we do not experience, but only infer, causation. J. S. Mill asserts that the idea of cause is merely a general induction from facts of observation. He gives the same explanation of all universal and necessary beliefs—not excepting our belief in the axioms of mathematics.(¹)

2. The theory that the notion of causality is Endogenous, or developed within, as held by Leibnitz, Kant, and Cousin. Sir William Hamilton also maintained that our idea of cause arises only from "a subjective necessity"—our inability to conceive of any thing except as an effect proceeding from a cause. Spencer holds that universal ideas are the results of organized experience, that is, the inherited experience of the race.

3. The theory that the notion of causality is Innate, or born within us—an essential attribute of our mental being. It is not implied in this view that the notion would ever arise in consciousness, except under the influence of the co-ordinate activity of the various departments of the mind. The notion of cause, for instance, though innate, may not be awakened into consciousness except by the discovery of uniform sequences in the external world, as is rather commonly held; or it may, as Maine de Biran, Reid, and others have believed, be roused into consciousness by observing the connection between acts of volition and the mental states or external changes which follow; or, as Coleridge thought, by the perception of the activity of our imaginations and the accompanying results. A belief in the innate character of the idea was entertained by Plato, by Carneades, by the Realists among the Schoolmen, by Descartes, and is held by the majority of modern metaphysicians.

(¹) J. S. Mill, "Logic," book ii., chap. v.

The distinction between the Innate and the Endogenous origin of the idea does not seem to me important. In either case it is a recognized and invariable characteristic of the mind —a universal datum of thought; and, in either case, it is considered as emerging in the field of consciousness only on the presentation of the appropriate occasion.

That the idea of causal relation is not the suggestion of experience, seems to be extremely obvious. Experience could afford only the idea of succession, or, at most, a fixed order of succession, like that of the individuals in a procession. It could never give rise to the notion of that relation between the terms which we denominate causal. And, again, should the concept of a causal relation arise as a general induction from a countless number of sequences, it could never yield us that certain conviction which we possess, that every assignable event proceeds from a cause. A moment's reflection upon our own mental states must convince us that we feel a certainty *beyond all doubt* that every event and every phenomenon is due to the exertion of some causal efficiency. The relation between cause and effect we feel to be more than a uniform sequence. Some energy has been put forth by cause, or has proceeded through, and emanates from, that which is called cause, to the effect.

In contemplating the essential nature of the causal relation, we perceive that it implies *sequence, efficiency, adequacy, direction,* and *application*. The potential cause exists before the effect; it exerts an efficiency to produce the effect, and does not stand simply as an invariable antecedent; it exerts an adequate efficiency, both in amount and kind; its efficiency is directed toward the effect still non-existent, and is applied to that from which the effect is evolved. These are simple constitutive ideas, whose shadowy and evanescent forms we can recognize inclosed in, or dependent on, the notion of causation.

Now, when we reflect that the naked and disentangled notion of cause is simply the intuition and accompanying belief, that every event proceeds from adequate efficiency, directed toward, and applied to, that substance, actual or potential, from which effect comes, it seems to me that we dismiss at once a mass of dialectic and scholastic verbiage which has darkened the discussion of causality ever since the days of Aristotle. If we view the subject in the clear light of the intuition in our own souls, it seems to be apparent that there can exist but *one species of cause*, and that is *efficient cause*—the entity in which efficiency originates.(¹) That which prompts efficiency to its exertion is *motive*, and not cause; and we introduce confusion to denominate it the "final cause." It is the "sufficient reason." Its relation to effect is recognized as essentially different from the relation between efficiency and effect. It is not the causal relation; and although the notion of motivity may

---

(¹) The term "efficient cause" is employed here in a restricted sense. It does not embrace, according to the views of Aristotle and the Schoolmen, any antecedent of an effect which is not the fountain and source of the efficiency on which the effect depends. Many modern physicists and naturalists employ the term "efficient cause" in the scholastic sense; but metaphysicians, though, for convenience, employing the term cause as the physicists do, make a clear distinction. J. S. Mill says, "I most fully agree with M. Comte that *ultimate*, or, in the phraseology of the metaphysicians, *efficient*, causes, which are conceived as not being phenomena, nor perceptible to the senses at all, are radically inaccessible to the human faculties. * * * When I speak of causation, I have nothing in view other than those constant relations" [of succession or of similarity] ("System of Logic," book ii., chap. v., § 9). Professor Jevons, who uses the term "cause" with great latitude of meaning, and seems, moreover, to misunderstand both Bacon and Mill, makes the same distinction, and for the same purpose: "We must not confuse this supremely difficult question [Is there any cause for the event?] with that into which inductive science inquires on the foundation of facts" ("Principles of Science," vol. i., p. 257). Professor Morris brings out the distinction with clearness ("The Final Cause," Proc. Phil. Soc., London, 1875).

arise simultaneously with the notion of cause, the two notions are clearly distinguishable.

Again, the material acted upon by efficiency, or from which or within which effect arises, is in no sense a cause. It may be an essential condition of the production of the effect, but we confound ideas again to designate it the "material cause." It sustains no causal relation to the effect.

Neither is the antecedent concept possessed by the causal agent clothed with the attribute of efficiency. The so-called "formal cause" is the preconception of the causal intelligence, and constitutes one of the numerous conditions of the realization of effect. Closely related to this is the "exemplary cause" of Pythagoras and Plato.

Neither, again, can the changed results which succeed the removal or change of an efficient cause be referred causally to the negation. "Negative cause" is an imaginary quantity. Effect proceeds from something real, and existent, and present, and efficient. "Negative cause" is a mere verbal contradiction. Nor is "modal cause" much more real; since mode is merely a state, or condition, or mode of action of that which *is* efficient, "substantial" and real cause.

These exclusions render it necessary to restrict the "general definition" of cause. The general idea of cause is not, as Aristotle affirms, "that without which another thing called effect can not be;" but rather, according to Wolf, "that which contains in itself the reason why another thing exists—*Ens quod in se continet rationem cur alterum existat.* Motive, material, intermediation, preconception, efficiency, being regarded as specific causes, we may abstract a general definition of cause; and we may render ourselves intelligible by using terms in such senses; but it must be constantly felt that "efficient cause," in the sense as qualified, is the only cause which is underlaid by our intuition of causality; and that, though the other Aristotelian and scholastic "causes" may be based on concepts, some of which are invariable concomitants of our notion of causation (cause in action), it should be the conceded prerogative of the eliminated intuition of causality to sanction the employment of the term "cause." I view cause, therefore, as a single and irresolvable idea; and the use of such an expression as "cause in the general sense" is an ætiological solecism.

Disencumbering myself of the verbal jargon of the past,(¹) and recognizing only one species of cause, I wish to abolish, further, except for mere convenience of phraseology, the distinction of "primary" and "secondary" causation. Secondary cause is simply the intermediation through which primary cause transmits efficiency. The very definition dethrones it as cause. The millstone is, in no proper sense, the cause of the flour. The hammer is not the cause of the contusion. These are media, or instruments, for the transmission of efficiency by primary causes. The naked intuition of causality is only an intuition of the relation between effect and primary, original moving cause.

In the next place, causal efficiency implies spontaneity. Dead substance may serve as the medium, or instrument, for the transmission of efficiency. Inanimate matter may occupy the place of so-called *secondary* causes; but a real or spontaneous cause it can never be. A dozen terms of secondary causation may intervene between effect and first cause, but first cause is necessarily implied in every instance—a first cause acting in and of itself, having inherent energy, put forth under the mandate of will, and consequently under the direction of intelligence. We

---

(¹) St. Clement says: "Now, all the causes may be shown in order in the case of the learner. The father is the *procatarctic* cause of learning; the teacher, the *synectic;* and the nature of the learner, the *co-operating cause;* and time holds the relation of cause *sine qua non.* * * * Causation is predicated in four ways: the *efficient* cause, as the statuary; and the *material*, as the brass; and the *form*, as the character; and the *end*, as the honor of the Gymnasiarch" (Clem. Alex., Strom., book viii., chap. ix.).

may *think* of efficient causation between the terms of the series of natural phenomena; but unless we can posit intelligence and will in the antecedent, the thought is illusory. We may say that the lightning has caused the destruction of a building; but unless we clothe lightning with the attributes of intelligence and will, the phrase can imply no more than secondary causation, which, as I have said, is no causation at all, in the sense implied in the intuition.

To get back through the chain of secondary causes, so called, to real or first cause, may demand the passage of a vast number of links—nay, an indefinite number of links; but real, voluntary, and intelligent cause must be disclosed at last. In the world of human activities, human will is seen standing as the first term of series of results, each of which becomes the instrumental cause of the succeeding term. In the natural world, the regress backward from phenomenon loses itself in a realm of mystery and impenetrableness; but human reason does not abate one jot of its confidence in the presence of intelligent efficiency at the initial end of the series. The Arabian philosopher Alfarabi says, as all change and all development must proceed from a cause, so the sum of all changes must flow from a First Cause. Albertus Magnus, in the face of the prevailing sentiment of antiquity, follows the instinct of causality to its legitimate conclusion, and affirms that even matter is an effect. Descartes denies that the *regressus in infinitum* affords the intellect any relief, and feels impelled to posit primordial causation in eternity, as the logical antecedent of the cosmos. Indeed, the notion of primordial causality is twin to the intuition of cause. To say absolutely that nothing in the universe exists except as an effect is to deny the possibility of all existence. The human mind promptly reposes itself on the idea of uncreated and uncaused cause. Wandering off into the realm of the undiscoverable, unable to climb the infinite steps which descend from primal efficiency, it feels that First Cause reigns at the beginning; and, in spite of the axiom of reason which dominates in all the cognizable realm, that "whatever exists has been caused to exist," the soul which rises to such heights as to gaze into the infinite and eternal, finds a supporting and unimpeachable testimony arising out of the obscure ground of its own consciousness, and affirming, in accents which interdict all doubt, an eternal *Self-existence*, filling the immensity which is mirrored in its own consciousness. Thus, I maintain that the idea of primordial cause—why may I not say the intuition of Deity?—is a datum of reason as clear, as necessary, as universal as the apperception of causality in the finite sphere.

This necessary idea of primordial causality is, to claim no more, but one remove from the intuition of Deity. As soon as reason recognizes the necessary truth of primitive causality—uncaused—without a term beyond, it passes by the necessary *law of substance* to the concept of *real being* in whom the attribute of primordial causality inheres. Without the consciousness of a process of thought, all which characterizes the absolute and infinite reveals itself as the investiture of the primitive causal existence, on whose will hangs all dependent existence.

This supreme datum—ultimate and initial—is not to be regarded as a mere possibility of thought. I do not embrace the doctrine that whatever is possible in thought is a reality in existence. The specialty of this ultimate theistic concept is its necessity and universality. Whether we be able to recognize one, two, or three steps leading to the concept of Deity, every step is taken in obedience to an inexorable law of the universal reason. It is simply the primitive notion of causality leading to the primitive notion of self-existent causality, combined with the primitive belief that every attribute implies real existence in which it inheres. Every link is a necessary and universal belief of humanity; and unless we are prepared to maintain the deceitfulness of *all* primitive beliefs, we must accept the conclusion that these also answer to realities; and the correlates for which they stand are facts in the system of existence.

This conclusion means: 1st. That efficient *causation* is a fact; 2d. All causation proceeds from intelligent *volition;* 3d. The reality of an *initial term* in the series bound by a causal nexus; 4th. A *real existence* at the beginning of things, clothed in all the attributes implied in the existence, not only of the cosmos of finite observation, but in the infinitudes of time and space whose reality is mirrored in human reason.

Having eliminated the datum of primordial causality, I suspend, for the moment, the claim that this becomes a necessary stepping-stone to the cognition of Deity, and invite your attention to a systematic unfolding of the necessary truths inclosed in the idea of efficient causation — premising only that such causation stands at the beginning of every series of events; that it implies intelligent will; and that the first causative effort put forth in the realm of existence was a primordial and creative one, and that nothing exists within the purview of reason to preclude a conviction that creative causation has been continuous.

Causation implies, FIRST of all, *the existence of a real cause.* Nothing could come into existence in the absence of an entity clothed with causative efficiency. Chance is not a cause. Cause is substantive; chance is modal. The ascription of any event or series of events to chance must be an act of ignorance; or it must be done with qualifications of the phrase which deprive it of all meaning. There may be an indifference or equipollency of probabilities, which leaves the determination of an event, in some cases, to conditions which can not be foreseen; and we may say there exist equal chances one way or the other; or, by an accommodation of language, that chance turns the scale, and causes the result which ensues. But this is a misuse of terms; since every one must perceive that whatever result ensues is produced by real causes, in which miscalled chances exert no more than a conditioning influence. The structure, harmony, and order of the cosmos have been ascribed to the "fortuitous concourse of atoms" having an eternal existence and eternal motion; and it has been assumed that such an origin of the cosmos dispenses completely with the doctrine of "creation" and an ordering intelligence. I do not assert that such an exclusion of Deity has been contemplated by the school of atomists, from Leucippus to Epicurus, and from Lucretius to Gassendi and Tyndall. Indeed, I believe that every one of the leading atomists has recognized divine existence, though some of them may have conceived his relation to the world as exceedingly remote and possibly unessential. Many recognized theists have equally maintained the eternity of matter, force, and motion; though it is impossible for me to comprehend how these postulates can be granted by philosophy. So far as I am able to discern, the atomistic theory demands Deity for its working. Its very data present three things to be accounted for: 1st. The eternal *atoms;* 2d. The eternal *motions;* 3d. The *correlations* presented by the world—correlations of structural part to structural part; correlations of structure to intelligible end; correlations of structures to persistent plans or archetypes; and especially correlations of an anticipatory character—all necessarily interpreted by reason in terms of intelligence, foresight, and beneficence. Now, to admit the eternity of an atom does not abolish the law of causality. An eternal atom needs a cause as truly as a finite one, unless, indeed, we are prepared to ascribe to it all those predicates which reason affirms of primordial, creative, but self-existent cause. Leibnitz conceived of monads endued with intelligence and will; but even such monads were held to be created things. The same must be affirmed of eternal motion. Its eternity does not strip it of the need of causation. An existence or a phenomenon persisting from eternity is still the effect of adequate causation. I am ready to admit the expression "caused from eternity;" though I should deny the *necessary* existence of matter or motion from eternity, or from any other assignable epoch. I can conceive that before the beginning of the existence of the present cosmos, or even its matter, Deity had ordained an infinite series of schemes of existence, none of which involved the employment of what we call matter. Thus, it seems to me, the fundamental postulate of what we call atomism can only be granted by creation. Still more does the existence of correlations in the world imply the thought and providence of a Being clothed with such attributes as creation implies. This thesis, however, which opens a wide field in science and philosophy, will be taken up hereafter. Finally, it still remains to determine the *nature* of the motions in the atomic universe; for it is important to know whether these are simply propagated from a primordial impulse, or generated from time to time as occasion demands; and if propagated undiminished from the beginning of existence, we must inquire whether they vary in quantity, quality, and direction, simply according to the mechanical laws of action and reaction, or receive from time to time the impress of extraneous power. The atomistic philosophy, therefore, is not necessarily atheistical; and the records show that it has not been so regarded by its adherents; while it must be confessed that, to shallow thinking, it may seem to present the current of events as a stream of flour ground out by the mechanical revolutions of a mill, with all inquiry respecting the origin of the mill and the grain conclusively silenced. Whatever aspect such a cosmology may present, it must be admitted that the fortuitousness of the concurrences and arrangements of the atoms is not, after all, a *cause* which accounts for the movements of the atoms. The atomistic theory, therefore, even if a true cosmology, can not denude existence of a real causative being.

In the NEXT place, *causative reality must be antecedent to all its effects.* To assert that effect can precede cause is to assert that a cause can act before it exists; while I have just shown that real existence is implied in the exertion of all causal efficiency. Indeed, the proposition would require no proof, if it had not been sometimes ignored in the attempt to thrust non-existence or modal existence—the negation of substantial existence—into the position of cause. The universe, as an effect, must be subsequent to its cause. The existence of matter can not run parallel with the being of Deity. Matter may be eternal in the mathematical sense; but the being of God is precedent both logically and historically. This is a necessary dictum of reason. In this discussion, I am affirming only necessary ideas.

In the THIRD place, the notion of causality implies *correlative subjectivity and objectivity*—the cause acting and the otherness toward which its efficiency is directed. In the field of ordinary human activity, man is the subjective factor, and matter the objective one. Man only acts upon matter. If my causal efficiency leave an impression upon wax, I act upon matter; if it produce a picture in the imagination of another, this is through the intermediation of matter—the tongue or the gesture on my part, and the auditory or optic nerve on the part of the other person. If my causal efficiency, in the form of a volition, produce a picture in my own imagination, the volition first impresses itself upon the cerebral organism, and thence succeeds the picture. I do not assert the *absolute* dependence of mind upon matter: I deny it; I only maintain that our normal—at least, our usual—mental acts are effected—objectified, through the intermediation of matter.

In the realm of creative activity, the objective datum is not actual, but potential. While only creative efficiency exists, otherness is a mere capacity of existence; and yet effectuation must be directed objectiveward. Potential effect must exist, ideally differentiated from cause; as, otherwise, cause, by the addition of effect to itself, would lose its identity; or we must accept the absurd proposition that creative action can take place while yet causal existence is incomplete. Whether, in this case, effect rise into existence *ab extra*, or be evolved from creative cause, *its relative objectivity is a necessity of thought.* The necessary *sequence* of effect, and the necessary *differentiation* of cause and effect—as subjective (and *in se*) unconditioned existence, and objective conditioned existence, rends the system of monism from centre to circumference. It is impossible to comprehend how that which is self-existent, and in itself absolute and unconditioned, can be one with that which is created, finite and dependent. If we assert the First Cause to be homogeneous with matter, we are lacking in the first datum of evidence that matter possesses a single one of the attributes which characterize First Cause. If we assert that matter is homogeneous with First Cause, we utter a simple hypothesis, and one which not only lacks all support from the field of human knowledge, but is in conflict with modern science, and the reflective thought of all time. We are bound to a dualism. It is safe to fall back on the *consensus gentium* and the intuitions of humanity in accepting as an axiom the proposition that the being who stands in the relation of cause is, in no sense, to be confounded with that which *is caused.*

The notion of causality implies, in the FOURTH place, the possession of *consciousness* by the causal efficiency. A cause without consciousness would sleep forever in potentiality. In order to become an actual cause, it must have knowledge of its own existence, and of the possibility, at least, of other existence, and of the possession of efficiency. It must have a further consciousness of all the relations subsisting between cause and effect, and of all the conditions which modify its causal activity. This necessity excludes the possibility of any system which is a pure, unconscious materialism, or a pure, unconscious dynamism. A mechanism called into being may run on through indefinite ages without the intervention of consciousness; but a conscious intelligence must have produced the mechanical structure and animated it with propulsive power. Such a conception of the cosmos may remove creative power to an indefinite distance from things present here and now; but yet it is not a godless scheme. How utterly and almost absurdly improbable it is, that a Being capable of creating a universe should never after exert his power in any way, I need only to remind you. How much evidence exists that that power is perpetually exerted, I hope will appear in the sequel.

In the FIFTH place, the notion of causation implies that the causal agent shall be able to form a conception of a specific non-existent effect, and shall form such a conception. This is the "formal" causality of the Aristotelians. The production of effect without premeditation does not develop the essential character of cause. If it were possible for me to produce effect without the antecedent conception of effect, my act, like the act of an unconscious thing, would be only an instance of secondary or mechanical causation. This is not to assert that every specific result which flows from my causal endeavor must have been previously discerned by me. Such claim would be a claim to indefinite foreknowledge, and consequently absurd. I do maintain, however, that in any case of causal effectiveness on my part, I have an antecedent conception of *some* effect, near or remote, at which I aim my efficiency, or which I contemplate as lying within the circumference of my efficiency. What series of secondary effects may flow from this contemplated one, assuming the character of secondary causes, no finite intelligence can completely foreknow. It is an incident of human limitations that no human being is able clearly to discern an end, and so gauge and direct his efficiency as not to touch and disturb the world of existence which environs it. It is, moreover, an incident of the ordained constitution of the world, that the energy put forth by me shall *not* be gathered up in an isolated effect, but shall run on in a stream of actions and reactions, indefinitely prolonged.

With reference to the activity of that cause which imposes conditions on all things, and is conditioned by nothing except its own will, we can not affirm those qualifications of foreknowledge which limit man. In the realm of involuntary existence, we can not hesitate to affirm that the least and remotest event transpires according to foresight, calculation, and purpose. This conclusion issues equally, whether we conceive the relation of God to the world to be "transient," as in a mechanical system, or "immanent," as held, pantheistically, by Hegel, or dualistically by some others. In the realm of voluntary existence, the relation of divine foreknowledge to the volition of finite beings presents a problem which has buffeted the world's attempts at a final solution; and I need not argue it here. My own belief holds to divine foreknowledge absolutely unlimited.

In the SIXTH place, the *consciousness of the principle of causality* must arise—the possibility of connecting efficiency with a given effect, and calling it from thought into actuality. However unnoticed may be our consciousness of subscribing to the truth of the judgment of causality, such recognition of its truth is implied in every act of volition. With complete ignorance of the nexus joining cause and effect, it would never occur to our intelligence that a contemplated effect, however desired, could be brought into existence; and all energy would lie as uninspired and unmoved as if intelligence itself were blotted out.

In the SEVENTH place, the effectuation of original causation implies the presentation of *motive*. Before efficiency acts, it must discern a reason why it should act. The motive to action, it is sometimes asserted, may exist either objectively or subjectively. If I extend my arm to shake the hand of a friend, the motive is objective; if I extend it to relieve a weariness caused by long use of the pen, the motive is said to be subjective; still more, if I desist from writing to relieve a wearied brain. But, as far as I can see, the motive, in every case, is properly objective to the mind. The efficient cause is the will, and the moving cause, or motive, must be something differentiated from it, even if existent in my body or my mind. In the last case the mind becomes subject-object, or object in reference to its own activity.

Motive, ascribed to the activity of the First Cause, is commonly known as "Final Cause;" and the doctrine of the existence of ends, or final causes in the world, is teleology. The belief that such ends may be discovered has been generally cherished since the most ancient times. The Old Testament abounds in teleological passages. Socrates defended the belief in divine existence from the structure of organized beings, maintaining that whatever exists for a use must be the work of intelligence. Aristotle based his proof of the existence of a supreme immaterial Spirit on the development in nature of objects whose form and structure indicate design, founding the reasoning on the general principle that all transition ($\kappa\ell\nu\eta\sigma\iota\varsigma$) from the potential to the actual depends on an actual cause. Again, he says, "All motion in nature is directed to an end." "God and nature do nothing in vain." The Stoics maintained that "the beauty and adaptation of the world can only have come from a thinking mind, and prove, therefore, the existence of Deity." "Deum agnoscimus ex operibus ejus," said Cicero[1] (we know God from his works). Lactantius, in his book "On the Workmanship of God; or, The Formation of Man," goes elaborately over the entire mechanism of the human body, and outdoes Paley in praising its utility, convenience, and beauty. Galen, the celebrated physician, believed that in the structural organization of animals is disclosed ade-

---

[1] Cicero, I. Tuscul.

quate proof of a designing intelligence. Gregory of Nyssa grounded the belief in God on the art and wisdom displayed in the order of the world. Cudworth, against the atheism of Hobbes and his followers, "vindicated the right of final causes to a place in physics;" and Samuel Parker, of the same period, "founded the belief in God's existence chiefly on the marks of design manifest in the structure of natural objects." With Newton, "the proof of God's existence is found in the exquisite art and intelligence which are exhibited to us in the construction of the world, and particularly in the organism of every living being." Locke held that the being of God is demonstrable by means of the cosmological and the teleological arguments; and Voltaire, agreeing with him, exclaims, "All nature cries out to us that God exists." Herbart, with all his skepticism, holds to the validity of the teleological argument for the being of God. Galileo, throughout his works, loses no opportunity to insist on final as well as efficient causes; and Cuvier made the belief in "ends" the guiding principle which conducted him to that marvelous insight of the structure and habits of animals long extinct, which is set forth especially in his "Ossemens Fossiles," and which conferred upon him, literally, the gift of seership. Such has been the general sentiment of the philosophic world, and such it still remains.([1]) Kant,

---

([1]) Compare M'Cosh, "Typical Forms and Special Ends in Creation;" Morris (G. S.), "The Final Cause as Principle of Cognition and Principle in Nature," Jour. Trans. Victoria Institute, or Phil. Soc. of Great Britain, 1875; Cocker, "The Theistic Conception of the World;" Hartmann (Edward von), "Wahrheit und Irrthum in Darwinismus. Eine kritische Darstellung der organischen Entwickelungstheorie," Berlin, 1875; Zeller, "Ueber die Aufgabe der Philosophie," p. 20 f.; Gyżicki (Georg von), "Philosophische Consequenzen der Lamarck-Darwin'schen Entwickelungstheorie," Leipzig und Heidelberg, 1876; Bianconi, "La Théorie Darwinienne et la Création," 1874; Krönig, "Das Dasein Gottes," 1874; Wigand, "Der Darwinismus und die Naturforschung Newtons und Cuviers," 2 Bde.; Duke of Argyll, "Anthropomorphism in Theology," 1875; Rudolph Schmid, "Die

however, while accepting theism as an article of faith, cast doubt on the validity of the teleological and other arguments in support of that belief;([1]) and the modern school of nescientists, while accepting divine existence, or, at least, proclaiming no argument against it, maintain that it is not competent for finite intelligence to ascribe motives to the Unknowable; and hence make light of all attempts to interpret nature in a theistic sense. Nevertheless, the doctrine of Final Cause is regaining its ground, both in science and philosophy. No assertions, however deducible from the postulates of a system of philosophy, can expel from credence a principle grounded in the necessary implications of thought. Professor Huxley says: "Perhaps the most remarkable service to the philosophy of biology rendered by Mr. Darwin is the reconciliation of teleology and morphology, and the explanation of the facts of both, which his views offer."([2]) "The teleological and mechanical views of nature are not, necessarily, mutually exclusive. On the contrary, the more purely a mechanist the speculator is, the more firmly does he assume a primordial molecular arrangement, of which all the phenomena of the universe are the consequences; and the more completely is he thereby at the mercy of the teleologist, who can always defy him to disprove that this primordial molecular arrangement was intended to evolve the phenomena of the universe."([3]) Similarly Von Hartmann, with his usual force: "Were the mechanism of the laws of nature not teleological, it would not be by any means a mechanism of orderly

---

Darwinischen Theorien und ihre Stellung zur Philosophie, Religion und Moral," 1876, p. 269–274.

([1]) Kant maintains that we are compelled to contemplate the world under the influence of the notion of final cause, but that this notion is only a regulative principle of thought, subjective in its origin, and not necessarily answering to objective reality.

([2]) Huxley, "Critiques and Addresses," Am. ed., p. 272.

([3]) *Ibid.*, p. 274.

laws, but a mindless chaos, an ox-headed, capricious power."(¹) Gyżicki says: "A voice speaks to us from the Universe, I am who is there, who was there, who will be there."(²) Professor Asa Gray's recent utterance is as follows: " Under the teleological aspect, which was once thought to be expelled from natural history, but which has come back in full force, a bur is an adaptation for the dissemination of seeds by cattle and other animals."(³) In short, at this moment little seems to be urged, on the part of science and philosophy, against the doctrine of Final Cause, save what we find in the late writings of L. Büchner, D. F. Strauss, Haeckel, O. Schmidt, Helmholtz, and the editor and some of the contributors of *Das Ausland*.

I join here in swelling the testimony of antiquity and of the large majority of thinkers of all ages, that Deity *is* proclaimed in the creation; that it is legitimate to deduce divine motives from the structure of the cosmos, and to point out motives as the moving causes of divine activity. I stated that the intuition of causality does not consider the magnitude of cause or

---

(¹) "Wäre der Mechanismus der Naturgesetze nicht teleologisch, so wäre er auch gar kein Mechanismus geordneter Gesetze, sondern ein blödsinniges Chaos stierköpfig eigensinniger Gewalten" ("Wahrheit und Irrthum in Darwinismus"). See, also, Von Hartmann's earlier work, "Philosophie des Unbewussten," though he seeks here, by absurd reasoning, to deny the existence of a conscious subject of the design for which he argues.

(²) Gyżicki, "Philosophische Consequenzen," p. 85.

(³) *American Naturalist*, vol. x., p. 1, Jan., 1876. Of similar purport are the utterances of Lyell, "Natural Selection not Incompatible with Natural Theology," London, 1861, pp. 29, 38; Owen, "Comparative Anatomy," and Trans. Zoöl. Soc. of London, vol. v., p. 90; A. Braun, "Bedeutung der Entwickelung in der Naturgeschichte," p. 49; K. E. von Baer, "Studien aus dem Gebiete der Naturwissenschaften," 1876, II. "Ueber den Zweck in den Vorgängen der Natur," p. 49–106, IV. "Ueber Zielstrebigkeit in den organischen Körpern ins besondere," p. 170–234 (see, however, a critical review of Von Baer by Seidlitz, "Beiträge zur Descendenz-Theorie," Leipzig, 1876).

effect. Effect may be infinite in magnitude or duration; but yet it demands a cause. So, I maintain, the intuition of intelligence from design does not consider the vastness of the intelligence, or of the being possessing it. The correlation between contrivance and intelligence is absolute. Wherever we discover contrivance, we feel impelled to recognize intelligence—however small a portion of the whole intelligence our apprehensions may grasp. It is intelligence, qualitatively, and not quantitatively, considered, which the intuition proclaims. I contemplate a structure in which part is shaped to part and acts with part, and the whole action subserves a necessary and beneficent end. Contemplating this, I proclaim *intention* and *intelligence.* My intuition knows no more of the finite or infinite character of its author than my hearers do before I declare what this piece of mechanism is. It is the correlation of parts, abstracted from authorship, in which I discern intelligence. Now, when I declare this piece of mechanism to be a model, with all the parts of a human hand—bones, ligaments, nerves, vessels, and coverings—every one exclaims, "How admirable and ingenious a contrivance!" But when I declare it to be the human hand itself, instead of a model from the manikin, the exclamation becomes, "Oh, we know nothing about any contrivance in that. Its Author is so superior to us in knowledge and power, that possibly it was not intelligence which planned the thing whose human copy reflects so much intelligence." The sentiment of all time and of all humanity is against such nonsense. It continues to see God's designs in nature. The universal common sense will sweep such a bastard affectation of philosophy into the realm of the "unknown" and "unknowable."

I acknowledge that a profound consciousness of the limitations of human thought and knowledge may suggest the indiscretion and the uncertainty of attributing designs to the cause of existence whose height and depth and breadth are equally immeasurable and impenetrable. I confess that the specific designs of omniscience, which, in some cases, we seem to have discovered, may be fatally misconceived by us. The same might be true of the product of human efforts. The question is not as to the existence of a specific design, but as to the existence of any design. I might grant, without detriment to the argument, that the ends of creation, if they exist, transcend so infinitely all human power of comprehension, that the full purpose of no combination of parts has as yet been revealed to our intelligence. Imagine this to be the case; would it be possible to suppress the conviction that the world and the parts of the world exist for a purpose? Could we even rid ourselves of the belief that in the adjustments of the human hand we had discovered at least a part of the purposes of that structure? Could we conceive of (infinite) causality exerting itself without a sufficient reason for so doing? It seems to me the answer is inseparable from the question. The denial of ends is the denial of the possibility of causation—the denial of all finite existence.

It is the custom of certain biologists to treat with levity the doctrine of final causes. I have sought diligently for their arguments, but I find only the reiterated assertion that the invariable laws of development of the individual and of the species, and the necessary influence of the environment, suffice for the determination of all structures which exist. Coupled with this is the customary disparagement of the attainments of those who hold to the necessity of final cause, as a condition of the activity of efficient cause;[1] and, not unfrequently, the allegation

---

[1] As an example of the argumentation to which I allude, see one of Haeckel's latest works, "Ziele und Wege der heutigen Entwickelungsgeschichte," Jena, Oct., 1875, which is a rejoinder to several of the leading opponents of his "monistic," pantheistic views. The most prominent feature of the book is his conspicuous contempt for all his foes. He does not condescend to reply by citations of pertinent evidence, but assails their

that the defenders of final cause repel the doctrine of efficient competency, and their scientific and private characters, with a profusion of sarcasm and a gay and reckless irony more worthy of a jester than of a philosopher in search of the profoundest truth. The late Professor Louis Agassiz, to whom all the world has paid its homage, is not more honored with an argument than Wilhelm His, and Alexander Goette, and Friederich Michaelis. The pages (78–85) devoted to a reply to Agassiz are occupied with ridicule of his reverent spirit, and gross disparagement of his scientific work and personal character. "Agassiz," says Haeckel, "has been so prominently set forth in recent times by orthodox theology, and specially by Christian philosophy, as the 'pious naturalist' adorned with the glory of a holy radiance, that we feel charmed to investigate a little more closely, *with the spectroscope*, the true nature of its changing Iris-hues." In place of argument and evidences to rebut the arguments of one of the first naturalists of the age, Haeckel now proceeds to impugn his honor, to charge him with dishonest appropriation of the work of others, as being an "indefatigable knight of industry" and the practitioner of "charlatanry." No cause can be so strong as not to suffer from such defense. That Haeckel is not so completely "without sin" as to be entitled to throw stones, appears clearly from the recorded opinions of his countrymen, and even his adherents. His affirms that some of Haeckel's figures (in his "Anthropogenie") purporting to be original are "theils höchst ungetreu" (His, "Unsere Körperform und das physiologische Problem ihrer Entstehung," p. 170). Semper, who pronounces Haeckel "The Apostle of a new Faith," and says that the gospel (Darwinism) according to Haeckel "ought to be the religion of every naturalist," nevertheless affirms that he could cite many similar instances; that, for instance, the section of the embryo of an earth-worm, taken from Kowalevsky, is "completely falsified, and that of *Amphioxus* partly so" (Semper, "Der Haeckelismus in der Zoologie," Hamburg, 1874, p. 36). His accuses Haeckel of a disposition to indulge in "a wanton sporting with facts, more dangerous still than his sporting with words." "According to my judgment," His continues, "he has, through his style of campaigning, himself forfeited all right to be counted in the circle of earnest scientists as one of equal birth." To which Semper adds, "I, on my part, indorse these words with the fullest conviction" (*op. cit.*, p. 36). Nevertheless, with such qualifications, I gladly concede to the researches of Haeckel a degree of originality, acuteness, and vigor which has seldom been equaled, and regard him as the source of a powerful impulse in recent biological studies.

causes.([1]) Let it be understood that the recognition or denial of the doctrine of final causes is a procedure lying exclusively in the field of deductive thought; and no amount of familiarity with the details of animal structure could constitute the slightest preparation for a decision. The most authoritative decision must be that prompted by the most attentive study of the laws of thought; while it is evident that those who derive the structural adaptations of nature from the orderly modes of change and succession, which are so apparent, do not penetrate to the discovery even of efficient cause, still less to a recognition of the infrangible law of "sufficient reason." They reach no principle, necessary and all-underlying, which reveals an incompatibility with the doctrine of final cause, resting, on its part, upon a universal datum of reason. They have discovered, possibly, the *method* of effectuation of results, and have not the discernment and candor to admit that method (law) is simply modal, and not causal, and, instead of being the limit of a rational analysis, itself implies an ulterior principle as an efficient datum; and a reason why, as the condition of the actualization of efficiency. The doctrine of derivation must be settled by an appeal to the facts of biology; it is a question of science. The doctrine of final cause, like that of supramaterial causation, must be settled by an appeal to the facts of reason; it is a question of philosophy.

In the EIGHTH place, the efficient cause, which, as we have seen, must be self-conscious and intelligent, may discern a *contingency* or *condition* which stands in some relation either to cause or effect, and may modify the amount or direction of the causal efficiency, or else the kind or amount of the effect.

([1]) "On one side stand the Dualists and Teleologists, who seek the *true causes* of soul-life, as of organic development, in ideas acting in organic bodies, consequently in purposive final causes" (Haeckel, "Ziele und Wege," p. 5). This charge was in effect made by Kant and Laplace, according to M'Cosh ("Typical Forms and Special Ends in Creation," p. 53, Eng. ed.).

A contingency influencing the effect directly is simply a secondary cause, and will be discussed hereafter. Moreover, contingency may be either disclosed or hidden. A contingency influencing the cause simply annexes a new term to motive, and constitutes a part of it. Such contingency must be disclosed, since nothing can constitute motive which is not cognized. It is external, nevertheless, and indirectly influences effect, through motive actuating cause. Under this analysis, contingency loses its importance as a distinct concept in the process of causation.

In the NINTH place, the influence of the contingency on the motive must be cognized. This is simply implied in the fact that the contingency becomes incorporated with the motive. This, as I have just stated, could not be if the contingency remained concealed.

In the TENTH place, the causal agent must be conscious of a *desire* to direct efficiency toward the contemplated effect. It must also be conscious of *freedom* to act according to desire. Without freedom, causation is simply intermediation, or secondary causation. The effect flows from that which coerces causal action. An act performed by an agent under constraint is, for the agent, an act not performed. He is merely the instrument in the hands of the will which controls.

In the ELEVENTH place, the concept of causality implies an *intention* to direct efficiency toward the contemplated effect. The intention to act must follow the consciousness of freedom to act, and must necessarily follow the desire to act. The desire can only be awakened in the presence of a known and contemplated and desirable effect. The intention to put forth causal efficiency implies also a cognition of cause as the necessary antecedent of effect. Intentionality, therefore, implies and incloses all these ideas. It follows that every effect, whether simple or complex, implies intentionality, and this implies intelligence. From the moment when we recognize the world as an effect, we are compelled, by the necessary laws of thought, to recognize also intelligence. I do not refer here to the *character* of the effect, but simply to the fact that the world *is* an effect. I shall show, hereafter, that the composition of the cosmical effect reveals an infinite realm of intentionality, and explains why the human mind, in all ages, has felt forced to recognize the existence of Supreme Intelligence as the correlative of the world. The steps by which the universal reason has ascended from the phenomena of nature to the creative efficiency have been seldom noted. The common mind, which is as richly furnished with intuitive judgments as the cultivated mind, seems to reach supreme causation by a leap. I have already expressed my belief in a direct intuition of Deity; but here is *another path* by which the common mind, as well as the philosophic mind, ascends to the very presence of the light which had been seen shining from without into the chambers of the soul. Intuition of Deity is the diffused light. Deduction to Deity is the discovery of the certain *path* to a better-comprehended existence. But yet this path is so short, the steps are so easily and so dexterously taken, that the common reason seems, even here, to leap, by one intuition, to God. Philosophy, instead of discovering and pointing out this way to God, plods and flounders in the very attempt to travel where common sense skips along with more than the agility of a kid. Philosophy has its use, however, in disclosing the fact that the path is a real one, on solid ground, and that the common mind, in rising habitually to God, is not winged by imagination to a bright cloud which floats merely in the air.

FINALLY, the consummation of the causal act implies the exertion of *will*. There must be an executive determination of conscious efficiency toward the contemplated effect which has awakened desire and purpose. All the other causative steps converge here. Will is the last condition of effect. Being the last condition, Will always implies Intelligence and Sensibility.

"Will is the synthesis of Reason and Power."(¹) In strict language, "intelligent will" is a tautological phrase.

Will is the only force in existence. Our earliest volitions disclose the transformations of will into efficiency. We have no revelation of any other source of efficiency. From will proceeds all intermediation; and back to will must be traced every thing which can be cognized as an effect. As the results of human volition are our earliest intimations of the nature of force, so back to will we return after the most discriminating analysis. Search the world through; consider the fall of an apple moved by terrestrial gravitation; the rush of the chemical atoms marshaled by their affinities; the quiver of the needle upon its pivot, struggling to maintain its fidelity to the pole; the reaction of the pent-up spring, actuating the mechanism of the watch; none of these energies find their explanation in themselves, nor in the matter which is moved by them. Think of the reaction of the spring as a phenomenon of inherent force, and you can not fail to inquire, "Where are the evidences of volition, of choice, of discernment, of desire, of purpose which the very act of original causation implies?" That energy is transmitted through the spring, and impinges upon an object, is apparent enough; but this still is but a sluice-way of force, and not a repository of force. Elasticity, magnetism, affinity — these are modes of intermediation by which cause reaches its ends. To this subject I intend to return.(²)

(¹) Cocker, "Theistic Conception of the World," p. 197.

(²) "In the only case in which we are admitted into any personal knowledge of the origin of force, we find it connected (possibly by intermediate links untraceable by our faculties, but yet indisputably *connected*) with volition, and, by inevitable consequence, with *motive*, with *intellect*, and with all those attributes of mind in which — and not in the possession of arms, legs, brains, and viscera — personality consists" (Sir John Herschel, "Familiar Lectures on Scientific Subjects," Amer. ed., p. 462).

"We can not predicate of any physical agency that it is abstractedly the

Will, then, closes the circuit of causation. Will completes and implies the exercise of the three classes of psychic activities which characterize personality. Intellect, Sensibility, Will—these are the prime factors of a personal differentiation from the objective datum of causality. Once before we reached the principle of duality. Now we perceive that one term of the duality must be a personality. It is impossible to interpret truly an effect without discovering Intellect, Sensibility, and Will; and it is impossible to think of these except as the attributes of a personal existence.

The term personality, however, is unfortunate and misleading. It is weakly anthropomorphic. Adopted as the antithesis of monism and pantheism, its associations carry the mind irresistibly into a narrow field of view. We must banish all thoughts of figure and locality; we must not think of motion, nor of body. Personality is *not* the alternative of divine immanence, as has been generally believed; but is compatible with the recognition of divine agency in all the phenomena of the natural world. This view, as we shall see, while it reproduces the simple theism of the primeval world, and those awe-inspiring conceptions of nature which characterize our Jewish Scriptures, promises to be the ultimate, but not distant, conclusion of the most advanced science and philosophy.

---

cause of another; and if, for the sake of convenience, the language of secondary causation be permissible, it should be only with reference to the special phenomena referred to, as it can never be generalized" (Grove, "Correlation of Physical Forces," Youmans's ed., p. 15). "An essential cause is unattainable [in the study of phenomena]. Causation is the will, Creation the act, of God" (*ib.*, p. 199). See, for numerous other citations, Cocker, "Theistic Conception of the World," p. 235-243; and the references already made in the present paper.

V.

THE DOCTRINE OF CAUSALITY—*CONTINUED*.

2. Causal Intermediation.

CAUSE is a word which I have used in a sense somewhat restricted. I have not admitted as real cause any agency supposed to be exerted, in the natural world, by what we call matter. The energy, however, which emerges *from* matter, and impinges *upon* matter, has generally been taken as the type of efficient causation. It has been assumed that energy may be pocketed in portions of matter, to be let loose on certain occasions, and produce effects. Not denying, for the moment, the possibility that matter may become the repository of force, it is impossible for me to conceive of matter as a fountain of force. A thing which is itself an effect must be an effect in all its parts and in all its attributes. All energy emanating from an effect must be itself an effect; and all results of its efficiency must be results of the first or original cause. Now, we may attach the term cause to that form of matter which immediately precedes a given effect;[1] we may attach it to the energy which proceeds from that form; but it must be apparent that the word cause, thus employed, means a very different thing from that implied when we speak of the ultimate efficiency which can not be viewed as an effect. It is a common phraseology, in speaking of a succession of serially dependent

---

[1] This is all that is meant by "cause" in the generality of discussions. J. S. Mill expressly shuts out all consideration of "efficiency" in connection with causes, holding the attainment of knowledge respecting efficient causes to transcend the powers of the human mind ("Logic," book ii., chap. v., §§ 2, 9).

events, to say that each is the effect of its predecessor, and, at the same time, the cause of its successor. To my mind, however, the difference of meaning between cause in this case and cause in the case of voluntary agency, is so great that different terms should be employed. The meanings are, indeed, antipodal. In the one case, we have intelligence and will; in the other, neither. In the one case, the energy is primitive; in the other, derivative. In the one case, the efficiency is self-moving; in the other, it is moved. In the one case we have that which is exclusively cause; in the other, that which is primarily effect.

The only escape from this antithesis is self-destruction. It is the admission that matter itself is sentient, cognitive, and voluntary. Heraclitus, it is true, conceived all matter to be animated; and Thales and other Hylozoists thought the world to be an immense animal. Leibnitz, also, conceived all existence to be composed of sentient monads. God, with him, is a monad; the soul is a monad; minerals are composed of monads. But Leibnitz is not a monist; there are spiritual monads as well as material; and between these all gradations of substance. But none of these philosophers clothed matter with absolute freedom of will. The Hylozoists recognized a supreme principle—be it water, or air, or fire, or chaos, or mind, as Anaxagoras suggested; and this principle introduced control, subordination, harmony, rhythm. The monads of Leibnitz, too, while capable of various degrees of thought, were controlled in their movements by mechanical laws; and the consonance between the psychical and bodily motions was effected only by a divine prearrangement or pre-established harmony. Thus the assumption of independent, originative volition in matter would be a new thing in philosophy—a theory sounding a dissonance with the tenor of human thought; and awaking in antagonism the historical instincts of humanity. Moreover, the investiture of matter with thinking and voluntary attributes would summon us to the funeral of God and the soul.

If matter thinks, there is no need to postulate spirit. If matter creates, and ordains, and co-ordinates, this is our god which we trample under our feet and sweep from our door-sills. Here, again, in reference to the insensibility of matter, the *consensus gentium* has been standing steadily on the rock to which reason must return, after long floundering in search of a more royal standing-place.

It is perfectly safe to assume that matter is not self-conscious and self-motive. Two alternatives remain. It may be conceived as absolutely passive and adynamic — a mere channel for the transmission of energy from some original fountain of force; or, as is conceivable, at least as a formula of words, it may be a repository of delegated force. The latter alternative approaches the current conception; which, however, represents natural force as a blind energy resident in matter, and constituting an essential property of matter. Let me inquire, first, what is involved in the popular idea that force inheres in matter. Under the prevailing conception, the myriad motions of the physical world are but the phenomena produced by the effort of force to reach a state of equilibrium. Gravitation is the cause of myriads of movements. The vapor of the atmosphere, condensed in rain-drops, descends to reach a resting-place which it does not find in the air. Fluent as the waters are, they find no rest on the hill-slope, but hurry off through rill and rivulet to the lowest levels attainable; and there they rest. There they would rest to all eternity, but for the intervention of another source of moving energy—the sun. Warmed more or less by the sun, vapory particles steal from the watery mass into the superincumbent atmosphere—absorbed, borne up, and transported by it. The unequal distribution of solar heat, by expanding portions of the atmosphere, changes their relative weight, and they no longer counterpoise adjacent portions, but are displaced by their lateral pressure. Hence arise vertical and horizontal movements of the air. Hence the relations of humidity to temperature are changed; and under certain conditions the excess of vapor is again disengaged as rain. Should the sun cease to emit heat, the waters of the world would soon settle to the lowest levels, and remain stagnant. The ascent of vapor is simply an effort to attain a position where equilibrium will ensue. The movement of winds is an effort to restore the impaired equilibrium of different positions of the atmosphere. The descent of rains and rivers is the search of the waters for equilibrium. So the flash of lightning in the clouds is the spiteful reaction of a disturbed equilibrium in the electric elements. The rebound of a spring of steel or a cylinder of compressed air is the recovery of that state of equilibrium which had been disturbed by some external agency. Reasoning in this way from the sources of the motions and changes which make up the world of physical phenomena, we are led to the conviction that all which we witness is merely the ferment of a set of forces struggling toward a state of rest, but mutually jostling each other in their progress, and undoing work which immediately must be done again.

These are the results supposed to be wrought out by the activity of forces inherent in matter. On this assumption, I wish to direct thought in two directions. The first thought is, that if these undiscerning mechanical forces *inhere* in matter, they must have been made inherent by some agent or cause. If so made, the event must have transpired in time. The theory necessitates an intelligent, uncaused Author of matter, with its properties. This is the current theistic conception.

The other thought is an anticipation of the *end* of this physical ferment, and the quest for some datum not involved in the final subsidence of cosmical activities. The transmission of heat from the sun to the earth, and from the earth's interior to external space, has been the physical cause of the terrestrial changes of millions of years. But the heat which escapes from the earth never returns to it; and the sun loses not only the thermal energy imparted to the earth and the other heavenly bodies, but the infinitely greater amounts disseminated through the unoccupied spaces of the universe. Hence the basis of the doctrine of the "dissipation of energy."(¹) The epoch is separated from us by only a finite interval, when these great perennial sources of physical activity shall have been exhausted, and, however the ferment may be prolonged by agencies impossible to compute, the whole world, the whole solar system, shall have settled at length into that condition of stagnation and death toward which creation is daily marching with strides as visible as the approach of those wintry frosts which are browning the meadows and shaking the scarlet leaflet to the ground. This impending crisis marks an end of the cosmical ferment as sharply as its historical purport pronounces a beginning; and leaves us at both extremities of existence, with no support but the same All-sufficiency already revealed in the dependent nature of force and motion and matter.

Such conclusions are necessarily involved in the popular idea that force inheres in matter. It remains to establish the possibility of the thesis. Is it thinkable, for instance, that a molecule of inert matter should be made the repository of an energy which should perpetually draw its neighboring molecule toward it, and of another energy which should perpetually repel it; or that these two forces should act respectively at certain distances, and cease to act at distances greater or less than these; or that, both forces acting, they should be found in equilibrium at several different intervals of distance between

---

(¹) The idea of the final refrigeration of the earth and sun, and, in short, the ultimate complete stagnation of the material universe, was shadowed forth by the author as an original speculation in the *Michigan Journal of Education* in 1860, and more explicitly in the *Ladies' Repository*, Cincinnati, for November and December, 1863, and January, 1864. The doctrine of the "dissipation of energy" seems to have been first broached by Sir William Thompson, Trans. Roy. Soc. Edinb., 1852.

the molecules? Is it thinkable that either atomic or molar matter is capable of exerting efficiency at a distance? Is it not a necessity of thought that efficiency requires presence in *space* as well as in *time*—activity *here* as well as *now?*([1]) I confess that, with all my efforts at abstraction and invention, I am unable to think "dead" matter—for that is the kind of which I speak—as acting, or as the seat of a "dead" energy which acts. If others can think this, and believe it, I commend them to that thread of thought, already disclosed, which leads hence, from this world of dependence, to the eternal Self-supporter revealed already in their intuitive consciousness.

Of delegated force residing in matter I can form no other conception than that it is actuated by the delegating power—a sort of form or husk, the substance and vitality within which is imparted from some source superior to matter. This conception, denying that force inheres in matter, presents it as an exotic power, exerting a vicarious activity, without essential dependence on its environment; but, like the hermit-crab, using it merely as a seat of operations. If such force is delegated, it is dependent, and destitute of autonomy; and it can

---

([1]) Gravitation has been regarded an instance of the exertion of (secondary) efficiency at a distance; but this was not the view of Newton. He repels the charge that the theory of gravitation is in conflict with the philosophical maxim that "a thing can not act where it is not." "It is inconceivable," he writes to Dr. Bentley, "that inanimate brute matter should, without the mediation of something else which is not material, operate upon and affect other matter *without mutual contact.* * * * That gravity should be innate, inherent, and essential to matter, so that one body may act on another at a distance, through a vacuum, without the mediation of any thing else, by and through which their action and force may be conveyed from one to another, is to me so great an absurdity, that I believe no man who, in philosophical matters, has a competent faculty of thinking can fall into it. Gravity must be caused by an agent acting constantly according to certain laws!" (Playfair, "Dissertation on the Progress of Mathematics and Physical Science").

only be a matter of mere speculation whether its accredited power is enduring, or requires to be instantly renewed. In any case, the very form of words implies a source of power superior to matter and material energy, and no interest remains in the question, save as a mere contingency of science.

The other alternative respecting the relation of matter to force conceives matter as purely adynamic. In this view, all natural force proceeds from a dynamic Intelligence superior to matter. Two sub-alternatives present themselves here also. Matter may serve merely as the vehicle which transmits primordial force; or it may be the seat of an immanent and ever-acting force. The first conception is not difficult to entertain. The activities of force are subordinated to laws of a mechanical and exact character. They come within the grasp of the science of quantity. But for the complexity of their mutual perturbations, it would be possible to chart their results for indefinite periods of time. As it is, the movements of planetary bodies, projectiles, tides, streams, and many other molar aggregates have been reduced to numerical expression which is very exact. Atoms and molecules elude our scrutiny, but chemistry is verging on an exact science, and we have some foreshadowings of the subjugation of the whole realm of atomic physics to the reign of calculable law. With such indications, it is eminently conceivable that the omniscient Disposer should be able to so discern the endless series of actions and reactions as to impart an initial impulse which should thrill through the chain of being in predetermined effects. The line of thought, however, here bifurcates again. Are the myriad phenomena of existence the unfolding results of a single primordial impulse, or of an impulse momentarily and instantly renewed? Either theory is rational. The former supposes divine agency to be separated from the present by the whole life-time of cosmic existence. The latter contemplates God as ever-presiding and ever-energizing. If, however, the cycles of events roll forth from a primordial impulse, they must inevitably reach at last a condition of rest. Phenomenon is but the disturbance of the equilibrium of force. All disturbances tend to repose. No cycle of motions can be self-perpetuating. To whatever extent we widen the cycle, by annexing new realms of dynamic activity, the widest realm is finite, and the universe of atomic agitations must finally become quiet. This is the same outcome reached when we reasoned on the *molar* activities of the cosmos. In philosophy, all roads lead to God. If we conceive the continuous renewal of the impulse applied at the periphery of existence, we bring Deity into intimate relations to the world—separated from phenomenon only by a film of matter. In this case, and indeed in either case, the question arises, Why should Deity choose to exert his energy from a distance? In the latter case, too, the human imagination is burdened with all the reluctance which is aroused in some minds at the contemplation of Deity as ever active in the sustentation of his universe. If, however, an active relation to the universe is admissible, the view which follows seems simpler and more plausible.

This view is, that natural force has no existence except as the direct effort of the Supreme Will. It supposes matter to be absolutely inert and naked of energy. Every form of force is a particular mode of divine activity. Every movement and every change reveals directly the presence of the Supreme Power; and man is surrounded by an array of admonitions of the divine presence the most awe-inspiring possible. Nay, man himself is the vehicle of the voice of God to his own sensorium. The changes of matter are in progress in our own bodies. Infinite agency permeates our very selves, assorting our nutrition, building us up, effecting repairs, wasting our tissues, and carrying us into the grave—nay, not forsaking us even there, but tenderly bearing the effete molecules which we can use no longer into new situations and collocations, to subserve other predetermined uses in the economy of nature.

Either phase of the theory of divine immanence, though the general doctrine, as I have said, has found many advocates, is obnoxious to an objection proceeding from the impotence of the human mind. It seems, at first, incompatible with the majesty of God to think of him as ever active and careful and cognizant of the affairs of the universe, and, most especially, of all their subordinate details. The relation even of creator and disposer, without the implication of immanent activity, has brought down the reproachful phrase, "carpenter theory" of the universe. Such misgivings and such reproaches are prompted only by human finiteness and incapacity. Activity is the central law of existence. Nothing exists for repose, but every thing for work. Indolence is a human invention. The only evidence of existence is action. Whatever ceases to act is dead. God, the author of life and fountain of living force, can not be less active than the modes of existence which represent him. But we must not overlook the meaning of omnipotence and omniscience and omnipresence. We must not overlook the fact that, with Deity, willing is accomplishing. We must not forget that God is without organs to be wearied or wasted with use. With Omniscience, the knowledge of *all* things is easier than, with us, the knowledge of one thing. With Omnipotence, the accomplishment of all things is easier than, with us, the accomplishment of one thing. After much reflection, this seems to me the most philosophic conception of the relation of the Supreme Being to the world.

The theories of matter and force which I have thus far discussed suppose matter to have a substantive existence. There is a counter-theory which regards matter merely a manifestation of force. In this view, the so-called properties of matter have no subjective ground. The resistances which it presents are not resistances of a material substance. The last two views presented—divine immanence *in* matter and divine immanence *through* matter—suggest the query, What, then, can matter be?

If the energies emanating from matter do not appertain to matter, then those modes of energy known as resistance, elasticity, adhesiveness, color, and the like, have no material ground. Extension and figure, which relate only to the space over which the energies just mentioned are active, are not properties of any material substances. Indeed, as all properties are but modes of energy, the properties of matter are completely detached from matter, and we are left to the conception of a substance without attributes.([1]) Such substance is a figment of the imagination. We know nothing, and can know nothing, of any substance save by its attributes. If the so-called properties of matter do not belong to matter, then matter as a ground of phenomena has no existence. But the properties of matter so called remain; they can not be ignored. Those forces which we have supposed to emanate from matter are realities. But it is not possible to thought to substitute abstract force or forces for all which we have regarded as forms of matter. Force can only be exerted by a real agent. Attribute does not float about creation without a substantial ground to rest on. Force is neither fatherless nor orphan, flitting about without haven and without allegiance. Force is efficiency sent forth by substantial existence. It is not force, indeed, which produces effects, but the *free-will* whence dynamic influence proceeds. Force is an attribute of will. Elasticity, resistance, color, which are both impressions made upon our sensorium, and thus subjective, and also energies exerted to produce those impressions, and thus objective—these, also, are attributes of will. The dynam-

---

([1]) This view is less accepted than it has been. Professor F. Schneider says, "The theory that the atoms have no extension in space and are merely centres of force * * * is, in view of the results of investigation in various provinces of molecular physics, no longer tenable" (Meyer, "Jahrbuch," for 1873). Nearly all physical speculations are now based on the assumption of the atomic constitution of matter (see Barker's Address before the Physical Section of the American Assoc. Adv. Science, Buffalo, 1876).

ical theory of matter, therefore, precipitates us immediately and irretrievably upon divine agency. We may loosely speak of atoms of matter as mere foci of force, and aggregates of matter as mere spheres of resistance; but such language is empty and vain. There must be something which exerts force. There must be something which resists.(¹)

Thus we find ourselves, by whatever path we pursue our explorations through the mysteries of matter and force, always confronted by the divine presence. We can not flee from Deity. There is no way to invent a world which must not depend first and last upon divine support. There is no way to think of an atom of matter, or that which may be called an atom, without conceiving it afloat in the breath of divine power.

Recapitulation of Possible Conceptions of Matter and Force.

A. The Dynamical conception of matter.
B. The Substantive conception of matter.
   I. Matter self-motive (Hylozoistic).
   II. Matter not self-motive.
      1. Endowed with force.
         (*a*) The force inherent (Popular view).
         (*b*) The force delegated.

(¹) Should the dynamical theory of matter become established, we should be forced into a modified pantheism. The theory means that no material, inert *substance* underlies the phenomena which we style the phenomena of matter. But reason declares that all phenomena are manifestations of *some* entity; and hence, if there be no matter, material phenomena are manifestations of Deity, and the substance or entity revealed by the properties of matter is Deity—*the material universe is Deity*. But if we ever find ourselves resting in this conclusion, we shall arise and re-affirm these unimpeachable dicta of reason—that reason which is the offspring of God: 1. Man possesses an independent identity and a free-will; 2. The Being whose activities constitute the phenomena of the universe, without the veil of matter intervening, is a *personality*—discerning ends, prompted by motives, executing by volition.

2. A mere channel for transmission of force.
   (a) The force initial or peripheral.
      (aa) One primordial impulse.
      (bb) Impulse constantly renewed.
   (b) The force proceeds from an immanent cause.

Science is sometimes heard to object to these theistic conceptions of matter and of the universe; but this is only because science does not philosophize. As I have before intimated, there is no fact of science from which philosophy can not find a path leading directly to God. If the scientist does not find the path, it is because he does not seek it. He contents himself with partial knowledge, rather than go beyond the data and the methods of science. Amusing himself with the means, he loses sight of the end. He is a man sent by the Almighty to rear a temple; and finding some prettily colored stones in the quarry, he entertains himself with these, instead of laying them in the massive wall. He is a child studying the alphabet, who thinks the acquisition of the letters the end of all learning.

The scientist sometimes declares that the admission of divine will, divine motive, divine providence, is the introduction of chaos or caprice into nature.(¹) All things, he says, move for-

---

(¹) "In the intellectual infancy of a savage state, man * * * regards all passing events as depending on the arbitrary volition of a superior, but invisible, power" (Draper, "Intellectual Development of Europe," p. 2). "As science demands the radical extirpation of caprice, and the absolute reliance upon law in nature, there arose with the growth of scientific notions a desire and determination to sweep from the field of theory this mob of gods and demons" (Tyndall, "Belfast Address," Appletons' ed., p. 88). It must be noticed, however, that when the order and certainty of phenomena under natural law are brought into antithesis with divine agency, it is some crude conception of supernaturalism which is disparaged—the Greek or mediæval anthropomorphism—and not the recognition of every kind and mode of divine agency in the world. Such passages are not intended to

ward with regularity under the dominion of law.([1]) It is absurd to attribute events to divine agency, when science demonstrates them the effects of the forces of matter, acting according to invariable law. The subjective natures of matter and of force are admitted to be involved in mystery. We may make it a matter of faith that divine agency has been concerned at some time and in some way; but the palpable phenomena and the fixed sequences are so obtrusive that, like the child or the savage, he is ready to recognize ultimate causal efficiency in the last-discovered antecedent, and satisfy himself with that. Long habituated to reason from sensible phenomena, he thinks nothing is real which can not be measured or weighed; or, if there be other realities, they are matters of opinion, or conjecture, or faith, which offer no reward for their search.

Now, I wish to assert emphatically, that, so far as I can discern, *any theory of divine immanence does not conflict with the doctrine of law, nor with the science based on the atomic doctrine.*

That law reigns in the world is an admirable fact, which I not only acknowledge, but argue, with rejoicing. The reign of law, however, is modal, and not efficient. Law effectuates

---

be taken in an atheistic sense. Dr. Draper says, "It is a more noble view of the government of this world to impute its order to a penetrating, primitive wisdom, which could foresee consequences through a future eternity, and provide for them in the original plan, at the outset, than to invoke the perpetual intervention of an ever-acting, spiritual agency" ("Intellectual Development of Europe," p. 74). Professor Tyndall says, "The profession of that atheism with which I am sometimes so lightly charged would, in my case, be an impossible answer to this question "(whether there are not in nature manifestations of knowledge and skill superior to man's)("Belfast Address," appendix, Appletons' ed., p. 102).

([1]) "The investigation of the aspects of the skies in past ages, and all predictions of its future, rest essentially upon the principle that no arbitrary volition ever intervenes, the gigantic mechanism moving impassively *in virtue of a mathematical law*" (Draper, "Intellectual Development of Europe," p. 3).

nothing. Law is the method according to which a lawgiver effectuates. Law never planned "equivalent proportions," and "inverse squares," and "ratios of squares and cubes," and "homological relations." Lawgiver planned these things; and whether he works or his dynamical agents work, it is lawgiver who observes these uniform methods from which formulated laws have been generalized. "The laws of nature," says Von Baer, "are the permanent expressions of the will of a Creative Principle."(¹) Even if it were conceivable that, in the absence of cosmical intelligence, the cosmos should go harmoniously, it is infinitely more rational to conceive correlation, fitness, utility, beauty, regularity, to proceed from an ordering mind. An ordering mind in nature does not imply caprice; it implies the very order which we observe; it is the necessary correlative and cause of order, harmony, law. It is supposable, certainly, that intelligence may impose upon itself fixed modes of activity. As the world is constituted, the happiness of man and beast depends upon fixed methods in nature. It is infinitely more probable that mind has planned correlations than that unguided force has fallen upon them by any chance. Mind is a better explanation of the structural affinities of animals than any principle of inheritance, unguided and unpurposed by mind. Mind is the best explanation, and the only explanation admissible in philosophy, of the complex of phenomena revealed in the panorama of nature.

Even should we receive the dynamical theory of matter, and recognize every lump of earth as only a manifestation of force, of which the real ground is the divine existence, still we may continue to reason and to conclude in the *same manner* as if the atomic constitution of matter were proved true. The theory of the solar system has been established on the assumed

---

(¹) K. E. Von Baer, "Studien aus dem Gebiete der Naturwissenschaften," p. 232.

truth of the Newtonian doctrine of gravitation; but a different doctrine is supposable, and different doctrines are, indeed, under discussion,(¹) which, while they would sweep the popular theory of gravitation from existence, would leave the principles of mathematical astronomy untouched, and would disclose no fundamental proposition which must be unlearned. Though the stone built into the dizzy tower of the cathedral be but a bundle of resistent forces exerted directly by Infinite Will, we have no cause to fear that Infinite Will is disposed to withdraw that exertion of energy, or for one instant to cease acting according to formulas prescribed from the beginning of the world.

I have discussed sufficiently the general relations of matter and force. I have pointed out the inevitable tendency of thought toward a theistic solution of the problem, under whatever aspect it may be presented. Thus I have reached certain general principles which I desire to apply to certain dogmatic propositions found in scientific literature.

Science proper is concerned only with the phenomena of causal intermediation. With primary causation, or the nature of efficiency in causation, it has nothing to do. Its data are, especially, the phenomena of the physical world. To these may be added the phenomena of society, the phenomena of the psychical activities, and the primary data given in the universal reason. But social, psychical, and rational phenomena are the data of science, in its recent acceptation, only so far as they may be employed inductively. Induction is commonly regarded the logic of science. Deduction is the logic of philosophy. Nevertheless, deduction may be employed to develop scientific quæsita. Such quæsita may belong to the realm of actuality or to that of potentiality. If the former, deduction becomes a seer; if the latter, a prophet. The predictions of astronomy

---

(¹) See Cocker, "Theistic Conception of the World," p. 210–222, for statements and references on this subject.

are prophetic deductions from principles induced from observation. The story of nebular geology is the revelation of a seer drawn out by the thread of deduction.([1]) On the basis of the theory of descent from a common stock, Haeckel and other evolutionists deductively infer the characters which the unknown stock must bear, and infer, guided by scattered facts, what must have been the nature of the ramifications. Such deductive inferences have been often confirmed by actual discovery. Marsh having traced, as he believed, the lineage of the one-toed horse back in time to a four-toed horse, predicted that from the deposits of some earlier geological period would be obtained evidences of the existence of a five-toed horse. In November, 1876, that prediction was fulfilled by the discovery of *Eohippus*.

As there is a science of mind, so we have a philosophy of science. Indeed, philosophy can not be strictly dissevered from science; as the annihilation of the data of science would impoverish philosophy. Philosophy would thus become a magnificent mill, with no corn to grind. It is unnatural, and indeed impossible, to work science and philosophy in separate fields; for they are yoked together. Every step of scientific reasoning employs a philosophic principle. Even induction, the much-vaunted engine of science, binds conclusion to scientific, or *à posteriori*, datum, by means of a philosophic, or *à priori*, datum. For instance, take the generalized proposition

---

([1]) I have long protested against the exaggerated importance which, since Bacon, science has been inclined to concede to the inductive method of investigation; noticing, as I have, that a large part of the reasoning of science—in fact, every thing which can properly be called reasoning—proceeds on *à priori* grounds (see a lecture on "Scientific Education," delivered at the dedication of the Judd Hall of Science of the Wesleyan University, in July, 1870; also "Sketches of Creation," March, 1870, pp. 52, 66, 435, 436). It is, of course, gratifying to find similar views set forth in a work of such authority as Jevons's "Principles of Science."

that the skins of Hottentots are black. The reasoning is skeletonized in the following syllogism:

> Whatever color of skin is possessed by A, B, C, and a hundred other Hottentots, must be the color of Hottentots in general.
>
> A, B, C, and a hundred other Hottentots, possess a black skin.
>
> Therefore, Hottentots in general possess black skins.

Now, it is an *à priori* datum of reason which validates the passage from the particular to the general in the major premise.

Moreover, what is the ground of belief that A, B, C, and a hundred other Hottentots, submitted to observation, are black? It is the antecedent and primitive belief that things *are* as our senses report them to us. This, again, is an *à priori* datum; and we observe that it lies at the very root of the initial process in all inductive or scientific reasoning—the verification of facts. No scientist thinks of the possibility of a flaw in his logic at this point; and, indeed, there is no occasion for it; the procedure is valid. I can not avoid adding, parenthetically, that the veracity of consciousness is worth no more in this case than in any other. The belief that *objects exist as sense reports them to us*, is no more binding than the belief that *intelligible correlations imply intelligence*. Accept the first proposition as true, it is idiocy to reject the latter. Reject the latter, it is idiocy to accept the first. *Credibile in uno, credibile in omnibus.*

Thus the antithesis of science and philosophy does not exist. Nor are their fields entirely apart. The scientist is bound to philosophize, and ought to philosophize, more than he does.([1])

([1]) The most eminent and original scientists feel least scruple at the employment of deductive data. Professor Tyndall says, "By an intellectual necessity, I cross the boundary of the experimental evidence, and discern in that matter which we, in our ignorance of its latent powers, and notwithstanding our professed reverence for its creator, have hitherto covered with opprobrium, the promise and potency of all terrestrial life" (Tyndall,

The philosopher depends on the data of science, and ought to be as profound a scientist as the scientist who is no philosopher. It is noteworthy that the most eminent philosophers have had the largest command of the treasury of science: witness Aristotle, Leibnitz, Comte, Whewell, Sir William Hamilton, Spencer. And the most eminent scientists have been most conversant with the ideas of philosophy: witness Aristotle, Galileo, Bruno, Gassendi, Newton, Cuvier, and Agassiz. Let science and philosophy, wedded by nature, remain undivorced.

Now let us turn the discussion to the implications and legitimate uses of the facts of causal intermediation, which constitute the peculiar data of science. Henceforward, I shall shape my phraseology with especial, though not exclusive, reference to physical science.

Causal intermediation or secondary causation implies, first, primary causation as the antecedent and responsible and only actual efficiency.

It implies, secondly, the absence, or latency, of the attributes characterizing primary cause. That is, it implies the absence of self-consciousness, cognition of the relation between cause and effect, motivity, intentionality, volition, and personality. These attributes do not belong to the world of natural phenomena, so far as we regard matter itself the ground of dynamic effort. If we posit in matter an exotheistic ground of energy, we necessitate a materialistic, hylozoistic pantheism, against

---

"Belfast Address," Appletons' ed., p. 89). And Haeckel: "Wer noch heute die Entwickelungsgeschichte als eine rein 'descriptive Wissenschaft' betrachtet — (eine Contradictio in adjecto) — wer noch heute den Unterschied zwischen Wissen und Wissenschaft, zwischen Kenntniss und Erkenntniss nicht kennt, der hat überhaupt unter den Vertretern wahrer Wissenschaft nicht mitzureden; und der verfolgt auch in der Entwickelungsgeschichte nur eine unterhaltende 'Gemüths- und Augen-Ergötzung,' aber keine wahrhaft wissenschaftlichen Ziele" (Haeckel, "Ziele und Wege," p. 4–5).

which it is scarcely necessary to direct an argument. If we posit in matter an endotheistic ground of energy, we reach a position from which the explanation of phenomena is simple, and consonant with the instincts of humanity and reason. It is scarcely necessary to say that whether we assume the exotheistic or endotheistic view of matter, its phenomena remain equally the legitimate data of scientific processes.

Thirdly, causal intermediation implies a *congruity* between antecedent and consequent. Like begets like. Modal activity does not come from mechanical action, but only material form and motion. Life is not generated by mire, nor thought secreted by brain; though life may be generated *in* mire, and *from* mire, by primary cause; and thought may issue from brain, or through brain, emanating from a thinking cause. This congruity is not necessary in original causation. Though matter, itself an effect, can not generate will, it may be generated *by* will. Though the dislodgment of a rock on a distant mountain-side might be repeated a thousand times, it could never produce a psychic motion in me; still less, a psychic power. Should psychic motion succeed, the fall of the rock could be no more than occasion; my will must be the cause. But will can cause the fall of the rock. Sitting in my chair, I can decree a train of instrumentalities which will dislodge the granite from its socket; as will may prompt a set of physical preparations in Boston, or determine the movements of a hundred thousand soldiers in the field. But even original cause, if finite, can not create matter or force; as it is impossible for finite intelligence to conceive how that event can be produced.([)

([) I find this law of (secondary) causation enunciated by Coleridge. "The law of causality," he says, "holds only between homogeneous things, *i. e.*, things having some common property" ("Biographia Literaria," chap. 8). So, also, Spinoza: "Quæ res nihil commune inter se habent, earum una alterius causa esse non potest" ("Ethica," book i.). J. S. Mill, however,

Fourthly, a relation of *efficiency* must subsist between the antecedent and consequent, even in secondary causation. But it does not follow that the antecedent is the source of the efficiency; it may only transmit it. In a question of secondary causation, therefore, two separate quæsita exist. First, does a relation of efficiency subsist between two given terms; second, if so, is the efficiency original or transmitted? The last question I have discussed generally, and have pointed out the various views which it is possible to entertain respecting the primordiality of the force manifest in the natural world. I have shown that there is but one possible view which does not conduct thought, ætiologically and necessarily, to a Prime Mover, the field of whose activity embraces not only matter, but every possible mode of existence.

Fifthly, causal intermediation is susceptible of arrest, or deflection, or acceleration, by *conditions*. Unlike conditions in primary causation, these exist only as a mechanical influence. They are the objective, in distinction from the subjective, conditions of primary causality.

These five principles are applicable in all reasoning from the phenomena of nature, whatever view we may take of the nature of matter, or the relations subsisting between matter and force. If we accept either phase of divine immanence, we may assume that Deity conditions himself *spontaneously* by the same laws as we are compelled to regard *necessary* laws, on the hypothesis of the inherency of force in matter.

The principles of *efficiency* and *conditionality* are the two rocks on which scientific reasoning has most frequently split. Sometimes a relation of succession or concomitance has been mistaken for an efficient relation. Sometimes a condition has

---

denounces the proposition as a fallacy ("System of Logic," p. 474). And yet he cites some admirable instances of the supremacy of the principle of congruity (p. 486–487).

been so mistaken. The line of false reasoning from neglect of the principle of conditionality bifurcates. There are, as I have before stated, two classes of conditions—those which are *subjective* to moving cause, and those which are *objective*. Conditions which enter into the constitution of motive are subjective. They co-exist with intentionality, and condition it. Conditions which modify or annul the efficiency proceeding from cause, either primary or secondary, are objective, and act mechanically. Organic conditions are objective; they are often privative or permissive. It is a somewhat frequent error of science to confound subjective and objective conditionality, as well as to transmute condition into efficiency. Those who fail or refuse to recognize intentionality in nature must consistently ignore all but objective conditions. Still, on their own standing-plane, they practice false induction when they clothe condition with efficiency.

I shall now attempt to point out and classify, by way of illustration, some leading examples of false philosophy in the methods of recent science. This task is difficult, and requires, probably, more acumen than I possess; but I shall venture, tentatively, to arrange these examples in five classes.

1. *Subjective Condition mistaken for Objective Condition, and then mistaken for Efficiency.*

The coadaptation, which every one has remarked, between organic nature and its physical environment has been the subject of different interpretations. De Maillet, Lamarck, Geoffroy-St.-Hilaire, and many others, down to Darwin and his disciples, have conceived the organism as impressed and fashioned by the direct influence of the environment. That is, the environment has been regarded as exerting an efficient causation, in the capacity of an objective condition. On the contrary, Cuvier, Agassiz, Dawson, and the whole line of believers in " Final Causes," from Socrates to M'Cosh, have maintained that the organism is *not* the product of the environment, but a product which intelligence has correlated with the environment. In other words, the environment has been the existent fact which *has conditioned the* INTENTION *of the causal intelligence.* If this latter view be correct, Lamarckianism and kindred theories, so far as they maintain that environment is the seat of causal efficiency, have mistaken a subjective condition for an objective one, and have then conceived it as exerting causal efficiency. The correctness of the Darwinian view, under the aspect just stated, it appears, depends on the proof of efficiency proceeding from environment to organism. But this does not seem to be probable. Admitting the environment to be, as it is in some cases, an objective as well as a subjective condition, *it is only a condition*—that is, it is a fact which stands either in a permissive relation to efficient cause, providing the possibility for the production of a certain result; or else, if efficiency emerges from it, it is only transmitted efficiency, the direction of which it determines within certain limits. In either case, efficiency does not reside in environment; but the latter case, moreover, is incapable of proof, since the efficient cause of organic growth acts in the organism; and the external conditions obviously sustain only a permissive relation to this activity.(¹) If external conditions permit only a dwarfed development, the efficient cause can proceed only to the limits assigned. If external conditions do not permit the elaboration of color-cells, the organism remains colorless. Often, however, we find

---

(¹) This discrimination has already been made by Huxley. "Conditions are not actively productive, but are passively permissive; they do not cause variation in any given direction, but they permit and favor a tendency in that direction which already exists (Huxley, "Critiques and Addresses," p. 276). I. H. Fichte, also, speaks pertinently to this point as a philosopher: "Nothing extraneous to any individual existence can transform it, but can only excite it to self-wrought development" ("Die Theistische Weltanschauung," Leipzig, 1873, p. 225).

structures in the organism which could not result from restrictive or privative conditions—such as the development of molars for trituration in animals having a digestive apparatus suited to a vegetable diet; or elongated and prehensile organs, as in the giraffe and the proboscideans, where the food is not attainable with the ordinary structure; or legs and lungs in aquatic embryos developing for terrestrial life, where the influence of the environment, if any were conceivable, would be exerted against the development of the organ. A triturating molar, an elongated tongue or snout, an unused pair of lungs growing in the water—these are not developments arrested by external conditions, but developments invited by external conditions, actual or future, and pushed forward by some force *acting in the organism*, and *acting with a discernment* of the character of the environment, either actual or future. Thus the environment exerts no efficiency whatever. It may condition in two ways, by limitation and by solicitation; while, in some cases, the structure is in *anticipation* of environment, though in these cases as truly conditioned by environment as in any other case. But all cases of conditioning environment are alike in failing to yield the evidence of efficient causation, even of the secondary kind. This critique is equally applicable to the doctrine of progressive improvement of animal life in geological time, conceived as the product of the improving conditions of the world.

2. *Subjective Condition mistaken for Efficiency.*

Here that which is a motive, or final cause, determining a method of activity, is mistaken for a necessary mode of existence, growing out of the assumed efficiency of secondary causes. One of the explanations of the fact of a method of evolution in nature falls under this head. That a method of evolution prevails can not, I think, be successfully disputed. It has been remarked by scientists since the times of Leibnitz, Laplace, and Von Baer; by sociologists from Plutarch to Comte and Buckle and Spencer; by theologians from St. Clement to modern thinkers. Some have attempted to explain evolution as an issue emerging, in every case, from some necessary relations of matter and the material forces. But evolution is a manifestation of order. Evolution implies foresight of an end involved in a beginning. It is a predetermined and permanent modality or mode of efficiency. A predetermined mode of action impresses intentionality. The method of evolution is a subjective condition. It conditions effectuation; but it does not effectuate.([1])

A general method of evolution, in a world full of differentiated sections of existence, implies various aspects of evolutionary manifestation and agency. There must be evolution in the cosmos; evolution of continents and seas; evolution of life and organic types; evolution of individuals; evolution of civilization; evolution of systems of education and of religion. Everywhere must be a procedure, as Spencer phrases it, from the more homogeneous to the more heterogeneous. Different forms of force or modes of energy must be manifest under the different circumstances. In the cosmos, speaking after the usual fashion, mechanical forces may suffice; in determining the succession of organic forms in the individual, in the race, or in the world, physiological forces may be instrumental; in sociology, education, and science, the force of ideas, variously conditioned, may effectuate the orderly advance; in the evolution of life, it is impossible to conceive of any thing short of immediate creative power, since between life and not-life, or between life and matter, is an incongruity which secondary causation is incompetent to bridge over.([2])

([1]) "The whole process of evolution is the manifestation of a power absolutely inscrutable to the intellect of man" (Tyndall, "Belfast Address," Appletons' ed., p. 91).

([2]) "If we look at matter as pictured by Democritus, and as defined for

But, admitting the reality of secondary efficiency proceeding from the material forms which constitute or environ the evolutionary series, I have shown that this implies primary causality and all which that concept incloses. If gravitation, and centrifugal force, and thermal exchanges are the intermedia of cosmic differentiations, there is a supreme Master whose will they administer. If inheritance, effectuated through physiological forces, results in specific deviations and race improvements, these are not the results of the law of heredity, since that law, like all others, marks only a rule of action ordained by a competent lawmaker. If the principle, or, more properly, the *mode*, designated as the "survival of the fittest"—which is only another phrase for "natural selection" and "sexual selection"— results in a slow improvement of the species, this is not because a mode effectuates any thing. The forces of life are the positive agents, and whatever subject controls these is the real cause of specific advance. And so, if successive acquisitions of ideas lead to the unfolding of more complicated and more advanced social systems, these ideas are but agencies employed by Intelligence which has contemplated ends concealed from every finite mind. As before intimated, however, I prefer to regard Supreme Intelligence as acting without intervention. In the evolution of life's beginnings, I again insist, no other conception is rationally possible. This is affirmed by Darwin and Huxley; and still more explicitly by the majority of those who hold to the derivation of species, and the general doctrine of evolution.

In the same category belong certain explanations offered of

---

generations in our scientific text-books, the notion of any form of life whatever coming out of it is utterly unimaginable" (Tyndall, "Belfast Address," Appletons' ed., p. 87). "Considered fundamentally, then, it is by the operation of an insoluble mystery that life on earth is evolved, species differentiated, and mind unfolded from their prepotent elements in the immeasurable past" (*ib.*, p. 91).

homological and teleological relations in the natural world; but I reserve my critique for a fuller discussion.

3. *Objective Condition mistaken for Efficiency.*

The universally recognized influence of physiological conditions on the psychical activities has led some thinkers to the extent of assigning these conditions to the position of cause of psychical activities. Thus, the body is the basis of mental phenomena, and mind is a figment. In reasoning against this view, I desire to say, *in limine*, that the theory annihilates both soul and immortality, and thus wars against the intuitions of humanity. This has always been a warfare of a hopeless kind. Next, the theory violates the principle of congruity. Unless the body is a voluntary actor, we have matter, as secondary cause, producing thought. This, as Tyndall insists, is inconceivable.[1] Obviously, bodily matter is only an objective condition of the permissive or privative variety. In the order of human nature, thought and will are manifest only through certain states of matter. The manifestation must be co-ordinated to the degree of permission. Nothing further needs to be said.

The "unconscious cerebration" of Carpenter is a materialistic phrase which seems to imply that brain is capable of elaborating thought during our periods of unconsciousness. Yet this interpretation is contrary to the positive tenor of Dr. Carpenter's teaching. By "unconscious cerebration" he means exactly the same thing as Sir William Hamilton means by "unconscious mental states" or "mental latency;"[2] and this

---

[1] "When we endeavor to pass * * * from the phenomena of physics to those of thought, we meet a problem which transcends any conceivable expansion of the powers we now possess" (Preface to the seventh ed. of "Belfast Address," Appletons' ed., p. 28). "The passage from the physics of the brain to the corresponding facts of consciousness is unthinkable" ("Scientific Materialism," Appletons' ed., p. 117).

[2] Hamilton, "Lectures on Metaphysics," Lect. XVIII.

means that the mind continues to act during suspended consciousness, as in sleep; and sometimes elaborates conclusions whose processes have escaped our notice. "Unconscious cerebration" of thought, in the literal sense, is a hypothesis amenable to all the objections just urged against the physiological causation of thought. It is the same thing.

I should add that the environment of organic forms, which plays so conspicuous a rôle in Lamarckian and Darwinian theories, seems sometimes to stand in the relation of an objective condition of the permissive variety. For instance, the existence of shell-bearing mollusks is permitted only by the existence of lime-yielding water. The growth of trees requiring silica in their constitution is possible only in soils affording silica; as a hundred other requirements or conditions of organic existence must be answered before each particular form of existence is permitted. Now, what have these permissive conditions to do with efficient causation? Obviously, the cause of whatever does grow acts in the organism, and co-ordinates its action to the external conditions. Efficiency implies will, which includes intelligence; and co-ordination also implies intelligence. Hence the assertion that a forest of pines is caused by a sandy soil is the acme of the illogical.

4. *Instrumental Relation mistaken for Cause.*

I have made allusion to a class of organic structures developed in antagonism to the environment, and hence, by no possibility, its product. It seems to be considered by some Darwinists a sufficient explanation of this phenomenon, that the organization is hereditary. The branchiæ of the tadpole do not disappear, and the lungs develop, during aquatic life, through the influence of the surroundings, but in obedience to the law of heredity. Well, this means that our tadpole acquires lungs at the same time that it must use gills, because its ancestors did this. But how did its ancestors get this peculiarity to transmit? Did they acquire lungs in the water through the influence of the environment? Oh no; it was a hereditary tendency with them also. But go back a hundred generations, or a thousand; go back to the first brood of tadpoles—there must have been a first brood—was there any hereditary tendency in them? It seems to me, to whatever distance we remove the *acquisition* of this hereditary tendency, we must necessarily recognize a *beginning*, at which air-breathing organs were acquired in the water *without the impulse of heredity*. We may conceive the amphibian characteristics to have been gradually assumed; but always, just in the same degree as amphibian characteristics *began* to develop, they began without the influence of heredity. The organic differential could never be so small as to elude the necessity of a causal influence, which the unfriendly element could not exert, and which, as each differential came first into existence, heredity could not be summoned to explain. In the several increments of its origin, the amphibian character was necessarily independent of heredity; in its integral development, therefore, heredity has nothing to do. The lungs of the tadpole can not be ascribed to the environment, whether we seek for its influence upon the individual or upon the species; and when we trace the increments of the organism, severally, back to their inception, the influence of heredity is excluded by hypothesis. We demand some cause which can originate a differential character *de novo*—independently of heredity and in opposition to the influence of surroundings—and, what is most significant of all, in *anticipation* of an environment which, in the animal's plan of life, will surround it at maturity. Heredity is but an *instrument* through which a needful organism is brought into existence, in spite of adverse influences, by some efficient cause capable of discerning physical adaptations, and realizing them in a manner conformable to general plans.

5. *Cause arbitrarily assumed.*

Here I would class Mr. Spencer's doctrine of "organized experiences." By this phrase he means that those necessary ideas, notions, beliefs, which I have shown to be innate, and which only a small school of empiricists can recognize as growth within the individual, are the result of a slow growth within the race. Now, *first* of all, such an acquirement, if it were such, would not be comparable with the inherited disposition of the pointer and setter, among dogs, since the latter is a case of complete transmission in a single generation, and not a gradually accumulated inheritance. *Secondly*, if these necessary concepts were gradually accumulated and strengthened, as the theory implies, they would be of different degrees of strength and clearness in individuals or races reared under different conditions. But no such disparity exists; nor is there the least evidence that they have added a particle to their strength since the date of earliest traditions. *Thirdly*, the hypothesis of incrementation violates the principle of heredity. Heredity transmits what it receives—nothing more. Heredity itself declares that these concepts have been transmitted from the *first man;* and that declaration I accept. *Fourthly*, the hypothesis violates the principle of congruity. The forces of heredity are physiological; the concepts which Spencer places at interest in their custody are ideas of the reason. "Men do not gather grapes of thorns, nor figs of thistles." This doctrine is a "*non causa pro causa.*"

Under the same category I would range the doctrine of abiogenesis, restricting the term to the generation of life by that which is non-life. Have we not learned that "like begets like?" This, at the outset, is another violation of the principle of congruity; and stands forth as such without a shred of apology to cover the naked absurdity of hurling absolute inertia into the chair of creative efficiency.

May I ask you to note particularly the force of the terms which I employ? In this discussion I always conceive of matter as absolutely inert—"gross"—"brute"—a *different* matter from that pangenetic entity in which Professor Tyndall sees every thing in potentiality. If we conceive matter self-efficient, or exerting a delegated efficiency, we can conceive it the cause, primary or mediate, of physical effects; but *life* is an entity which has nothing in common with matter; and, though it may be revealed in forms of matter styled organic, its commencement demands a cause generically differentiated from matter. This is not to assert that the cause of life acts invariably through a pre-existent germ. The rule does not preclude exceptions. We all believe, in fact, that life upon the earth has descended from one or many absolute beginnings. If life has been once or more introduced without the intervention of germs, it may have been so introduced in a myriad instances, running down to yesterday. But to conceive the potency of life *shut up in matter* is either to wander from the accepted signification of the term, or to confound simple material concomitance with efficient causation.

The views which have opened before me during the progress of these discussions have rolled forth with a copiousness by which I have felt embarrassed. Would that I had conceived them with clearer eyes, and phrased them with more expressive words! I thought, when I assigned two lectures to the discussion of the doctrine of causality, I should be able to exhaust the well of my deepest convictions, and give ample attention to those views, sometimes attributed to science, which impinge against the eternal principles of truth revealed in human reason. But I have only given you the conspectus of a discussion. I have lifted the veil; I have afforded a glimpse within the adytum of truth; I can do no more. I beg you to rend the veil with your own hand; enter and commune.

VI.

THE DOCTRINE OF INTENTIONALITY.

In my fourth lecture I stated, in effect, that faith in God may be based on—

I. The feeling or intuition of his existence.

II. The knowledge of his existence.

This knowledge I stated to be attainable in various ways, among which are—

1. The common consent of mankind.
2. The intuition of causality (Ætiological).
3. The evidence of intentionality in nature (Teleological).

It will be remembered that in the attempt to develop the ideas inclosed in the necessary concept of original causality, I enunciated intentionality as one of them; and pointed out the fact that in every effect where intention is manifest, mind is implied. I also reminded you that the world is full of instances of intentionality, since it is full of facts of co-ordination, which we necessarily apprehend as the result of intention.

Now, the intentionality of which I am to speak in particular is not that of which we become convinced in viewing the world simply as an effect. The mere fact of simple causation does evince intentionality; but the fact of *co-ordination* of effects evinces reflective intentionality. It yields additional evidence of the activity of mind. It is this stronger evidence to which I invite your attention.

Philosophically speaking, it is not necessary to spread before you an extended array of examples. If that primitive judgment is valid by which we deduce intelligence from correlation, then the discovery of a single instance of correlation in all the universe makes just as strong a case in defense of theism as the production of a hundred instances. The battle-ground, in these times, is on the threshold of the teleological argument. Nescience meets us at the door, and attempts to bar us completely upon the outside. It proposes to invalidate the very basal proposition which lies deeper than Socrates, or Galileo, or Butler, or Paley ever explored—unconscious as they were that all their reasoning assumed an antecedent truth which could be challenged. The prior proposition of teleology is the affirmation that *intelligence is implied in intelligible correlations.*

The general tenor of my last two lectures is an argument which may be applied to the support of this proposition. For this reason, I shall not enter here upon any preliminary discussion. I need only remind you that the truth of this proposition is revealed in the universal reason of humanity—like the truth of the axioms of geometry; that, being a simple truth, a first step in reasoning, there are no steps by which it is possible to reach it with an argument; that, in the sphere of human affairs, its validity has never been questioned, and that, in the realm of nature, its invalidity is only the recent claim of a limited number of thinkers; that even these do not *assert* its invalidity, but only its possible invalidity, since the effects which we observe in the natural world emanate from a source which entirely transcends our apprehensions; and that these thinkers, nevertheless, generally incline to recognize the world as the product of intelligence akin to our own, while they regard it most becoming to science and philosophy to restrict themselves to the phenomena of the finite. I remind you, lastly, that this intuition is one which takes no cognizance of the distinction between finite and infinite; but renders its testimony as emphatically and unreservedly when it interprets a phenomenon in the natural world as when it enters the shop of an artisan; that the impeachment of the authority of this intuition is an implied impeachment of all, and the logical result is, to precipitate man into a wilderness of misleading and Fichtean unrealities—a very insanity of philosophy.

This is the skeleton of a treatment of the fundamental question, which has been incidentally filled out, in parts, in the progress of the last two lectures, and the full development of which must satisfy the most exacting of the validity of the basis of the teleological argument.

Though one instance of design is as good as a hundred in fixing a philosophical conviction, it is not as good as a hundred in moving the religious nature. There are two avenues to religious conviction; one is the *rational*, the other the *emotional*. Both are excellent ways; but some are too feeble to pursue the rational, while others are too proud to pursue the emotional. Both roads converge at the same end, and the Judge who sits there never asks the individual by what route he has traveled. Now, while a display of the economy of nature is not purely an appeal to the emotional, like the effort of the religious exhorter, it is partly so. Every one is aware of awakened emotions in contemplating nature. These spring not simply from the beauty, or sublimity, or complexity, or vastness of nature; but there is irresistibly mingled with the sentiments which these characteristics awaken, a feeling of reverence and awe, in view of the manifestation of God. And can it be that the instinct is illusory which so quietly, so universally, and so instantly ascends from the harmonies and grandeur of the world to an adequate Author of these manifestations, already revealed in the soul? No. The very emotions, then, which the contemplation of nature awakens imply the truth of the fundamental principle of teleology. But because the wonders of the universe awaken emotions—religious emotions—the multiplication of instances may strengthen a religious nature which never dreams of the philosophic explanation of its emotions, and is innocent of the possibility of reflective doubt. More than this, it may turn the balance in a noble mind, in which religious faith is beginning to cower before the arrogant demeanor of a vigorous intellect.

The correlations discoverable in nature may, I think, be all embraced under two general heads: MECHANICAL CORRELATIONS and MODAL CORRELATIONS. The former are coadaptations of parts of a structure intended for action; they imply *contrivance*, by which the principles of mechanics are made operative and effective in forms shaped and coadjusted in the requisite manner. The parts thus become either instruments or the constituents of a machinery. Such are the chiseling beak of the woodpecker, the climbing beak of the parrot, and the straining beak of the duck. Such are the muscles which extend and flex the forearm, and that admirable bony and ligamentous structure which gives breadth and prehensile power and marvelous dexterity to the human hand. But there is another concept which coexists with that of contrivance in every instance of natural mechanism. *The mechanism subserves some objective end.* It generally subserves utility or beauty. The sufficient reason for its existence is not subjective in the designer, but objective in some sentient being whose happiness is promoted by it. It might still be a mechanism demonstrative of intelligence, if it sustained no relation to the happiness of sentient beings—the sufficient reason for its existence residing in the consciousness of the designer. I mention the relation of utility only as an objective fact, not as a necessary correlation of contrivance. It enhances, however, the significance of the contrivance to find not only its parts adapted to each other, but the whole adapted to utility. As a mechanism, it implies intelligence; as a useful mechanism, it implies intelligence twice-told.

Modal correlations are coadaptations of parts or wholes in conformity to *plan*. They imply, 1st, the conception of a plan; 2d, the ordering of effects so as to give expression to the plan. Plans in nature are as various as the fields in which effects are displayed. We recognize them in the organization of the body of man, in that of each of the types of animals, and in the general conception of an animal at large. We recognize them in the correlation of the intellectual faculties, in the moral faculties, in the voluntary faculties, and in the interactivities of all the faculties. We recognize plan in the system of correlations between the psychic and bodily natures; we discern it in the structure of the solar system, in the geological history of the world, in the interaction of the physical forces, and in the progressive changes of the cosmos as a whole and in its parts. We discover plan in the disengagement of results through the method of *evolution*, and in the subordination and action of the *various agencies* employed by the Prime Evolver in working the plan—be those agencies physical forces, heredity, natural selection, sexual selection, hybridity, prolonged gestation, accelerated or retarded development of the embryo, occasional extraordinary births, parthenogenesis, influence of the environment, or an inherent conative quality of nature.([1]) Each of these agencies, or systems of instrumental effectuation, has been set forth as operative, more or less, in the evolution of organic series. I believe them all influential. I believe the tendency of each of these agencies may be, generally, toward the evolutionary result. But I recognize each system of agencies operated according to a method which regulates its particular activities; and, most of all, I recognize *higher* plan in the thoughtful convergence of all these thought-elaborated systems toward one harmonious, homogeneous result—evolution. Evolution is the method of methods; and is

---

([1]) In a little work entitled "The Doctrine of Evolution," the present writer has endeavored to give a popular exposition of the general subject, and of the various opinions entertained respecting the *Causes* of the assumed derivation of species.

one of the strongest possible attestations of the dominion of thought in the universe. Evolution in itself, however, is *only a method* of effectuation. It implies, 1st, a Designer of the method; 2d, an Operator of the method. Evolution possesses no efficiency. He who contents himself with discovering this method in nature contributes nothing to the philosophy of causality. He leads us along the rills of phenomena, but only tantalizes the innate thirst to drink from the fountain of truth.(¹)

In historical order, the recognition and study of mechanical correlations long preceded the recognition of modal correlations. The former were styled teleological, as they disclosed an *end*, which seemed to be sought by a designer. Modal correlations also disclose conformity to plan as an end to be sought; and hence may also be styled teleological. But the end in one case is objective utility toward sentient beings; in the other, it is objective conformity to a subjective concept. This conformity may, at the same time, be designed for a useful end; and thus, even the dominance of plan may reveal a characteristically teleological character. But the distinction between mechanical teleology and modal is so clear and fundamental, and the term teleology has become so definitely restricted, by long usage, to the mechanical kind, that I shall employ another term to express modal teleology. In the comparative

---

(¹) I have taken great pleasure in the perusal of a work by Rudolf Schmid, Stadtpfarrer in Friedrichshafen, entitled "Die Darwin'schen Theorien und ihre Stellung zur Philosophie, Religion und Moral," Stuttgart, 1876, in which the complete compatibility of the derivative hypothesis with the Christian religion is intelligently maintained. Wigand's earlier work ("Der Darwinismus und die Naturforschung Newtons und Cuviers, Beiträge zur Methodik der Naturforschung und zur Speciesfrage," 2 Bd., Braunschweig, 1874–1876) assumes, in this respect, a similar position. See, also, K. E. Von Baer, "Studien aus dem Gebiet der Naturwissenschaften," St. Petersburg, 1876, containing two papers on Teleology and one on Darwinism.

study of organic structures, those which are built upon a common plan are said to be homologous. Thus nails, hollow horns, hoofs, and hair are homologous, because equally outgrowths from the dermis. Transferring the term to this discussion, homology is the doctrine that PLAN *implies intelligence;* while teleology is the doctrine that CONTRIVANCE *implies intelligence.*

The theologians of a recent period were reluctant to admit the existence of plans and archetypes, through fear that they might be incompatible with the doctrine of ends, so clearly substantiated. The execution of the plan might be claimed as the sole end. But we have learned that the intervention of the homological plan is the quickest way to the teleological end. Homology supervenes on teleology. The two always co-exist. No useful design is realized except in subordination to a general method. The existence of the method does not nullify the end which it subserves; it sheds a light upon it and enhances its meaning. Moreover, in homological relations an *objective end* is discoverable, sharply distinct from the teleological end, though co-existing with it. This is the influence of intelligible plan upon the human intelligence, before which it is wrought out. This might be termed psychic teleology, in distinction from ordinary mechanical teleology. Psychic teleology is further distinguishable into noetic (addressed to the intelligence) and æsthetic (addressed to the consciousness of the beautiful). I have long felt convinced that the revelations of lofty thought and all-penetrating prescience, with which the scheme of nature is enriched, were intended to stir the intellect of man, and lift it up toward the realities which transcend the sphere of sense. "God geometrizes," says Plato, beautifully and truthfully. Let us strive to think the thoughts of God. Not less have I been convinced that the beautiful in nature has a teleological meaning. It implies man fore-ordained; it implies æsthetic cognition and æsthetic susceptibility; and purposes by the exercise of this order of faculties to multiply the sources of happiness.

The doctrine of homology in organic structures, after having enjoyed great favor from the time of Goethe to Richard Owen, has fallen, like teleology, into a degree of disfavor with a certain class of anatomists, who think the principle of heredity is sufficient to account for all the affiliations of structure which group forms together under the shadow of one plan. Now, let us open the way for heredity, by all means. It is one of the intelligible *instrumentalities* by which Intelligence effectuates the objectization of plans. If animals belonging to different species, genera, or orders exemplify an identical plan of structure, and it can be shown that they have descended from a common ancestry, then all hail heredity! We have discovered the method and agency by which directive Intelligence transmits and perpetuates the objective expression of its conceptions. But, let it be observed, *first*, that this conclusion must be based on discovery, and not on conjecture; and, *secondly*, that the discovery will not be the disclosure of efficiency, but only of the mode of activity of efficiency. Heredity accounts for nothing; it is only the objective condition of resemblances in structure.

The theological uses of teleology have been almost exhaustively worked out by Paley.[1] He has, indeed, employed but a limited number of instances of design in nature, and has followed in the path blazed out by Socrates and Xenophon twenty-three centuries since; but he has selected admirable and fruitful examples, and has pressed them on this side and that, until it is impossible to extract further meaning from them, or from any other example of the teleological class. Since Paley's time, however, the extension of our knowledge of organic

---

[1] The design revealed in the structure of the human body was gone over with singular fullness and elaborateness by Lactantius in his book on the "Workmanship of God, or the Formation of Man."

structures, particularly the lower forms of animals, has vastly enriched the treasury of examples to select from; and Bell,([1]) Owen,([2]) Balfour,([3]) Clark,([4]) Chadbourne([5]) and many others, not omitting Cooke,([6]) in chemistry, have supplemented the archdeacon's imperishable labors; while in the field of astronomy, Chalmers([7]) and Mitchel([8]) have continued the work begun by Galileo, and Kepler, and Newton.([9]) In the science of geology, new facts and new views have shown to how large an extent the physical and organic changes of the world have constituted a *preparation for man*.

The field of homological correlations, for reasons already indicated, has been less worked in the interests of theology, though Dr. M'Cosh has ably broken the ground.([10]) I therefore invite your attention to a few illustrative examples.

([1]) "Bridgewater Treatise."

([2]) Exeter Hall Lecture: "The Power of God in his Animal Creation."

([3]) "The Religion of Botany."

([4]) "Mind in Nature."

([5]) "Lectures on Natural Theology."

([6]) "Religion and Chemistry."

([7]) "Natural Theology," vol. i., book ii., chap. iii.: "A Series of Discourses on the Christian Revelation, viewed in Connection with the Modern Astronomy."

([8]) "The Astronomy of the Bible."

([9]) Darwin in his various works has brought together a large fund of instances of mechanical and modal adaptations in the organic world.

([10]) "Method of the Divine Government," book ii.; and "Typical Forms and Special Ends in Creation." The theological significance of homology has been fully appreciated by Richard Owen and by Louis Agassiz, as may be learned from many of their writings. See, also, Whewell, "Philosophy of the Inductive Sciences." Older writers recognizing the theological bearing of homological relations of things are Plato, "Leges," book iv.; book x., cap. ix.; book xii.; book xiii., cap. xiii.; Cicero, "De Natura Deorum," lib. ii., cap. v., vii., xx., xxxii., xxxv., xliv.; Plutarch, "De Plac.," i., vi.; Samuel Clark, "Demonstration of the Being and Attributes of God;" Newton, "Optics." Spinoza says, "The laws of nature are noth-

The first example is the existence of *fundamental types of animal structure*. Cuvier, and most naturalists after him, have recognized four—Vertebrates, Articulates, Mollusks, and Radiates. Whether, as some believe, more than these should be recognized, or not, the persistence of these, from the dawn of animal life upon the earth,([1]) is a fact of profound significance. The existing world affords almost an infinitude of situations for the occupancy of animal forms. It is one of the intelligible economies of nature to populate all these situations with animal life. The solid land, the water, and the air teem with tribes innumerable. The grassy plain, the reeking jungle, the gloomy forest, the mountain solitude, the wilderness of rifted granite blocks—these all are the chosen retreats of air-breathing animals, severally correlated, in all their structures and instincts, to their diversified habitats. Not alone upon the surface of the earth do forms of life declare the existence of a co-ordinating intelligence. The woodchuck burrows in the earth to find a place of shelter and protection; the mole, to abide there. The beaver resorts to the water for safety and

---

ing else than the eternal decrees of God;" and similarly K. E. Von Baer: "Die Naturgesetze sind die permanenten Willensausserungen eines Schaffenden Principes" (Studien, p. 232); and Montesquieu affirms, "Ceux qui ont dit qu'une Fatalité aveugle a produit tous les effets que nous voyons dans le monde, ont dit une grande absurdité; car quelle plus grande absurdité, qu'une fatalité aveugle qui aurait produit des êtres intelligents?" (Those who have declared that a blind necessity has produced all the effects which we see in the world, have declared a grand absurdity; for what greater absurdity than a blind necessity which should have produced intelligent beings?) ("Esprit des Lois," I., i.) See, also, the references under "Original Causality" in the present work.

([1]) I do not ignore the Dawn-animal (*Eozöon*), which, as far as we know, was the earliest manifestation of life, and could not be ranged under any one of the four types named. I speak generally, and conceive the dawn of life to mean the appearance of the teeming populations of the Silurian —the first great age of animalization.

for a home; while the squirrel seeks his in the tree. Of the water-breathing tribes, some seek fresh water, some brackish, and some brine. Some thrive best in cold water; some in mild. Certain animals are confined to shallow waters; others retire to the dim and quiet depths of the ocean. Some are fond of an agitated stream; others loll in the stagnant pool. Of those which inhabit the air, some discover the fitting conditions near the town, some in the meadow, some in the forest, and others among the lightning-blasted pines which cling to the dizzy mountain-cliff. Even the types of insects are found swarming in all conceivable situations—darting like a beam of light through the air, crawling over the ground, burrowing beneath the bark of a tree, diving under the water or dancing upon its surface, fervid with activity at high noon, or flitting among crepuscular shadows, or prowling about in the dead of night. And thus, in respect to endurance of temperatures, how varied are animal natures! From the heats of the tropical plain to the rigors of the arctic ice-floe; from the bee humming in the sunny vale, to the coleopter skipping upon the surface of high Alpine glaciers; from the infusorian which withstands the temperature of boiling water, to the ovum lodged in a crevice upon the bark of a tree, and resisting, without injury, the piercing frost of a wintry night—in all terrestrial temperatures, as in all conceivable situations, the plan of animal life has found a suitable home for some percipient creature to dwell in.

And yet a world teeming with populations, conformed and adapted to situations too various for enumeration, presents us but four, or at most, but few, fundamental plans of animal structure. Throughout the world — over the vast stretch of continents, through the awful depths of the oceans — whatever the emergencies, however extreme the situation, the scheme of life clings to the few types. If this persistence of plan is amazing, what shall be said of the fact that the same plans have persisted through *all the ages of the habitable world* — through the period of tepid oceans lashed by cyclic storms; over the dripping shores just emerging from the briny ooze; under the shade of ferns and sigillariæ nurtured by a carbon-laden atmosphere, and reeking with the moisture of a continental jungle; under all the changing phases and vicissitudes of ever-widening land-areas, and ever-shrinking oceans, and ever-upspringing mountains, and ever-wasting islands; in the progress of appearing and disappearing populations; extinctions of species and genera and families; unfolding of comprehensive types, specialization of faunas, and gradual approximation to a fitness for the advent of man? Is there not intelligible purpose here—in such a restriction of plans to meet such an infinitude of emergencies? Why have not the external conditions, in their revolutions, revolutionized the plans of animal structure? Why has not the perpetual survival of the fittest evolved a plan of life which would fail to recognize either of the others as its remotest ancestor? If lines of descent, as derivationists believe, have diverged from the molluscan to the vertebrate type, how is it that the lowest orders of *all* the types have persisted to the present, and each of the types, on its first appearance in the world, was as clearly characterized as after the lapse of hundreds of thousands of years? Because Intelligence planned and ordained these types of structure; and to whatever uses heredity and natural selection have been appointed, they have never had the license to override the primordial decree.

Contemplate one of these types with more particularity. The skeleton may be taken as expressing the fundamental conception of the vertebrate type. This, in man, presents an extreme diversity of forms. In the vertebral column and in the ribs we have series of similar forms; but the two pairs of limbs would be regarded as dissimilar, while the cranium as a whole, or in its several parts, seems to offer no hint of resemblance to any other bones in the body. If, however, we compare with this skeleton the skeletons of other vertebrates, in descending order, to the fish, we observe that the bones of the different parts of the body present a constantly diminishing degree of differentiation from each other. We thus arrive at the discovery that the entire length of the skeleton is but a series of similar segments, differently modified in different parts of the body, to constitute the various bony bases of the organs which subserve the needs of the animal.([1]) We find that each one of these segments—taking no account of the modifications—consists essentially of a central, more or less cylindrical bone, commonly known as "vertebra" (and, in human anatomy, as "body of the vertebra"), supporting above a bony arch consisting of two pieces on each side of the median line of the animal, with a central piece, or key-stone, completing the arch, and supporting below another bony arch similarly constituted. When all these segments are placed together in a series, the "centrums" form the mass of the "backbone;" the upper, or "neural," arches form the channel in which the spinal marrow is lodged; and the lower, or "hæmal," arches inclose the cavity which holds the visceral organs. The cranium embraces four segments. The brain-box is made by the expansion and flattening of the bones which enter into the constitution of the four neural arches. As the brain is only a prolongation of the spinal marrow, the skull is only a prolongation of the vertebral column. The ribs are the lower, or hæmal, arches of the body, while the two jaws are the hæmal arches of the two anterior segments of the cranium. In the fish, the hæmal arches of the three anterior segments of the cranium are distinctly seen in the bones of the upper jaw, the lower jaw, and the tongue. The limbs are viewed as appendages. The pelvis, when it ex-

---

([1]) For an elementary elucidation of this subject, see Owen, "The Skeleton and the Teeth;" also Huxley, "Anat. Vert. Animals," chap. i.

ists, is a hæmal arch, and answers, like each of the jaws, to a pair of ribs, including the cartilages, connecting them with the sternum. Posteriorly, the hæmal arches diminish by disappearance of distal parts, and then disappear. Farther back, the centrums of the vertebræ generally diminish, as also the neural arches, and so gradually dwindle into the caudal appendage. It is a plan of organic structure that tail and brain are in inverse proportion. In mankind the tail is reduced to the *os coccygis*.

The vertebrate "archetype," so called, is a series of bony segments, consisting of centrums and upper and lower arches, each formed of its several pieces. This, of course, has no *actual* existence; but the skeleton of every actual vertebrate is composed of more or less of the archetype, with the bony pieces more or less varied in shape, though never varied in their relative positions and connections. The ends of the animal's existence are sometimes best effected with numerous segments, as in the serpent; sometimes with few, as in the mammal. The abdominal hæmal (lower) arches are sometimes complete, with their five pieces, as in the alligator and the lizard; those of man, and most vertebrates, have two of the pieces (one on each side) cartilaginous or wanting. In the latter case, of course, the central piece is also wanting. In the alligator, these arches become abbreviated, and their sides soldered together, beneath the tail, to constitute the "chevron" bones; in the ox they are entirely obsolete. In most mammals, one of the hæmal arches is strengthened and consolidated into a pelvis; in the fish the pelvis is absent. In reptiles, the vertebræ which support the pelvis remain distinct; in mammals they are consolidated in a "sacrum." In the fish, the pieces which enter into the constitution of the skull remain distinct, and thus afford a clue to the archetypal constitution of all skulls; in man, the pieces of the brain-box are so coalesced that its conformity to the archetype is much obscured. In most vertebrates, two pairs of appendages are present; in others we find but one pair—either anterior or posterior; and in still others both pairs are absent. In the fish we find the anterior pair articulated to the posterior neural arch of the cranium; in most vertebrates they are detached, and the proximal pieces, or "scapulæ," are imbedded in the dorsal muscles of the thorax. Thus the forms of the pieces of the skeleton are endlessly varied, and their relative dimensions are equally so—as well as the extent to which contiguous pieces are consolidated together, or "anchylosed." But every bone which is present can always be recognized as a piece of the archetype, and can be referred to its place in the archetypal segment.

This archetype expresses the *plan* of the vertebrate as far as the bony structure is concerned; but the nervous, vascular, respiratory, nutritive, and other departments of the organism are correlated with it, and, similarly, give expression to the plan. Each of the other fundamental plans of animal structure might be shown to manifest a similar conformity to an archetype. Each class, also, conforms to a class-archetype, which is a methodical and constant modification of the fundamental archetype.

The vertebrate skeleton, in the progress of geological time, has undergone what may be described as a gradual development or evolution. Fishes were the earliest representatives of the type; and here the skeleton presented, as it still presents, the minimum modification of the archetype. The different segments approach most nearly to identity. Batrachian reptiles next appeared, and then the tribes of scaly reptiles, with the skeleton successively more differentiated. In birds, which next came upon the scene, the skeleton was further specialized; while in mammals, the last class in order of appearance, the archetype, through the superadded modifications which it has undergone, is thrown into a state of comparative, but not impenetrable, disguise. Nevertheless, the archetypal conception runs through the entire series of beings, stretching down through eons of vast and unknown duration.

Now, what means this persistence of an idea—this imperishability of an abstract thought? Shall we say that these forms, having descended from a common stock, retain their fundamental resemblances through the influence of the law of inheritance? Or shall we maintain, with Cuvier and Agassiz, that the first representative of each class, ordinal, generic, and specific type is a new existence—a special creation? The latter view seems, at first, more consonant with the theistic instincts of man; but let us consider what the other view necessarily implies. It is the law of inheritance to perpetuate *identity*. This alone, then, would not account for continuous or periodical accretions of improvement. Moreover, if genetic affiliations run from end to end of the vertebrate line, they must run from end to end of the animal line; and this conclusion vastly augments the magnitude of the obstacles, the least of which heredity is incompetent to surmount. If the hereditary lineage is a fact, we must seek for some other cause to account for the wide divergencies which conflict with the principle of heredity. Shall we say that diversified conditions of existence have deflected the genetic line in various directions? These, I have said, can not be regarded as real causes, nor, generally, the seat of activity of real cause. The cause which effectuates whatever results in animal forms, acts in the animal organism exactly where the principle of heredity operates, and through exactly the same instrumentalities which heredity employs. There exists in the animal, then, a tendency to persistence of form, and an antagonizing tendency to divergence of form—a force centripetal and a force centrifugal. If we call the centripetal force heredity, what name have we for the centrifugal? Shall we call it an inherent tendency to divergence, as heredity is an inherent tendency to parallelism? The character of inherent tendency does not satisfy the requirements. This, like any other unintelligent force, must act *in a straight line;* but the divergences for which we seek to account are as sinuous as the myriad conditions to which the structures of animals are co-ordinated. The force producing them discerns the various conditions, and varies its action to conform to them. Discernment is an act of intelligence, and does not belong to matter. There must be, consequently, an external intelligence acting, or directing activity, within the organism. How shall we dodge this exit of the argument?

The doctrine of derivation implies, then, that external intelligence acts perpetually in the organism. The doctrine of successive creations implies that intelligence acts periodically; and is, therefore, the less theistic view. Derivation necessitates continual creation; and Descartes expressed this idea, long ago, in reference to the perpetuation of his own existence; while the Cuvierian view necessitates only occasional creations. Science is not yet prepared to settle unreservedly upon either of these views. There remain great, apparently not insuperable, difficulties in the way of the doctrine of derivation of organic forms; but, most assuredly, we may remain content to leave science to work out the problem at its opportunity.

The persistence of the vertebrate idea means, therefore, the overshadowing presence and efficiency of intelligence. The homological conformities are ordered by intention. The teleological subserviencies are arranged by intention. The whole world-wide and time-long panorama of vertebrate life is a never-ceasing and never-dimming revelation of God.

I desire to unfold this view with other details. Consider a particular portion of the vertebrate skeleton. The anterior appendages of vertebrates are composed, osteologically, of a definite series of pieces—scapula, humerus, radius and ulna, carpals, metacarpals, and phalanges. Preliminarily, observe that the posterior appendages are composed of an identical series of bones identically coadjusted. Now, when we consider the different uses of the anterior and posterior extremities, in many of the vertebrates, especially in man, it is remarkable that the same plan of structure is employed for both; and we feel compelled to admit that not alone the needs of the animal, nor the conditions of its existence, have guided the efficiency which produced limbs; but an abstract concept—conformity to a plan—has also been a guiding motive.

Next, consider the variations which have been played upon this membral archetype as a fundamental theme in the evolution of the anterior pair of extremities. We contemplate the arm and hand of man, and deem the member admirably adapted to the function of grasping and lifting; but the arm of the cat or dog, which neither grasps nor lifts, but performs other functions with admirable dexterity, has the same osteological composition. The broad, shovel-like hand of the mole, affixed to the extremity of a twisted fore-arm, shows us again the same bones teleologically modified to serve the behests of a different group of instincts, and the needs of a different bodily system. In the ox and horse the same series of bones is teleologically modified for simple locomotion on the land; and this function is better performed with this species of extremity than would be possible with the modification existing in the mole, the monkey, or almost any other quadruped. As these herbivora are the predestined prey of carnivores, and prey themselves upon no other animal, this endowment of fleetness is something co-ordinated to their exposed situation, while, at the same time, it becomes effective only through the further co-ordination of instinctive alertness and timidity. Next, the same membral archetype is further modified for aërial locomotion. In the bat, a wing is formed by the extension of a thin membrane over the elongated phalangeal frame-work. In the bird, the phalangeal frame-work, on the contrary, is foreshortened, consolidated, and obsolescent; and becomes, with the fore-arm, a solid base of support for an expansion of quills and feathers—themselves a marvelous structure, presenting a maximum of surface and strength with a minimum of material and weight. Lastly, the fish has wings for the watery element. Its pectoral fins present a bony composition in which the membral archetype is shadowed forth without ambiguity; as the abdominal fins answer, homologically, to the posterior extremities.

Now, it is futile to assert that, through all this range of conditions and co-ordinated instincts and functions, the environment is the efficient cause of modifications. In the self-same atmosphere, and sunlight, and temperature, the insectivorous bat presents us one modification, the insectivorous swallow another. So, under the same conditions, the honey-loving humming-bird possesses the same plan of wing as the carrion-eating vulture, but a fundamentally different one from the honey-loving butterfly! The resemblances and the differences exist in defiance of the nature of environment. There is a more occult principle which reigns in the system of morphology. It is not heredity; for that is essentially antagonistic to variation. The whole problem resolves itself, as soon as we recognize the existence of fundamental plans in nature, deflected endlessly, in conformity to the endless conditions which surround animals founded upon the same or different fundamental plans, class-plans, ordinal plans, family plans, or generic plans. Intelligence is the solution of all problems which surround us.

It will be interesting to still further specialize our mention of membral homologies. The recent researches of Professors Leidy, Marsh, and Cope have brought to light the former existence, in our Western regions, of several quadrupeds possessing structural affinities with the domestic horse. In the Eocene, or oldest Tertiary deposits of Wyoming and Utah, are found the remains of equine quadrupeds of the size of a fox, but having four hoofs in front (three behind). They belong to the genus *Orohippus*. In the Miocene, or next following stage, occur, in Oregon and Nebraska, the remains of *Miohip-*

pus and *Mesohippus*, about the size of a sheep, and having three hoofed digits before, of which the middle one is the largest. In the Pliocene, or next younger stage of the Tertiary, we find the remains of the *Anchippus*, *Hipparion*, and *Protohippus*, having the bulk of an ass, and ranging from Oregon through Nebraska to Texas. These genera are characterized by the possession of a stout middle digit, and a lateral one on each side not reaching the ground. There also occurs, in the Pliocene of Nebraska, another generic type, *Pliohippus*, in which the lateral hooflets have become reduced to a pair of "splint-bones," as in the domestic horse. Lastly, the same conformation exists in the remains of the genus *Equus*, discovered in the Quaternary, and having the size of the domestic horse, but belonging to a species which has become extinct.

We have here a chronological succession of forms possessing the highest interest. Between *Orohippus* and *Equus*, the oldest and newest of these equine genera, and representing the two extremes in structure, we may interpolate *Miohippus* and *Protohippus*, representing the intermediate structures. This gradation is intelligibly set forth in the conformation of the digits of the anterior extremity.

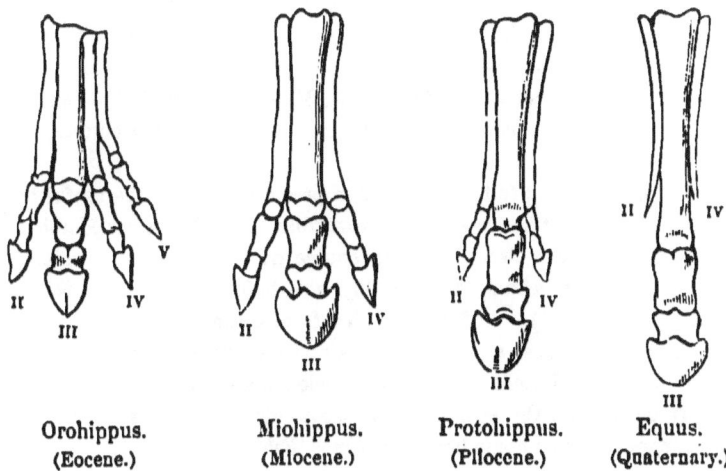

Orohippus.   Miohippus.   Protohippus.   Equus.
(Eocene.)   (Miocene.)   (Pliocene.)   (Quaternary.)

Here a certain order of change seems clearly to be established; and we may project the line of analogies deductively both into the past and the future. It seems legitimate to anticipate that an equine genus of later origin may yet exist, in which the "splint-bones" shall have completely disappeared; and to conjecture, with Professor Marsh,([1]) that, at some period earlier than the epoch of *Orohippus*, an equine quadruped probably existed having five toes before and four behind; and, at a still earlier period, a genus possessing five toes before and five behind, according to the norm of vertebrates.([2])

Two possible explanations of this series of phenomena present themselves. Both must recognize the existence of correlation of structure, which constitutes plan. We may assume that these successive forms sustain *no* genetic relationship, but are distinct creations—the continuity subsisting only in thought; or we may assume that each is lineally descended from its predecessor. This idea is favored by the succession in time corresponding to the gradation in type; by the circumstance that the several types are so related geographically as not to imply improbable migrations; and by the fact that with the manifest progress in the structure of the anterior extremities co-existed a regular advance in the assemblage of characters—in the increasing size; in the relative enlargement of the brain; in the

---

([1]) Amer. Jour. Sci. and Arts, vol. vii., March, 1874, p. 257. Compare, however, opposing considerations by Owen, "Anatomy of Vertebrates," vol. iii., pp. 792, 793.

([2]) It is a striking fulfillment of this prediction—a fact as useful here as in a scientific treatise—that in November, 1876, Professor Marsh announced the actual discovery of an equine quadruped having rudiments of the fifth digits behind, and, probably, also before (Amer. Jour. Sci. and Arts [3], xli., p. 401). Professor Marsh informed the writer that he sought methodically for these remains among a vast quantity of material obtained from the lowest Eocene beds ("Coryphodon beds") of New Mexico, distinctly older than the strata which had yielded *Orohippus*. This new, archaic, pentedactyl horse has been named *Eohippus*.

gradual elongation of the head and neck; in the widening of the "diastema" (space for the bit); in the disappearance of the first premolars and of the fangs of the molars; in the lengthening of the crowns of the molars; in the diminishing size of the canines and the enlargement of the incisors, with the acquisition of the characteristic pit of the modern horse. To these indications must be added the analogies of embryonic development,[1] and of similar series of forms in other orders of animals and other geologic ages.[2]

---

[1] "The embryonic life of man is almost an epitome of the animal kingdom, beginning with characters common to the moners and the worms, and ending with the Vertebrates" (Packard, "Life Histories of Animals, including Man," p. 239). According to Haeckel, the stages of the human embryo exemplify not less than twenty-two types of organization in a regular progression. These may be generalized as follows: Structureless protoplasm (moner), egg, morula, planula, gastrula (sack-stage), ascidian (exhibiting what some regard the homologue of a spinal marrow), amphioxus, low shark, amphibian, monotreme, marsupial, lemuroid, tailed monkey, tailless ape, Papuans ("Anthropogenie," Lectures XIV.-XIX.).

[2] Leidy, "The Ancient Fauna of Nebraska," Smithsonian Contributions to Knowledge, 1853; "Extinct Mammalia of Dakota and Nebraska," in Journal Acad. Nat. Sci., Philadelphia, vol. vii., 1869; "Extinct Vertebrate Fauna of the Western Territories," Hayden Survey, 1873. Cope, "Extinct Batrachia and Reptilia of N. Amer.;" Proc. Amer. Phil. Soc., 1869, Feb., 1873; Proc. Acad. Nat. Sci., Philadelphia, Jan., 1873, Feb., 1873, Aug., 1874, 1875 (p. 261), May, 1876, July, 1876; Bulletin U. S. Geol. Surv. Territories, No. 1; Hayden Survey, Annual Rep., 1873, pp. 498, 519; Hayden Rep., vol. ii., 4to; Wheeler Survey, Systematic Catalogue, Vertebrata, New Mexico, 1875; Ann. Rep. Chief of Engineers, 1874, p. 604. Marsh, Amer. Jour. Sci. and Arts (3), July, 1871, Sept., 1872, May, 1873, March, 1874, March, 1875, Nov., 1876; *New York Tribune* extra, No. 8. The descent of the horse was discussed by Professor Huxley in his New York lectures (see *Tribune* extra, No. 36).

The extinct *Palæotherium, Anchitherium,* and *Hipparion* of the Old World are similarly connected with the modern horse. Modern birds are connected, through sundry intermediate forms, with the Dinosaurian reptiles; the Eocene Amblypoda (Cope) are a type connecting the elephantine

I think, nevertheless, that we are not authorized to assume a genealogical descent satisfactorily proved by the simple fact of a graduated succession of forms; and to proceed, as some scientists do, on this basis of evidence, to discourse about the genealogy of the horse with as little reserve as we feel in treating of the royal line of the Prince of Wales. This assumed genealogy implies that one generic form may be derived from another; while all the facts which have fallen under our observation fail to supply a single species certainly derived from another.(¹) While this is the case, the circumstance of *consecutiveness* falls far short of logical proof of descent. A *link*

---

and equine types with the regularly clawed quadrupeds; the Creodonta are intermediate between Insectivores, Carnivores, and lowest Quadrumana; the Tœniodonta are intermediate between Creodonta, Edentates, and Rodents; *Anaptomorphus* connects Lemurs and true Monkeys, and *Tomitherium* connects Lemurs with Creodonta. Thus, as we trace the records of mammalian life backward to the commencement of the Eocene, we find forms presenting an ever-diminishing amount of differentiation — forms less and less distinct from each other — forms more and more "generalized," "synthetic," "comprehensive," or "undecomposed" — forms approaching more and more closely to a small-brained, five-toed, plantigrade stock or primitive ancestor, from which, according to derivative doctrine, have ·diverged the various lines which terminate in the living types of mammals. However we may interpret this retral convergence toward an ancient Eocene stock, the fact is demonstrated (compare Dana, "Manual of Geology," pp. 382, 597).

(¹) "I doubt whether any case of perfectly fertile hybrid animal can be considered as thoroughly well authenticated" (Darwin, "Origin of Species," Amer. ed., p. 223). "In extremely rare exceptions the fertility persists in the offspring, but it is much diminished. It diminishes still more in the grandchildren, and it is extinguished in the third or fourth generation at the most" (Quatrefages, "Natural History of Man," Amer. ed., p. 25). On the other hand, see Notes C, D, and E, by the editor of the above-named work, in reference to unlimited fertility of hybrids of the common and the Chinese goose, and of two species of woodpeckers. On these hybrids of geese, as well as hybrid plants, see, also, Darwin, "Origin of Species," p. 222. On hybrid woodpeckers, see Baird, Pacif. R. R. Rep., ix., 122.

missing destroys the chain of evidence. The lack (if such really exists) of conclusive evidence of the possibility of the derivation of a species is as total and fatal a failure of proof, in this case, as if there were no order in the succession, or as if the succession were one of inorganic instead of organic structure. I attempted once to expose this fatal inconsequence by publishing an ironical *jeu-d'esprit* on the "Genealogy of Ships."(¹) My little projectile elicited a number of responses,(²) of which two maintained that my implied argument was unsound in consequence of the disparity in the natures of ships and animals.(³) Indeed, that disparity, which I was supposed stupidly to have overlooked, furnished the very gist of my little argument. It was that which gave the theory of derivation (as far as proof from succession goes) a *reductio ad absurdum*.

But suppose a genetic descent provable, as, in view of the whole range of evidence, it seems to be. That alternative is precisely as satisfactory to theology as the other. We shall

(¹) *New York Tribune*, May 16th, 1874. The idea had been previously set forth by the writer in "The Doctrine of Evolution," 1874, pp. 90, 91.

(²) *New York Tribune*, May 25th, and June 2d, 1874.

(³) Still, Wallace asks, "Are not improved steam-engines or clocks the *lineal* descendants of some existing steam-engine or clock?" ("Natural Selection," p. 295). The analogy is also brought out by Von Hartmann, and exactly the same point is made. "Wenn z. B. gesagt wird, dass der gothische Dom aus dem romanischen, dieser aus der Basilika, und diese aus einer Art römischer Markthallen entstanden sei, wenn ferner zwischen den genannten Typen flüssige Uebergangsformen aufgezeigt werden, so wird doch niemand daraus folgern, dass etwa ein bestimmtes Bauwerk im gothischen Baustil jemals durch effectiven Umbau der Rundbögen in Spitzbögen hervorgegangen sei" (Von Hartmann, "Wahrheit und Irrthum in Darwinismus," 1875, pp. 12, 15, 16). It is a case exactly similar when we affirm, as Von Hartmann does, and others before him, that the systematic relations of minerals are no proof of genetic affinity, or that the derivatively related hyperbola, parabola, ellipse, circle, and right line have no other than an *ideal relation*.

then know that the intelligible plan of membral structure is perpetuated by descent; and that, instead of occasional creations to renew the expression of its existence, the method is, *to exert creative power perpetually*, whenever and wherever the activities which result in descent are in existence.

The class of homological relations may be legitimately extended beyond the range of organic structures. Homology implies correlations which express plan. I have already said that evolution is a vast plan; and that the various series of instrumentalities through which evolution is effected give expression to so many plans of effectuation, and imply in their separate as well as their concerted action an ordering Intelligence. The plan of world-life involves one of the grandest of these conspiring series of effects.

The plan of world-life!—it is simply a process of cooling. The plan of the cosmos!—it is simply a system of exchanges of temperature in search of an equilibrium. The proofs of this stupendous induction are excluded by the circumstances which surround me. The great fact suffices to illustrate my argument. The primordial condition of cosmical matter is either that of a fire-mist, or an antecedent non-luminous vapor which, by condensation, becomes a fire-mist. This condition is exemplified in the irresolvable nebulæ. Excess of heat is relieved by escape of heat. Sometimes a curdled or discontinuous condition of the fire-mist ensues, as exemplified in resolvable nebulæ. Sometimes a condensation about the centre gives rise to a "planetary nebula." Sometimes a rotary motion is generated, which develops the form of the "spiral" nebula. Sometimes the curve of rotation returns to itself, and the mass, as a total, is held in equilibrium while it rotates. In course of time, the peripheral portion becomes segregated, and produces an "annular" nebula. In the nebular history with which we are best acquainted, annulation seems to be a normal stage of the evolution. According to the theory which best harmonizes with the facts, and best accounts for them, a succession of detached rings, continuing to rotate, results, by successive ruptures and condensation, in a series of planetary bodies, constituting a system. It is conceivable, as I have elsewhere suggested,([1]) that a ring may preserve its equilibrium for an exceptionally prolonged period, during which a sort of stratification ensues, segregating an indefinite number of rings, so that the delayed rupture should result in an indefinite number of small planetary bodies grouped at a somewhat uniform distance from the centre of rotation. This might account for an asteroidal zone. The residual sphere of fire-mist remains all the time a central sun. The planetary masses suffer cooling and annulation, like the primary. Their annuli break up into satellites. In one case within our own system, we note the stratification of the annulus, which I have suggested as a step toward an asteroidal group. But the Saturnian rings have escaped the contingency of rupture till they seem to have cooled to the condition of dust. All the planets and satellites, self-luminous at first, become incrusted and darkened. All suns are marching toward the same goal. Before complete liquefaction ensues, darkened clouds of cooler matters float in their fiery photosphere, or ensue on the outburst of mineral vapors from the central nucleus. A sun in this condition is a "variable star." Such is our own sun. After the incrustation of a cosmical body, a long period ensues, during which the consolidating crust suffers many ruptures, permitting the imprisoned fires to pour forth, and send an unwonted gleam through the universe. These are the "temporary stars." The "white" stars, the "yellow" stars, and the "red," are only suns in progressive

---

([1]) "The Geology of the Stars," in "Half-hour Recreations in Popular Science," No. VII., p. 285. In this essay the probable succession of cosmical conditions is more fully set forth. See, also, articles in *Methodist Quarterly Review* for April, 1873, and January, 1874; also, "Sketches of Creation," where the terrestrial history is more especially dwelt upon.

stages of cooling, after which follow the variable stars and the temporary stars. In the lapse of time, after the incrustation of a cosmical body, clouds of watery vapor gather about it, and a cyclical storm descends upon its surface. In such a condition is Jupiter; and such a condition has left its records upon our earth. Then areas of dry land begin to emerge; the storms abate, and the procession of animals begins its march across the scene. The zoic period is exemplified in our own earth, and probably also, but more advanced, in Mars. In the lapse of ages, the cosmical mass becomes cooled to the centre; the waters and the atmosphere are absorbed; organic existence is swept from being, and the body hangs a mere *fossil world*, like the moon, to admonish us of a fate impending over all worlds.[1]

Such, in most respects, is the best accepted view of the sweep of cosmical events. What a picture to spread before the im-

---

[1] It is a noteworthy circumstance that the three great morphological conceptions of modern science have been broached by thinkers who are commonly reputed to have been indifferent to religion, and who are even popularly accused of presenting their hypotheses as substitutes for supernatural creative activity. Goethe discovered that the leaf is the archetype of all the structures of the plant. Oken first exhibited a vertebra as the archetype of a cranial segment. Laplace generalized the history of planetary worlds. These three discoveries were equally regarded by religionists as atheistical in tendency, and were earnestly opposed; but they are now equally approved by science, and equally adapted to exalt our apprehension of supreme wisdom and power. The doctrine in relation to plants and animals is a morphology, and probably a phylogeny; in relation to planetary, and, as now completely generalized, to cosmical existence, it is also a morphology, and almost demonstrably a phylogeny or material continuity. If the phylogenetic relations of plants and animals shall ever be fully established, we shall have in that doctrine (the derivation of species) another example of a scientific doctrine first employed in the interests of atheism (only, however, by the opponents of the doctrine), then established, and found to be a weapon peculiarly available in the interests of theism.

agination! What a generalization to address to the intellect! What a stupendous plan to utter the name of the Infinite, and awaken the religious sentiments of the soul! What an all-embracing unity of method is here to proclaim one empire, one lawgiver, one God!([1])

It is time that I leave the discussion to your reflections. My heart has burned with a desire to break through the crust of sensible things, which obscures the spiritual eye-sight, and help you to glimpse the sublime realities of the realm of thought and spirit, which "is not far from every one of us." How feeble have been my efforts!—may the Source of Truth to whom I have aspired forgive my failures! But, however impuissant may have been my endeavors to rise to the substantial First Principle of all, may I exhort you to seek still its revelation in the facts and thoughts of nature which lie around you. FEAR NO TRUTH—embrace all truth, for it is God's and yours; and as embassadors of God, take all His Truth, and use it to convince the world.

([1]) Further illustrations of "intentionality" in nature will be found in the last paper of this volume.

VII.

REASON FOR THE FAITH.(¹)

"It is of much more importance to give our assent to doctrines upon grounds of reason and wisdom than on that of faith merely."—ORIGEN, *Contra Celsum*, book i., chap. xiii.

"Which subject he [Cyprian] did not handle as he ought to have done; for he [Demetrian] ought to have been refuted, not by the testimonies of Scripture, which he plainly considered vain, fictitious, and false, but by arguments and reason."—LACTANTIUS, *Institutiones Divinæ*, book v., chap. iv.

TIME, which keeps all appointments, has brought the anniversary of culminating interest in collegiate life. You who have labored assiduously and long, through the rigorous curriculum, have seen the events of the final trial and triumph slowly rising in the horizon. We who have watched your efforts and prayed for your success, experience more keenly than ever the sense of responsibility for faithfulness to our trusts. I feel it a relief that the present occasion affords an opportunity to impress upon you, and all who hear me, a few words of wisdom, which, of all the lessons you have learned, I would commend to the deepest and warmest and most exclusive place of lodgment in your heart. As our relations to the world of invisible realities transcend in importance all other human interests, I have thought it might be useful to bring before you a systematic statement of the Reason of the Faith which, as Christians, we entertain. I shall undertake, therefore, to present a conspectus of the rationale of Christian belief. I shall

---

(¹) A baccalaureate address to the candidates for graduation in the College of the Liberal Arts of the Syracuse University.

speak, not as a divine, resting on Scriptural authority, but as a scientist and philosopher, seeking after the authority on which Scripture itself rests.

I feel that an inquiry of this kind may be peculiarly appropriate to the intellectual mood of the times. It is a questioning, iconoclastic age, which holds nothing sacred because it has been revered; and demands that even divine existence, divine providence, and religious faith commend themselves to human reason. I feel that I hazard nothing in accepting that issue. Bishop Butler tells us, "Reason is the only faculty we have wherewith to judge concerning any thing, even revelation itself." From that starting-point I see an open highway to a theistic faith and a Christian life.

Many obstacles to the progress of our argument will disappear on a summary statement of the *causes* of the modern phase of skepticism. We shall see that these causes are emotional, superficial, or inconsequential, and hence are not such causes as he who appeals to logic can pronounce sufficient; and that he who pleads them is not standing squarely to the battle-front, but is skulking under subterfuges.

The first cause of skepticism is *the evil heart.* It is the old clamor of the appetites and passions to be released from the restraints which all religions impose. It is, therefore, not peculiar to our times; but stands by perpetually to prompt and abet the questionings of the intellect.

The second cause is *the enforced abandonment of certain positions of traditional faith, necessitated by the progress of human knowledge.* Thus, it used to be maintained, by authority of the Church, that the earth was the centre of the universe. It was a heresy to assert the doctrine of the habitability of other worlds. The Jesuit Scheiner was compelled to publish anonymously his discovery of the spots on the solar disk. Not yet wholly silenced are the murmurs of dissent from the doctrine of the high antiquity of the world; or the reality of physical death before the sin of our first parents; or the local character of the Noachian deluge. Still more audible are the sounds of disapproval when we assert that the history of planets is a slow evolution of results wrought out by forces still active, and according to methods exemplified before our eyes. And, again, how slow have we been to discern and admit the fact that, to our apprehension, all spiritual manifestations are conditioned by matter! Yet on all these questions the Church is taking, as it must take, an affirmative position. Men not controlled by their religious instincts, seeing the abandonment of old positions which it once defended with arguments and anathemas, and sometimes with cruelties, hastily assume that Christian faith has nothing whatever in it which can stand persistently the tests of reason and science. But every one must perceive the inconclusive character of such reasoning. In fact, it is no reasoning at all, but an illogical generalization, like that of a man who, from sundry unsuccessful attempts to digest a supper of oyster-shells, should conclude that the human stomach is not adapted to oysters. The most puerile intelligence must discern that the position of the earth in the universe can not be a question of religious faith, but is a question of observation and mathematical calculation. Whether other worlds are habitable, must be inferred from data which address themselves to the intellect. Whether the procedure in world-making has been slow, and according to the method of evolution, is of no consequence in the question of divine existence, or of creative and formative activity. It has been natural, in times past, to associate all generally accepted doctrines and dogmas with beliefs which are strictly religious; and then to forget the distinctions among the beliefs incorporated in the religious system. An age of intellectual sluggishness would favor such confounding of doctrines; an age of mental activity would be sure to expose the fallacy, and involve religious and secular truth in common peril. Against this we must guard. The world truly moves, as Galileo asserted; but prayer may still be a human duty, as the Church maintained.

The third cause of skepticism *is the habit of rash and disingenuous generalizations on the part of the evil-disposed*. There are those who would rejoice to see science and Christian faith in irreconcilable conflict. There are others who sincerely believe that they sustain no natural relations to each other. Persons of the former class make haste to seize upon every new development, or suggestion, or intimation which makes its appearance in the field of science, and, without waiting for that due certification which is the first canon of Baconian generalization, they proclaim oracularly the final overthrow of the "superstition of Christianity." Thus, when relics of pottery were announced as found at a certain depth beneath the alluvium of the Nile, all the world was at once informed that the Bible contained egregious misstatements respecting the antiquity of the human race; and the whole system based upon such authority must be abandoned. It was not the careful scientist who made this proclamation. It *was* the careful scientist, M. de Lanoye, who proceeded to test the alleged fact, and was thereupon led to publish to the world his conclusion, that geological Egypt is an alluvium twenty-six feet in maximum thickness, laid upon a bottom of marine sand; that of this alluvium four-tenths (0.4134) of a foot is deposited in one hundred years; so that the whole Nilotic deposit is but six thousand three hundred and fifty years old. So, when human relics were exhumed from the Mississippi delta, even Sir Charles Lyell was disposed to yield to the plausible claim of immense antiquity for our race; but now Humphreys and Abbot, in their patient and masterly study of the hydraulics of the Mississippi valley, formally enunciate the conclusion that the entire delta does not exceed five thousand years in age. So with the illogical claim that the discovery of the perpetual conservation and convertibility of physical force proves the mechanism of the universe self-sustaining.

Suppose this true, does it prove that force is self-existent, and self-convertible, and self-conservative? Is it proved—granting heat to be "a mode of motion"—that motion can take place without a mover? Is it proved—granting the method of creation to be an evolution—that there was no intelligence to devise the method, no power to evolve? The claim that this and similar propositions, even supposing them proved, militate fatally against religious faith is shallow, if it is not malignant. The whole foundation of religious faith rests behind all these questions, and too deep for their agitation to disturb.

The fourth cause of skepticism *is the cowardice of believers*. Unwittingly, if not stupidly, they second the attacks of the preceding class. The evil-wisher dogmatically asserts that such and such conflicts exist. The weak-kneed believer is too prone to admit that it appears to be so—that it is so; and then, as he can not ignore his religious instincts, there is no alternative but to arraign science as their foe. He acknowledges the *status belli;* but then, instead of seizing his sword, he incases himself in coat of mail, and meekly stands the raps, to the infinite contempt of those who feel that he ought to surrender his position or defend it. Shame! If I have ever felt indignation, it has been at the sight of these believers cowed by such whips of straw. Accept no unauthoritative interpretation of the facts of nature, or application of them to matters of faith. Accept no unattested statement of the facts. Be sure you stick to the letter of the allegations of science, and avoid premature inferences—especially inferences made by third parties, who possess no qualifications for scientific investigation. Do not attribute to original scientists opinions which they do not avow. Your field is too narrow to enable you to discern what theological beliefs may seem most truthful to them. Stick to that which the scientific world recognizes as well established; and never surrender your faith in religion or science at the bidding of either bully or upstart.

A fifth cause of skepticism *is the mistaking of the non-essential for the fundamental in matters of theology.* How fatal and how frequent has been this error! The whole history of theological dogma and hierarchical oppression is an illustration of our point. The numerous attempts to which allusion has already been made, to decide questions of science by decree of council or pope, have repeatedly involved the Christian faith in confusion and reproach. It is hazardous to make Christianity sponsor for crude theorizers in natural science. Their default becomes a stain upon her name. If she voluntarily vouches for their opinions, and stakes her integrity upon their soundness, the world will be inclined to leave her to the consequences of their overthrow. Christian truth needs keep no disreputable company. Even in the domain of ecclesiasticism the Church has failed to preserve the distinction between human opinion and rational truth. As Socrates was condemned, under a polytheistic religion, for asserting the heresy of monotheism, so modern bigots have inflicted persecutions for opinions far less radical than that. For denying the spiritual supremacy of the pope, fifty thousand Protestants suffered death on St. Bartholomew's; and Servetus was burned at the stake by his fellow Protestants for maintaining the *homoiousian* view of the nature of Christ, in opposition to the orthodox *homoousian.* In the same spirit we have seen Hyacinthe and Döllinger excommunicated and anathematized for denying the dogma of infallibility.

We confess no approval of such deeds as these; but yet are there not modern and Protestant dogmas upon which men ought to be permitted to differ, without the accusation of unchristian heresy? Does the safety of Christianity demand that we all profess a uniform belief in respect to the specific unity of the human races; in respect to the method of human creation; in respect to the antiquity of man; in respect to the spiritual condition of the heathen; in respect to baptismal regeneration; in respect to predestination, infant salvation, and apostolical succession? I hold it to be perilous to the interests of fundamental truth to stake its credibility on the fortunes of a human opinion.

Now, I think it will be admitted that radical skepticism, founded on any such pretexts as above specified, has no right to existence in the mind of any man who professes to follow the leading of reason. The light of reason, when we discern it, leads, as I think it can be shown, in quite the contrary direction. Let us look about us in this light, and discover where, in the realm of realities, we find ourselves situated. We shall not attempt to *elaborate* the argument, but to take you to the top of a mountain, whence you can survey the field. You may explore it hereafter at your leisure.

I. *The Necessity of Some Religion is upon us.*

Few men have brought themselves to the point of denying this. Yet this admission implies much. For the sake of learning *how much*, let us review the evidences.

Every one of us is conscious of the presence, in his own mind, of certain religious notions, sentiments, and impulses. These may differ, in different persons, in every particular except two—1st, they exist; 2d, they are religious. They have a Supreme Intelligent Power for their object, and tend to express themselves in certain religious acts. This religious consciousness is something so universal in Christian communities, that we might feel justified in pronouncing it an original and indestructible constituent of human nature, like the notion of number or of self-personality. But, as it is easy to assert that all this is the result of education, let us take a wider view, and attempt to discover the natural religious status of man with the influence of education eliminated.

Taking a comprehensive view of peoples in the history of the world who have attained to any considerable degree of intellectual activity, we can not fail to be struck by the *universal* exhibition of religious phenomena. The religious sentiment has been no less conspicuous and controlling than the acquisitive or the maternal. Out of the religious consciousness of the great nations that have rested for ages in isolation from their neighbors have grown up twelve great systems which have dominated over nine-tenths of the populations of the world. Five of these have originated with the Aryan race, three with the Semitic, two with the Chinese, and one each with the Cushites and the Egyptians. Besides these, the Peruvian and Aztec systems of religion, if we may rely upon the Spanish chroniclers, are almost equally worthy to be embraced in the enumeration.

Egypt, the seat of the oldest civilization which the world has seen, was for centuries the theatre of the most elaborate ceremonials. The very government of the country, as among all primitive peoples, was hierarchical—a fact which of itself demonstrates the dominance of the religious sentiments in the ancient land of Mizraim.

The Cushites, who belonged, perhaps, to the Turanian race, planted, 2700 years B.C., the first civilization known in the region of Susiana and Babylonia. Invaded and gradually absorbed by Phœnicians, Babylonians, and Assyrians, they bequeathed their religion, as well as their civilization, to their Semitic conquerors, and thus perpetuated their religious beliefs and ceremonies through a period of twenty-five centuries.

At a date not long subsequent to the rise of Cushite civilization, Abraham went out from Ur of the Chaldees, an old Cushite city, into Egypt, and became the founder of the Jewish theocratic system, which, as we all know, usurped all political functions, and illustrated in Jewish history the potency of the religious factor of human nature.

Out of Judaism came forth Christianity, the second great Semitic religion. We have nothing to do here with the divinity of its founder. We cite Christianity as a secular phenomenon, illustrating further the power of the religious instincts to assert themselves and control the lives and destinies of millions of subjects. According to Berghaus, nearly thirty-one per cent. of the population of the globe are now adherents of this system.

Islamism was the third great Semitic religion, springing up six hundred years after Christ, and swaying the sceptre, at one time, over Arabia, Persia, Syria, Jerusalem, Egypt, Spain, Gaul, Asia Minor, and Turkey. In later periods it has extended into the eastern and central parts of Africa, where its adherents number one hundred millions of souls. It prevails in parts of Russia, in Persia, Afghanistan, Beloochistan, Tartary, India, China, and the Malay Archipelago, comprising at present nearly sixteen per cent. of the population of the world.

Of Aryan religions, the oldest is Brahmanism, arising about 2000 B.C., spreading over India, and maintaining sway, in our own times, over more than thirteen per cent. of the population of the world.

Zoroastrianism appeared next. It was originally an improved or restored Brahmanism, and is still perpetuated, to a limited extent, in the form of Parseeism. It had, at one time, extended itself so far as to threaten to become the religion of the East. Had the battles of Marathon and Salamis been lost, Jupiter might have succumbed to Ormuzd, and Magianism become the worship of the peninsula and isles of Greece.

Buddhism was the third great Aryan religion. It rose in the North of India about 477 B.C. It was the Protestantism of the Brahmanic people, marking a revulsion of the religious instincts of humanity from the corrupt and unsatisfying worship which had supplanted primitive Brahmanism. It holds powerful sway in many of the surrounding countries, and, though itself corrupted, counts among its adherents thirty-one per cent. of the population of the world.

Hellenic mythology was a fourth system of Aryan religion,

first embodied in form by Hesiod, and afterward greatly enriched by Homer. Whatever we may think of it as a humanitarian cultus, the religious character of Greek mythology can not be gainsaid. Nor can there be a difference of opinion in reference to the pervading character of its influence in society, in literature, in art, and in political life, in all the regions to which Grecian dominion extended.

Among religions of Mongolian origin, the first of which we have any knowledge, is Tao-ism, founded by Lao-tse about 600 B.C. This, with Confucianism, which arose about 500 B.C., and Buddhism, an Aryan religion, constitute the three great state religions of China and Japan, with their hundreds of millions of adherents.

Now, in this phenomenon of vast, pervading, and persistent religious systems, we have a fact which can not be otherwise than full of significance. I think it may be fairly assumed that no such general expression of religious feelings and beliefs would have been at all likely to obtain, had there not been a common religious principle or law implanted in human nature. But scan the contents of these ethnic religions carefully, and what do we find to be the common properties of all? I have analyzed these systems with care and candor, and, after eliminating every thing of a circumstantial character, I have found them to yield me the following constant factors: The first great fact of the ethnic religions is *Deity;* the second is the sense of *Moral Obligation;* the third is faith in *Immortality;* the fourth is *Prayer;* the fifth is *Sacred Symbolism;* the sixth is a body of *Sacred Writings.* These great facts — the preambles of the Christian system — are no more the peculiar property of Christianity than of Islam or Buddhism. These primitive faiths are absolutely the common possession of humanity—if we neglect the tenth part of the race resting in a state of savagism. We must feel compelled to admit that the Author of our nature has implanted a body of intuitions, which lead universally and necessarily to the formulating of a body of doctrines which constitute the very marrow of the religion of Christianity.

But we summon the barbaric hordes to render a similar testimony. It has been repeatedly asserted that some of the lowest tribes of savages are utterly destitute of religious ideas. Now, if this were proved true, the state of the facts might be that nine hundred and ninety-nine thousandths of the human family are known to manifest such ideas, while one thousandth are incapable of making any definable religious manifestations. The nine hundred and ninety-nine thousandths embrace all the normally developed representatives of humanity, while the one thousandth consists of a few squalid, miserable outcasts, in whom it is almost equally difficult to discern an *intellect* above that of the brute. Now, who can honestly hesitate to decide which fraction represents the norm of humanity? Which fraction has the right to testify for humanity?

But I do not desire to leave the subject even in this position. I have critically and patiently examined the evidences in respect to all those tribes reported destitute of religious ideas, and these are my conclusions on the general subject of the religion of savages:

1. Travelers report nearly all savages with whom they have had intercourse as addicted to some kind of religious practices.

2. Christian missionaries have often reported savages destitute of religion, when a careful study of the facts has shown simply that their religious practices were abhorrent to Christianity. In citing and execrating these unchristian rites, these missionaries do virtually testify to the existence of the religious principle among them.

3. Other travelers, irreverent toward Christianity, have similarly reported a destitution of all religion, because they have failed to discern the essentially religious character of certain

rites and observances which to civilized eyes are vicious, cruel, or absurd.

4. Of some tribes reported without religion, it is certain that our information is yet insufficient to enable us to assert a negative opinion.

5. But three tribes are known to me, of whom I should consider it a fair representation of the ascertained facts to assert that no religious consciousness has been discovered. These are the Andamaners, the Gran Chacos of South America, and the Arafuras of Vorkay.

6. The religious condition of savages presents us, as might be expected, a graduated scale of religious intelligence. The higher savages recognize, more or less distinctly, the existence of one supreme, beneficent Creator, with or without the notion of a devil, but accompanied, generally, by a belief in many subordinate deities. In the next step below, the idea of one beneficent Deity becomes more or less vague; but the belief in good and evil spirits is controlling. In the third grade, all notions of a beneficent Deity disappear, and the Supreme Power assumes the character of a malignant divinity. This faith is generally accompanied by a belief in subordinate divinities. In the fourth grade, the evil deity is superseded by an undefined faith in many evil but powerful spirits. In the fifth grade, the notion of spirits of every kind becomes extremely vague, and nothing remains but a *sensus numinis* — an undefined sentiment of the supernatural. In the sixth and lowest grade, we detect no trace of a consciousness of any existence above themselves and the material objects by which they are surrounded. Through all these grades, except the lowest, a belief in future existence accompanies the theistic concept; and some form of worship is everywhere present, varying from prayer and the use of temples and altars, through adoration of sun, moon, stars, mountains, elements, as the divine embodiments and intercessors, to rude sacrifices, sorcery, and witchcraft.

And all this is our conclusion in reference to that one-tenth of the human family not embraced under the influence and control of one of the twelve great ethnic religions.

But my researches have led me even farther than this. We have gained some intimations of the religious character of peoples whose existence antedates all our histories and traditions. Among the relics of the Hewn-stone Age we find ruined hearths, with the remnants of the feasts which commemorated the dead, in accordance with a custom still extant in China; and, mingled with the bones of the dead, are arrow-heads and trinkets which, like the beads and hatchets of the American Indians, were undoubtedly votive offerings, intelligibly proclaiming a belief that the departed had not passed beyond the sphere of consciousness, but still lived in another land. In the Polished-stone Age these evidences become more positive, and are accompanied by relics of rude inclosures which, to our eyes, seem prophetic of the temple-building of later times. In the Bronze Age we find, added to all the foregoing evidences, the ruins of massive temples—as at Stonehenge and Abury, in England—in which primitive men seem to have assembled to pay worship to the supreme power to whose mercy they consigned their dead in the populous burial-places with which they surrounded their rude temples.

This array of evidences, it seems to me, ought to be regarded as conclusive that the religious instinct is native to man. There are certain ethical propositions in which all mankind are agreed. Man is gifted by nature with certain religious intuitions which, as all intuitions must do, have exerted a controlling influence over his life. In other words, man is created for religion, adapted to religion, predisposed to religion; and this is the key to the religious phenomena of the race. It is futile to ignore the evidences or resist the religious law of our being. Whether there be a God or not; whether prayer be futile or not; whether hope of hereafter be vain or not; whether devotions and rites be absurd or not, all this is contemplated and determined and ordained in the constitution of our nature. And so, I repeat, *the necessity of some religion is upon us.*

II. *Constructive or Deductive Theistic Belief.*

To most minds it would be sufficient to have proved that religion is the law of human existence. No question of the validity and binding character of the law would be entertained. Deity, and the fundamental propositions which depend upon divine existence, would be at once conceded. But, in reality, a vast field of *positive* evidence remains to be examined. The theistic proposition, with all its corollaries, may be built upon the intuitions of the reason; and I proceed to sketch the method by which the idea of God may be logically constructed.

By intuitions of the reason, we mean those apperceptions of simple truths which are common to all human intelligences: like the intuition of externality; the intuition of self; the intuition of causality; the intuition of reality or substance. They are the most elementary propositions, like the axioms of mathematics, into which all complex knowledges, on analysis, resolve themselves. Like the axioms of mathematics, these propositions are self-evident. They neither require proof nor admit of proof. We do not believe them because they have been proved or taught. We intuit the truth of them, and believe them because we feel that we must. It is only a belief — a primitive elementary belief — and yet we feel that it is knowledge; there is no knowledge of which we are more certain, or upon which we feel it more safe to rest.

Great care must be exercised in determining what beliefs are really primordial. The criteria generally relied upon are *universality* and *necessity*.

These beliefs, we say, are spontaneous. But we must have the candor to admit that a certain school of philosophers, from Locke to J. S. Mill, maintain that they come to us from without. We can not, of course, argue the question at length, but we may make note of the following points: 1. The *onus probandi* rests with the sensationalists. 2. These beliefs bear no quantitative nor qualitative relation to experience; being as clear and controlling in the infant as in the adult, in the savage as in the philosopher. 3. If all primitive beliefs are grounded in observation, certainty in any universal proposition is an impossibility; and yet no one asks to be more confident of any truth than that "the whole of a thing is equal to the sum of all its parts," or that "every change is the effect of some adequate cause." 4. Since, on the sensational hypothesis, we could not construct universal propositions possessing absolute certainty, every step we should take in the progress of an argument would lead us farther and farther from certainty. And yet, in the demonstration of a proposition in geometry, we feel that every step is immovably secure, and the conclusion as certain as the axioms on which it rests. 5. On the sensational hypothesis, I could have no certain knowledge of substance or reality. I should float in a world of appearances, without being able to make a single affirmation that would yield me the satisfaction of certainty. 6. Certain primitive beliefs, like that in the existence of space and time, can not possibly be the sequences of experience. Space and time are not the objects of experience; but, on the contrary, as Kant has observed, they are the antecedent conditions of the possibility of experience. 7. The idea of cause can not possibly be referred to experience, since that, at best, would afford us only a strong presumption that any given effect had a cause; while, in fact, we feel the most unreserved certainty that *every* effect has a cause. 8. The whole doctrine of sensationalism rests upon a *petitio principii*, since the primitive beliefs are the very condition of the possibility of experience. Experience implies that we know the consciousness has been impressed by something; but this knowledge is the very intuition which J. S. Mill proposes to set down as the result of experience. Now, it is obvious that if intuition is the necessary antecedent of experience, it can not be the necessary sequent of experience.

For such reasons, briefly stated, I maintain that the primitive beliefs found in existence in all minds are spontaneous, inborn, and necessary.

The question of the authority of these beliefs is still another one. Suppose they are inborn, what do they mean? Do they correspond to realities? Do they represent things as they are? If all men must believe in a world external to themselves, are we certain that such a world is a reality? If I must believe that every event or change implies a cause, have I warrant for assuming that this belief corresponds to the reality of things? This is a question of the utmost importance. Few philosophers, whatever their opinion of the origin of these beliefs, have had the temerity to impeach their authority. As before, it is impracticable to argue the question here, but I may offer, again, a few considerations.

1. There are some intuitions which can not be questioned without involving the questioner in self-stultification. In every act of consciousness there is a dual character—first, the consciousness of *self* as thinking; and, second, the consciousness of something *not self*. The first belief in logical order is the belief in the reality of the *act* of consciousness. Now, if I doubt the reality of the act of consciousness, I must be conscious of some contradiction or absurdity upon which I may base a doubt; so that, in the very act of denying the testimony of consciousness, I must appeal to consciousness for proof. The doubt annihilates itself. It is impossible to doubt the authority of consciousness in this case. From similar considerations appears the self-stultification of doubting the testimony of consciousness in respect to the reality of that which is not self.

In regard to the contents of consciousness, or the particular knowledge or report brought by consciousness, this witness is not necessarily veracious; and we have to examine its credibility. Our belief in its testimony is, however, one of the primitive beliefs of the human mind; and it must stand or fall with the others.

2. The validity of the primitive beliefs ought to be presumed until the contrary is proved. The universal assent of mankind, the impossibility of mental or bodily activity not predicated on the validity of these beliefs, afford the strongest presumption that they correspond to realities.

3. They exert the most absolute control over our lives. We rest upon them with the most unreserved confidence. I believe the external world a reality, and shape every act by that conviction. I have a representation of a past sensation, and call it a recollection, and fully believe the representation truthful; I take my oath upon it; I stake my life upon it.

4. These beliefs, or intuitions, are closely analogous to the instincts of the lower animals. The instincts act as regulative and controlling principles of the actions of the animal; and no one thinks of asserting that they do not answer to certain realities to which they are correlated. The primitive beliefs are equally regulative and controlling principles of human actions. They are, in truth, a species of instinct of the reason, and we are bound to presume they answer equally to realities in the world in which we are placed.

5. The primitive beliefs establish a complex and wonderful, but beneficent, correlation between man and the world in which he seems to live; or, rather, they give efficiency to a correlation already existing. Now, can it be admitted that a body of beliefs, whose activity opens a field of co-ordinations so complicated, so vast, so admirable, and so beneficent, and whose activity only saves all that is from a state of nugatoriness, is, after all, but a body of beliefs which mislead us, and answer to nothing which is real? a vast machinery without a real object to act upon, or a real end to be sought in its action?

6. If I deny the veracity of consciousness as to the external world, I abandon all evidence that the world appears to me as it is—nay, I have no evidence of the existence of the external world; I must ever remain in doubt whether these are real trees, and skies, and persons, and voices, or merely images flitting before my consciousness, like the phantasms of a diseased vision. Nay, worse than this; if consciousness is a false witness in respect to external objects, it may be equally false in respect to subjective reality. I do not know even that I suffer, or move, or think. To my own existence even I can not certify. I seem to be something, surrounded by something, and engaged in doing something; but all this seeming may be illusory. I can only assert that phantasms exist; nay, I can not even assert this, for my consciousness of phantasms may be illusory. Alas! could a more pitiable condition of a rational intelligence be conceived? Yet this is the logical consequence of denying, in a single particular, the authority of consciousness. Hear what Fichte says, who followed out this dreary philosophy to its issue:

"I know absolutely nothing of any existence, not even my own. I myself know nothing, and am nothing. Images there are; they constitute all that apparently exists; and what they know of themselves is after the manner of images—images that pass and vanish without there being aught to witness their transition—that consist, in fact, of the images of images, without significance and without aim. I am myself one of these images; nay, I am not even thus much, but only a confused image of images."

It is scarcely necessary to state that no philosopher has carried such a philosophy into consistent practice. Even in his speculations, Fichte reached, at length, a sounder conclusion. In his "Practical Philosophy," written later in life, he says: "I have found the instrument by which to *seize on this reality*, and therewith, in all likelihood, on every other. * * * The instrument I mean is Belief. * * * All my conviction is only Belief." And so the prince of doubters came around, in his old age, to the position which we shall be safe in assuming at the outset.

Now, let us make an application of the positions proved. We have shown that the human mind finds itself in possession of certain primitive beliefs, which are the ultimate constituents of all that which we call knowledge. We have shown that these beliefs arise spontaneously from within, and are not the outgrowth or consequence of external conditions. We have shown that it is necessary to accord them absolute authority; and that, consequently, they correspond to realities, about which it is futile, absurd, and impossible to entertain doubts. We have shown that among the primitive and universal beliefs of man is the belief in divine existence and its corollaries. It follows, therefore, that divine existence is a reality; and all those propositions of the ethnic religions which cluster around it and flow out of it are propositions which answer to realities, and which a sound philosophy calls upon us to accept.

I have assumed that the theistic notion is primitively a direct intuition. I have reflected much upon the subject. I find myself in accord with Jacobi and Schleiermacher, and probably Sir William Hamilton, in this respect. I entertain a strengthening conviction that by no other means could rude savages rise to any notion of divine existence. Yet there is a less direct method by which reason may ascend through a brief, spontaneous, deductive process to the theistic concept. Let us examine the steps.

The *intuition of real being* leads to the affirmation of such axiomatic judgments as the following: "Every quality implies substance to which it belongs;" "Every attribute implies real being." A moment's reflection will show that it is impossible to conceive the contraries of such propositions. They necessarily condition all thought. But, from what we have shown, these propositions must not only *seem* true, but must *be* true.

The *intuition of causality* leads to the affirmation of the axiomatic judgment that "Every effect implies an adequate cause." The intuition of effect as depending upon cause is accompanied by the notion of *conditioned existence*. The relation of effect to cause suggests a remoter cause of which the first cause was the effect; and, similarly, the remoter cause is presented as sustaining the relation of effect to a cause still more remote; and so on *ad infinitum*. The simple intuition of causality, therefore, leaves us at last with an endless series of effects still unaccounted for. Or perhaps, more correctly, we have no intuition of real cause, but only of secondary cause, until we reach the notion of *primordial causation*. This notion satisfies the reason; and, though we can give no account of its mode of existence, we rest satisfied in the belief that efficient or primordial causation is a fact. The notion of primordial causation is accompanied by the notion of *unconditioned existence;* and this is accompanied by the notion of *infinity*. I do not mean to assert that this is the origin of the notion of infinity; I only desire it to appear that this notion exists among the notions which cluster around the intuition of causality.

We might pause here and apply these principles to the phenomena of the universe. Here is a series of effects. Trace them to their causes, and these, in turn, put on the character of effects. Thus the universe appears, at first, an endless chain of events sustaining mutually the relations of cause and effect. But now arises the notion of primordial causation, unconditioned existence, and infinity; and the mind feels relief in ascribing the chain of events to unconditioned primordial power. This is the "Ætiological Argument." The ontological intuition now assigns primordial power to real existence, and we have a faithful concept of an Infinite, Unconditioned, Causative Being.

In the next place, the *intuition of intelligence* leads to the affirmation of such axiomatic judgments as these: "Adaptation of means to ends implies intelligence;" "Contrivance implies intelligence;" "Correlation of ideas implies intelligence." Applying these principles to the universe, we are led to declare that every instance of mechanism in the animal economy is the product of intelligence. Organic contrivances are suited to particular ends, because intelligence so ordained. This is the "Teleological Argument." The ontological intuition transfers this intelligence to real being, and we have an Intelligent Being as the author of organic contrivances. Again, the relationships of *plan* and *method* which subsist among animals of different orders and classes, and between the successive stages of an evolution in the organic or inorganic world, are evidences of the exercise of intelligence; and here we have what I have called the "Homological Argument," which reaches real being, as before, through the ontological intuition.

Next, we have the *intuition of ethicality*, which leads to the affirmation that certain acts are essentially right, and others essentially wrong. This is accompanied by the notion of *duty* or obligation; and this implies a tribunal which imposes the obligation—an authority which must not be evaded. The ontological intuition implants this authority in real being, and we reach the concept of supreme justice and a Moral Governor. This law of justice we find exemplified in the world of nature and humanity. This may be styled the "Ethical Argument."

Finally, we discover in our minds *the intuition of goodness*—that is, goodness is a quality the notion of which arises spontaneously. It forms the rational basis of prayer, and supposes that justice is approachable for forgiveness. We look about us in the world of nature, and discover numerous relations existing which are distinctly beneficent. They are inwrought in the contrivances and plans of creation. We affirm, therefore, that here are not only evidences of intelligence, but also of goodness. Thus we reach an argument which may be styled the

"*Agathological.*" The intuition of real being transfers the attribute of goodness to an entity, and we get the concept of a Being possessed of goodness as vast as the creation.

Now, finally, summing up the results, we find that these four primordial intuitions—the intuition of causality, the intuition of intelligence, the intuition of ethicality, and the intuition of goodness, supply our minds with the necessary concepts of infinite power, infinite intelligence, infinite justice, and infinite goodness; while the intuition of real being affirms that these are necessarily the attributes of a real being—and that being, endowed with these attributes, is God. The Deity, then, which exists in the sanctions of the reason is a Real Being, a First Cause, a Moral Governor, unconditioned and infinite in intelligence and goodness, and approachable by prayer.

This, I confess, is but a bare outline of the method of the rational argument. I fear the subject is too abstruse to be entertaining, but I shall not regret it if I have given you occasion for close attention and subsequent study.

III. *Deductions from the Theistic Proposition.*

We thus arrive at the formal proposition that God exists— God, infinite; unconditioned, without beginning of years; the cause of all things; the fountain of justice and of moral law; as infinite in goodness as in power; pleased to cause happiness or to remove distress; apprecable by those who have merited the frown of his justice, or have fallen into the pit of suffering. How much is implied in this conclusion! And yet we are bound to it. Whether an intuition direct, or a spontaneous, deductive conclusion from the axioms of reason, we know not how to evade it. The conviction of its truth comes into our minds—imbeds itself there; it sets up a dominion there; it sways a sceptre over our lives, and over all human lives. And, still more, we are glad to receive it: we give it hospitality, and it comforts us; it resolves our doubts; it dissipates our fears; it affords a resting-place for the reason and the conscience; nay, we rejoice with joy unspeakable to have found a way to a solution of the mysteries which surround us; to have reached a Being who is both a potentate and a friend, and whose character answers to all the deepest longings of the human soul. Oh, how many millions have been comforted in leaning upon this arm! How many hearts have been eased in breathing the passionate or the tender requests of trusting prayer! How blank, and desolate, and utterly miserable would the world of humanity be without this faith!

How irrelevant, how heartless, to be reminded that all this is something which we can not understand, and to which, therefore, we can not yield a rational assent! What boots it that the method of divine existence be all "unthinkable?" that the act of creation from nothing is "unthinkable?" that the world is governed by immutable law, and our feeble prayers must be futile? Shall we abandon the citadel we have won because unable to carry it on our backs? We make no pretense of comprehending God and his ways; but we feel certified of certain predicates respecting God. Nor does reason demand that a proposition shall be comprehended before we can yield it a rational assent. We have followed the lead of reason in reaching a proposition which is "unthinkable." Indeed, we can give to thought no exposition of the grounds of a single one of our primitive beliefs. Shall we renounce them because their ground is "unthinkable?" Shall we deny infinite space because "unthinkable," or infinite duration? Finite space and finite duration are equally "unthinkable;" and yet, are we not certain that time and space are either finite or infinite? Let us stick to our conquests; we have won them fairly.

But we must go farther. We have found out a Being infinitely powerful, wise, and good. We know another being finite, imperfect, and consciously responsible to the first for all his acts. We find this finite being infinitely correlated to the infinite one—the product of his creation; dependent; an offender against his justice; the recipient of his goodness; hopeful of his mercy; aspiring to present and future happiness. We find him longing for communion with a loving God; a loving God desiring communion with him, and having all power at his control for opening communion with his feeble subject. What, now, I ask, is probable in the case? What is probable if we reason as in a court of justice in reference to the influence of motives?

1. It is probable that this communion will be established. It will not be alone the voice of prayer ascending from the subject to the ear of God. It will be also a response coming down to the consciousness of the petitioner. It will be a communication of good tidings, of good-will, and of providential purposes. This will be the common privilege of humanity. In exceptional cases it will become remarkably clear and complete.

2. It is probable that, in the history of the world, numerous instances would occur in which these extraordinary communications would be put on record, and preserved as written revelations from God; and that bodies of such writings would become the sacred books of the peoples to whom they were communicated.

3. There is no antecedent improbability that these communications would come to representatives of various races and peoples. Infinite goodness would be as likely to favor one race as another; and no race would be expected to perform the superhuman work of consulting the records of all the other races in search of the mind of God.

> "Who shall say that to no mortal
> Heaven e'er oped its mystic portal,
> Gave no dream or revelation
> Save to one peculiar nation?
> Souls sincere, now voiceless, nameless,
> Knelt at altars fired and flameless,
> Asked of Nature, asked of Reason,
> Sought through every sign and season,

> Seeking God; through darkness groping,
> Waiting, striving, longing, hoping,
> Weeping, praying, panting, pining,
> For the light on Israel shining!
> Oh, it must be! God's sweet kindness
> Pities erring human blindness;
> And the soul whose pure endeavor
> Strives toward God, shall live forever;
> Live by the great Father's favor,
> Saved by an unheard-of Saviour."(¹)—G. L. TAYLOR.

4. It would unavoidably be the case that these communications would be somewhat tinctured by the human media through which they should come. They would necessarily suffer from the imperfections of the human intellect; the cloudiness of the spiritual apprehensions which should take hold on the thoughts of God, and the defects of human languages. It would follow that the most spiritually minded nation or race would receive the purest and completest revelation of the mind of Deity.

(¹) St. Clement of Alexandria regards the Greek philosophy as probably given by inspiration. "Perchance, too, philosophy was given to the Greeks directly and primarily, till the Lord should call the Greeks" (Strom., book i., chap. v.). * * * "But all [the philosophers], in my opinion, are illuminated by the dawn of light" (Strom., book i., chap. xiii.). * * * "So, then, the barbarian and Hellenic philosophy has torn off a fragment of eternal truth" (Strom., book i., chap. xiii.). In his "Exhortation to the Heathen," after quoting admiringly from Plato, Antisthenes, Socrates, Xenophon, Cleanthes, and the Pythagoreans, he concludes as follows: "For the knowledge of God, these utterances, written by those we have mentioned, through the inspiration of God, and selected by us, may suffice" (Cohortatio, chap. vii., *ad finem*). So Lactantius, after quoting with approbation from Cicero's "Republic," adds: "Who that is acquainted with the mystery of God could so significantly relate the law of God as a man far removed from the knowledge of the truth has set forth the law? But I consider that they who speak true things unconsciously are to be regarded as though they prophesied [divinent] under the influence of some spirit" ("Institutiones Divinæ," book vi., chap. viii.).

5. I think it should be expected that the full import of the communications would transcend the intelligence of the human recipient, and would frequently transcend the general intelligence of his race. The thoughts and methods of infinite wisdom, expressed in the plainest of human words, must sometimes remain inscrutable. Hence divine revelations might involve some mysteries and some uninterpretable statements. These should not be hastily rejected, but should be reverently accepted on the authority of their author. This is the dictate of the highest reason. As the very germs of all our knowledge are but simple acts of faith, for which we can furnish no grounds, so here, in the opposite direction, faith supersedes knowledge, without robbing us of that sense of assurance and satisfaction which is the proper attribute of knowledge. The progress of human inquiry may be expected to resolve some of these mysteries; but others must resist all efforts to penetrate them.

IV. *The Christian Scriptures answer to these Deductions.*

1. They assume the idea of God pre-existent in the human mind. Indeed, there could be no revelation from God to a race not possessed already of some notion of God. It would be like the attempt to explain the hues of the violet to a man born blind.

2. The Christian Scriptures set forth, on the whole, *such* a God as exists already in human thought—the Creator and Preserver of all things; infinite in wisdom, power, and goodness; the source of moral law; the lover of men; the hearer and answerer of prayer. They inculcate the privilege and the duty of prayer and devotion; they teach the reality of spiritual existence, and promise a future life.

3. At the same time, we detect some of the stains and imperfections of humanity transmitted to the sacred record; as the color of the glass imparts its hues to the light which it

transmits. The Hebrew people had not attained to that degree of secular knowledge, and intellectual culture, and æsthetic refinement, which enabled their inspired writers to leave a record which, in all its details of style, should commend itself to the highest refinement the race was destined to attain. Vastly superior as were their notions of Deity to any entertained by contemporaneous peoples, yet they were unable to divest themselves, at times, of those very anthropomorphic conceptions which disfigure the mythologies of the Greeks and other ancient nations. God is pictured sometimes as having human organs; as walking among men; as arguing with men, indulging in anger, and visiting his enemies with vengeance. We must have the sagacity, however, to penetrate beneath the anthropomorphic garb of the sacred teachings, and discover there the spiritual Being of purity and beneficence whose attributes, in other portions of our Scriptures, are so adequately and so eloquently described. These blemishes, which indeed play a much less important part than has been pretended, have been unwarrantably magnified and misunderstood; and have been made the pretext for rejecting the whole body of written revelation. We shall do ourselves injustice not to judge these Scriptures candidly, and not to concede to them all that truthfulness and authority which comport with the antecedent presumptions which we have established.

4. After all that can be charged against the tracery of human imperfection which may be detected in the style of certain portions of our Scriptures, we must not only acknowledge them a general fulfillment of the antecedent presumptions, but we must claim for them a wonderful degree of consonance with the developments of truth which have come to the uninspired mind of man in the progress of the ages. It is doubtful whether science can ever successfully impeach any important statement of our Scriptures, when fairly interpreted. This is the result which we had grounds to expect. This circumstance

alone, to the mind of one who has not examined the ground we have been over, ought to be strong evidence of their superhuman origin. Written ages before the birth of the modern sciences, there was the utmost liability for mere human authorship to fall into the most egregious misstatements respecting the phenomena of the natural world; but, in point of fact, some of the statements of our Scriptures were so far in advance even of the science of the nineteenth century, that we are only just beginning to understand them. Here is a harmony, at least, which answers to all the antecedent demands.

V. *Our Reasonable Duty.*

As pendants to the grand positions which we have established, some most important lessons ought to follow.

1. The religious consciousness of man is an innate part of his nature; it inherits as high a nobility as the intellect; and honesty, and self-respect, and mental health, and reverence for truth, unite their demands that the religious nature be exercised and cultured. Devotion toward God is as much a law of our being as attachment to a child. Prayer is as natural and efficient an utterance of the human soul as the infant pleadings which move a mother's heart. Faith in the being and providence and word of God is as rational as faith in that primitive intuition which leads unresisting assent, through all the grades of thinkable knowledge, to that other and upper sphere of truth which faith only can touch.

2. If God has written his name upon every human heart, then the feeblest and most inadequate gropings after the presence of God should command our respect; and the rude dance and ghastly sacrifice should excite our pity for those who, like children crying in the night, feel that a comforter exists, though they know not how to search. And though we can neither bow the knee at mosque of Islam or shrine of Buddha, let it be remembered that the adherents of these religious systems

are moved by the self-same spirit of devotion as leads us to the temple of Christian worship.

3. Cherish a veneration for our Christian Scriptures. They embody the purest written revelation which God has ever imparted to man, and afford us precious lessons which can never be reached by unaided efforts of the intellect.

4. Betray no fear that any word of truth will clash with any other. Have faith in truth; have faith in all truth. Be man enough to treat truth with impartiality. Be as hospitable to a moral truth as to an intellectual. Round out your spiritual nature with a just and generous nurture of all its faculties. Honor God by honoring every department of the human nature which he has constituted.

5. Be men of science, but be devout men. I exhort you to this in no professional mood. We come up from a survey of the deep and eternal foundations of truth, and proclaim that on one basis rest the systems of theology and the systems of science. If you would live the truth, be devout in being wise —nay, be wise in being devout. Honor philosophy, but do not forget that this includes a religious philosophy. Enrich the soul with religious emotions, that they may fertilize and inspire the intellect. Seize upon every intellectual discovery to strengthen, correct, and purify the religious faith. Labor for the union of science and religion in all their aims. Thank God, I see their slow approximation begun. They begin to understand each other. They begin to respect each other. They begin to extend hands for a cordial greeting. The blessed day of their wedding will come. I can discern the roseate dawn. With prophetic ear I catch the strains of the rising epithalamium that shall bring rejoicing to the hearts of all the nations, and shall be caught up by angels and archangels dwelling in the sunlight of Eternal Truth.

VIII.

THE CONFLICTS OF FAITH.[1]

THIS day and this occasion are consecrated equally to the contemplation of those truths most intimately related to the religious nature of man. These young persons whom I especially address are on the eve of the completion of a long and earnest course of secular study; and yet we desire to freight our latest admonitions with thoughts which shall fortify those faiths which take hold on the things unseen and unsecular. We live in an age the most glorious and most to be desired that has ever dawned in the history of man; and yet, in this advanced and progressive age, we hear a strange and unexpected clangor of arms in the world, proceeding from what at first appears to be a desperate conflict between the champions of religious faith and the champions of that learning which makes our age so glorious; and, in the midst of this din, we want to ask you to stop, and go with us to a mount of observation and contemplation, where we may dispassionately view the whole field of the facts, and discern, if possible, the meaning of the noisy conflict around us.

The *Battle-fields of Faith* have been many and bloody. They are scattered along the whole march of human history. No wonder the unphilosophic have deemed the conflict mortal, and more than once declared that either religion or science must go under; that they can not live together in the same world in peace. No wonder that, in a period of ecclesiastical ascend-

---

[1] A baccalaureate address to the graduating class of 1874, in the College of the Liberal Arts of the Syracuse University.

ency, science has been clipped of her plumes and chained to an effete and fungoid carcass. No wonder, again, that, in an interval of strangulation of the voice of religious faith, secularism should have trampled religion in the mud.

But religion still lives; and science still marches on. What does it mean? In the economy of existence, may it not be that both are ordained to live? And may it not be that both are ordained to live in amity and mutual respect? Or is their incessant conflict an incident of the law of progress through antagonism? As affliction mellows the soul of man, and adversity whets its powers, perhaps religion and science are appointed to be mutually whetstones to each other, and their collisions are but the friction which sharpens and improves.

If we gaze for a moment at the human *powers* which prompt to this incessant struggle, what do we see? The religious phenomena of the race are as universal and obtrusive as the intellectual. The religious activities are equally uniform in their essential nature; the dominion of the religious instincts is equally controlling. Notions of supernatural creative power, of moral government, of personal responsibility, are as universal accompaniments of human life as notions of reality, of causality, of externality, or the distinction between self and not-self. The prompting to prayer and sacrifice, and the confidence in their efficacy, are factors of humanity as positive as the longing and the seeking of the infant for its food, or the impulse of the understanding to inquire after causes of things. The religious sentiments, it may be rigorously shown, are a native endowment of human nature. The promptings to prayer and worship, and the sense of accountability, by all the reasoning of Lubbock and Darwin, and Burton and Comte, have not been proved less a primordial constituent of man than are the intellectual discernments which stand correlated to another sphere of ideas.

We have, then, for our present purpose, two groups of intuitions or feelings—the intellectual and the moral. Among the latter, let it be distinctly understood, must be ranged the sentiment of Deity, the sentiment of accountability, the sentiment of right and wrong, the sentiment of prayer, the sentiment of piacular offerings, the sentiment of future life. I am willing to denominate these feelings as sentiments. In the lowest conditions of the human mind, I confess they are but feeble sentiments; and yet I desire to impress the psychological fact, that the intuitions belonging to the intellectual group are also but feelings or affections of the mind. I desire also, by way of a caution, to remark, that the vague *sensus numinis* which I here denominate the sentiment of the supernatural is not our only avenue to the cognition of Deity.

Among the intuitions of the intellect must be ranked such as the following: A thing cannot exist and not exist at the same time. That which impresses my senses is external to me. It is also a reality. Every attribute implies substance; every effect, a cause. The whole is equal to the sum of all its parts, and is greater than any of its parts.

It is not my purpose to prove that there are realities corresponding to the primitive beliefs existing in the human soul. I desire merely to remind you—and that, only in passing—that we have the same ground for accepting the reality of the correlates of the ethical beliefs as of the intellectual beliefs; that the universal and ineradicable beliefs in divinity, right, and duty answer to verities as absolute as our beliefs in the things testified by perception or memory. To impeach one witness is to impeach all. To deny the validity of our primitive beliefs is to plunge us into the fearful abyss of nihilism, which is a suicide instigated by a metaphysical insanity.

We must admit that these two groups of mental powers are absolutely co-ordinate in legitimacy, in authority, in significance. This proposition, which I am not attempting to-day to prove, can not be too profoundly pondered. The religious faculties of man have a right to existence and activity. No apology is needed for their exercise—none for the assertion of their rights—none for the imperious sway which they exert, and always have exerted, over the lives of men. But, though equal and like in a certain sense, in another sense they are unequal and unlike. Each group of powers has its sphere. The conscience discerns the fact that right, and wrong, and duty, and accountability exist, and prompts unremittingly to some line of action in harmony with its discernments. But it does not determine *what* line of action this shall be. The intellect must discern the act most conformable to the law of right and duty. This is a judgment. The ethical nature makes discernments, and feels duty, and urges to right action; but these states all concern the abstract; the intellect supplies the concretes—the particular things—between which the discernments are to be made, by which the feeling of duty is aroused, or toward which action is to be urged. Moral discernments, duty, and obligation are verities of one class; particular acts or particular facts are verities of another. The ethical sentiments are a heart yearning for a consummation; the intellect is the eye which discovers the way to it. The heart of man cries out for God; it *feels* the being of God; it demands to be shown its God. The infant intellect opens its eye, and, behold! the glory of the *sun* is everywhere; the sun is the most powerful and glorious object within reach of the senses: the intellect introduces the sun to the religious consciousness as its God. The religious nature accepts it, and pays it worship. In another land, the supreme and terrible majesty of *mountains* impresses the intellect as the grandest manifestation in the visible world, and these become the gods on which the poor, blind heart wastes its adoration. Again, it is the *ocean,* or the *sky,* or the *storm* which the soul rests upon in its groping for the felt Deity. But

"The thoughts of men
Are widened with the process of the suns."

By-and-by, the intellect perceives that it does not belong to material objects to exert the attributes of divinity; and then the sun and moon and mountains become the *manifestations* or the *abodes* of divinity. The mind of the infant race could only picture Deity as a human form, with human passions; and, under such guises, it represented Deity to the religious nature. The fancies of anthropomorphism were hardly swept from the minds of the Jewish writers — or else they were permitted to employ anthropomorphic language to suit their utterances to the mental status of their times.

The religious nature is a set of impulses and accompanying beliefs in the reality of their objects. It enacts its laws and enforces them inexorably. No man may think he can evade them. The intellectual powers take cognizance of the natural truth which furnishes the means and modes of gratification of the ethical powers. If the intellect be undeveloped, the religious mandates may drive mankind to fetichism, to idolatry, to polytheism—to juggernaut or the funeral pyre. The religious nature *must act*. If intellect fail to open a rational avenue for its exercise, it rushes blindly into imbecilities, superstition, bigotry, dogmatism, persecution. But it has a right to act according to the best light which reason affords; and when it acts thus, it acts rightly, it acts righteously. Many a poor Buddhist will enjoy a higher seat in heaven, I believe, than the enlightened in our own ranks who are struggling to think their religious promptings a superstition.

Hence arise the conflicts. The soul that has fixed its religious affections upon the sun or the mountain is loath to remove them when assured that neither sun nor mountain can possibly exert divine attributes. The intellect utters this disparaging declaration, and the religious nature revolts at such profanity. Out upon that knowledge which would rob us of our gods! Such unbridled daring must be restrained. The intellect beholds the religious nature paying its devotions to a senseless object, and derides its credulity. And yet the religious faith remains subjectively legitimate and rational. It is only the objective exercise of it which assumes an absurd form. After a protest and a struggle, religious faith may settle upon another form which, for the time, commends itself to the most enlightened judgment of man; and from this, in the further progress of thought, it may also be driven. Thus, while intellect is ever progressive, faith, like love, is conservative. Thus intellect is ever pointing in derision at the fogyism of faith; and faith retaliates with scorn at the irreverence of intellect. It is the nature of religious faith to recognize sacredness. That with which divinity has been associated in our minds is sacred; and faith can learn, only by a painful effort, to count it otherwise. Intellect cares only for the reality of things. It dethrones the idols of humanity the moment it discerns there is no divinity in them. It takes no comfort in deceiving itself; it has no patience with deception. But its scope is finite; its discernments are often obscure, and its judgments erroneous. It is well for man that his religious faith tends to immobility; it serves as ballast to a ship with too much canvas.

Thus the antagonism is self-regulative. When the sway of the intellect is in excess, the religious nature revolts; when the religious nature runs riot, the intellect shames it back to sobriety and reason. Faith has always been prone to commit the error of clothing with sanctity things merely external and strictly secular. Its creeds have enumerated too many particulars. They have attempted to embody all the existing beliefs, and have thus subjected themselves to many an unnecessary shock, as the progress of intellect has disclosed their untenability. No reproaches are to be cast for such reasons. Such is the law of human progress. Intellectual and ethical rights are equipollent. Alternating secularism and superstition are but the vibrations of a psychological balance caused by the accidents which transpire in human affairs.

Such general views crowd themselves upon our candid attention. It does not remain to seek the illustrations, for they lie before our minds already. We follow back the highway of human history, and see the altars of religion smoking in an unbroken series. We need not recede farther than the dawn of Greek philosophy to note man's jealousy of the honor of his gods. Oh, how sublime have been the intellectual struggles of humanity! How had honest thought tugged at the problems of existence before yet our Saviour had appeared to shed upon them the light of a new revelation! The ever-present feeling and the ever-present manifestation of divine existence and causation prompted the thoughtful Greek to seek for a closer knowledge of the reality. Most of the Greek philosophers had no doubt of the existence and unity of the ultimate Cause, but its nature remained inscrutable. Protagoras, discouraged with the search, proclaimed that truth is relative, and nothing can be affirmed respecting divine existence. Athenian piety was shocked. Protagoras was accused and condemned as an atheist; and private owners of copies of his work were commanded to give them up to be burned in the market-place.

Aristarchus of Samos had the fortune to disquiet popular orthodoxy by asserting that the earth is not the centre of the universe, but revolves about the sun. This honest and correct opinion earned him the charge of impiety from Cleanthes the Stoic. It is not needful to rehearse the story of "Galileo with his woes" to remind you how precisely the history of thought revolves in an orbit. Aristarchus had not the appliances to demonstrate the truth of the heliocentric theory, and conservative faith continued to hug, for nineteen hundred years, the dead body of an effete astronomy.

Socrates is not generally reputed to have borne a character less reverent toward divine things than the majority of his Athenian countrymen. In fact, according to the pictures which Plato and Xenophon have produced of their master, Socrates struggled surprisingly near to the spiritual discernment, purity, forbearance, and fortitude which have characterized sufferers for the Christian faith. His very divergence from the prevalent theism of Athens — his very approximation toward the Christian stand-point—was made the ground of the accusation against him, and he died a noble martyr to his religious opinions. It is instructive to note the language of the indictment: "Socrates is a public offender in not recognizing the gods which the State recognizes, introducing other and new divinities; he is also an offender in corrupting the youth." He was not less honest, less conscientious, less pure, less devout; but his honesty, conscience, purity, and devotion were not conformed to the dominant type; and he reasoned with the youth of Athens to teach them his purer and nobler and more rational faith. But his sublime death was followed by a revulsion in public sentiment. His prosecutors were themselves punished, and his faith was nurtured to a splendid maturity in the philosophy of Plato.

In its relation to our theme, the persecution and martyrdom of Christ, viewed only as a witness to the truth, are full of illustration. Teaching a purer morality and a loftier and more spiritual devotion than his nation believed in, he was counted a religious offender—a heretic—a defamer of the Mosaic law; a profaner of the holy temple; a violator of the Sabbath; a tolerator of evil-doers; a usurper of divine prerogatives; and so the conservatism of the national faith must vindicate the integrity of the Jewish religion, even to the death of the Author of our Christianity. But, as Jesus' teaching was the mind of God— as it demonstrated itself true—it must prevail. Innocent blood was again the nutriment of the truth, and Christianity was destined to reign in the ascendant.

The struggles of religious faith have not always been with the enemies of faith. Indeed, the general proposition may be enunciated, that blank unbelief has seldom lifted its hand against religious faith. The conflict has generally been between two factions of its own adherents. Old faiths have been antagonized by new interpretations either of nature or of sacred Scripture. Sometimes one of the combatants has professed comparative indifference for the interests of religion; but, as a rule, both parties have floated the banner of religious belief.

Old faiths die hard. Though Judaism, and, still more, Christianity, commended themselves to the ethical and intellectual natures of men, the popular Greek theology retained a wonderful hold upon their minds; and powerful sects devoted themselves to vain efforts to harmonize Greek mythology with the purer religions. By a natural revulsion, the excessive spirituality of Plato had been succeeded by earnest questionings, and a gradual ascendency of theories more exclusively intellectual. Thus followed, in graduated order, the Peripatetic philosophy, the Stoic, the Epicurean, and then the Skeptical. It was now time for the religious nature of man to assert itself again. Judaism had assumed a prominent position, and its theocracy afforded a welcome relief for human faith oppressed by the incongruities of the old Hellenic myths. Philo accordingly attempted to co-adapt the two; and now for a period waged a conflict between Jewish-Alexandrian theosophy, on one hand, and pure Judaism and rising Christianity, on the other.

Gnosticism, in its various sects, marked a similar conflict of faiths. In general, it was an attempt to reduce the Christian system to a philosophy; but Judaism, Hellenism, and Parseeism were powerfully contending factors. At length the decree of Justinian closed the schools of philosophy at Athens (529 A.D.); and out of the residual conflict between Judaizing Christianity and aristocratic Gnosticism came forth, at Rome, the Catholic form of Christian faith.

It is not my purpose to present a history of the conflicts which religious conservatism has waged with intellectual radicalism. I wish, however, to impress the thought already announced, that those conflicts have not been generally between faith and skepticism, but between *forms* of faith. This is especially exemplified in the history of thought during the ages of ecclesiastical supremacy commonly known as the scholastic period. So firmly had the Christian system become established that all intellectual efforts were directed to the harmonizing with it of all science and philosophy. Science and philosophy, for twelve hundred years, were but the molders and welders for a stereotyped form of religious faith. It can not be supposed that during this reign of tradition the intellect of man always wore its chains with composure. On the one hand was the established body of beliefs—secular as well as religious—to which the Christian world had assented in the second century (about 175 A.D.) of our era. On the other hand were the products of continued speculation and investigation. Many old views of nature were antagonized by the progress of discovery. If the new conclusions were tenable, the old faith must give way. If the old faith must be maintained, the new views must be suppressed. It has always been a painful dilemma. Who is able to act as umpire between the high authority of intellect and the imperious power of faith? You well know the history of these fearful collisions—how, for a millennium, the sceptre was in the hand of the Church, and intellect, free-born, crouched a slave at her feet. Still, the utterances of intellect could never be fully stifled. Her sober judgments stared every man in the face. The Church might hold to the flatness of the earth, but, somehow, sailors observed a distinct convexity, and Columbus and other captains proved that it could be circumnavigated. The Church might affirm the immaculate character of the sun's face; but whoever looked through the instrument of Galileo must see the spots. The Church might deny the habitability of other worlds; but there was Mars revealed with its land and waters, like our own globe, and the presumption of habitability could not be resisted. How could these things be? The question must have presented itself to many minds with painful urgency. Could there be two orders of truth? The old views of natural things seemed to be in accordance with the accepted books of divine revelation. Could it be that the testimonies of the senses and of reason are in discordance with these infallible revelations? Even to such a conclusion did the mind's distress impel it. Pomponatius maintained that there *are* two orders of truth—the philosophical and the theological, and that, accepting all the dicta of the Church, he was still at liberty, in the domain of reason, to subscribe to judgments which contradicted them. The Church, however, condemned the doctrine. It is analogous, nevertheless, to such tenets as those of Sir William Hamilton and Mansel in reference to the Unconditioned and the Unknowable, which compel them, in view of a supposed impotency of the reason, to attenuate our knowledge of God into a mere faith, which, after all, philosophy does not deign to indorse.

Against this mediæval slavery of the intellect the great reformation of the sixteenth century was a rebellion. The mention of this reformation recalls the fearful shocks of a commotion which has hardly yet subsided. The intellect of man instinctively sided with the reformers. But the absolute freedom of thought; the unity of truth; the sacredness of natural truth; the correct view of the relative functions and prerogatives of the rational and the religious consciousness—these were attainments too exalted above the condition to which the mind had been consigned for a thousand years, to be reached by the advances of a single generation. Even Luther thought it incumbent upon him to anathematize the "reprehensible doctrine" of the Sorbonne, that "whatever is demonstrated true in philosophy must also be accepted as true in theology;" while of Aristotle he declared, "If he had not been of the flesh, I should not hesitate to affirm him to have been truly a devil." It is due to Luther to state that he afterward modified these opinions to a large extent. Melanchthon, his co-reformer, though better disposed toward philosophy, was scarcely better prepared to recognize freedom of opinion; for he applauded the execution of heretics, and pronounced the burning of Servetus a "pious and memorable example for all posterity."

The rebellion against intellectual servitude being inaugurated, many a valiant champion ventured to draw his sword. Bacon and Hobbes—though the latter, by a natural revulsion, went too far—have been regarded as the leaders in the final and full emancipation of philosophy from its subserviency to ecclesiastical traditions. Descartes (1596–1650), Spinoza (1632–1677), Leibnitz (1646–1716), Berkeley (1684–1753), Voltaire (1694–1778), Hume (1711–1776), Rousseau (1712–1778), and Kant (1724–1804) are the great lights of what is generally known as rationalistic religion—recognizing the fundamental doctrines of Christianity, but giving a free rein to speculation in every field, and tending, in certain cases, toward materialism; in others, toward some form of pantheism.

The pendulum of thought was now vibrating toward the opposite extreme. Intoxicated with freedom, the intellect began to hate its former master. It was now, in turn, the effort of philosophy to degrade and enslave religion. Hobbes (1651) and Lord Herbert (1624) began the attempt, and it was eagerly followed up in France by Bayle, Diderot (1713–1784), D'Alembert (1717–1783), Von Holbach (1723–1789), Volney (1751–1820), and others; and a bloody revolution having thrown political power into the hands of the skeptics, the travesty of government reached its climax in the enthronement of reason and the attempt to efface every record of religion.

This terror was more than the religious instincts of man could bear without revolt. They arose again in their majesty, and regained an acknowledgment of their right to sway the lives of men. For more than half a century religion and philosophy—which had become now more exclusively a philosophy of nature—observed toward each other outwardly a decent and somewhat cordial respect. Religious faith had marched up to a position abreast of modern science, and science exercised its full freedom to conquer new realms and make chaos of old theories. But it was plain enough that the peace between the two was not a complete *entente cordiale;* it was only an armistice. Faith watched with jealousy the manœuvres and proclamations of science, and science made the existing faith, at times, the subject of contemptuous remark. Both parties congratulated themselves on the evidences of progress. Science took just pride in her splendid superstructures of astronomy, geology, and physics; and religion felt relieved to have shaken off the effete appendages and crude accessories of her system, only to find its beauty and solidity more abundantly revealed. But the reconciliation of science and religion was not yet.

During the last three decades, the human intellect has made strides which have set the world agog. It is really amazed at its own achievements. It has become self-complaisant, if not self-conceited. It shows signs of overconfidence and usurpation. I speak of the human moods of some of the representatives of this progress. Scientific positions which were deemed impregnable less than a generation ago have been swept by a storm of new ideas. Many of the fogs and mists which have always obscured the vision of the race have been dissolved, and the intellectual atmosphere immediately around us has been wonderfully clarified. True it is that still beyond are banks of cloud darkly bounding the horizon, and new and loftier Alps of thought which remain to be scaled; and these revelations of labors yet to achieve temper the mind's elation with humility; but the advances of thought have been so general all along the front line of the sciences, that he who holds wholly to the scientific faiths of his father embraces forms as dead as Egyptian mummies. Every system of belief—educational, political, religious—which involved, or in any of its outposts rested on, the interpretations of nature which were current a third of a century since, must fail to-day to quadrate perfectly with the existing body of recognized scientific truth. So it has happened that science, which, for the time being, is the dominant phase of philosophy, is getting into a quarrel again with religious faith.

In spite of all the lessons of history, we still incline to embrace non-essentials in our creed. It is the law of religious faith to consecrate and cherish all which the intelligence holds true. Faith is a doting mother who lavishes indiscriminate affection upon the proper members of her family and those who are only adventitious comers; and when she must relinquish the latter, she clasps them in her arms, suffuses them with tears, and yields only when the last entreaty fails. There is something touching in faith's fidelity to the objects it has loved. But yet it seems to be true that even modern Christianity, as Christlieb sagaciously concedes, has been willing, sometimes, to make itself responsible for positions not at all vital to its interests, and the holding of which turns with to-morrow's thinking or to-morrow's experiment in the laboratory. Christianity may be likened to a splendid palace which the great Builder founded on a rock, digging deep, and bolting it to the granite. When he had gone, those who were sent to occupy and defend, built wings which spread themselves upon the sand; and the floods came, and the sands were washed away, and the wings crumbled into a ruin; but the body of the palace stood unmoved in its original strength and majesty. And others came to occupy the palace, and they too built extensions, and the tempest came and moved them from their place, and left them crushed, chaotic masses; but the body of the stately palace stood, for it was anchored to the rock.

It can not be denied that the world is witnessing to-day another ebb-tide of religious sentiment. The reconciliation of our Scriptures and our faiths with existing knowledge must, in some points, be effected by changed methods. It is sometimes painful to admit it; but it is always manly; and with our antecedent knowledge of both the imprescriptible rights and the rational defenses of religious faith, and of the irrefragable authority of the spirit of our written revelation, there is no ground for apprehensions; and any undue reluctance to correct or prune is worse than a refusal to look through Galileo's telescope lest we witness the crescent of Venus: it is a denial of the crescent after having it demonstrated to our eyes. Such reluctance will tend to avert the respect of the large number whose convictions will ever be controlled by the data of secular thought, and whose intelligence and respectability will, in turn, control a large proportion of the unthinking masses, already predisposed by their natures and indulgences to relieve themselves of the restraints of religion.

I have aimed to float your thoughts rapidly over the successive waves of religious manifestation which have diversified the history of the civilized world. I have desired to make it clear that the existing collision of new ideas with religious faith is but a natural recurrence of the same phenomenon which the world witnessed in the latter part of the last century, culminating in the bloody revolution of France; and, earlier, in the great reformation under Luther; and, still earlier, in the struggle from which the early Catholic Church was born, and in the crucifixion of our Lord, and in the Pyrrhonism of the post-Socratic age, and in the atomism of the materialistic Leucippus, following on the exalted spiritual philosophy of Anaxagoras. I desire to inspire your minds with a confidence that the interests of religion are by no means in peril. It is unmanly to be found quaking with fear. Faith is to experience another renaissance. It may not be easy, it may not now be possible, to explain how all discordances are to be reconciled; but I entertain the strongest confidence that all the conflicts of the passing hour will only result in the elimination of a body of truth—religious and secular—more beautiful and lovely than any upon which human thought has yet been fixed. I wish you to feel brave. I wish you to feel strong. I wish you to feel jubilant. I would like to lift my arm as high as heaven to signify my steadfast faith in the fortunes of our Christianity. I would like to speak with a voice which all the terrified should hear and take heart again. I would like to raise a shout which should fill the world at the joy I feel over the coming reconciliation of the contending forces, and the final establishment of the harmony and sacredness of all that truth which God has constituted us to accept—for which philosophers have thought, or poets dreamed, or martyrs bled.

But more than faith sustains me. I am not enveloped in impenetrable fog. I have a prophetic discernment of the methods by which the new reconciliation is to be effected. It is not a new faith that we are to receive; it is the old, old faith in a bright new vesture. Look, I pray you, at the tendencies of the conflicts which the opposing battalions are waging to-day. Is the strife between Moses and geology? To my mind the inspired epic of Moses presents an accordance with the geological history of the world which is almost, if not quite, supernatural; and is made more intelligible and more wonderful in the light which science has thrown upon it. Even admitting the impossibility of a circumstantial harmony, all conflict has forever vanished.

Is the strife waged over the antiquity of the human race? Let us candidly arrange three preliminaries: 1. The absolute age of Adam's race is not revealed, and has only been deduced by human calculations based on an assumption of the continuity of the genealogies given in Scripture—an assumption which is not insisted upon by all Christian theologians. 2. The Scriptural authority bearing on this question may have exclusive reference to the Caucasian race, as Dr. M'Causland, Dr. Whedon, and many others maintain; and the antiquity of this race may be much less than that of some other races, though there be a blood affinity between them. On the scientific side, the following propositions may be maintained: 1. All science testifies that the advent of our species is comparatively recent; more recent than any of the great revolutions of the globe; more recent than the advent of the other great types of organic life. 2. All the great changes which the Caucasian race have witnessed may have transpired within a few thousand years. The final disappearance of the continental glaciers; the extinction of numerous animal and vegetal species; the erosion and transposition of continental shores, and the desiccation of vast seas and lakes — these are all phenomena on which our race has probably gazed; but according to the chronometry of changes transpiring before our eyes, they do not imply that the origin of the race remounts to an antiquity exceeding eight to twelve thousand years. But suppose twenty thousand years appear more probable, what forbids?

Is the strife over the destruction of men by a great deluge? I discover, first, that the Bible does not compel me to believe it speaks of a deluge covering all the continents simultaneously; and, secondly, that history, tradition, and geology preserve the knowledge of post-Adamic deluges which brought destruction over all the world known to the sufferers.

Is the strife over the specific unity of human kind? Then we may bear in mind these positions: 1. There is much reason to believe, with M'Causland, that the Mosaic history of primeval man refers only to the Caucasian race, and that, consequently, the alleged consanguinity is no more than all people admit. 2. Even if this be true, anatomical and physiological science demonstrate that all the races are still of one blood and one structure, as every psychologist admits they are of one mental and moral constitution. 3. If we hold to the common parentage of all the races, we assume a position far advanced toward

10*

the admission that still lower types of organization are, also, but older or more divergent conditions of the common stock; and we become involuntary defenders of a doctrine of development. 4. If any theory of the derivative origin of species ever becomes established, the unity of human kind follows as a corollary.

Is the existing conflict waged over the origin of species? I hold it to be exactly like a fight over the question of the origin of coal. It is simply a question of fact. The truth is to be found out by searching, and to be revealed to the understanding. Religious faith has no more to do with it than with the contents of a freight-car. But doesn't the Bible teach that God created man and other forms of life? Yes, and so does reason; and so, I believe, does science. It is impossible to conceive of organic existence except as the result of supernatural creative power. But is it not the miller who reduces wheat to flour when he constructs a water-wheel, and causes it to turn the stone which pulverizes the grain? And is it not God who makes man when he arranges a line of genealogical succession which ends in man? And would not man still be the work of Deity, if no supernatural power were interposed between the initial act and the human result? I think so; and still I feel at liberty to entertain a growing conviction that even if species have a derivative origin, there is not one moment between the initial act and the final result when the impress of intelligent will is removed. In this view, not only is every species, but also every individual, the result of direct creation; but both are creations according to preordained and uniform methods. But, finally, I desire to say for myself that the derivative origin of species seems not to be proved; and hence, for the time being, I must believe that each organic type is a primordial, and not an indirect, creation.

Is the conflict to-day over the origin of life in general? Do Pouchet and Wyman and Bastian assert — what I hold is not yet proved by observation—that under certain circumstances living animals and plants come into being without the intervention of germs? Well, that is the very thing for which we contend in asserting that the first representatives of all organic types were *not* generated, but created. Do you assert that this so-called spontaneous origin of life does not answer to the theological idea of creation? Then I would ask two questions in turn: What warrant has any one for denominating such an origin of life spontaneous? And, in case of any primordial creation by supernatural agency, what set of circumstances and appearances would you expect to witness? Would you look for hands molding a microscopic animal form? Or would you not rather expect such form to be molded by agencies invisible and immaterial? That is what the doctrine of archegenesis asserts. It is not necessary to assume that forces which have no basis but matter elaborate the living result. Human reason affirms that every result proceeds from intelligent volition. And so, when Dr. Bastian points us to a living form rising into being from a germless fluid, I would cry out, Behold the fact of creation! Look upon the very presence of Deity!

Does Maudsley, Bain, or Carpenter—Büchner, Vogt, or Barker—assert or imply that mental manifestations are so far determined by cerebral conditions that we are prompted to regard thought a mere secretion of the brain—mind but a function of matter? Then I rise in the name of the universal consciousness to denounce the absurdity. If it is only nervous matter which thinks, then all the testimony of my being is perjury. Nature itself is a lie. But I am prepared to maintain from the platform of science that no such doctrine as the unification of all species of force is established, short of an ultimate synthesis of all in one supreme intelligent Will. In the realm of inorganic matter we discover, besides the correlated physical forces, a force of gravitation, a force of molecular attraction, and a force of molecular repulsion. In the world of organization we have revealed a force of vitality and a force of Will. Now, here are forms of energy which have never yet been mutually transformed. To say that a man's mental manifestations are conditioned by the state of his brain, and this by the food which he consumes, is only to state a truism which the world has never denied. But does this prove that mentality has no cause but brain? The movement of the locomotive is conditioned by the switch; but does this fact make the switch the cause of the locomotive's motion? Its motion is correlated to the switch, as mentality is to the bias which brain gives it; but neither motion in the one case, nor mentality in the other, can be rationally referred to any influence the exercise of which implies the antecedent and independent existence of the thing influenced.

Now, to be candid, I am not aware that the physicists of the day, save in one or two instances, have actually avowed a disbelief in the reality of spiritual forces. Some of them have explicitly avowed the contrary; and I am inclined to think most of them, if led to give expression on the subject at all, would agree in substance with the positions I have assumed. But that dreadful materialism! Where does it come from? Why, it is the joint child of our ignorance and our fears. Come, let us cease whining, and stand upon the prerogatives of reason. We know that mind is a factor of existence, and so does everybody. We will quit setting up ghosts to frighten ourselves withal.

Such are the principal fields of controversy between science and religious faith at the present day. None of them appear to me so bloody and desperate as to the eyes of some of my friends. With an antecedent and immovable persuasion of the indestructibility of the basis of our Christian faith, I contemplate this warfare with the loftiest and most serene composure. Indifferent as to *what* may be proved true, I am only anxious to know that it *is* true, and embrace it. I hold devoutly to the utterance of the Sorbonne, that whatever can be proved true in philosophy must also be true in theology. It is of less interest to know by what particular means the doctrines of science can be harmonized with the spirit of the Bible, than to know that complete harmony reigns, and that by the ordination of God.

I have attempted to vindicate the religious nature of man; to assert its right to activity; to explain and illustrate its mode of activity, and its relations to the intellect; to commend to you a profound respect for every form of religious manifestation; to confirm you in an unalterable faith in the perpetuity of our religion; to guard you against superstition and bigotry, and the entanglement of your faith with questions of human opinion; to make you strong Christians, valiant Christians, ever ready to face your enemy and vindicate your faith; to plant you on a rock whence the storms of hell shall be unable to move you.

If history and philosophy and psychology concur in proving that man is not man without religion, then it follows that there is no human relation from which the duties and observances of religion ought to be excluded. We can no more shake off our religion than our skin; how, then, can there be a place where it is proper to disown it? In the operations of business, in the halls of legislation, in the organization of states, in the university, in the high school, in the primary school—everywhere, according to our reasoning, have the religious instincts the right to assert themselves and qualify our determinations. Man, however, is free to do violence to these instincts—even to belie and deny them; but what right has such a man to object to my compliance with the law of my being and the law of humanity? What right has he to interpose an unnatural and monstrous protest against the recognition of the religious hemisphere of our being in any of the processes or stages of education? Education must be secularized? It is unnatural. It is monstrous. It is impracticable. It is *impossible*. Do you say that in a free country we should not impose our opinions upon those who dissent? Religion is *not* an opinion; it is a law of humanity, like respiration and hunger. It is Heaven that imposes religion upon us all—upon the objector as well as me. And what shall we say of the man of religion who panders to the feigned scruples of the objector, and joins with him in voting religion out of school? Whose mind does his vote represent in committing this impiety? Certainly not his own. And does not the very principle of equality which he professes to respect dictate that he give himself a representation instead of affording a perverted nature a double one? Oh, sacrilege! oh, blindness! Never will a majority of sincere objectors expel religion from its rightful place in any of the affairs of men. If it is ever done, it will be through the weakness and ignorance of religious men.

Religious faith is an ineradicable constituent of human character. It is ordained to live and act as long as the race survives. But its mode of action is receptive, emotional, propulsive; that of the intellect is cognitive, discriminating, directive. Faith is tender, reverent, conservative, safe; intellect is bloodless, profane, iconoclastic, daring. Superficially viewed, they have almost always been regarded as the antitheses of each other. The true view is, that they mutually antagonize and qualify each other to produce a whole which constitutes the excellence of a human soul—as molecular attractions and repulsions in their eternal antagonism marshal quivering atoms into stable masses; as centrifugal and centripetal forces conspire, by opposition, to create and maintain the circling harmonies of the cosmos.

They are unlike, but not incompatible. Though each has its sphere, it can never be admitted that faith and science must remain apart. "The mingling of science with religion," says Bacon, "leads to unbelief; and the mingling of religion with science, to extravagance." To all this the drift of my arguments is opposed. One can appreciate the force of the aphorism in an age when a set of arbitrary dogmas was called religion, and fallible interpretation had power to disfranchise intellect; but strange it seems that men should still maintain that no necessary or possible correlation can subsist between the thoughts embodied in God's two revelations; or that science is authorized to put faith in a test-tube, or theology to set stakes to science. The peace to be established between the two is not what Bacon intimates — a sullen non-intercourse. It is the peace of mutual recognition and mutual understanding. Religion will learn that whatever is true is hers, and must be incorporated into her system. Science will learn that many things must be true in theology which can not be gauged by her methods. Philosophy will yet convince her, when the exhilaration of her heyday is past, that underneath the isolated patch of ground on which she stands stretches the broad rock of fundamental truth, that bears up, in equal majesty and equal strength, the fabric of the Christian system. Then shall she learn that the most imperious demand of philosophy is to accept some things which are above all philosophy and all science; that, in short, faith is the very apotheosis of reason.

There is a story told by Casalis, the African traveler, which I have read and reread, and seldom without tears. It illustrates and proves, better than all argument, how inseparable from humanity is the feeling of religion; and how deep and mysterious it is, even in the breast of the lowest savages. I present you the account, and leave you to ponder its meaning. Arbrousset, the missionary, had been explaining the tidings of the Gospel to one of the noblest of the savage Kaffirs, when he raised himself up and made reply. "Your tidings," said he, as reported by Arbrousset, "are what I want; and I was seeking before I knew you, as you shall hear and judge for yourselves. Twelve years ago I went to feed my flocks. The weather was hazy. I sat down upon a rock and asked myself sorrowful questions; yes, sorrowful, because I was unable to answer them. 'Who has touched the stars with his hands? On what pillars do they rest?' I asked myself. 'The waters are never weary; they know no other law than to flow, without ceasing, from morning till night, and from night till morning; but where do they stop? And who makes them flow thus? The clouds, also, come and go, and burst in water over the earth. Whence come they? Who sends them? The diviners certainly do not give us rain, for how could they do it? And why do I not see them, with my own eyes, when they go up to heaven to fetch it? I can not see the wind; but what is it? Who brings it, makes it blow and roar and terrify us? Do I know how the corn sprouts? Yesterday there was not a blade in my field; to-day I returned to the field and found some. Who can have given to the earth the wisdom and power to produce it?' Then I buried my face in both my hands."

This is the cry of infant humanity in the dark. This is the call of nature for its God. This is the yearning which can only be eased by a form of faith. This is the prayer of the soul which Deity only can hush. This is the murmur of a spiritual power which is mightier than ocean-billows; which can no more be extirpated from existence than the energies which hurl the planets in their circuits. Oh, let us be calm! Oh, let us be trustful, and confident, and brave—and wait reverently for God to vindicate his own everlasting TRUTH!

IX.

THOUGHTS ON CAUSALITY, WITH REFERENCES TO PHASES OF RECENT SCIENCE.

When I was in London last July, I received an invitation to participate in the approaching Belfast meeting of the British Association for the Advancement of Science. Had I known that the occasion was to be signalized by some of the most notable utterances of the century, I might have resisted the strong pressure which was urging me to the Continent. As it was, I went from London to the Alps, while Tyndall proceeded from the Alps to London. The latter, as President of the British Association, delivered an address, the noise of which reached me at Chamonix. It is only since my return to America, however, that I have had the opportunity to learn precisely what the great physicist uttered, and how considerable a commotion it occasioned in the newspapers of this country.

The gathering to which I refer was the scene of other notable utterances from a scientist no less distinguished, and no less worthy of distinction. The two addresses of Tyndall and Huxley exemplify well a characteristic of recent science, which, by many, has been deplored as a tendency to positivism and consequential materialism. To these two productions I might add two recent and powerful works by Haeckel, of Jena, the latest of which has also fallen into my hands since my return to America. I refer to Haeckel's "Natural History of Creation,"[1] and his "Anthropogeny."[2]

---

[1] "Natürliche Schöpfungsgeschichte, 4te. verbesserte Auflage," Berlin, 1873, 8vo, pp. 688.

[2] "Anthropogenie, Entwickelungsgeschichte des Menschen," Leipzig, 1874, 8vo, pp. 732.

In studying these latest emanations from the evolutionist school of science, I have been deeply impressed by four observations: 1. The great learning and scientific acumen of their authors. 2. Their strict adherence to the study of material phenomena, and their customary reticence upon questions which receive no direct light from physical observations. 3. The wide-spread popular misapprehension of these men in respect to the subjects of their reticence, and of the bearing of their scientific opinions upon those subjects. 4. The existence of latent fallacies affecting in common, to a certain extent, some of their fundamental positions.

With the view of eliciting into prominence the common fundamental principles of such writers, and applying to them what I believe to be true philosophic and universal criteria of correct thinking, I begin by presenting the line of reasoning embodied in the address of Professor Tyndall.

This address is a panoramic survey of the history of thought and speculation on the origin and substratum of phenomena, and concludes that, so far as the inquiries of science are concerned, there has always been manifest a tendency in leading minds to rest, as an ultimate datum, upon the proposition that atoms and molecules are ultimate existences, and their interaction is the cause of all material and mental phenomena. Yet the author repeatedly recognizes the necessity of admitting the existence of some inscrutable energy farther back than the remotest cause attainable by human research.

The first efforts at reasoning traced events to superhuman agency exerted by numerous beings called gods, but the conception of whom was strictly anthropomorphic. Science was born in the desire to find fixed and orderly energies with which to replace the capricious wills of the primitive gods. While yet in its cradle, science manifested a consciousness of its mission, in attacking and destroying the contemporary religious faiths and pretensions. In seeking from below, instead of above, the causes of phenomena, ancient Greek speculation struck into the fundamental idea that atoms and molecules are the ultimate constituents of the cosmos. Democritus, who is pronounced a philosopher superior to Plato or Aristotle, first gave precision and form to this idea. He held to the eternity of the atoms, the materiality of the soul, and denied chance. He first advanced the idea of *vortices in the genesis of worlds*. Empedocles suggested that those combinations which were suited to their ends *maintain themselves from their very nature*, and thus launched the thought which has taken form, in our own time, as the doctrine of the "survival of the fittest." Epicurus, while actuated by an equal desire to discover law and order in the phenomena of the universe, and thus dispel the superstitions of the existing religions, did not reject the belief in divine existence; and was himself a worshiper of the gods. Lucretius, if he admitted divine existence, maintained that the world shows no proof of intelligent design, and that all things have been caused by the shock of the atoms, while the fittest combinations have persisted. He is thought to have suggested the *nebular hypothesis* to Kant. As to Socrates, Plato, and Aristotle, they imposed a yoke on the human mind which remains, to some extent, unbroken to the present day.

This auspicious inauguration of the advance of science was arrested by the quickening of the religious feeling through the introduction of Christianity, which made the mistake of adopting Biblical interpretation as the criterion of all truth.([1]) The

---

([1]) In the Second and Third lectures of the present work I have given a summary of the facts connected with the relations subsisting between the early Christian Church and contemporary systems of thought. I have shown that it was only through the abnormal aggrandizement of the ecclesiastical power that the *councils of the Church* (not Christianity, except so far as implicated in the acts of those who professed it) attained to an attitude where they were enabled to dictate terms to intellect; and that, in doing this, they violated not more the rights of intellect than the spirit of primitive Christianity.

philosophy of Aristotle sanctioned and aided the *à priori* methods of the schoolmen; and, though science made positive advances in Arabia, the bond of tradition was not seriously wrenched in Europe till the time of Copernicus and Bruno. Bacon strengthened the incipient bias toward inductive methods; and Descartes, though setting out from a first principle, unconsciously abandoned it, to present the cosmos as a pure mechanism. The full establishment of monotheism was favorable to the conception of the universe which presents it as a system of physical effects; and Gassendi signalized the possible compatibility of theology with a revived Epicureanism. The doctrine of atoms, which started with Democritus,([2]) has since grown into general acceptance. But while Democritus conceived the atoms dead, Gassendi, and, more recently, Clerk-Maxwell, have looked upon them as "prepared materials," thus suggesting either the postulate or the inference of an antecedent preparer. Tyndall agrees with Kant in denying the power of reason to bridge the chasm which separates the atoms from their Maker.

In an imaginary discussion between Bishop Butler and a disciple of Lucretius, the close correlation between states of mind and conditions of the brain is pointed out; but it is admitted that the impinging of dead atoms upon dead atoms can never result in sensation or any other phenomenon of consciousness. This admission does not appear in the address as originally published, but there is no reason to infer that the author's position has been changed.

Professor Tyndall, proceeding to the phenomena and the problem of the succession of organic forms in geological time, iterates his belief in the genealogical continuity of the series, and follows with a sketch of the origin of the doctrine of

---

([2]) Democritus, in fact, was a pupil of Leucippus, a disciple of the Eleatics. Leucippus seems to be the real originator of the atomic philosophy (Ueberweg, "Hist. Phil.," vol. i., p. 67).

transmutation or derivation of species, and of the grounds on which the Darwinian phase of the doctrine reposes. Mr. Darwin and Professor Huxley receive high encomiums. Repetitions here would be irksome. It is asserted that variations occur under domestication and in a state of nature; that infinitesimal variations transmitted through generations become greatly accumulated and augmented; that the external conditions which are concomitant with these variations are "true causes;" that Darwin rejects teleology, even while bringing forward some of the most striking examples of apparent design; that instincts are only inherited and accumulated experiences; and, finally, that Darwinism has become firmly rooted in the convictions of thinking minds.

In the recent progress of scientific research, the doctrine of the conservation of energy has become established; and this principle is held to embrace organic nature as truly as inorganic. Next, the origin of mind itself has come specially under review; and Spencer is maintained to have established for it a developmental history parallel with that established by Darwin for the physical organism. Eyes and other organs of the senses are but portions of a primitively homogeneous mass differentiated by the influence of light and other external agents. The tactual sense is observed to possess a development correlative with the intelligence of animals; and the inference is that it determines such intelligence. Instincts and intuitions are but the accumulated experience of races, transmitted from generation to generation. Space and time are " elements of thought," or, as Kant phrases it, " forms of intuition," instead of objective realities.[1]

---

[1] The phrase "elements of thought" as here used is too loose for philosophy. Space and time are not the "elements," but the concomitants, and probably the conditions, of thought. "Forms of intuition" is more exact; but still, "conditions of intuition," or "conditions of the possibility of intuition and thought," would be better.

The author now approaches the critical point of his discussion. Having admitted that the scientist often feels himself impelled to pass beyond the field of physical phenomena, and from phenomena to induce an abstract generalization under which an entire category of phenomena may be ranged—as in the case of the force of gravitation—it is not strange that Lucretius should have reached the generalization that his atoms were endowed with life; or that Darwin should have permitted himself to be understood as abstracting creative power, exercised in a limited number of initial cases, as the antecedent and cause of the series of organized beings. Darwin, our author thinks, should speak with clearness at this juncture, and assume the responsibility of carrying derivative development back, not only to one primitive stock, but to unorganized matter itself. At the same time, he admits that the doctrine of spontaneous generation is not yet proved, though he seems to regard that achievement as not very remote.

We stand now in the presence of that matter so uniformly defined as dead. We have traced life from its highest manifestations, through all its gradations, to granulated, vivified protoplasm. Life is everywhere associated with matter. We know nothing of life save as associated with matter. Is there any terrestrial life which does not depend for its maintenance and its origin upon matter? "Here the vision of the mind authoritatively supplements the vision of the eye. By an intellectual necessity," he says, "I cross the boundary of the experimental evidence, and discern in that matter which we, in our ignorance of its latent powers, and notwithstanding our professed reverence for its creator, have hitherto covered with opprobrium—the promise and potency of all terrestrial life."

Here, then, he reaches the goal toward which recent theories in science seemed to impel him. This, indeed, is a sort of materialism; but we must have the candor to permit the distinguished physicist to explain the sense in which he embraces materialism. In harmony with Spencer, and in opposition to Mill, Fichte, Berkeley, and Hume, Professor Tyndall entertains no question as to the existence of an external world; though we have no evidence that it is as it seems to be. "Our states of consciousness," he says, "are symbols of an outside entity which produces them and determines the order of their succession, but the real nature of which we can never know. In fact, the whole process of evolution is the manifestation of a power absolutely inscrutable to the intellect of man.* * * Considered fundamentally, then, it is by the operation of an insoluble mystery that life on earth is evolved, species differentiated, and mind unfolded, from their prepotent elements in the immeasurable past" (p. 91).

The facts of the religious consciousness of man are repeatedly recognized. "The facts of religious feeling are to me as certain as the facts of consciousness" (p. 24, Appleton & Co.'s ed.). "Physical science can not cover all the demands of man's nature" (p. 42). Speaking of facts of consciousness which have prescriptive rights quite as strong as those of the understanding, he says, "There is also that deep-set feeling, which, since the earliest dawn of history, and probably for ages prior to all history, incorporated itself in the religions of the world. You who have escaped from these religions into the high and dry light of the intellect may deride them; but in so doing, you deride accidents of form merely, and fail to touch the immovable basis of the religious sentiment in the nature of man. To yield this sentiment reasonable satisfaction is the problem of problems at the present hour" (p. 93). It will be noticed that he relegates religion to the realm of emotion. This force is something "capable of being guided to noble issues in the region of emotion, which is its proper and elevated sphere"([1]) (p. 93). Finally, while claiming for sci-

---

([1]) On this subject, see the present writer's views expressed in the First Lecture, p. 22–25.

ence a rightful and complete exemption from the restraints of all religious theories, schemes, or systems, he asserts an equal right of the ethical nature to free exercise. "The advance of man's understanding in the path of knowledge, and those unquenchable claims of his moral and emotional nature which the understanding can never satisfy, are here equally set forth" (p. 97). In an address delivered two months subsequently to his Belfast manifesto, Professor Tyndall, raising the question whether there are not in nature manifestations of knowledge and skill superior to man's, replies, "My friends, the profession of that atheism with which I am sometimes so lightly charged would, in my case, be an impossible answer to this question" (p. 102).

The ethical bearing of scientific materialism is found further set forth in an address delivered by the same speaker in 1868. After explaining the invariable relation of physics to consciousness, and alleging that, "given the state of the brain, the corresponding thought or feeling might be inferred; or given the thought or feeling, the corresponding state of the brain might be inferred, he asks, "How inferred? It would be at the bottom not a case of logical inference at all, but of empirical association.* * * The passage from the physics of the brain to the corresponding facts of consciousness is unthinkable (p. 117).* * * In affirming that the growth of the body is mechanical, and that thought as exercised by us has its correlative in the physics of the brain, I think the position of the materialist is stated as far as that position is a tenable one. I think the materialist will be able, finally, to maintain this position against all attacks; but I do not think, in the present condition of the human mind, that he can pass beyond this position. I do not think he is entitled to say that his molecular groupings and his molecular motions *explain* every thing. In reality, they explain nothing. The utmost he can affirm is the association of two classes of phenomena, of whose real bond of union he is in absolute ignorance" (p. 118).

The foregoing digest indicates that the celebrated Belfast address is an attempt to show that the most penetrating minds of all ages have felt themselves borne toward the conviction that the ultimate datum of scientific, and, perhaps, of philosophic, investigation must be matter. It asserts that this is the general, or at least the forming, conviction of men of science at the present day; that all activities in the realm of life and mind, as well as in that of organization, are intimately connected sequents or concomitants of the interactions of the atoms, and that back of this basis of phenomena, whatever we may feel impelled to believe, there is nothing which can be reached by real knowledge; though we are compelled to recognize a profound and mysterious reality to which our ethical feelings are co-ordinated. It is unfair to hurl at Professor Tyndall the charge of atheism in the philosophic sense. He distinctly repels the imputation. It is uncandid, after his careful qualifications, to charge him with materialism in that ordinary sense which excludes the notion of Deity back of matter. When he avows materialism, he means that within the region of the data of science he discovers every thing originating from antecedents under the recognized laws of matter and force. There certainly *is* something, he says, behind matter and force; but he follows Spencer in refusing to subscribe to any predicates respecting it. He is hardly a material pantheist, for he distinctly declares that sensation and thought can not come from dead matter; and implies that though existence emerges from matter, its ground is farther back. He certainly belongs to the nescience school of theists, in which Hamilton and Mansel are older masters than Spencer; and there seems little propriety and less occasion for his assuming the burden of a confession so opprobrious as materialism.

I desire to make the analysis of this address the occasion for shaping a statement of fundamental principles which ought to regulate the procedures of scientist, philosopher, and theologian alike. We are all equally attempting to cleave through the dense darkness which environs us, to reach the truth of things. That we live in a universe of phenomena is generally admitted. We are therefore realities, and we all act on the assumption that there are other realities shadowed forth in the realm of appearances. No reasoning, nevertheless, can prove the existence of an external world; and the history of thought shows that it is possible, in individual cases, to stifle the universal belief that it exists. But if these phenomena represent realities, we are still uncertain that they represent realities *as they are.* Universal belief again affirms that they do; and yet there is room for doubt.

If we trust the indications of the shifting phenomena, the world of realities is the theatre of perpetual movement, change, and transformation. We find rooted in universal belief a conviction that all these changes are severally the results of appropriate causes; and that the realities themselves are equally effects of adequate causation. It is a law of mind to look upon every phenomenon as an effect, and to couple effect with cause. It is the province of science to catalogue phenomena, to classify them, to note their relations of antecedence and sequence and formulate laws; and, from observed uniformities of sequence, to lift the veil from the future and the past. It is the province of philosophy to pass beyond the phenomenon and inquire, not what is its antecedent, but what is its cause; to pass from immediate and accessible causes to remote ones, and from these to ultimate, efficient causation. Philosophy, when it has attained this limit, becomes theology. Theology is the granary in which the fruitage of science and philosophy is garnered. Religion is the activity of that department of our nature which feels its ground and sanction in the supreme Reality in which the successes of science, philosophy, and theology converge.

Though searchers after truth may be ranged as scientists, philosophers, and theologians, it is seldom the case that either shuts himself closely in his own field. The scientist from phenomena induces laws; and from the postulates of his own mind deduces causes, such as gravitation, affinity, electricity. The modern philosopher combines the data furnished in reason with the conclusions yielded by science; and the theologian pursues all paths and all methods which seem to tend toward a last solution of the mystery of being and events.

It is a misfortune, as it seems to me, for either to restrict his investigations to a single field. The practice begets indifference to certain classes of data, and ends in bigotry, misunderstanding, and hostility. Our common nature covers, in each individual, the whole ground, and it seems to me narrow and pernicious for the truth-seeker to tie himself up to a single method.

Science, in its modern acceptation, does not lead to causes —still less, to primordial cause. The search for these is the legitimate object of philosophy. Science, strictly speaking, knows only phenomena with their groupings and orders of sequence. It talks much of forces, but these are only hypotheses, verbal symbols of unknown quantities which may be one thing or another. Moreover, when the scientist steps into the realm of abstract realities, he is playing the rôle of philosopher.[1]

I have said the bond between effect and cause is a universal

---

[1] So natural and legitimate is philosophizing that the most emphasized scientist finds himself continually tempted beyond the limits of science. The earnest hunt for truth renders the mind oblivious of the boundary-lines between the territories of science and philosophy. "*By an intellectual necessity,*" as Professor Tyndall truthfully admits, "*it crosses the boundary of the experimental evidence,*" and demands of philosophy the extradition of truth which had eluded pursuit in the realm of positive science. See further on this subject in the Fifth Lecture.

datum of reason. I think no modern philosopher will maintain that existence or phenomenon can be the product of chance. In ruling chance, however, from the throne of the universe, it may be well to offer an explanation and a discrimination. We must recognize such a thing as chance; and we ought to understand what it is and what it is not. If I throw down a couple of dice, it is impossible to calculate what will turn up. We say the result is wholly a matter of chance. I may chance to turn up one ace; it may be two. But the contingency of the result is not the cause of it. The two aces concur by chance; but chance did not put forth the efficiency which moved each dice precisely so far and no farther. The movement of the dice is as absolutely the effect of the forces exerted by my hand, by gravity, and by elasticity, as if I had deliberately laid each one down with the ace up. I have not the ability so to measure and adjust the force and direction of my muscular effort as to produce a preappointed movement and lodgment of the dice; and there is, consequently, some range of possible movement and possible place of rest for the dice. But whatever movement transpires, and whatever may result in the position of the dice, ordinary physical forces were the cause—the proximate cause—of all. Chance, in this case, is simply a field of possibility. It is a range of values of an unknown quantity, within certain limits. It is a name for our inability to gauge precisely the forces which act—our ignorance of the precise result which they will produce.

The case is not fundamentally altered when, for the dice, we substitute the atoms of a universe. The field of possible results is inconceivably enlarged; but we must feel equally certain that, whatever adjustment the atoms assume, there has been some adequate cause or set of causes to move them to their places. We say that any particular adjustment is the result of chance; but it is absolutely certain that, whatever the adjustment, there were forces moving the atoms in such directions and with such velocities as to produce precisely that adjustment. The chance of which we speak is no more a cause in this case than in that of the dice.

Chance is essentially a negation of cause. The moment I assert that a result *is caused*, the idea of chance is necessarily excluded. Were there no cause but chance in the universe— even supposing the atoms of matter to exist—every thing would rest in a state of immobility, stagnation. There would be no further effect than the birth of matter.

But suppose the existence of matter and orderly acting forces to be granted, there is much more in the collocations of the atoms of the universe than can be attributed to causes acting without discernment. We are not authorized to assert that the disposition of the atoms is the result even of blind attractions and repulsions; since, as can be shown, there are numberless adjustments in which harmony, beauty, fitness, and utility have been the directive or conditioning force; and these are qualities sustaining relations only to intelligence.

Whatever character, then, philosophy may authorize chance to assume, she can not concede to it the character of cause. Existence can not be the result of chance. No mode of existence can be the result of chance.[1]

It is one of the results of science to prove that that which had been regarded as a cause is only an effect. The more we know, the longer the chain of intermediate causation seems to be. Primitive man recognizes no interval between cause and first cause. Every event in the natural world is looked upon as the direct product of supernatural causation. This is not a theoretical opinion, but a historical fact, which I have ascertained after abundant research. The relics of this habit perpet-

---

[1] On *chance* and *probabilities*, the reader may consult De Morgan, "Probability," p. 23; Mill, "Logic," book iii., chap. xvii.; M'Cosh, "Typical Forms," pp. 40, 41, etc.; Venn, "Logic of Chance," 1876.

uated themselves among the Greeks until the dawn of Greek philosophy; and we are assured by Draper and Tyndall, and the professions of the philosophers themselves, that the aim of philosophy, in which, in ancient times, all science was merged, was, to demonstrate that events do not transpire through the direct intervention of the gods, but according to the orderly methods of physical law. With such gods as ruled in the Greek pantheon, there must have been much to stimulate philosophy and forward its aims.

Advancing from the lowest stage of barbarism, the first step in reflection discloses the law of invariable antecedence and sequence among physical phenomena; and the mind attaches its ineradicable notion of cause to the invariable antecedent. Here arises the notion of *physical causation*. But the invariable antecedent is now regarded the effect of first cause, acting in the guise of a supernatural power. Here is one term interposed between first cause and ultimate phenomenon.

The next step in reflection discloses the same fact in regard to the observed physical cause as had been noted at first in regard to the last phenomenon. This is also the effect of a physical cause; and the mind now finds two terms of intermediate causation interposed between assumed first cause and ultimate phenomenon. The opportunity presents itself, at this stage, for another observation which, in the development of science, becomes extremely significant. The recognized intermediate causes of two separate phenomena appear, in many cases, as the effects of the same cause. The number of assumed first causes is therefore much less than the number of intermediate causes in the first order of remove from phenomenon.

With the further advance of reflection, it is ascertained that the assumed first cause is again the effect of remoter causation; and so its aspect changes to that of an intermediate cause, and we find three terms interposed between phenomenon and newly assumed first cause. At the same time, it is observed that, in many cases, two of the previously assumed first causes are, in common, the effect of one first cause thus removed by three terms from phenomenon.

Thus continues, through the instrumentality of researches of the scientific kind, the process of interpolating new terms of intermediate or secondary causation; and parallel with the retreat of primary causation into the ever-dimmer distance is a diminution in the number of assumed first causes. The tendency of lines of causation or series of effects to converge has been noted by every thinker. This zone of secondary causes is the peculiar field of science.

Before proceeding further, one suggestive fact should be conspicuously held up to view. The human mind all along holds fast to its notion of primary causation. Disappointed and deceived a hundred times, its faith in the reality is not one whit abated. Reluctantly and sorrowfully driven from post to post, it moves on into the unexplored darkness, full of confidence that the object of its trust will be found at last. Look, further, at the notion which it always frames of the character of its primary cause. True it is that the hue of humanity is reflected over it. The first cause *does* assume human attributes. In the rude conditions of society, they are bodily as well as spiritual; but afterward purely spiritual. Man is conscious of the exercise of a power of causation on his own part, and he knows nothing of any other mode of essential causation. As long as all that he sees and investigates in the universe is found coordinated to the powers and methods of his own intellect, it would be an impossible philosophy to assume that primary cause, when discovered, should not exert its efficiency in a manner harmonious with the indications of all the rest of the universe. The mind of humanity, therefore, invests its primary cause with volition and intelligence. It may be said that humanity's conceptions in this and many other things are destitute of demonstrable foundation. I do not wish to meet the objection now, but would suggest that sound reasoning demands that we proceed from grounds which are strongly probable, rather than from the total negation of them because not demonstrated. The fallacy of asserting that a given position can not be demonstrated true, and then proceeding to reason as if it were demonstrated untrue, is a somewhat fashionable one, and has served as the basis of a great deal of bulky and ostentatious, if not very substantial, philosophizing.

Another observation to be made at this point has reference to the relative influence of polytheistic and monotheistic conceptions upon the body and the march of science. It is the characteristic of polytheism to stand ready to recognize an indefinite number of first causes; thus necessarily retarding, instead of stimulating, the search for intermediate causes. Monotheism, while recognizing but one absolutely first cause, must either favor the tendency of lines of causation to converge at a point, by the continual interpolation of secondary causes, or else must yield to the anthropopathic instinct of uncultured mind, in assuming an indefinite number of points of application of causal efficiency. This latter alternative would evidently be the resort of a monotheism not yet sufficiently exalted in scientific knowledge to be able to appreciate the full meaning of that convergence toward a unity which is disclosed in the genealogical lines of phenomena. To the first alternative it would be driven by a clearer understanding of the significance of the history of opinion; and when once fully intrenched in that position, it would contemplate with satisfaction, rather than alarm, the progress of science in breaking through the unexplored barriers which separate the last found causes from the One Universal Cause.

We turn back now to scrutinize the field of secondary causation in which physical science occupies itself. It is purely a phenomenal world. The data of physical science, strictly speaking, do not consist of *causes* made manifest in sensible phenomena, but of sensible phenomena themselves, certain ones of which sustain to each other the relation of invariable antecedence and sequence.(¹) The body of positive science is restricted to these. When, in obedience to a law of our minds, we connect the necessary notion of causation with a given invariable antecedence, we perform a legitimate act of philosophic thinking; but we neither know the *modus operandi* of the causation, nor whether the causation inheres in the antecedent or acts through it, nor whether such causation is primary, or separated by an indefinite number of terms from primary cause. It is only an accommodated and symbolical form of expression when I say, for instance, that friction causes electrical phenomena. I only know that electrical phenomena follow friction. Friction may be the cause proximate, or it may not be. That it is the first cause no one will pretend; but how many removes separate it from first cause no one can conjecture.

Physical science may conveniently and harmlessly assume that causation inheres in the antecedent; but the habit of so doing must not generate a belief that the assumption represents a verity. Science may forbear to inquire—nay, in its own character, it can not inquire—whether efficient causation inhere in the material substance back of the phenomenon which stands as invariable antecedent; or whether the remotest phenomenal

---

(¹) Certain language which Professor Morris has published since this paper was written (and published) is singularly coincident with some of our expressions. It is a pleasure to learn that he has independently thought the same thoughts, and to call attention to the acute analysis by which he eliminates the principle of final cause as a necessary principle of cognition and of the contemplation of nature. "The laws," he says, "of such [mechanical] action are laws of phenomenal sequence, and not of causation. So-called mechanical causes are not true causes" ("The Final Cause as Principle of Cognition and Principle in Nature," in Jour. Phil. Soc. of Great Britain, 1875). For further references, see the foot-note on page 96 of the present work.

antecedent reached by science represents substantial first cause. Should the scientist refrain from instituting such inquiries, he should neither be reproached, on the one hand, with the charge of apathy touching questions of primary causation, nor himself commit the mistake, on the other, of assuming that inquiries in his actual field have led him to real causes. Still less should he dogmatically deny that real causation is posited outside of the phenomenal world in which his labors are conducted—beyond the last term which he has discovered with his microscope, or dissolved in his alembic, or discerned with the *Vorstellungskraft* of his imagination.

The method of science, I repeat, is chiefly inductive; that of philosophy, chiefly deductive. The science of antiquity and of the Middle Ages was essentially a body of conclusions derived deductively; and the inevitable and glaring absurdities of the method and its results, contrasted with the brilliant successes of the inductive method of modern times, have caused many scientists to look upon deductive processes with an unmerited degree of distrust, or even disdain. This has led them, since scientific induction can not be carried into the field of first principles, to reject as unsafe and unworthy of consideration the results of *à priori* reasoning. Hence has sprung up the miscalled "positive philosophy." This tendency has gone too far, and it is quite time to return to the natural method, which appreciates and weighs with impartiality the evidence afforded both by reason and the senses; and does not refuse to search for causes in the realm of immaterial things, because there they would elude the verification of the crucible and the balance. Deduction, dealing with necessary truths and admitted principles, is a permissible and safe procedure, and so natural and available, that not unfrequently the scientist himself falls into the use of it, at the same time that he professes to observe rigorously the canons of scientific induction.

The test of a physical truth—that it must be capable of mental presentation—is legitimate; but a moment's reflection will convince any one that it is an impossible test in the whole field of abstract ideas. By what sort of process, for instance, would Professor Tyndall bring before his mind's eye a *Vorstellung* of cheapness, or ambition, or despair, or even the generalization induced from a body of phenomena?

In this phenomenal world science disposes its data according to their resemblances, concomitancies, and sequences. An observed invariable sequence is styled a law. In the generalized faith that a certain sequence will remain invariable, science forecasts terms which lie in the future; and, in a similar faith that it has always been invariable, science retraces the pathway of phenomena into the inaccessible past. But it is of the utmost importance to refrain from endowing the word *law* with the notion of efficiency. We say loosely that the law of chemical affinities causes the disengagement of carbonic acid when chalk and sulphuric acid are brought together; that it is a law of life that the stomach should not be dissolved by its own juices; that it is the law of the "survival of the fittest" which causes the progressive improvement (either assumed or proved) in the successive generations of a species in the state of nature. We are apt to think that when we have ranged a phenomenon under its appropriate order of sequence, we have pointed out its cause; whereas, laws are only uniformities of juxtaposition of phenomena. There is no efficacy in law. It is not a force, but only the method of activity of force or the order of its effects. The law which expresses the relations subsisting between the intensity of gravity and the masses and distances of bodies, when applied to a certain assemblage of phenomena, renders them intelligible in a certain sense; it discloses the consummate harmony subsisting among them, and reveals correlations which seem to be the work of intelligence; but we deceive ourselves when we imagine that the law produces a single result. The law itself is a result—an induction from the order of the phenomena which a mistaken science summons it to explain. If a progressive improvement of race is an outcome of the continuous "survival of the fittest," then this order of sequence is a law; and in accordance with it, we shall expect every race left to itself to undergo a gradual improvement; but such order of sequence is no more a cause in this case than in any other. The immediate causes of this result are the agencies which destroy the individuals not "fittest to survive," or, more accurately, the forces concerned in the continuance of the species, under the conditions (extermination of the weakest), through the surviving individuals.

Still employing the term cause in the symbolical sense customary with science, there is another set of circumstances which ought not to escape notice in scrutinizing the principles of causality. I refer to conditions of causation — sometimes called conditioning causes. There are conditions indeed to the efficiency of every cause — conditions of its operativeness in any degree; and there are others which merely modify its operation; and, not unfrequently, the two characters are united in one condition. There is danger of confounding conditions with causes. I agree to write a book, for instance, on the condition that my publishers will put it in print. It will not be written with that condition left out. But the publisher does not thereby become the author of my book. The dilute acid in the battery will attack the zinc only on condition that you connect the zinc and platinum externally by means of a conductor; but this does not render the conductor the agent which dissolves the zinc. I build a wall behind my grape-trellis, and I find the ripening of the fruit accelerated; but it is not the wall which does the work: it is still, as before, the sun. The amount of light emitted by my lamp is determined, within certain limits, by the height of the wick; but this does not render the wick the cause of the light. The varying wick is only a varying condition of a varying result (oxidation) of a varying activity of a constant physical cause—chemical affinity between oil and oxygen. Similarly, the amount of thought which I can evolve is conditioned by all the various affections and conditions of the brain. My poetry and my philosophy are indeed correlated to brain and blood and oxygen and beefsteak, but only in the same way that my boots are correlated to calf-skin and tan-bark and black-wax. These condition the exercise of the boot-maker's skill; beefsteak conditions the exercise of mine. It is quite true that the activity in both cases has other conditions; but it is also true that none of the conditions can be elevated to the dignity of causes. The physical scientist is sometimes hoodwinked by the exact graduation of mental activity to the condition of the brain, and commits the mistake of clothing condition with the character of cause. As well assert that the wick secretes the light.

A similar departure from correct reasoning is the assignment of the "environment" as the cause of organic modifications. I shall not deny that organic modifications are generally correlated to the environment, and vary with the environment, and as a sequence of its variations. Though I have observed that organism bears no fixed, and therefore necessary, relation to environment, and even sometimes ignores it, I will assume that the correspondence is always as uniform as a certain school of derivationists pictures it. What then? This is, after all, but a conditioning cause. It seems to me to imply a lack of close discrimination to assert, for instance, that increased cold causes an animal's fur to grow longer. If it grow longer with increase of cold, and as a sequence of it, the immediate cause is evidently the increased amount of assimilation at the growing points of the hairs. That cold is the cause of this, there is no ground for asserting. But if it were the cause, cold itself is the effect of a remoter cause—the diminution of heat-vibrations; and this is the result of a decrease of energy in the *cause of heat-vibrations*, whatever that may be. When the common potato is grown in a dry and sterile soil, it deteriorates in size and quality; and the Darwinist would assert that these changes are caused by the change in the environment; while, in fact, they are only conditioned by it. The change in the soil is the condition of the assimilation of less material; it is the condition of the less energetic action of the vital forces. Whatever result ensues, it is these forces which cause it. The crane's long legs and the duck's broad bill are co-ordinated to their environment, and have been fashioned as they are by some cause. It is evident that the environment has been the condition with reference to which the conformation was produced. But there is no particle of proof that the environment produced them. It would be interesting to contemplate Professor Tyndall in the effort to represent to his mind's eye the process by which pond water wove the web of a duck's foot; or that by which the consumption of clover-heads fashioned a persistent pulp in the molar of the rabbit, while forest fruits determined a limited growth in the molar of its fellow-rodent, the squirrel. The whole doctrine of organic transformations, or formations, through the influence of external conditions, is infected with this fallacy of reasoning. I am not denying the co-ordinations alleged, but I choose to trace them to intelligible and real causes.

The scientist, in pronouncing upon causal relations among his phenomena, is in danger of committing the logical error of *post hoc, propter hoc*. The fundamental conception of the doctrine of the derivation of species, under any of its aspects, is a case of *post hoc, propter hoc*. While there is not an undoubted instance of the derivation of a genuine species, its possibility is a mere hypothesis;[1] and the assertion that *all* species are de-

[1] The author would be sorry to indulge in dogmatism on this question. Recent observations have shown the possibility of structural changes of great significance, one of the most interesting of which is cited from the *Zeitschrift für Wissenschaftliche Zoölogie*, which represents a minute

rivative is a somewhat hazardous assumption. The direct observations which we have been able to make on the serial rela-

---

crustacean varying, with increase of the saltness of the water, from a specific form known as *Artemia salina* to another specific form known as *Artemia Milhauseni*, and with decrease in the saltness of the water varying inversely (*Popular Science Monthly*, vol. ix., p. 122). Even this is less striking than the transformation of *Siredon lichenoides* (observed by Professor Marsh) induced, under change of habitat, by which a transition was effected not only from one supposed species to another, but from one recognized genus to another, and even from a group (Perennibranchiata) commonly regarded as of ordinal value, to another group (Caducibranchiata) often regarded as a distinct order. Obviously, however, such examples remain, for the present, open to the explanation that naturalists have overestimated or underestimated the relative value of different categories of characters (mistaking certain ones for specific which are only varietal), or have assumed as adult and ultimate states those which are merely developmental; as in the remarkable instances of Medusæ, where, as an illustration, the embryonic stages of a single individual were described as four genera, *Scyphistoma*, *Strobila*, *Ephyra*, and *Aurelia* (Packard, "Life Histories of Animals," p. 68; Clark, "Mind in Nature," p. 67-72).

Since the foregoing note was penned, the researches of American zoölogists have made it appear that a large proportion of the recognized species of birds, mammals, and fresh-water mollusks of our country are no more than geographical varieties, having, of course, common origins. Yet we have been no less positive about the fixity of these supposed specific types than, on the same grounds, we might continue to be, in respect to specific types still recognized. If we must admit that so many "good species" have had common origins, we may as well admit that all good species have been probably derived from common origins, and thus the barrier to acceptance of the derivative hypothesis would be completely broken down. In the judgment of the writer, the evidence for derivation has been continually accumulating, and, *pari passu*, the difficulties encountered by it have disappeared. This admission, however, concerns the theory only as *a mode of succession of phenomena* and as *an explanation of the material conditions and physiological instrumentalities* under which and through which the succession is effectuated by some cause existing without the province of science. It is made, also, in view of the entire range of evidence—geo-

tions of species disclose the existence of obstacles which, so far as we know, have never been surmounted. The fossil treasures of our continent furnish us, in successive ages, a series of equine quadrupeds with a progressively diminishing development of toes, ending with the solidungulate horse. Derivation assumes that these belong to one genealogical line; while it is perfectly obvious that this set of facts, taken by itself, is entirely consistent with the creation hypothesis. The gigantic basal inconsequence of a theory which deduces material continuity from a simple succession of terms is, nevertheless, greatly palliated by its harmony and parallelism with the phenomena of embryonic development, and with recently established facts of variability of species; and I do not think any man authorized to deny dogmatically that specific derivation is the method of nature.

Equally unfounded in reason or science is Mr. Spencer's assumption that instincts are inherited and accumulated experiences "registered in the organism," and that our intuitive ideas are "organically remembered" experiences. No glimmer of evidence exists of any such connection between instinct or intuition and ancestry; while all attainable evidence shows that, besides the absolute lack of qualitative resemblance between instinct or intuition and its alleged cause, the instincts and intu-

---

logical, zoölogical, embryological, and morphological—and not on the naked evidence of a few nicely graduated successions of forms.

On the geographical variations of American species, see, for *Birds*, Baird, "The Distribution and Migration of North American Birds," in Amer. Jour. Sci. and Arts, vol. xli., Jan. and March, 1866; Allen, Proc. Boston Soc. Nat. Hist., vol. xv.; Ridgway, Amer. Jour. Sci. (3), iv., Dec., 1872, and vol. v.; for *Mammals*, Baird, "Pacific R. R. Reports," vol. viii.; Allen, Proc. Boston Soc. Nat. Hist., 1874, vol. xv.; for *Birds* and *Mammals*, Yarrow, "Wheeler Survey," vol. v., chap. i., 1876; Morse, Popular Science Monthly, Nov. and Dec., 1876; for *Mollusks*, Cooper, Proc. Cal. Acad. Nat. Sci., vol. v., p. 128; Weatherby, Proc. Cincinnati Soc. Nat. Sci., June, 1876.

itions are the most absolutely fixed and secularly invariable elements in the system of life, and are as distinctly operative in the brute as in man.

Not unfrequently the phenomena which challenge our investigation sustain relations of simple concomitancy or parallelism; and when such relations appear tolerably uniform, it is natural to suspect some intercausal connection between them, while in truth nothing of the kind may exist; and their parallelism may result from a common relation to some higher cause. The improvement of the tactual sense in the ascending series of animal forms proceeds *pari passu*, with improving intelligence; and Mr. Spencer has assumed, accordingly, that intelligence is developed by improved tactual organs. Now, there is much better reason for affirming that improved intelligence causes improved organs; for it is obvious, from considerations already presented, that external conditions are not causes at all, but, at best, only conditions; and still less could they become the cause of a result qualitatively diverse; while intelligence, as we are conscious, is gifted with the power of causation. But in truth neither is the cause of the other; though superior intelligence is the condition of improved coordinate faculties in the organism which is its instrument. The whole catalogue of needs and accompanying instruments for their gratification belongs to this category; as well as the parallel phenomena of mind and brain, from which Dr. Carpenter has illogically generalized his strange doctrine of "unconscious cerebration," while others have been led to conceive of thought as a "secretion of the brain."

The assignment of an uncertified antecedent for cause is but one degree worse than the assignment of an inadequate cause. As no stream can flow higher than its source, so no cause can produce an effect greater than itself. This recognized necessity of things is disregarded in that phase of the derivative theory which contemplates organic traits augmented by inheritance. Inheritance transmits what it receives—no more. If, in the course of generations, a character become more and more developed, we discover the action of a constant force loading more and more into the vehicle of inheritance.

We must now endeavor to approach more closely to the real objective ground of phenomena. We have assumed that an external world is a reality. We all know that its phenomena have been investigated by Science until the chain of causation has been traced back to portions of matter which elude observation; and, by a leap, she has concluded that divisibility extends to those inconceivably smaller portions called molecules and atoms. These supposed atoms are, then, the ultimate realities of science; and all other forms and conditions of material substance result from their mutual interactions. The interactions of atoms and their resulting aggregates are admitted to be the effects of causes. The universal and individual reason would rebel against the converse hypothesis. Now, those causes lying out upon the utmost verge of intellectual exploration have been designated forces. Their modes of activity are their "laws," and produce, severally, those correlate orders of phenomenal sequence called the "laws" of phenomena. Now, force, it must be perceived, is the name of an entity unknown to science. It is another symbolical term employed for convenience, the symbolism of which, as in other cases, long usage is liable to disguise. We are absolutely certain, nevertheless, that the cause called force is a reality.

Where, now, does this reality reside? I do not inquire where it acts, but where, in reference to matter, is its own subjective essence? Here opinion bifurcates. A few maintain that matter itself is the subjective ground of force, while others believe that force is external to matter. Suppose we assume matter itself to be the author of energy. The supposition involves the absurdity of confounding subject and object. Moreover, as matter must be either intelligent or unintelligent, we may suppose, at first, that it is unintelligent. If unintelligent, then the interaction of dead atoms gives rise to a universe of phenomena among which are life, volition, and thought. I am willing to consider as final the admissions of Tyndall and Dubois-Reymond on this point, both of whom explicitly assert the impossibility of eliciting intellectual fire from the collision of dead atoms.([1]) If the force-atom is not unintelligent, it is intelligent, and we have a universe with an infinitude of atomic intelligences, acting, nevertheless, in infinite and eternal harmony among themselves; or else the universe as a whole is one intelligence, and objectivity in respect to it is totally annihilated. Every thing which *is*, is not a manifestation of the Supreme, but a part of it. Of these two alternatives, the first is a more startling hypothesis than that of the living monads of Leibnitz; since these were not the seat of ultimate cause, but subsisted under it. It may be pronounced infinitely improbable, and dismissed from consideration. The second alternative, which identifies nature with one supreme intelligence, is pantheism, the credibility of which I have no space, at present, to discuss, beyond the suggestion already laid down.([2])

The other supposition which may be made in reference to the ultimate seat of energy views it as external to matter—that is, an entity of which matter is neither a part nor the whole. This entity may be considered as intelligent or unintelligent. If unintelligent, we have no cause for life, volition, and intelligence more promising than when we sought it from unintelligent atoms. If we suppose the ultimate ground of force to be intelligent, we have an adequate explanation of vi-

---

([1]) Tyndall, "Belfast Address," pp. 68, 87; Dubois-Reymond, "Ueber die Grenzen des Naturerkennens," pp. 20, 29.

([2]) Helmholtz considers matter resting and inactive in itself, but yet, in some strange way, as animated with varying forces. The definition implies that the ultimate cause—that is, the cause of the atomic forces with which matter is endowed—is something external to matter.

tal and mental phenomena in the world, and an immediate and all-sufficient explanation of the rational method which knits creation into a web of relationships.

This conception of supreme, intelligent power, enthroned at the fountain head of phenomena, and displaying its activity in force acting upon atoms and aggregates of matter, does not differ, so far as this qualification goes, from the conceptions set forth by Spencer, Huxley, Tyndall, and Dubois-Reymond. Organization, like crystallization, flows from an impulse imparted to material atoms.

Now, let us look at the significance of this position. The whole range of molecular activities proceeds from the exertion of intelligent activity from without. That is, wherever and whenever those activities exist, there such energy is exerted. If molecular attraction and repulsion, which number organization among their results, are but force exerted from without by supreme intelligent cause, then such cause has been active, not alone at the beginning of existence, but through the whole history of molecular activities since the world began; and continues to act in the myriad phenomena of daily observation. The only alternative to this sweeping conclusion is that which contemplates supreme cause as exerting only an initial energy, the currents of which sweep through infinite years and infinite existence. This would imply that the molecular forces of the present are either exerted by dead matter, or are not original, but simply transmitted, forces. The first supposition is contrary to the premise. The second is the view commonly entertained; and it resolves the universe into a dead mechanism. There are grave difficulties which oppose it. First, the molecular activities of to-day are universally believed to be identical in nature with those which have always been manifest in matter, and hence, if the first motions were imparted by intelligent being, all are. Secondly, we have no knowledge or room to conjecture that molecular force has undergone any change since the morning of material existence. Thirdly, it is out of harmony with the facts of the moral consciousness to posit supreme causation at a point so remote from the present. Fourthly, the molecular forces are probably one: this is the demand of philosophy and the foreshadowed verdict of science. The atoms also, by the general admission of physicists, are of one kind. Now, it is unreasonable to affirm that one identical, unintelligent, involuntary force or impulse, acting upon one unintelligent, involuntary set of atoms, can give rise to the varied classes of material phenomena. It seems to me a far more rational resort to abandon the hypothesis of blind impulse running on in pursuance of an initial energy, and recognize, as Sir William Thompson has himself suggested, the immediate presence of first cause in all the passing activities of the material world.

This, of course, is a restoration of the very power which, according to Tyndall, antiquity invoked science to overthrow. But science herself has brought us to a situation which suggests and commends this alternative. It does not follow, however, that the universe must be again subjected to the dominion of capricious will. It is demonstrable that the universe is not so ruled; and, in view of the conclusion reached, it appears that supreme spontaneity wills to act according to fixed methods. It is surely as easy to refer the regularity of phenomena to discerning mind as to blind mechanism.

It is a common phraseology of science to speak of heat, light, and other forms of energy as "modes of motion." This form of expression is inexact, and opens the way to logical subreptions and other fallacious procedures. A mode of motion is some kind of motion, and, as such, implies *a thing moved* and *a mover*. The thing moved is an atom or molecule; the mover is the real energy to which thought is habitually directed when we speak of molecular force. Motion, instead of being an ultimate physical cause, is merely an effect. Now, it is true that the real cause may produce—does produce, various modes of motion, one of which may be styled heat; another, light; and so on; and these motions, in accordance with the law of "continuity of motion," or "persistence of force," may be propagated indefinitely along the lines which characterize respectively the several species of energy so named. Used in this sense, however, heat and light are no longer energies; and exact science should desist from discoursing about them as such.

Now, it seems to me that, by a defensible process of reasoning, the conclusion has been reached that the ultimate ground of physical force is voluntary intelligence. This ground may be reached from another datum. The only mode of causation of which we have any knowledge is that of which we are conscious—the exercise of free-will suggested by motive, prompted by desire, and directed by intelligence. By a compulsion of the reason, we feel ourselves under the necessity, when thinking of cause, to think of it as we know it. This mandate of the universal reason possesses the same authority as any other; and, if we recognize at all the validity of our necessary intuitions, or the authority of the common consent of humanity, we are bound to recognize the truth of this indication of the nature of causation.

Again, it is a datum of the universal consciousness that relations of order, fitness, adaptation, utility, imply intelligence. Now, the universe abounds in relations which, within the sphere of human affairs, would be pronounced such relations; and hence, by a necessary law of reason, we affirm that the cause of the universe is intelligent; and this attribute, by the necessary law of substance, we posit in real being.([1])

([1]) It may be observed that Kant's opinion of the insufficiency of the cosmological and teleological arguments for the existence of God is determined by his neglect of the "law of substance," or the ontological intuition which carries the reason across the chasm which separates the world of phenomena from the realm of real being.

If, then, a voluntary intelligence is the ultimate ground of all causation, and this intelligence chooses to act according to methods so uniform that, as in the movements of a piece of mechanism, sequences can be predicated on given relations of things, it only remains to make two further important points. The first is, that we discern more than a single mode of activity; in other words, the forces of nature are not all mutually convertible. Some of the molecular forces seem to be so. Heat may perhaps be transformed into electricity; electricity into heat, and so on. And yet even among these we note a want of similarity. Magnetism and electricity are polar forces; but it is not probable that heat, light, and affinity are such. Though light and heat are both molecular vibrations, and hence congeneric, they can hardly be regarded as conspecific, equivalent, and intertransmutable, since they are vibrations of different intensities. Electricity, magnetism, chemical and cohesive attractions, though sustaining undoubted correlations with heat and light, are not known to be vibrations or modes of motion; and it seems like a stretch of evidence to pronounce them conspecific with phenomena which are such. Repulsion, moreover, is a molecular force looming distinctly above the horizon of discovery; and there are indications that its intensity is inversely as the *fifth* power of the distance, while chemical affinity varies inversely as the *cube* of the distance. Gravity is a force varying inversely as the *square* of the distance; and it is, moreover, a force which has never, to our knowledge, resulted from the transformation of any other force; nor does it sustain quantitative or any other correlations with any other force—seeming to be entirely unique, and the most mysterious of the catalogue of forces. Here, then, in the field of inorganic nature, we find forces producing three classes of phenomena—attractions, repulsions, and vibrations. Of the attractions, certain ones affect aggregates, and others atoms and molecules; the former are again differentiated into non-polar (gravitation) and polar (magnetism and electricity), while the latter embrace cohesion and affinity. The vibrations, moreover, are different intensities, as before stated. We have, therefore, three different genera of inorganic force, and at least five species.([1]) Within a few years we confidently expected to find their respective lines of sequence converging at the farther limit of the phenomenal world; but here we are at that limit, and we find five separate threads of causation emerging from the realm beyond that boundary.

In addition to this, we have the phenomena of life, back of which we discern a force which, so far as we know, is not a transformation of any other form of force. True it is, that the vehicle, and instrument, and sensible expression of life is a material organism, whose building up is chiefly the work of molecular forces. True it is, that the mode of expression and manifestation of life is and must be co-ordinated to this sole and material medium of expression. But that which we call life plays the part of a force which conditions the activity of the molecular forces; has never been produced by the transmutation of any of them; can not be approached by any of the methods of physics, nor brought, like a physical force, within the grasp of numerical formulation.

The other point to be noted is, that the supreme, intelligent Spontaneity, as we are thus led by science and reason to think it, is revealed to us in our own mental constitution, whose laws

[1] Attractions between:
- Aggregates:
  - Non-polar .... (inverse square) .. Gravitation.
  - Polar:
    - In magnets .... Magnetism.
    - In electrics .... Electricity.
- Atoms and Molecules:
  - Atoms, and like molecules .... Cohesion.
  - Unlike molecules .... (inverse cube) ... Affinity.

Repulsions .... (inverse fifth power). Repulsion.

Vibrations of:
- Low intensity .... Heat.
- High intensity .... Light.

Mechanical force and motion, so far as I can see, are always effects of one or more of the above forms of force, or of animal volition, or of vital force.

afford us the only attainable ground of certainty; whose delegated spontaneity is a picture of the absolute Will; whose intelligence takes hold on the thoughts expressed in the cosmos, and finds them comprehensible, admirable, and satisfying; and whose conscience, while it finds among men the fitting theatre for its activities, discovers, in the supreme entity which we have disclosed, the sufficient ground for its authority and basis for its hopes.

Let me now attempt, in a concise manner, by way of recapitulation, to draw out in historical order the steps and circumstances in the genesis and constitution of our notion of causation in the existing universe.

1. I dismiss the consideration of all secondary causation. The phrase is a misnomer. There is no real cause which can be disclosed as an effect; *first cause is only cause.* That must be an intelligent spontaneity, and must act without intermediation or "instrumental causation."

2. The notion of causation implies *correlative subjectivity and objectivity* — a thing acting and a thing acted upon — a causative spontaneity and a possibility of its action otherwise than in and upon itself. In all causation, except a primordial creative act, objectivity is a reality—in primordial creation it is a potentiality. This dual necessity of subjective agent and objective possibility of effect implies, in every case of actual causative effort, a differentiation of active and passive existence; and hence renders irrational the theory of "monism" and its corollary "pantheism" under all its aspects.

3. The *subject must be self-conscious* — conscious of its own existence and power of determination. This necessity is the ground of "personality;" and it implies that the subject is a "free agent."

4. The subject *must form a concept of an effect*—a thing not yet existing, or an event not yet enacted.

5. The subject must be *conscious of the relation between effect*

12

and cause — the intuition of causality must arise in the consciousness. This intuition certainly embraces the notion of efficiency and adequacy; and, in all cases of intermediate causation, it implies, also, that the effect must be congeneric with its cause. In intermediate causation we have merely a given energy transmitted—no new energy put forth. This must retain through an indefinite series of terms the same quality and quantity as belonged to the initial and only logically causative act. Original causation, on the contrary, is not bound by any qualitative relation between cause and effect — though, in the finite sphere, subject to other conditions which may variously restrict the field of effects.

6. The subject must be conscious of *motive prompting to produce the effect conceived*. There must always be a *reason why* an intelligence acts one way rather than another. This necessary "reason why" is often styled the "final cause."

7. The subject *may cognize a contingency existing*—that is, a fact constant or varying which sustains some established relation to the effect contemplated. Such fact, if it exist, becomes a "condition" or "conditioning cause."

8. The subject must become *conscious of the influence of the contingency* (if it exist) *upon the conscious motive*—adding to or taking from it.

9. The subject must next be conscious of a *desire to produce the effect conceived*. This desire would be modified in a manner co-ordinated with the contingently modified motive.

10. The subject must next be conscious of a formed *intention to produce the effect*. "Intentionality," whose genesis arises at this point, incloses all the mental acts which precede—self-consciousness, intuition of causal relation, motivity, perception of conditionality (if existing), and desire (conditionally modified).

11. The subject must finally *will the effect*—modified by the contingent fact, if it exist.

This is the whole process of original causation as represented in individual consciousness, which, unless the harmonies of the universe be fatally misleading, is the finite reflection of the method of infinite causation.

In the case, however, of finite causality, as in the human will, every effect external to the mind itself must be reached through instrumentalities. In most cases, the final determination does not reach immediately the external result toward which volition is ultimately directed. It reaches, nevertheless, another result which, however it may escape observation, is the effect which figures in the foregoing account. This effect is a muscular movement adapted to serve as the first term in the series of intermediate causes. After this, the whole history of causal efficiency, as above laid down, must necessarily be repeated for each separate term in the series of intermediate causes. In the mean time, complications arise. The instruments employed become effective on condition that the forces of nature prove regularly operative; and thus supreme causation may be summoned to conspire with human volition in the accomplishment of the most trivial result.

X.

IS GOD COGNIZABLE BY REASON?[1]

"Knowledge, accordingly, is characterized by faith; and faith, by a kind of divine, mutual, and reciprocal correspondence, becomes characterized by knowledge."—CLEMENS ALEX., *Stromata*, book ii., chap. iv.

"THE existence of God," writes one of the most original of the scholastic fathers, who is said to have rescued Aristotle from atheism and secured him for orthodoxy, "*can be known by natural reason*, as is said in the first of Romans; and this and other truths of the same kind are not properly so much articles of faith as *preambles to these articles*, our faith presupposing natural knowledge, as grace presupposes nature."[2] This thought is the theme of the volume before us.

We have here a contribution to religious philosophy which is an honor to American letters. The treatment is worthy of the theme, and the theme is worthy of philosophy. It is an essay at the old problem so profoundly pondered by Socrates and Plato, Anselm and Leibnitz, Descartes and Newton, Barrow and Butler—the attempt to construct a formal proof of an affirmation which rises spontaneously in the human soul, and around which cluster the profoundest emotions and the highest hopes of humanity.

The lapse of twenty-five centuries has not diminished the interest of the human mind in the legitimate grounds of its irre-

---

[1] "Christianity and Greek Philosophy; or, the Relations between Spontaneous and Reflective Thought in Greece and the Positive Teaching of Christ and his Apostles." By B. F. Cocker, D.D., Professor of Moral and Mental Philosophy in the University of Michigan. New York, 1870.

[2] Aquinas, "Summa Theologiæ," art. iii., Quæst. 2.

sistible theistic faith. The keenness of the search has indeed been sharpened. Every new unfolding of truth in the realm of science or the empyrean of speculation is promptly questioned as to the testimony which it has to render respecting the supreme ground of all truth. Modern thought holds no system too sacred for its scrutiny. Decayed timbers must be hewed out; and, if the fabric fall in the excision, the remorseless axe must do its work.

It is a questioning, relentless, irreverent spirit. It strikes many a blow heedlessly, recklessly, malignantly. Commissioned to cut out the effete and the false, its appetite seems whetted for mere destruction. Christianity appears before its bar to show cause why it should not be expunged as a superstition; and even the ancient religion of humanity is challenged again and again to uncover its granite foundations, and demonstrate its right to stand.

It is not an age in which Christian believers can rest securely upon their traditions. If Christian faith survives, it will not be through the grace of its enemies, but the vigor of its defenders. In the midst of the conflict, it does not need even the weapon of an enemy to inflict a wound. Christian believers must arm themselves with the alertness and learning of their times; and it must ever be remembered that the antique armor which once served for adequate defense is not a muniment against the implements of modern warfare. No, the intellectual activity of the age must pervade the ranks of Christianity. The Christian system, being grounded in reason, rests securely beneath the ægis of reason. Its field is as wide as the realm of reason. All philosophy and all science are its legal inheritance.

Christianity must recognize its alliance with all truth. It is not, indeed, peculiarly a system of philosophy, but it is a *fundamental tone* to which all science and philosophy must be attuned; not because Christianity is our faith, but because underneath Christianity lie the eternal foundations on which reposes *all that is true;* and any system resting on other foundation floats in air. Because Christianity is co-ordinated with all real truth, it is concerned in every discovery of truth, and stands foremost in welcoming and assimilating results, and stimulating original thought. For the same reason, the teacher or defender of Christianity must place himself in relations with the whole field of thought before he can discern the system in its symmetry, or know what is alien to it, and what is its own. The defense of Christianity, in our times, is a conflict located upon the field reached in the march of modern thought. Thunders, *ex cathedrâ*, are no longer heard in the camp of the enemy. They are like the sounding of gongs over the heads of the sappers attacking the deep foundations of the fortress, or the scolding of cowards frightened to the covert of their caves. Go out, strike the Philistines at Gath, and the God of David will strengthen your arm.

The work of Dr. Cocker is, in effect, a brave defense of the fundamental truths of Christianity. It is a grammar of religious thought, illustrated by citations from Grecian thinkers. It is an attempt to introduce to personal consciousness the axioms of religious philosophy, and familiarize it with their characteristics and implications. But the method is not alone abstract. The necessary laws and tendencies of human thought are illustrated by the history of Greek philosophy; and the necessary relation of all correct thinking to a correct conception of the Christian system is also exemplified in the gradual preparation of the philosophic mind of Greece for the reception of ideas peculiarly Christian.

The work consists essentially of three parts: 1. *The fundamental ideas of religious philosophy.* 2. *Illustration of these in the results of Grecian speculation.* 3. *Christian revelation a final disclosure divinely correlated to the religious instincts of man and the previous education of the race.* Such, at least, if not the strict arrangement of the work, is a classification of its ideas, of which we now proceed to give a condensed statement.

In the preliminary chapter, the author passes in review the city and the men of Athens, and the physical features of the Grecian peninsula in general. In commenting upon the connection between national character and physical surroundings, he takes occasion to remark that the latter are merely modifying forces; while human spontaneity—reason and will—in connection with a superintending Providence, are the fundamental forces which give direction to national development. Human will impresses even the face of nature;[1] and, although great men are generally mere mouth-pieces of their generation, they seem sometimes appointed by Divine Providence to antagonize the spirit of their age, and achieve moral revolutions. Still, physical surroundings impart individuality to national character; and this is well exemplified in the Hellenic traits. The central position of Greece in the civilized world led to a *commercial* development, and this was favored by a maritime climate. The configuration of the surface and the shore-line contributed to *individuality;* its scenery impressed the *æsthetic* character. The Athenians were ardent, vivacious, and of independent spirit. Their intellect tended to observation and thought, and their language was adapted to be the vehicle of the highest philosophy, and the medium of the loftiest civilization attainable without Christianity.

Before proceeding to discuss the religion of the Athenians, our author furnishes a condensed and masterly exhibit of the philosophy of religion in general. Defining religion as "a form of thought, feeling, and action which has the *Divine* for its ob-

---

[1] On the "Power of Mind over Nature," see Cocker, in *Methodist Quarterly Review*, January and April, 1870; and Marsh, "Man and Nature;" and, on human will as an original spontaneous cause, see "Whedon on the Will," p. 42, and elsewhere; also Cocker, in *Methodist Quarterly Review*, October, 1864.

ject, basis, and end," and enunciating the fact of history and ethnology that "religious ideas and sentiments have prevailed among all nations," he runs his scalpel through the joints of the various theories of religious phenomena which do not recognize their germs in the constitution of the human mind. This chapter, by itself, is a neat, clean-cut monograph, and might well be made a tract for more general reading. The Comtean theory, that *religious phenomena have arisen from the fear of unseen powers*, falls with the overthrow of Comte's theory of the "law of the three states" in human development—the theological, the metaphysical, and the positive.(¹) The Hegelian theory, that *religion is a part of an evolution of the Absolute, attaining its fullest self-consciousness in philosophy*, next receives an exposition (if exposition be possible) and an exposure(²)—for propositions which categorically contradict the axioms of reason(³) admit only of exposure, and not of refutation. The theory of Jacobi and Schleiermacher, that *religion has its foundation in feeling*, is indefensible, since feeling can not be the source of ideas; and, further, any *cognition* of Deity alleged as *correlated* to the feeling of the Divine must be logically preceded by *ideas of reason*.(⁴) The theory of Cousin,

---

(¹) P. 57–65. See, also, a sharp criticism of this fundamental position in Huxley's "Lay Sermons, Addresses, and Reviews," p. 156–164; and for a consummate dissection of the "Philosophie Positive," see Martineau's "Essays," vol. i., p. 1–62.

(²) P. 65–69.

(³) Like this: "Being and nothing are identical." The fundamental principle of Hegelianism is the paradox that "contraries are identical." But, since the time of Aristotle, the "law of non-contradiction" has been accepted by all logicians as a fundamental law of thought.

(⁴) P. 70–77. Is not this criticism based on a misconception of the sense in which Jacobi employs the term "feeling?" All mental states may be regarded as "feeling." Brown uses "feeling" for consciousness ("Philosophy of the Human Mind," § xi.). All cognition involves a kind of *intellectual feeling*—the subjective factor of consciousness. J. S. Mill

that *religion has its outbirth in the spontaneous apperceptions of the reason*, is stated and substantiated as a rational account of the genesis of the *idea of God*, but found defective as a philosophy of the phenomena of religion (p. 78-86). Finally, the theory that *religious phenomena had their origin in external revelation*, is shown to be unsatisfactory,([1]) because, 1. It is improbable that truths so important should have been intrusted to tradition alone; 2. The theory does not account for the *universality* of religious beliefs and practices; 3. Verbal revelation could *convey no ideas* to a being destitute of antecedent notions of divine things (p. 86-95).

As the result of this survey, our author concludes with the following proposition: "The universal phenomenon of religion has originated in the *a priori* apperceptions of reason, and the natural, instinctive feelings of the heart, which, from age to age, have been vitalized, unfolded, and perfected by supernatural communications and testamentary revelations (p. 97). It thus contains an element of REASON, an element of FEELING, and an element of REVELATION.

The way is now opened for a statement of the higher characteristics of the religion of the Athenians. Numerous evidences, presented to the eyes of St. Paul as he entered their city, convinced him that they were "every way more than or-

---

uses the term in this sense, "Every thing is a feeling of which the mind is conscious" ("System of Logic," American edit., p. 34). The *sensus numinis* evidently is not supposed to be a distinct definable cognition, but only the analogue of the *sensus vagus*, or vital sense, in the field of sensations. Jacobi calls it "*Glaube*," and compares it with our "faith" in the intuitions of sense; and, finally, in a later work ("Ueber das Unternehmen des Kriticismus, die Vernunft zu Verstande zu bringen," 1802), the faculty which he had before called "Faith" he now names "Reason"—*Vernunft*. This would make the corresponding "feeling" something more specific than the *sensus vagus*—a real intuition of God.

([1]) On this, see Cocker, in *Methodist Quarterly Review*, April, 1862.

dinarily religious."(¹) This character the apostle had reason to ascribe to them in a sense entirely strict and legitimate. Religion, in its essential character, being something more than a system of dogmatic teaching, and consisting in "a mode of thought, feeling, and action determined by our consciousness of dependence on a Supreme Being" (p. 107), the numberless temples and shrines of Athens testified to their excessive "carefulness about religion." Leaving their idolatries and superstitions for the moment in the background, certain noble and normal outcrops of the religious nature were clearly discernible in the religious philosophy of the Athenians. They had some faith in the being and providence of God (p. 107–109). They felt a consciousness of dependence upon God (p. 110–117). One of their own poets (Aratus) had said:

> "Jove's presence fills all space, upholds this ball;
> All need his aid; his power sustains us all,
>   For we his offspring are."(²)

The same sentiment had been hymned in the same city by Cleanthes. This feeling of dependence and sense of obligation lie at the foundation of all religion. The Athenians also *possessed the religious emotions flowing from the feeling of dependence*—fear of offending the divinity which they felt over them, and an instinctive yearning after the Invisible. Finally, they felt *a consciousness of sin, and made piacular sacrifices.*

But, turning to contemplate the dark side of the Athenian religion, we are confronted by the shocking realities of polytheism and idolatry. Modern inquiry, however, in penetrating beneath the exterior of these religious monstrosities, finds them

---

(¹) This is Cudworth's rendering of κατὰ πάντα ὡς δεισιδαιμονεσίρους (Acts xvii., 22), and with this exegetical writers substantially agree. The first chapter on the religion of the Athenians appeared in the *Methodist Quarterly Review* for April, 1869.

(²) Aratus, "The Phenomena," book v., 5.

to be mere excrescences upon a purer and simpler faith—a degeneracy from a state of primitive monotheism which seems to underlie the religion of humanity.(¹) And even during the reign of these abominations, the *élite* in the realm of thought looked upon them with horror, and denounced them with a boldness tempered only by an instinctive respect for popular opinions. The genesis and significance of the Greek mythology are discussed in this connection in words which ought to be made the preamble to every Christian text-book of the classical authors (p. 128–160). We commend the discussion earnestly to the attention of those bees in the world of thought who love to extract the honey even of poisonous flowers. Our author regards the Grecian mythology as a grand symbolic representation of the Divine as manifested in nature and Providence (p. 139).(²)

We reach here the heart of the discussion: *Is God cognizable by Reason?* If a religious nature and destination appertain to man; if certain fundamental principles are found underlying the Grecian and all other religions; if it be a clear presumption that the reason of man is furnished with necessary ideas or laws of thought correlated to the instinct and emotion of worship, let us see whether it be possible to give these ideas an articulate expression, and reproduce the spontaneous and instantaneous deduction by which reason bridges the gulf which

---

(¹) This position is earnestly controverted by certain writers, who hold that mankind has undergone a continuous and uniform development, religiously, from a state of fetichism, and that fetichism is incompatible with a sense of theistic unity. Having given this subject, however, an independent study, we have been surprised at the copiousness of the proof that Dr. Cocker's position is a valid one.

(²) He draws largely from the learned dissertation on this subject by Cudworth, "Intellectual System of the Universe," especially chap. iv. The reader will fall upon a coincident line of thought in Müller, "Chips from a German Workshop," vol. ii., p. 142–169.

separate the changeful and finite from the permanent, infinite, and eternal.

I. The idea of God is a common phenomenon of the universal intelligence. The proofs of this (pp. 89, 90) are found in common observation, in the voice of history, and in the concurrent testimony of travelers among savage tribes.

II. The idea of God, in its completeness, is not held to be a simple, direct, and immediate intuition of the reason alone, independently of all experience and all knowledge of the external world. It is a complex idea—a logical deduction from self-evident truths given in sense, conscience, and reason. The logical evolution of the theistic concept begins with the disengagement of certain ideas formulating themselves in primitive judgments which the mind intuitively perceives to be true necessarily and universally. Such are "Every event implies a cause;" "Every attribute implies a substance." These *à priori* judgments constitute the major premise of the theistic syllogism. The minor premise is furnished by the facts of experience and observation. From these facts, the *à priori* laws of reason necessitate, as a conclusion, the affirmation of a God as the only valid explanation of the phenomena. Historically, or actually, the process is reversed. The phenomena of experience first come before the mind, and, in their presence, the latent laws of thought or primitive ideas of the reason are roused into efficiency, and the judgment, by a natural and spontaneous logic, free from all reflection, and, consequently, from all possibility of error, affirms a necessary relation between the facts of experience and the *à priori* ideas of the reason.(¹) The demonstration consists necessarily of *à priori* as well as *à posteriori* elements. It is of no use to point to the events and changes of the material universe as proof of the existence of a *First Cause*,

---

(¹) For a lucid treatment of this subject, see Cocker, *Methodist Quarterly Review*, April, 1862.

unless we take account of the universal and necessary truth that "every change refers itself to an adequate cause." There is no logical conclusiveness in the assertion of Paley, that "*experience* teaches us that a designer must be a person," because, as Hume justly remarks, our "experience" is narrowed down to a mere point, and "can not be a rule for a universe; but there is an infinitude of force in that *dictum* of reason that "intelligence, self-consciousness, and self-determination necessarily constitute personality."

III. The universe demands a God as its adequate explanation. The attempts of Positivism are futile and absurd. Mankind can not be prevented from striving to pass beyond phenomena. Positivism is possible only through transcendental ideas. We can not even have a cognition of phenomena without the play of the regulative ideas of the reason. No notion of realities underlying phenomena can be given by the phenomena themselves. It is given by reason in the presence of phenomena. These *à posteriori* and *à priori* data mutually condition each other. The relation between them is a law of thought and *a law of things*. It is a universal and necessary correlation which impels us to affirm that a living power is the correlative of the changing phases of the sensible world; and intelligence the correlative of the order which we discover in them. The author has given us an exhaustive table of the facts of the universe, material and mental, which may be regarded as " hints and adumbration of the ultimate ground, and reason, and cause of the universe" (p. 175–177).

It thus appears that the phenomena of the universe can not be explained on the basis of Positivism; and this, though we admit, as Descartes, Pascal, Leibnitz, Saisset, Mahan, and others have mistakenly and fatally done, that the universe is infinite. Its infinity is only a mathematical infinity, which might more correctly be styled *indefinity*. Infinity is not predicable of quantity. This principle solves the problem of Kant's "Antinomies," and constitutes a complete refutation of Hume on the eternity of the universe.(¹)

IV. In the field of consciousness are discovered elements or principles which, in their regular and normal development, transcend the limits of consciousness, and attain to a knowledge of Absolute Being, Absolute Reason, Absolute Good—that is, *God*. The mind is in possession of universal, necessary, absolute ideas, as the idea of space, the idea of cause. Reason, distinct from sense, is the organ or faculty for the cognition of these ideas. Their elimination from the mass of mixed knowledge in the mind is a work which has engaged the attention of Plato, Aristotle, Kant, Cousin, and others, but it is yet incomplete. Our author presents a neat, compact, and symmetrical table of the principal ideas of this class. Here, in two pages, is the quintessence of the speculative thought of two chiliads of years.

Our author next passes in review, through two chapters, those philosophic theories which lead to the *denial that God is cognizable by reason*. Our appropriate limits do not permit a reproduction of even the gist of the discussion. J. S. Mill and the Idealists, Comte and the Materialists, Hamilton and the Nescientists, Watson and the Dogmatists, are taken in hand by turns, and in a few incisive sentences, each of which reaches to the marrow of the subject, each school is shown to be doing violence to the inexorable laws of thought. Positivism infracts the principle of causality in denying that we can proceed beyond a knowledge of phenomena and their laws. It dishonors the principle of intentionality in affirming that we can only know what *is*, and never *why* it is.(²)

(¹) P. 178–184. This principle has been presented and applied with masterly analysis and force by a writer in the *North American Review*, No. CCV., art. iii., 1864.

(²) In this connection our author rather discredits the "nebular hypothesis," fortifying himself with an array of authorities. It might be said,

The Hamiltonian philosophy of the unconditioned is shown to involve a discrediting of one portion of the testimony of consciousness, and thus a conflict with the fundamental principle of the natural-realistic school. The further examination of this subject is especially able. The Dogmatic theologians are shown to attack the principle of causality in affirming that philosophy can only attain to the idea of an "eternal succession" of phenomena. They attack the principle of the unconditioned in denying that human reason passes spontaneously from the finite to the notion of the infinite. They invalidate, also, the principle of unity and the evidence of the moral intuitions, and fail to discern the real meaning of certain passages of Scripture.([1])

The next six chapters are devoted to an examination of the historical development of Greek philosophy. This may be regarded as another form of proof of the proposition that *God is cognizable by reason.* An inductive generalization from the facts of Greek speculation leads to the affirmation of the proposition. More strictly speaking, however, this part of the work

---

however, that the first cited—Sir William Herschel—was the real originator of the hypothesis (Sir William Herschel in "Philosophical Transactions" for 1811). If this theory is to be decided by a vote, we may cite in the affirmative Arago, Dana, Dawson, Helmholz, Hunt (T. S.), Huggins, Lockyer, Meunier, Mill (J. S.), Newcomb, Nichol, Sæmann, Schellen, Thomson (Sir William), Tyndall, Young, and the generality of geologists and astronomers of the present day. Objectors and objections which date back twenty-five years have lost all weight, in consequence of the new data (especially spectroscopic) furnished by recent science. The reader may consult further the present writer's articles on the "Unity of the Physical World," in the *Methodist Quarterly Review* for April, 1873, and Jan., 1874. [It appears that the author himself (of the work under review) is inclined to yield at the present time to the weight of authority in support of the "nebular hypothesis." See "Theistic Conception of the World," pp. 104, 105, 143, etc.]

([1]) For instance, Acts xvii., 27; Romans i., 19-21, 32.

may be viewed as a citation of illustrations or confirmations of the main thesis.

Following Zeller in the grouping of the schools of Greece, we find that the Pre-Socratic were *physical* in the point of view from which they contemplated the problems of speculative philosophy; the Socratic were *psychological*, and the Post-Socratic were *ethical*. The first make the world the great centre of inquiry; the second, the "ideas" of things — truth and being; the third fall back upon the practical conduct of life as the chief interest in philosophy. We can not follow the author through his compact but lucid digest of the opinions of these noble pioneers of thought. The six chapters form a neat and concise compend of the history of Greek philosophy; not a mere chronological table of facts, but a body of facts imbedded in a matrix of thought—such an exposition as discloses the spinal marrow—the common subjective, animating principle of those three centuries of manly mental struggle. We can only make disconnected reference to some of the prominent conclusions from this survey.

The bifurcation of speculative thought began in the Pre-Socratic age. The Ionian school, from their stand-point, tended toward Sensationalism; and the Italian, from theirs, toward Idealism. The issue, theologically, was material pantheism, on one hand, and ideal pantheism, on the other. These divergent streams of thought had their common source in one fundamental principle or law of the human mind—*the intuition of unity*, or "the desire to comprehend all the facts of the universe in a single formula, and consummate all conditional knowledge in the unity of unconditioned existence." The radical error of Sensationalism is the denial of the validity of the testimony of consciousness in reference to suprasensuous phenomena; while the fatal fault of Idealism is a similar denial in reference to sensuous phenomena. Both alike, by discrediting consciousness in one affirmation, virtually discredit it in all, and set us afloat in an atmosphere of phantoms. From such philosophy no theistic result is possible, save universal skepticism. Accordingly, the Sophists signalize the completion of the first cycle of philosophic thought.

It is interesting to note another evidence that, even in abstract thinking, "there is nothing new under the sun." Hegelianism existed two thousand years before Hegel. Parmenides of Elea held that all phenomenal existences are but modes of the Absolute, and seems to have been the inventor of the aphorisms, "All is one, " "Thought and being are identical." We might add, however, that Heraclitus had previously asserted that contradictory propositions may be consistent.([1])

Socrates, by the inductive use of the phenomena of consciousness, was a patron of the inductive method — a method which Francis Bacon no more originated than he did the other laws of thought. Plato enunciated the "law of sufficient reason"—universally attributed to Leibnitz—in these words: "Whatever is generated is necessarily generated from a certain αἰτίαν"—ground, reason, cause—"for it is wholly impossible that any thing should be generated without a cause." The Ontology of Plato, after having served as a starting-point for other philosophers for a period of twenty centuries, remains to-day nearly the most perfect system extant. The Aristotelian Organon has equally survived the criticisms of the entire course of philosophy. Aristotle proposed three forms of theistic proof: 1. The Ontological, based on our necessary idea of an eternal and immutable *substance*. 2. The Cosmological, based on our necessary idea of *causality* as the correlative of effect, and *intelligence* as the correlative of harmony and contrivance.([2]) 3. The Moral proof.

([1]) Aristotle, "Ethic. Nic.," lib. viii., 1.

([2]) Cosmological, as here used = Ætcological, Cocker + Cosmological, Cocker + Teleological, Cocker = Cosmological, Kant + Physio-Theological, Kant. See sequel of this article.

Pyrrhonism marks the transition from the Socratic to the Post-Socratic schools. In the latter, Epicureanism manifests a decline of the spirit of ontological speculation, and Stoicism signalizes its almost complete supersedure by the ethical spirit.

For us, however, the most important aspects of Greek philosophy are its theological results. These are gathered together in the last two chapters of the work under review. No thoughtful person can glance over this summary without being convinced that Greek philosophy had an important propædeutic office to perform for Christianity. The object of all philosophy is to systematize the results of thought, and attain to a basis of certainty. Its especial aim is the disclosure of the Supreme Reality which underlies the phenomenal world. The correlation of the human mind to the Divine renders this a hopeful effort. Again, the Author of nature is the Author of revelation. The "true light which lighteth every man that cometh into the world" "shone on the mind of Anaxagoras, and Socrates, and Plato, as well as on the mind of Rahab, Cornelius, and the Syrophenician woman, and in a higher form, and with a clearer and richer effulgence, on the minds of Moses, Isaiah, Paul, and John." No wonder, then, that in the teachings of Socrates and Plato we find a striking *harmony* of sentiment, and even form of expression, with some parts of the Christian revelation; and in the speculations of Plato "catch glimpses of a world of ideas not unlike that which Christianity discloses, and hear words not unfamiliar to those who spake as they were moved by the Holy Ghost" (p. 459).

Christianity, if its enunciations would not be nugatory, must sustain some relations to human reason, and to the progressive developments of human thought in the ages before Christ. "Christianity did not break suddenly upon the world as a new commandment, altogether unconnected with the past, and wanting in all points of sympathy and contact with the then present. It proceeded along lines of thought which had been laid through ages of preparation; it clothed itself in forms of speech which had been molded by centuries of education; and it appropriated to itself a moral and intellectual culture which had been effected by long periods of severest discipline. It was, in fact, the consummation of the whole moral and religious history of the world" (pp. 461, 462). Greek civilization sustained direct preparatory relations to the Christian system. It was the most perfect civilization which the world had yet witnessed, and the highest attainable by human nature without the specific reinforcement of moral and religious ideas and demonstrations which was now impending in Christianity. This civilization the conquests of Alexander propagated from Antioch and Alexandria. The Greek language, enriched by Plato and Aristotle, was not only the most copious and perfect of all tongues, but was also the most perfectly adapted to serve as the vehicle of moral and religious, and even Christian, ideas. Greek philosophy, too, had gradually educated the human mind to the contemplation of that purity, holiness, justice, and spirituality which were to characterize pre-eminently the Christian teaching. But philosophy had done its utmost, and mankind had not yet attained to a full and impressive sense of the majesty and holiness and presence of God. It was a moment of despair. It was the grand climacteric in the life of humanity. Paul appeared and preached Christ, and the heart of the Greek bounded responsively.

Let us see a little more specifically what service Greek philosophy rendered to Christianity. We have said it served as an education of the intellect of the race, as Judaism served for the discipline of the religious nature. But all logical training of the intellect leads it toward the same Supreme Reality which Hebrew revelation discloses directly. The growth of philosophy is a reverent approximation toward God. Mankind, like children, first accepted God with a spontaneous faith. Then, like the youth, they plunged into misguided speculations, fruitless sophisms, and distressing doubts. Lastly, like the man of matured wisdom, they attained an age of reflective consciousness, and glimpsed with clearer vision the God who had been at first simply an object of blind faith. In the history of Greece, the Homeric age was the national childhood; the Pre-Socratic the transitional, and the Post-Socratic the philosophic, age. In these facts of intellectual and religious history we discern a true development and a progressive preparation. It is discernible—

I. In the field of theistic conceptions. In this field its tendency was to dethrone the false gods and enthrone the true one. This is seen—

1. In the release of the popular mind from polytheistic notions, and the purifying and spiritualizing of the theistic idea. The idea of a Supreme Power is not the product of philosophy. It is the immanent, spontaneous thought of humanity. Without tuition, or suggestion, man sees God in the impressive phenomena of nature transpiring around him. He translates her mysterious manifestations in the light of the feeling of the divine which bathes his soul. The sun, the mountain, and the storm command his veneration as the manifestations of the felt Deity. Then, in the lapse of time, he forgets their symbolical character and worships them as gods, or as the dwelling-places of gods. He becomes a polytheist; and, in attempting to embody his necessarily anthropomorphic conceptions of his gods, he is led into idolatry. But now, when the era of reflection and inquiry arrives, he discovers the absurdity of many of his theistic notions, and the stubborn inscrutableness of the divine nature, and he begins to fear he has been wholly deluded. He doubts. He surrenders himself to speculation; he seeks for that which must be the first principle of all things. He fancies it discovered in "water," or "air," or "fire." Unsatisfied, he seeks it in "numbers" or in purely abstract "ideas," or it may be an Anaxagoras glimpses it in "mind." But the human

soul still longs for a personal God. "The heart of man cries out for the living God." These abstractions are unsatisfying, and humanity is again skeptical and restless. Now, Socrates and Plato introvert the mental gaze, and, in the analysis of thought, discover elements which at once announce themselves to consciousness as out of necessary relation to the things of time and sense—ideas, truths which are seen to be necessary, universal, and eternal—truths which would beam in the firmament of mind though the worlds cease to exist. These are rays from the eternal source of truth. Here, in this world of ideas, is the only solid ground on which faith and reason may embrace each other. In this eternal reality is the absolute ground of all causality, all thought, all beauty, all goodness.

Such was the progress of theistic speculation in Greece. The inevitable tendency toward a unity served to gradually undermine the popular polytheistic faith which had usurped the simple theism of the earlier ages. The Eleatics rejected the gross anthropomorphism of the Homeric theology. Socrates held that the Supreme Being is the immaterial, infinite Governor of all; that the world bears the stamp of his intelligence, and that he is the author and vindicator of all moral laws. Plato earnestly inveighs against the anthropomorphism and polytheism of the Greek mythology; and having himself risen to purer conceptions of the Deity, he insists that he ought to be represented as he is—without imperfections, the author of all good, and the punisher of sin. "There is no imperfection," says Plato, "in the beauty or goodness of God;" "he is a God of truth, and can not lie;" "he is a being of perfect simplicity and truth in deed and word."[1] Aristotle, though less spiritual, enunciates views entirely incompatible with the popular mythology of the Greeks. Thus, the popular notions of divine existence which had been current from the time of Orpheus and Homer,

---

[1] Plato, "Republic," book ii., § 18-21.

were gradually dissipated, and the way was cleared for Christian theism.

The preparatory office of Greek philosophy, in the region of speculative thought, is seen—

2. In the development of the theistic argument in a logical form. The growth of Greek philosophy evolved in due succession every form of argument employed by modern writers in proof of the being of God. Our author inclines to except the "moral argument;" but we believe that Plato's ontological proof of the existence of the Supreme Good ought to be regarded as involving the moral argument. This, as we shall attempt to show, is but a single aspect or branch of the ontological. We might add the statement more distinctly than Dr. Cocker has presented it, that the argument from "Common Consent" is as old as Socrates.([1]) Universal beliefs were made by the Stoics an argument for the existence of God; and before the Stoics, Alexander of Aphrodisias ascribed great authority to widely prevalent beliefs, "since," he asserts, "mankind generally do not greatly err from the truth."([2]) Cicero declares that "in any matter whatever the consent of all nations is to be reckoned a law of nature;"([3]) and such opinions have received the sanction of modern philosophy.([4])

The four arguments most conspicuously embodied in the philosophy of the ancients are thus formulated by Dr. Cocker (p. 487–494):

(1.) The *Ætiological*([5]) proof, or the argument based on the

---

([1]) Plato, "Apology," § 32.

([2]) "De Fato," ii.; Ritter, "History of Ancient Philosophy," vol. iv., p. 242.

([3]) Cicero, "Tuscul.," i., 13.

([4]) Grotius, "De Jure Belli et Pacis," ii.; Butler, "Analogy" (Introduction); Quatrefages, *Revue des Deux Mondes*, 1860–1861; Saisset, "Essay on Religious Philosophy" (Edinburgh translation), i., 33, note.

([5]) This is the Cosmological proof of Kant.

principle of causality, which may be presented in the following form:

> "All genesis, or becoming, supposes a permanent and uncaused Being, adequate to the production of all phenomena:
>
> "The sensible universe is a perpetual genesis, a succession of appearances; it is always becoming, and never really is:
>
> "Therefore, it must have its cause and origin in a permanent and unoriginated Being adequate to its production."

This argument is enunciated more or less articulately by most of the Greek philosophers, especially Pythagoras, Xenophanes, Zeno of Elea, Anaxagoras, Empedocles, Plato, and Aristotle.

(2.) The *Cosmological*([1]) proof, or the argument based on the principle of order, and thus presented:

> "Order, proportion, harmony, are the product and expression of mind:
>
> "The created universe reveals order, proportion, and harmony:
>
> "Therefore, the created universe is the product of mind."

The fundamental law of thought which underlies this mode of proof was clearly recognized by Pythagoras, and is also elaborated by Plato in his Philosophy of Beauty.

(3.) The *Teleological*([2]) proof, or the argument based on the

---

([1]) This is embraced under the Physico-theological of Kant. The present, however, is a more legitimate use of the word than Kant has made of it, since the primary (and, with the Greeks, the usual) signification of κόσμος is "order." Moreover, as Pythagoras, who first applied κόσμος to the universe, designed especially to express its (numerical) order, Kant has clearly violated the rule of preoccupancy in the attempt to divert the word to another use.

([2]) Embraced under the Physico-theological argument of Kant.

principle of intentionality or final cause, and is presented in the following form:

"The choice and adaptation of means to the accomplishment of special ends suppose an intelligent purpose, a designing mind:

"In the universe we see such choice and adaptation of means to ends:

"Therefore, the universe is the product of an intelligent, personal cause."

This is especially the Socratic proof; but it was also employed by Plato and Aristotle.

(4.) The *Ontological* or *Ideological* proof, or the argument grounded on necessary and absolute ideas, which may be thrown into the following syllogism:

"Every attribute or quality implies a subject, and absolute modes necessarily suppose absolute being:

"Necessary and absolute truths or ideas are revealed in human reason as absolute modes:

"Therefore, universal, necessary, and absolute ideas are modes of the absolute subject—that is, God, the foundation and source of all truth."

This is especially the Platonic mode of proof.

The preparatory office of Greek philosophy is seen—

II. In the department of *ethical* ideas and principles.

1. In the awakening and enthronement of conscience as a law of duty, and the elevation and purification of the moral idea. Here we find an order of succession in the evolution of moral ideas corresponding with that observed in the field of speculative thought. These stages are traceable equally in the individual and the national mind. We recognize (1) in the age of Homer, Hesiod, and the Gnomic poets, and the Seven Wise Men, a period of "popular and unconscious morality;" (2) in the following age, beginning with Protagoras, a "transitional, skeptical, or sophistical period;" and (3) in the So-

cratic age "the philosophic or conscious" period of morality. We must refer the reader to the pages of our author (p. 495–505) for the illustrations and proofs.

2. In the fact that, by an experiment conducted on the largest scale, it demonstrated the insufficiency of reason to elaborate a perfect ideal of moral excellence, and develop the moral forces necessary to secure its realization. The moral idea in Socrates, Plato, Epictetus, Marcus Aurelius, and Seneca rose to a sublime height, and developed a noble and heroic character. Yet the cardinal virtues of the ancient ethical systems are prudence, justice, temperance, and courage. The gentler virtues—humility, meekness, forgiveness of injuries, love of enemies, universal benevolence ("graces which give beauty to character and bless society")—are scarcely known. The inculcation of humility, forbearance, and forgiveness by Epictetus and Seneca is not clearly an attainment of philosophy unillumined by the spirit of contemporary Christianity. Socrates, "the noblest of all the Grecians," had no world-wide sympathies which concerned themselves with interests beyond the limits of his nationality. "Plato, in his solicitude to reduce his ideal state to a harmonious whole answering to his idea of justice, sacrificed the individual. He superseded private property, broke up the relations of family and home, degraded woman, and tolerated slavery" (p. 507). Plato himself asserted the inadequacy of human teaching and effort, and announced that "virtue is the gift of God."[1]

III. In the department of religious feeling and *sentiment*, the propædeutic office of Greek philosophy is further seen.

1. "It awakened in man the sense of distance and estrangement from God, and the need of a mediator—'a daysman betwixt us that might lay his hand upon us both.'" The first

---

[1] On the insufficiency of philosophy, see the concluding portion of Farrar's "Seekers after God," p. 318–336.

stage of human history recognized the divine as near. Nature was the supernatural. The second, or reflective, stage removed God to the region of the unseen. It made him abstract and difficult to discern. Man now longed for an approachable Father, Counselor, Friend. Humanity was thus prepared for the announcement of an incarnation.

2. It deepened the consciousness of guilt, and awakened a desire for redemption. In the Homeric period the idea of wrong-doing was certainly present, but it was vague and gross. The sentiment uppermost in the great tragedians is the invincibility of the moral law. "The sinner must suffer for his sins." "But after the law comes the gospel. First the controversy, then the reconciliation. A dim consciousness of sin and retribution as a fact, and of reconciliation as a *want*, seems to have revealed itself even in the darkest periods of human history. This consciousness underlies not a few of the Greek tragedies" (p. 516). Offended justice is appeased by divine interpositions. The office assigned to Jove's son, Apollo, in the "Prometheus Unbound," is certainly suggestive of the Christian doctrine of *reconciliation*. Plato more than once betrays his longing for a divine helper. The obstacles to virtue, as he says, are great, and insurmountable to feeble man. Plato admits it with a spirit of sadness, and says it is the work of God to restore fallen humanity. He lets fall obscure hints of a coming Conqueror of sin, an Assuager of pain, an Averter of evil; but he indulges rather in desires than in hopes.[1] The experience of

---

[1] Socrates, in express words, prophesies the future advent of some heaven-sent Guide (Xenophon, "Memorabilia," I., iv., 14; Plato, "Alcib.," ii.). In the "Republic" Plato employs these singularly suggestive words: "Thus he who is constituted just shall be scourged, shall be stretched on the rack, shall be bound, have his eyes put out; and at last, having suffered all evils, shall be crucified" (cited from Clem. Alex., Strom., book v., chap. xiv., where other foreshadowings of the Redeemer are referred to). The expectation of a Redeemer seems to have been very wide-spread. Dr.

Plato found its counterpart in the experience of Paul prior to his conversion. "What I do, I approve not; for I do not what I would, but what I hate." "Oh, wretched man that I am! who shall deliver me from the body of this death?" But Paul, conscious of deliverance, was enabled to say, "I thank God, through Jesus Christ our Lord;" while Plato could only desire and hope and wait for the coming Deliverer.

The history of religions and philosophies is thus the confirmation of Christianity.([1]) We may, indeed, regard the revelation of God in the human soul to be as genuine and authentic, though not as clear and influential, as the revelation in the person and teaching of Christ. These two revelations are harmonious, and must be so. Greek philosophy had made the calculation, from the data of human consciousness, that a Saviour was needed—that a Saviour must be predicated. Paul came to Athens, and pointed out the Saviour whose want had been

---

Curry has expressed the opinion that the idea of vicarious suffering is intuitive (lecture before the students of Drew Theol. Sem., Feb. 4th, 1874). However this may be, Dr. J. P. Newman cites it from the Japanese (see letter on "Religion in Japan," in *Christian Advocate*, N. Y., Oct., 1873), and from the Chinese (see letter on "Tauism in China," *ibid.*, Feb. 19th, 1874); and it is notorious that the expectation of a deliverer was found existing among the Pueblos, Navajoes, Aztecs, and others (Whipple, "Pacific Railroad Reports," vol. iii., part iii., chap. iii., p. 46; *ibid.*, p. 42; Prescott's "Conquest of Mexico," vol. i., pp. 60, 312). On this subject compare, also, M'Cosh, "Method of the Divine Government," book iv., chap. ii.

([1]) "Philosophy," says Clement, "was a school-master to bring men to Christ" (Clem. Alex., Strom., i., § 28). "Philosophy, before the coming of the Lord, was necessary to the Greeks for righteousness, and now it proves useful for godliness, being in some sort a preliminary discipline—$\pi\rho o\pi a\iota\delta\epsilon\iota a$ $\tau\iota\varsigma$ $o\check{v}\sigma a$—for those who reap the fruits of the faith through demonstration" (*ibid.*, i., 5, § 28). "Philosophy was given as a peculiar testament—$\delta\iota a\theta\acute{\eta}\kappa\eta\nu$—to the Greeks as forming the basis of the Christian philosophy" (*ibid.*, Strom., vi., 8, § 67; see, also, "Cohortatio," chap. vi.). Similar testimony has been abundantly rendered by Augustine, Origen, Lactantius, and Justin Martyr.

felt—giving sight to the blind instinct that had been feeling after God, and preaching a Gospel which fulfilled the prophetic longings of the struggling ages of Greek philosophy.

Such is the line of argument pursued by the author of "Christianity and Greek Philosophy." We must refer the reader to the work itself for an idea of the fullness and symmetry with which the discussion is evolved. We may yet state that it embraces in its compass neat monographic treatments of a number of subsidiary theses. Often, nevertheless, the full discussion of a topic must be gathered from widely separated pages; and this, perhaps, is a defect in the arrangement of the work.

The work shows the signs of study and erudition upon every page. But it is not simply a *learned* treatise, for the author possesses a remarkably keen and penetrating insight into subjects of speculative inquiry, and hews out, with trenchant blade, and in rapid succession, clean-cut blocks of thought to fit into the beautiful structure of his growing argument. His mind's eye sees with the clearness of noonday in realms which are thick darkness to ordinary vision. He revels, with playful unconsciousness of effort, among the ponderous problems of metaphysical research, shedding upon each the light of a brilliant intellect, transmitted through a style as pellucid as crystal. His pages resound from beginning to end with the changes rung upon his favorite ontological conceptions. Indeed, the only fault of the book seems to arise from the circumstance that the author is so completely possessed by his favorite thought that it is always present in his mind, whatever subsidiary theme he handles, and, like a ruling passion, always finds some avenue to utterance. This leads sometimes to a premature broaching of the heart of an impending discussion, and, by a division of forces, somewhat weakens, in some cases, the effect of the presentation. Thus, in treating Plato, he lets fall something of Plato's ontology on almost every page. Quite a full statement is presented three times: first, in treating of Plato's Psychology; second, under the head of Dialectic; and, finally, under Ontology proper. That the author's positive theistic system, ultimately argued out so lucidly in its various aspects, is considerably scattered in presentation, will be apparent from the attempt to make all the references on any leading topic—as *philosophies of religious phenomena* (p. 55–95, 172–176, 203–223); *the materialistic philosophy of religion* (p. 55–65, 172–176, 203–223, 293, 311); *the Platonistic philosophy, and its relations to Christianity* (p. 328–387, 492–493, 502–504, 507–509, 517–519); *the doctrine of "Final Causes"* (p. 211–223, 320–324, 405, 413, 489–491). Still, these peculiarities proceed from the influence of a strongly dominant idea, and the tendency is to make it a dominant idea in the reader's mind. In perpetually turning the subject over, he always exposes some new side. Every presentation is in fresh phrase, and is brought forward from a different direction. If the shadows of coming conclusions are sometimes cast before, they at least serve, like "prophetic types" in geological history, to proclaim a unity of thought in the progress of the evolution. The style is dignified, enriched with a copious vocabulary, forcible, sometimes sententious, and always remarkably transparent. It is somewhat freighted with brief quotations and foreign words; but these almost always add some meaning to the text. The comprehensibility of the work would be improved if its skeletal structure were a little less disguised; though, in the subordinate parts, the method is as noticeable as it is admirable. A detailed analysis, showing the subordination of parts, would very much aid the student and the general reader. This suggestion is made under the conviction that it is a treatise which might be studied with great profit by all intelligent clergymen and candidates for the ministry. Indeed, as before stated, the subjects treated and the views presented can not, in the present age, be safely passed by without earnest study by the "defenders of the faith."

In reviewing the work of Dr. Cocker we had purposed to avoid any general discussion of the question of the knowability of God through the powers of reason. Our estimate of this work is so high that we thought it would prove a better service to the reader to present simply a miniature portrait of its method than to attempt an original discussion. We conclude, therefore, by making a mere memorandum—partly by way of *résumé*—of the various forms of theistic proof, showing that every proof inevitably hinges on the validity of a primitive belief or intuition of reason.

I. THE ARGUMENT FROM COMMON CONSENT.—We find religious impressions, faiths, and practices a universal fact of humanity. (1) They existed, if we rightly interpret the indications, even in the Stone Age of the life of humanity.[1] (2) They are abundantly exemplified in the existence and prevalence of great religious systems among those portions of the human family that have risen above the stage of savageism.[2] (3) They characterize the life of the lowest savages. We are aware of contradictory statements.[3] Formerly, missionaries denied the lowest savages a spark of religious fire, through zeal for the importance of written revelation. Recently, their theological antipodes have made the same denial, for the pur-

---

[1] Quatrefages, "Rapport sur le Progrès de l'Anthropologie," 1868; Duke of Argyll, "Primeval Man;" Figuier, "Primitive Man;" and many other authorities. This position is questioned (we think through the influence of preconceived opinions) by Lubbock, "Prehistoric Times," and "Origin of Civilization;" and Vogt, "Lectures on Prehistoric Man."

[2] See, for condensed and accessible accounts of these, (in addition to the work of Dr. Cocker), Clark, "The Ten Great Religions" (to these ten we would add Lao-tseism and the systems of the Aztecs and Peruvians); Moffat, "A Comparative History of Religions;" Müller, "Chips from a German Workshop," vols. i., ii., iii. ; and "Lectures on the Science of Religion, with Papers on Buddhism."

[3] Sir John Lubbock's works, cited above; Burton, "Abeokuta," vol. i., p. 179 ; Darwin, "Descent of Man," etc.

pose of undermining the foundations of Christianity. We have examined the specifications and charges in detail, and our judgment is, that the charges are "not proved." However gratifying it would be to spread the facts before our readers, we must forbear.(¹) (4) The fact has impressed itself upon the minds of thoughtful writers in all ages. We could quote Alexander of Aphrodisias, Socrates, Plato, Zeno of Cittium, Cicero, St. Paul, Augustine, Galen, Anselm, Descartes, Leibnitz, Barrow, Butler, Herder, Ritter, Ad. Pictet, Carpenter, Calderwood, M'Cosh, Spencer, and many others, to prove that if theistic ideas do not exist fully formed in the minds of lowest savages, they manifest, at least, a religious susceptibility and predisposition which could not exist without a connatural foundation.

But it is not necessary that these ideas, or even predispositions, should be established in every case. There are whole tribes, as there are single individuals, which can not reasonably be taken as tests and standards of normal humanity. We may throw them out if we choose.

Could we go no farther, we have in these universal phenomena the data for a "philosophy of religion." *Why* this common consent? We have listened to the solution of Comte; we have strained our mental vision till we feel symptoms of strabismus in endeavoring to reconcile the paradoxes of Hegel; but we remain unsatisfied. The religious consciousness is a *characteristic of humanity*, and we demand the sanction of its affirmations. We feel borne toward the conclusion that the voice of humanity is the voice of truth. This is the verdict of the ages. Πάντων μέτρον ὁ ἄνθρωπος—*vox populi vox Dei*—the sentiment of humanity is the utterance of God.

(¹) A summary of the results of a study of the religious nature of savages has been more recently given by the present writer in the *Methodist Quarterly Review* for January and July, 1875.

But is such an argument a demonstration? It is, *if* the voice of humanity is the voice of truth. The conclusion hinges on the validity of a primitive necessary belief. Is that which mankind necessarily believes to be taken as a presentation of the reality of things?

Let us see if it be possible to rise to a knowledge of God by any chain of thought which does not involve this link.

II. THE ARGUMENT FROM DIRECT "REVELATION."—Here, it seems at first, is an unimpeachable demonstration. But suppose ourselves in a position to witness the immediate manifestations of the Divine presence, and to listen to the audible voice of God, what proof have we that the phenomenon is not an illusion of our senses? or that any of our sensations are not illusory? We receive an impression upon our *sensorium*, and *believe because we must;* but that is all. What sanction has our belief? Next, suppose we had the best of grounds for assuming the reality of *something* making the outward manifestation, how could we know that reality to be such as mankind conceives the nature of God to be? Without an antecedent notion of God, the sensible manifestation could only announce itself as a finite phenomenon. Whence the notions of intelligence, goodness, infinity, rising up in the soul in presence of a finite phenomenon? This "revelation," instead of imparting a primordial knowledge of God, simply awakens into consciousness a pre-existing knowledge. With us who no longer witness such sensible revelations of God, but receive them only by tradition, it is obvious that the demonstration must be weakened rather than strengthened. Revelation, therefore, can not possibly be a revelation of God's existence and attributes; and, in order that it may become efficient at all, as a divine revelation, there must be an antecedent concept of the Being revealed. We come round, then, to the point from which we started—Whence this concept, and what is its meaning?

III. THE ARGUMENT FROM IMMEDIATE INTUITION.—As all

men seem to themselves to know of the Divine, and are unconscious of any process or effort by which they have attained to this knowledge, have we not here a clear case of immediate intuition? To this question Jacobi and Schleiermacher and many others respond affirmatively. This is probably the meaning of the theism of Hamilton and Mansel; and no other theism was possible to Kant without virtual self-contradiction. We refer to the pages of Dr. Cocker for an exposition and criticism of this philosophy; but for ourselves, we feel like confessing a leaning toward it. We can not here argue the point; nor do we wish to intimate that there is not another avenue of approach to the theistic concept. We believe there is. But here we are confronted still by the old question. Consciousness reports directly (in this view) the reality of the Divine, and we irresistibly believe the report. Now, what authority has consciousness to report thus? Does the presence of this necessary belief imply a reality? We must make a further effort to flank this difficulty.

IV. THE ÆTIOLOGICAL ARGUMENT.—We turn here into the domain of necessary ideas. We place our feet on the principle of universal causality, and rise from the observation of contingent causes to the concept of primordial causation. This concept is a revelation of causation adequate to the formation of the world and all the visible or conceivable universe. But as nothing, quantitatively considered, can be infinite, but only *indefinite*, this principle does not lift us to infinite causation. The power is not that of an absolute cause, but only a world-maker, a demiurge, and this does not answer to the human conception of Deity. But, further, the argument only bears us to the necessary *idea* of primary causality; and though we do, indeed, discover beyond this the necessary *idea* of absolute cause —self-existence—it furnishes us no means to bridge the gulf between necessary ideas and necessary realities. True, the reason supplies us with the means of passing from mode to subject, but this is extraneous to the purlieus of the present argument. This method, therefore, of itself breaks off before reaching our objective point; and, moreover, it will be noted that, whatever the uses to which it may be put, its validity rests, again, on the trustworthiness of that judgment which affirms that *every effect must have a cause.* What sanction has reason for affirming this judgment? What validity appertains to our belief in the principle of causality? Let us make another tack.

V. THE TELEOLOGICAL ARGUMENT. — Restricting this to cases of the mechanical sort, we affirm that the contrivances discoverable in nature proclaim intelligence operative in nature. Here we are met at the threshold by the objection that we know nothing about *designs* in nature;([1]) and the only reply we can make is, that we feel fully persuaded that contrivance implies intention, and therefore intelligence, and that we feel this necessity to be the same in the domain of nature as in that of humanity. Still, it is only a primitive belief. But there is further difficulty. The evidence carries us, at best, only to the idea of necessary intelligence as the adequate explanation of the mechanism of the universe. This, again, apart from any other proof, is not infinite intelligence, but only intelligence *indefinite* in degree—such intelligence as is demanded by the system of nature—and, in addition, it is only *intelligence*, and nothing more. The argument does not lead us to the idea of being and personality; and so, like the preceding argument, it leaves faith dangling in mid-heaven, and groping around desperately for a firm support. We hasten to the next alternative.

VI. THE HOMOLOGICAL([2]) ARGUMENT. — As this phrase is

([1]) This "conclusion [that design is revealed in nature] could not bear, perhaps, the strictest transcendental critique" (Kant, "Critique of Pure Reason," English translation, p. 435). This objection is echoed and re-echoed in the pages of Hamilton, Spencer, and others.

([2]) This is the Cosmological argument of Cocker, or a branch of the Physico-theological of Kant.

a stranger in the category of theistic arguments, we explain the meaning to be, an argument based on proofs of intelligence drawn from the existence of intelligible methods — plans in nature. We need not amplify the explanation or the argument. It is at once apparent that, however convincing the proofs of intelligence, the argument lands us exactly where the teleological does, and faith still feels itself afloat without an anchorage.

VII. THE ONTOLOGICAL ARGUMENT.—Here we deal with essential realities—the ground and source of all cognizable modes and attributes, whether contingent or uncontingent. We find in our minds the necessary idea of existence—reality—and feel impelled to predicate a necessary *something* distinct from the world, and which constitutes the ground and reason of its existence. This is the *only* argument furnished by reason which attains to real being. There are three orders of cognizable manifestations, giving rise to three corresponding orders of ontological concepts:

1. *Phenomena of the Objectivity* (*extension, form, color, etc.*). —Ontological principles, applied to these phenomena, supply a form of real being which is contingent, *finite*, and MATERIAL.

2. *Phenomena of the Subjectivity* (*the mental states*).—Ontological principles, applied to these phenomena, supply a form of real being which is self-conscious, free, intelligent, moral, and IMMATERIAL, but still *finite* and *conditioned*.

3. *Necessary Ideas.*—These are not properly phenomena of mind. The consciousness of their presence is such. No phenomena of the finite can claim a necessary existence. Some of the necessary ideas which reason discovers in its domain are the following: The ideas of (1) Substance or Reality; (2) Causality, with its derivatives, Will, Liberty, Motivity, Intelligence, Unity, and Personality; (3) Intelligence; (4) Liberty; (5) Ethicality—the idea of right and wrong; (6) Duty; (7) Personality; (8) Unity; (9) Infinity; (10) Absolutivity. (Per-

haps the 10th is also derivable from the idea of causality. It will be observed that while certain of our necessary ideas seem to be primitive and intuitive, they may also arise through a brief, spontaneous process of deductive derivation. Kant says Liberty is not directly cognized, but only a deduction from the concept of Duty; but in this he contradicts himself and the verdict of common consciousness. To us it seems, however, that while the idea of Liberty is simple and spontaneous, it is also summoned into the field of consciousness as a correlative of the idea of causality — coupled, or not, with the idea of Duty.)

Ontological principles, applied to the existence of necessary ideas, present them as modes of the absolute, proclaiming necessary, *infinite*, and *unconditioned* Being as their subject. Therefore, the ontological argument shows that *if* necessary ideas exist, there is a necessary subject to which they must be referred as their adequate cause and ground. We repeat, then, that necessary ideas exist—

(1.) Arising spontaneously in our own minds in presence of the phenomena of the external world, but transcending all which we can conceive of the extent, duration, or degrees of contingent existence, and clothing themselves with the attribute of absolutivity. Such are our transcendental ideas of substantivity, causality, intelligence, etc.

(2.) Further illustrated and emphasized by a thoughtful contemplation of the cosmos. For instance:

Intelligence is exemplified in (*a*) Relations of *contrivance* (the Teleological proof); (*b*) Relations of *plan* (the Homological proof);

Primordial causality and its derivatives:
Unity,
Motivity,
Self-determination, } = Personality; are exemplified in relations of cause and effect (the Ætiological proof).
Self-consciousness,

These three and other([1]) similar modes of argumentation thus contribute *predicates*, which the Ontological argument affirms of real being. These predicates, together with those supplied directly and spontaneously by the mind, make up the whole possible conception of *Perfect Being*, or DEITY.

We desire, in passing, to offer a few words in reference to Kant's criticism of the theistic proofs from speculative reason. He is commonly represented as having visited them with a Waterloo overthrow. He enumerates three arguments: (1) The Physico-theological (= Teleological, Cocker + Cosmological, Cocker = Socratic = Argument from "Final Causes"); (2) The Cosmological (= Ætiological, Cocker = Peripatetic or Aristotelian = Leibnitzian, in part); (3) The Ontological (= Ontological, Cocker = Platonic or Ideological, or argument from absolute modes + Anselmian, or argument from Perfect Being = Newtonian [as far as it goes], founded on space and time, viewed [erroneously] as attributes of Deity and symbols of infinity = Leibnitzian, founded on the principle of "sufficient reason"). "More than these [proofs] there are not, and more, even, there can not be."([2]) His criticisms of the first two are just; and, it ought to be added, his praise of the first is generous, though reserved. His strictures of the Ontological argument are keen, but, it seems to us, contradictory to reason, and even to some of his own later ontological propositions. He asserts that the Ontological argument proves the necessity of *something* as the

---

([1]) Similarly we might frame an *ethical* argument, based on the principle of ethicality as major, and the demonstrations of justice in the world as minor, premise; also an *agathological* argument, based on the idea of goodness and its manifestations in nature. But these arguments, guided by nature, reach only to *indefinite* intelligence, causality, justice, and goodness, when we are obliged to turn to the reason to furnish the concepts of *absolute* attributes; and still another effort of reason is demanded to view these absolutes as modes of being.

([2]) Kant, "Critique of Pure Reason," Haywood's translation, p. 411.

ground of the necessary idea, but it renders demonstrable *no predicate* of that necessary something. Is it substance, reality, necessity? In his "Critique of Practical Reason" he admits, similarly, the concept of Duty, and then asserts that it has an objective, real existence. But, on the contrary, he holds that Necessary Being remains only an idea. We can not pass from the idea of Necessary Being to the *qualitative*, objective actuality. This is simply, so far as we understand it, a confession of the impotency of reason in all attempts to comprehend Necessary Being. We reach here the idea of the undefinable, incomprehensible ("unknowable," Spencer, Hamilton, etc.) "something" which we can not render to our intelligence, except as to its real and necessary existence; and this impotency *is simply the confession of all the theistic ages.*

We pause to inquire whether it is essential that we be able to go farther. Of this Necessary Being all predicates are *possible* which are not contradictory to reason; and even if no predicate were *demonstrable*, we should be precluded from the *possibility* of speculative atheism, or the possibility of disproof of any of the Christian predicates of Deity; while the *hypothesis* of a self-existent Creator and Father would remain the only rational explanation of the world, and we should be bound to accept it as an inductive generalization of the highest possible degree of probability.

But we hold that there *are* predicates of the (so-styled) undefinable which must be affirmed if we would not dishonor our intuitions. If the world logically refer itself, through reason, to Necessary Being, then the *intelligence* which Kant cheerfully acknowledges revealed in the world so refers itself; and intelligence is a necessary predicate of Necessary Being.

But the great transcendental philosopher raises a difficulty deeper than this, which strikes the axe into the very roots of the Ontological argument. That which appears necessary to our reason may not be necessary *absolutely*. The necessity of our judgments must be distinguished from the necessity of things.(¹) "The principle of causality has no meaning at all, and no sign of its use, excepting only in the sensible world."(²) "The statement that a triangle must have three angles is only a necessary judgment, and not a necessity of things.(³) From this premise, it follows that we can not logically trace the chain of causation beyond the limits of the existing world, and affirm *absolute primordial causality*. We can affirm only causation as a prefix of the existing order. Now, if this were all, it appears that the principle of causality possesses the same validity and the same extent of dominion as the ideas of geometry. That is, the theistic proposition, on the showing of Kant, is just as demonstrable as a theorem in mathematics, though both are propositions limited to the *existing order of things*, and not depending as absolutes upon the necessity of things *in totis possibilibus*.

This is certainly pushing a firm foot-hold for reasoning as far as most minds would ask to carry it. If transcendental philosophy goes to the limit of affirming an intelligent Creator of the existing order of things, we may breathe freely; that is as far as any of our arguments have pretended to go; and we set down Kant as a speculative *theist in the same sense as Butler and Paley*. His exceptions to the transcendental argument (for the three or four so called are finally but one) lie entirely beyond any thing thought of by ordinary theists. Besides, most

---

(¹) Thus also, Hamilton: "It is not competent to argue that what can not be comprehended as possible by us is impossible in reality" ("Metaphysics," p. 552). And Professor Stephen Alexander: "The relations of things are matters of constitution and arrangement. * * * One part of space is not diverse from another, nor does one day of the week of course succeed another *because we may choose to think* so, but because the Creator has formed (or conformed) them so" (Amer. Jour. of Science) [2], vii., p. 180).

(²) Kant, *op. cit.*, p. 413.   (³) *Ibid.*, p. 424.

thinkers will affirm the truths of mathematics to be a "necessity of things," and the properties of a triangle to hold good under any possible (not to say conceivable) constitution; and hence, also, the principle of causality and the principle of intelligence grow out of the necessity of things, and not the existing constitution of things; and hence, finally, the proof of an intelligent Creator is the proof of Absolute Being.

After all, we are inclined to think, with Leibnitz, that there exists a more direct road to the Absolute Intelligence, and that it may be directly predicated on transcendental grounds.([1]) As the existing order of things is not the only order conceivable as a possibility, and as the relations of different possible orders must be intelligent relations, there must be an *Understanding* which lies back, not only of the existing intelligible world, but of every possible constitution of things; and this Understanding must be the predicate of a real Being—a Being thus unconditioned by any possible law out of itself.

Finally, we desire to direct attention to the fact that on whatever ultimate the last predicate of reason rests, we are obliged to accept it—though we do it cheerfully and necessarily—simply because the denial of it appears absurd. Simple, primitive belief, therefore, is the very root of the highest certainty attainable.

([1]) Leibnitz, "Essais de Théodicé," *ad initium.* The Leibnitzian argument, reduced to distinct propositions, is as follows: 1. "There must be a first Reason of things (Ætiological); 2. The reason must be out of the world, and a necessary self-existence (Ætiological); 3. It must also be intelligent. *Proof:* To understand the relation of all possible worlds and the grounds of choice of this world (Cosmological, Cocker); 4. It must have self-determination to make the choice (Ætiological); 5. It must have power to render the choice efficient (Ætiological); 6. Power belongs to substance—it tends to Being (Ontological); 7. Wisdom or understanding tends to truth [reality] (Ontological); 8. Will tends to goodness [the Perfect Good] (Ontological); 9. This Intelligent Cause tends to all that is possible—therefore infinite every way (Ætiological); 10. There is only room for ONE, as all is linked together (Ontological).

Must we, then, confess that all our knowledge rests on a basis which admits of doubt? Never was a more important question raised in the whole annals of humanity. It is of supreme importance to discern the absolute and irrecusable validity of the primitive beliefs. They are the molecules of philosophy. In the last analysis of our knowledge, we find an element which we hesitate to pronounce knowledge, because it is only belief; and we are not satisfied to pronounce it belief, because we feel that it is knowledge. All our knowledge resolves itself into primitive judgments which we affirm, because we *intuit the reality.* Intuitive knowledge is identical with primitive belief, and philosophy is a deduction from intuitive knowledge.

It was not our purpose to attempt to enforce the authority of the primitive beliefs, but merely to point them out as the key-stones of human knowledge, and to remind the reader that the *impeachment of one is the dethronement of all.* To attack the authority of the belief in efficient causality is not only to launch us upon a universe of chance, but to surround us, as Fichte confessed, by a phantasmagoria of unrealities and illusions. To dishonor our belief in Absolute Being as the ground of our necessary idea of Absolute Being is, by a fell touch, to break the electric communication which unites the world of finite existence with the realm of eternal Realities, and plunge the unhappy soul into the abyss of nihilism. On the contrary, to assert the authority of our belief in the reality either of the external world or of the world within ourselves, is, by implication, to announce the authority of that universal faith of humanity which affirms Supreme Divinity; it is to recognize intelligence, power, goodness, justice, in the ordinations of the visible universe, and to make these attributes the predicates of the Absolute and Perfect Being revealed in the inmost chamber of human reason.

XI.

GOD IN THE WORLD.(¹)

"I am not oblivious of what is babbled by some, who in their ignorance are frightened at every noise, and say that we ought to occupy ourselves with what is most necessary, and which contains the faith; and that we should pass over what is beyond and superfluous, which wears out and detains us to no purpose in things which conduce nothing to the great end."—CLEMENT OF ALEXANDRIA, *Stromata*, book i., chap. 1.

PEOPLE still live who sincerely believe that Mr. Moody's method is the only one requisite to convince the world of religious truth. They have heard of the loudly proclaimed "conflict between Science and Religion," but they maintain that the only way to a pacification is through "evangelical teaching." They have seen the young, in the formative stage of opinion, yielding with an irresistible deference to the evidences which science arrays before the human understanding; but they still proclaim that well-established science, in certain of its forms, is false, and must not be trusted. "Tyndall, Huxley, Spencer, and Darwin" must be put down; and the way to do it is to "preach the Lord Jesus Christ." These are literal and recent quotations from the lips and pens of excellent Christian divines, and are not made in any spirit of levity or disparagement.(²) Nevertheless, we do not think it neces-

---

(¹) "The Theistic Conception of the World: an Essay in Opposition to Certain Tendencies of Modern Thought;" by B. F. Cocker, D.D., LL.D., Professor of Moral and Mental Philosophy in the University of Michigan, author of "Christianity and Greek Philosophy," New York, Harper & Brothers, 1875.

(²) While we write, a Doctor of Divinity is advertised as about to pub-

sary to support our statements by giving names and places; while we have no right to attach names to opinions privately expressed. We wish only to define a position which we think wholly mistaken and indefensible. We shall be the last to utter a word of depreciation of evangelical efforts. By all means, let them be assiduously promoted. We sincerely honor Mr. Moody and his fellow-evangelists. We only maintain that a large and increasing class of persons exists who can not be reached by such efforts, as long as certain antecedent and fun-

---

lish "a series of masterly discourses * * * in opposition to the celebrated doctrines and theories of all the celebrated materialists." * * * "He will expose and refute the theories of Tyndall, Spencer, Huxley, Darwin, and others of that school." If this divine undertake so broad a task, we fear he will bring religion into renewed and unmerited disrespect. He is eminently able to serve the cause of religious truth by "preaching the Lord Jesus Christ," and convincing such as are accessible to his presentations; but he will sorely disparage—not science, but Christianity, by convincing his auditors that an inherent alienation exists between the two. Should he penetrate understandingly the subject-matter taught by "that school," the "scales would fall from his eyes," and he would feel less eager to parade the assumed "materialism" of "Tyndall, Spencer, Huxley, Darwin, and others." We do not say that these scientists are exemplars of fervent piety; we do not affirm that they are "evangelical;" but we do maintain that they are not amenable to the charges of which multitudes think them guilty. Our meaning will become obvious as we proceed, setting forth, in our progress, the matured estimate of modern science which is embodied in the work under review.

In similar error was another Doctor of Divinity whom we call to mind, and who, during a meeting of the American Association for the Advancement of Science, announced a Sunday sermon on the Warfare of Science against Religion—or something to that effect. At the same moment an eminent scientist was advertised to speak on the *harmony* between science and religion. Such harmony has been set forth time and again by members of the Association on the Sunday occurring during the session; and scarcely a presidential address has been delivered during the existence of the Association which did not, more or less at length, affirm the friendship of science for the fundamental doctrines of the Christian faith.

damental questions of evidence remain unsettled in their minds. We will briefly explain our position.

The work of Dr. Cocker assumes that a conviction of religious truth may be legitimately grounded on data disclosed as the ultimate results of analytical inquiry. The existence of the work implies that though the belief of the multitude may be prompted by their feelings — reverence for teachers, hope of future happiness, devotional susceptibilities — there is a considerable number who demand the *proofs of the realities* which must stand as correlates to the religious feelings.

Belief is a conviction of the truth of some proposition. Conviction always rests on some ground; there is some reason why we believe. Sometimes its ground is *testimony* to a fact observed. Sometimes it is simply *authority*. A entertains a certain belief, and B, presuming A's belief to represent truth, adopts it, and can give no other reason for his faith. Sometimes belief — sincere belief — is generated or biased by our *interests*; intellectual discernment becomes perverted, and the grounds of belief are not revealed to us in their true light. Sometimes belief is based on the results of a *personal scrutiny* of evidence. George Smith, who has seen and deciphered the Chaldean inscriptions, may feel a confidence in the veracity of our ancient Scriptures no stronger — perhaps even less unreserved — than that of the servant-girl who acquires it from her faithful pastor; but his belief rests on a basis not traditionary. We who have not deciphered these inscriptions may still accept, without reserve, the testimony of the antiquary, and, with a knowledge of the nature of the evidence, may build a faith as firm and as logical as that of the original decipherer. Similarly, the chemist notes the transformations which take place in the test-tube, and acquires an original belief in the principle of chemical affinities. He measures and weighs the products of these reactions, and, finding that the compounds present him with definite multiples of the simples, he attains to a belief in the doctrine of "chemical equivalents," and the doctrine of the atomic constitution of matter. The philosopher, introverting his scrutiny, notes the facts of consciousness, and grounds on direct observation his belief in the reality of his conscious states. Here belief becomes knowledge; there is no normal contingency which can invalidate or qualify this intuitive knowledge that he thinks and feels. He finds existent, also, a belief that the *something* to which consciousness refers its states is a reality, and *such* a reality as is represented in this reference. This belief respecting the existence of an objective reality, and its nature, is accepted by all men as knowledge. It is knowledge exalted above all contingency. These ultimate data disclose an absolute identification of knowledge and belief. Once more, the philosopher discerns reflected in consciousness certain other primary truths which exclude the possibility of all conditionality—such as the principle of causality, the principle of substance, and the principle of intentionality. These he feels to be more indestructible even than matter itself. All knowledge, all science, is but a superstructure built up of these ultimate atoms of truth. The ground of a primary belief is neither testimony, nor authority, nor sensuous observation, nor inductive inference, nor deductive consequence. It is a ground more unassailable than any of these. It is a directness and a singleness of intuition of one transcendental and eternal truth. A religious belief is not secure from the attacks of doubt till, by a process of reflection, it has been resolved into these ultimate and adamantine elements.

Now, a moment's reflection suffices to show that men's beliefs possess various degrees of validity. Nor is the ardor of belief graduated to its validity—unless it be in an inverse ratio. One man rests belief on grounds which would not be satisfactory to another. Some persons, like children, willingly adopt beliefs; while others must themselves bring the grounds of belief under the careful inspection of the intellect. Some persons with warm feelings may be easily prepossessed by beliefs which, in others of cooler natures, must be built on evidence comprehended and weighed; and in persons of similar emotional characteristics, proneness to take advice of the feelings is inversely as the control of intellect.

The *religious* feelings hold the first place in respect to influence over the lives of men. They are not the product of occasional concurrences of circumstances; their existence does not depend on conditions of poverty or wealth, power or subjection, sickness or health, age or sex: they sway the actions of men through the presentation of interests which range not alone over the entire period of mortal existence, but through the dimly glimpsed vistas of an eternal life. All other interests, all other motives, are limited by circumstances, and transitory in duration, save as they condition the religious feelings which, like the dome of the sky, cover and embrace all that there is in human life.

Yet men differ no less in the intensity and dominance of religious feeling than in intellect, or amiability, or physique. Differences which exist absolutely may be counteracted or exaggerated by the other differences which exist—differences in intellect, in education, in fortune, in personal associations. The final resultant of all the forces which influence human actions may be, in one case, an irrepressible religious predisposition; in another, an emotionless, questioning, religious circumspection. The first individual will possess an exuberance of religious faith, though he may be unable to give a reason for it; but will remain legitimately cheerful and happy. The second may deny all religion, though equally unable to give a reason for his denial; but remain unsettled and anxious. Tertullian could believe even *because* belief was impossible;(¹) Pyrrho

---

(¹) Tertullian seems to have been fond of paradoxes. Besides his *Credo quia impossibile*, which Sir Thomas Brown says he learned out of Tertul-

would not believe even when doubt became absurd. Between Tertullian and Pyrrho stand all gradations.

There is a class of individuals richly gifted with religious susceptibilities, but yet subject to the strong influence of habits of intellectual inquiry. In their ordinary moods, belief can only exist under the previous sanction of intellect; but in a roused condition of the religious nature, belief bursts into being *at the bidding of the higher intuitions;* and ratiocinative intellect comes afterward merely to sanction its existence.

The intelligent reader can not hesitate to give indorsement to these propositions. Can there be any difficulty in applying them to the work of convincing men of religious truth? The religious predisposition exists in all men; in most men it is strong. The great mass of people, then, need no arguments; they need only persuasion; they need arrested attention, aroused religious emotions, quickened religious perceptions. To accomplish this must be always the chief work of the religious teacher. It is legitimate; for we maintain not only that the essential propositions of the religion of Jesus are capable of authentication by the most rigorous logic, but that there is a higher apperception of their truth which is glimpsed most clearly by those who attain to the sublimest conditions of religious exaltation. To convince through the emotions—emotions profound and pervading enough to be calm and clear—is to open the intuitional eye, and anticipate the affirmation of reflective intellect.

True it is that the religious teacher whose own belief rests on authority or religious predisposition, may throw the sanctity of religion over tenets which are purely secular or even

---

lian, as an easy solution of knotty problems, the worthy father has left us the following: *Non pudet, quia pudendum est; Prorsus credibile est, quia ineptum est; Certum est, quia impossibile* ("De Carn., Christ.," v.); *Merito damnantur licet damnent; Ad leonem damnanda Christianum potius ad leonem.*

baseless; and he may thus become the propagator of a volume of crude, if not false and damaging, "theology." How sadly is this danger illustrated in the history of even the modern church! True it is, too, that the subject of religious exaltation is sometimes simultaneously the subject of a nervous exaltation which quickens the imagination and the whole range of sensibilities; and in consequence of this, the religious intuition becomes fogged, or even confounded with imaginative and physiological impulses. These extravagances of both religious teacher and religious pupil are to be diligently corrected by invoking the calm influences of intellect.

But a different phenomenon and a different demand are presented by that respectable minority of persons in whom the religious predisposition can not be evoked. Though they do not, by any means, embrace all the thinkers, they constitute, on the whole, a thinking class. The ideas which elevate our civilization, and the enterprises which advance the happiness of the race, originate with them. They unite with strong motive, executive power. They are accessible to argument as well as persuasion. Their attitude toward the tenets and institutions of Christianity will be determined by the claims and pretensions of professing Christians; by the results of a study of Christian evidences; by the awakening power which is brought to bear upon them; by education, example, friendships, or other accidents.

Among the influences which will determine the attitude of this class will be the allegations of conflict between the system of religion and the system of knowledge. Science is at work in dusky basement, and high tower, and scented field; and now and then a new-fledged thought flies forth, like another dove, to typify the mind of the All-Father. Then some representative of the first class, from his lofty attitude of religious enthusiasm, and pellucid faith, and beautiful communion, proclaims that the idea is out of harmony with the system which his faith has consecrated; it is a false idea; it must be put down. Accordingly, he begins to denounce "unsanctified" learning, and to preach "faith and repentance" more earnestly than ever.(¹) Meantime the thoughtful minority examine the claims of this new announcement from the laboratory or observatory. *It seems sustained by evidence; our preacher has said nothing germane to this evidence; if the system which faith indorses is inconsistent with this, it must be inconsistent with truth.* We must consider the system more deliberately. We feel predisposed toward it; but if its apostles affirm its incompatibility with what seems to us good reason, we must hold aloof; for reason, as one of the fathers has said, is our only means of judging of the truth of any matter whatever, even of revelation itself. So argue the conservative minority. Do we not see half our young men standing in this attitude? The spirit of God may reach them; but the heart's door may even be bolted against the spirit of God.

Now, turning toward the author and propagator of this terrible new teaching in science, they may, quite possibly, find a man completely antipodal to him of exalted religious intuitions. Whether from deficiency of religious endowment, or as the result of some mental revulsion caused by religious delinquencies or extravagances in others, he may be seen preserving the most inviolable reticence respecting his own faith and the bearing of his new science upon the current faith of his neighbors. Here is ground for painful apprehension. Our friend in the minority—the young man in college, the man shadowing forth

---

(¹) "Some who think themselves naturally gifted do not wish to touch either philosophy or logic; nay, more, they do not wish to learn natural science. They demand bare faith alone".(Clemens Alex., Strom., book i., chap. ix.). "But, as they say that a man can be a believer without learning, so, also, we assert that it is impossible for a man without learning to comprehend the things which are declared in the faith" (*ibid.*, book i., chap. vi.).

a creed to shape his life—will certainly prolong his hesitance; his questionings will become bolder; he will recede visibly from alliance with religion. But should the man of science happen to be a doubting Xeniades or D'Alembert, or a scoffing Von Holbach, or misanthropic Rousseau, he may even corroborate the fatal charge of the pure religionist, and leave our seeker after truth to ponder over the problem, What must be the result when immovable religious faith is impinged upon by the irresistible force of rational evidence?

Here is a dilemma more painful than can be described, and it seems to us that he who contributes to rescue the victim from between the millstones of doubt performs a religious service for his fellow-man. The verdict which comes from the lofty elevation of a faith which ignores the grounds of doubt is false. The verdict which comes from the sullen depths of a doubt which ignores the grounds of faith is also false. The conflict, friend, is imaginary. Heavenly faith will receive from imperial science the kiss of reconciliation.

It is the effort to show that Christian faith sounds no dissonance with the universal scheme of truth which occupies the author of the work before us. *He* does not look unmoved upon the wide paralysis of faith and hope caused by the pernicious influence of this uneducated crusade against science, and this soulless contempt for religion. He presents us a conception of the world, as framed and sustained by profoundest scientific investigation, and shows us that it implies God. Here is the text-book for the wavering, and for those who would counsel the wavering. Here is the resolvent for their scientific doubts—doubts which can not be dissipated by the fervor of a hymn, nor exorcised by the authority of a sermon—the most stubborn and invincible of all the obstacles to religious life.

Let us examine this work. It is not a theory framed by the author. It shows a thorough familiarity with all recent authorities in physical science; and its copious array of citations, concatenated together, would almost constitute a manual of science in the words of the masters themselves. Indeed, we feel moved to express our wonder, *in limine*, that an author so thoroughly familiar with the questions discussed should feel it necessary to fortify his statements by quoting so largely the dicta of scientists and philosophers. Dr. Cocker, philosopher as he is, is also a scientist, and he possesses the prerogative of speaking by authority, yet he seems reluctant to rest his own logical convictions on their merits. One feels sometimes disappointed that he does not leave a well-reasoned and well-put truth to rest without the bolster of authority. One is led to suspect he may be deficient in the dogmatic spirit. He seems distrustful, at times, of his judgments in matters of physical science; but no person can read the work without feeling that the author's information and clearness of head make him the equal of those whom he cites for confirmation; and this all the more when it is remembered that the disputed points in physical science lie rather within the territory of philosophy than of physics. The explanation of this exuberance of literature is undoubtedly to be found in the author's purpose to put the representatives of science themselves upon the stand, to testify in their own words, and thus forestall all charges of misinterpretation. This purpose is judicious, and hastens the finality of the existing controversy. But, aside from such object, the reader will thank the author for opening so many avenues of collateral reading and study.

Viewed as a whole — in its conception, method, and argument — the work is a finished product of broad philosophical reflection, and sheds a genuine lustre upon American authorship. It is a pure and lofty cosmic philosophy. It supplies the co-hemisphere of his former work,([1]) and rounds out with completeness a sphere of cosmo-theistic reflection. He has given

---

([1]) "Christianity and Greek Philosophy."

us the relations of Christianity to ancient thought, and the relations of Christianity to modern thought. In the former, he has not developed as great detail as Cudworth in the "Intellectual System of the Universe;" in the latter, his details of science occupy the physical rather than the organic field, as in M'Cosh's "Typical Forms and Special Ends in Creation." Cudworth and M'Cosh have diverged to great distances in certain directions — and so, indeed, have Paley, and Butler, and Chalmers, and the "Bridgewater Treatises;" but Dr. Cocker has described a complete circumference by keeping himself constantly near the central and fundamental position. He has given a great range of proof; others have adduced a greater variety of illustrations. Spencer([1]) and Fisk,([2]) as far as comparisons may be made, have furnished each an admirable and masterly organon, and Mahan([3]) has given a more ostentatious metaphysic; but we think the reader of these authors has need to exercise a degree of discrimination between sound and unsound which is not required in the study of Dr. Cocker.

Starting with the fundamental inquiries which have exercised the thinking world in all ages, the author leads us by steps of reasoning, as lucid as logical, through the realms of philosophy, science, and revelation, to the necessary and vivid conception of a personal, Intelligent Will, as the originator, conservator, and governor of the world.

Four answers, he tells us, have been given to the question, What is the First Principle of all things? "In the beginning was MATTER;" "In the beginning was FORCE;" "In the beginning was THOUGHT;" "In the beginning was WILL." The first and second answers coalesce with Atheism; the third, with Pantheism; the fourth is the creed of Theism; and this is the answer which is rendered alike by our Sacred Scriptures and by the testimony of recent science.

([1]) "A System of Philosophy."   ([2]) "Cosmic Philosophy."
([3]) "Natural Theology."

The idea of God is a common phenomenon of the universal intelligence of our race. An inquiry into the essential nature of the divine originative existence thus revealed discloses it as "an unconditioned will, or self-directive power seeing its own way, and having the reason and law of its action in itself alone." Will is conceived as implying *reason, affection,* and *efficiency.* This determination of the nature of the first principle is sanctioned by both philosophy and science. Grove, Sir John Herschel, Carpenter, Wallace, the Duke of Argyll, Laycock, Murphy, Challis, and even Comte, unite in affirming that intelligent will is the only rational explanation of the existence and order of the universe. All our acquired conceptions of God fall into harmony with this idea. Whether contemplated under the category of being, attribute, or relation; whether in the light of reason or of revelation; our total conception of the Supreme Cause finds its synthetic expression in WILL.

In discussing the question, What conception are we to form of the nature and mode of the first origination? the author first considers it in its hermeneutical and metaphysical aspects, arriving at the conclusion that it is the purpose of Scripture to teach the absolute origination of all existence by the Power of God, and that the same conclusion is the outcome of the most defensible line of philosophic reasoning in respect to the existence of space and time, matter and force. The absolute ideas of *immensity* and *eternity* he finds imbedded in the depths of consciousness; and he is led, by a subtle process of reasoning, to regard immensity and eternity as attributes of God; while space and time are relations between co-existing things and successive events, and, *apart from things and events, have no reality.* Matter, also, derives its existence from the divine will—produced, not out of nothing, but out of the eternal potentialities of the divine nature. The establishment of the conditionality of the existence of time, space, and matter relieves natural theology of those fatal embarrassments involved in the admissions of Chalmers, Martineau, Mahan, and others. "The creative act was not conditioned by time, or space, or matter."

The conclusion we freely indorse; but it seems to us the discussion of the question respecting the nature of space and time is not yet closed. The affirmation that space and time have no reality apart from things and events is not thoroughly satisfying. It is difficult to apprehend how the existence of body (we use the term for any entity possessing extension) can condition the existence of space. If space, as we all agree, is the condition of the existence of body, then the existence of space is the logical antecedent of the existence of body, and it must be possible to contemplate spatial existence abstracted from bodily existence — that is, with body non-existent. Let the attempt be made; think all material existence annihilated except two atoms of matter. Space, as our author admits, still exists. The space once occupied by matter annihilated, it seems to us, also exists as before. Now think the last two atoms annihilated, and space, our author says, exists no longer; nothing but the immensity of God remains, as before creation began. But for us the space still exists. The fallacy in Dr. Cocker's reasoning, if we may venture the opinion, is a *fallacy of definition;* it consists in adopting an arbitrary definition, and one which does not answer to the universal idea of space. Space, he says, "is the relation of co-existing material things— that is, the relation of position, distance, direction, hereness, thereness." Accordingly he says, "Let one atom of matter be created, and we have extension." That we grant, for extension is an essential property of matter. "Let a second atom be created, and there is now a relation of distance, position, direction—that is, there is *space.*" The existence of the relations alleged is obvious, but we appeal to the common consciousness for the verdict that such relations are *not space.* Having assigned such a definition to space, the conclusion is self-evident that space was created in the creation of matter, for the conclusion is embraced in the definition; and (as similar reasoning may be employed in reference to time) that time was created in the creation of matter; and that, as a corollary, space and time have no eternal and necessary existence; and creative efficiency was in no way conditioned by them. These propositions are all but different forms of the definition. The last is a most important conclusion for natural theology; nay, we agree with the author, that a system of natural theology is baseless which does not rest on this corner-stone. But we feel fully persuaded of our title to this corner-stone, even if not derived from the authority alleged: we possess a more valid title than one resting on an erroneous definition.

What is that title? it will be asked. Our first and highest title is based on the necessary intuition of First Cause. The universal intelligence entertains the idea of First Cause; accepts its reality; can not be driven from a belief in it. There must be one cause which does not exist as an effect. No existence can be prior to that which has the sole capacity to confer existence. Neither space, time, matter, nor material force can assert possession of that capacity. It is only when we attempt to reconcile this spontaneous concept of the necessary limitation of the existence of space, time, matter, and force with the formulated processes and products of reflective thought, that difficulty is discovered and doubt arises. But suppose the method of this harmony undiscoverable; we are not bound to point it out. Our difficulty is disclosed in a deductive inference several removes, perhaps, from the first truths from which we argue. Every step opens a possibility of fallacy. Our belief in absolute creation is *primary;* it possesses higher authority than any deduction—still more, a deduction which conflicts with it.

But we may *endeavor* to deduce conclusions which shall quadrate with the highest law of belief. The existence of body implies the existence of space; for there can be no extension—not even an atom's extension—without space. It also implies the existence of time; for we can not separate existence from duration: a thing whose existence has no duration has no actual existence. Space and time, then, are concapacities of body—the conditions of the possibility of body. Time is the sole capacity of unextended being. But time and space have no *dependence* on body or succession. Time exists logically before succession, and space before body; and we are able to think them as so actually existing. Neither time nor space is the capacity or condition of *absolute* existence. As to absolute being, we can not affirm that it exists *in* time or space— in eternity or immensity. *God exists.* Here and there, prior and subsequent, have no meaning in relation to the Absolute. Space and time, immensity and eternity, are not needed for the existence of God; *nor are they attributes of God:* they are created to serve as the capacities of other existence, or the conditions of the potentialities of other existence. Of the nonexistence of space and time we can, indeed, form no conception or idea; our reason knows no denomination in which to formulate that negation; we are part of the same system as space and time, and our intelligence is made the measure of the system to which we belong, and not another unimaginable system which may be possible with God. Nor is it necessary to form the concept of divine existence manifest, cognizable in all space and all time past and future, and yet characterized by activity not transitive through time and space. There are few things which may be confidently predicated of the Absolute by finite intelligence; and we may be certain that of the legitimate predicates of the Absolute, nearly all must transcend the grasp of human reason to the same extent as his causality existing out of relation to time and space.

We proceed, now, with our résumé. A survey of the passing phenomena of the actual world soon transports thought backward to a beginning. That the existing *order* had a beginning, is a thesis less debatable than the creation of *matter.* The leading representatives of science accord with each other and with the showing of Sacred Scripture on this point. Little less contrariety of conviction now obtains in reference to the limitation of cosmical existence in the opposite direction. Science and revelation with one voice prophesy an end. If science conduct us backward to a condition of matter which, for her, must be regarded as a beginning, what has she to testify in reference to the nature of matter, and thence, by inference, in reference to the origin of matter? This question affords the author the opportunity to bring science to the witness-box; and the verdict made up from its testimony is alternative: Either matter is simply a phenomenon of force, and therefore referable to an original creative entity as its ground, or else it is to be regarded, in each of its atoms, as "a manufactured article and a subordinate agent," "precluding the idea of its being eternal and self-existent." This, let it be remembered, is the verdict of recent science. Here let the person troubled about the atheistical tendencies of modern science take hope again, and trust to the voice of God which he hears, as Socrates heard it,([1]) perpetually uttered in his own consciousness. Science—*physical* science—affirms that all its data—its *ultimate* data—*are things created.*

Holding, then, to the creation of time, space, and matter, and to the finiteness of the existing order, what was the *method* of its beginning? That some motive or sufficient reason for creating was necessary to condition the divine will to activity, is maintained both on purely metaphysical grounds and on the admission of philosophers and scientists. The doctrine of

---

([1]) "I am attended by a supernatural intimation which has been assigned me from a child, by Divine appointment. This is a voice which, when it comes, prevents what I am about to do" (Plato, "Theages," xi.).

final cause, then, instead of being exploded, is acquiring new strength under the sanction of such names as Laycock, Sir William Thomson, Bacon, Müller, and even J. S. Mill. "The highest law of the universe," concludes our author, "must be a *teleological* idea to which all nature-forces and all causal connections are subordinated. This ultimate purpose forms, as it were, a complete net-work of higher teleological connections above the web of mere aiteological connections which pervades the universe." As to the nature of the supreme teleological law of the universe, finite intellect may judge inadequately or erroneously; but our Christian Scripture reveals its character as a purpose to "communicate of the divine blessedness to intelligent personal being." Reasoning from this fundamental principle, it must be inferred that the self-manifestation of God in creation would be *gradual, cumulative, conservative*, and *harmonious*. A critical examination of the sacred narrative, in reference to its general purpose and its literary character, shows that this *à priori* inference is sustained; and an inquisition of the facts and conclusions of science demonstrates a complete consonance with the meaning educed from the sacred text.

In drawing out the parallel chronologies of Genesis and geology, we notice but one point which is open to our adverse criticism. With Lange and many others, Dr. Cocker recognizes only the first verse of Genesis as belonging to the "exordium" or "proëmium;" we feel quite confident the real exordium embraces the first and *second* verses. What is the subject of the statement in the opening of the second verse? The EARTH. "And the *earth* was formless and empty." Now, according to the author, this was before the creation of "light"—the luminosity of the matter out of which the earth was to be fashioned. Is such an interpretation reasonable? Next, the succeeding clauses depict events *in relation to the earth*. "And darkness was upon the face of the abyss; and the spirit of God brooded upon the face of the waters."(¹) Now, this was an "abyss" revealed in the condition of the *earth*, just mentioned; and these "waters" belonged to the *earth*, and not to outer space. It is only in the third verse that the primeval fact in creation is enunciated; *this is the beginning of the narrative*. The statements of the second verse are to be regarded as detached glimpses—foreshadowings—of some of the mighty events which are to pass before us in the hymn; as when, in the proëmial passage of the "Paradise Lost," Milton sings,

> "Of man's first disobedience, and the fruit
> Of that forbidden tree whose mortal taste
> Brought death into the world, *and all our woes*,
> With loss of Eden," etc.

Here, as is universal with the epic poets, some salient facts of the narrative are pre-announced. We always picture the sacred writer as gazing upon an inspired vision. The first and highest fact of all is the disclosure of God as absolute originator. Next, as the panorama of creation passes rapidly before him, his attention is particularly arrested, 1. By the formless and empty condition of the arid, scorching surface of the primeval crust; 2. By the chaos—the disorder of, and the absence of correlations in, the features of that surface and the promiscuity of the aërial envelope; 3. The darkness which hid the earth when the gathered mantle of aqueous vapors excluded the ancient sunlight; 4. The ocean precipitated, and myriad

---

(¹) Our author says "vapors," and quotes Lange: "The 'waters' of verse 2 is quite another thing than the water proper of the third creative day; it is the fluid (or gaseous) form of the earth in its first condition." Now, its first condition was not liquid—if that is what is meant by "fluid" —and an incandescent gaseous fluid would be a singular condition of matter to which to apply a term immediately afterward applied to *waters*. This is a virtual arraignment of the good discrimination, and, so far, the authority, of the narrative.

forms of life *hatching* from the waters vivified by the "brooding" "spirit of God." Of these conspicuous features of the divine work he makes a memorandum; and then returns to the beginning to recount the series of events in its completeness and order. And thus he begins: "God said, 'Let light be;' and light was."

No difficulty arises from the use of the word "evening," on the theory that the first "day" began with the creation of light. "Evening" and "morning" are not here equivalent to darkness and light; they are poetically expressive of the "beginning" and "end" of a demiurgic day. If the "evening" of the first day means the darkness which preceded the creation of light, what means the evening of the second day, which followed the creation of light? We think the interpretation here suggested to be demanded equally by critical exegesis and by science.

The next question which arises concerns the present relation of the Creator to the creation. The key-note of the discussion respecting the conservation of the world is struck in the copious citations from Sacred Scripture, and the authorities of the Church, which represent God as continuously exerting a conserving efficiency, without which creation would sink immediately into non-existence. Divergent from such a recognition of divine power are the views of certain "advanced thinkers," which our author now proceeds to examine. The first school, represented by such writers as Professor Tyndall, Dr. H. Bence Jones, and Dr. Bastian, hold to "the absolute inseparability of matter and force." While subscribing to the doctrine of primordial creation, they maintain that the phenomena of the universe are perpetuated through the inherent and unwasted energy imparted to matter in the beginning. The second school, represented by such men as Professors Owen, Huxley, and Baden Powell, "deny the ultimate distinction between matter and force, and regard both as phenomenal manifestations of some 'unknown substratum'—a supramaterial PHYSIS ($\phi \acute{v} \sigma \iota \varsigma$), which is identical with the divine substance." This is a phase of thought which verges toward Pantheism. "A third and intermediate school assumes the existence of a plastic nature (*vis formativa*) intermediate between the Creator and his work, by which the phenomena of nature are produced." This hypothesis was propounded by Cudworth, and probably possesses a close affinity with the old theory of the *anima mundi*; but it may be doubted whether the "animating principle" of Harvey, the *materiæ vita* of Hunter, or the "organic force" of Müller, or "plastic force" of the Schoolmen, is similarly intended to imply the existence of any separate intelligence. The theory has been lately reproduced by Dr. Laycock and Mr. Murphy, under the name of "unconscious organizing intelligence." To what, it may be asked, does this intelligence pertain? If to matter, the theory means Atheism; if to spirit, it means Pantheism.

Now, every conception of the world which makes it self-supporting, self-evolving, with Deity standing merely as a remote, unapproachable prefix, however sanctioned by any theology styling itself orthodox, is essentially atheistic and in conflict with Scripture; but, happily, also, a conception which is incompatible with the deductions which we are compelled to draw from the data of reason and science. In the defense of this thesis, our author displays an admirable familiarity with the theories and speculations of physical science, and gives, we think, the two most charming chapters of his work. Our limits do not permit even an abstract of his method; and we can only commend this masterly discussion to the studious attention of those who desire to acquaint themselves with the real positions of the scientists named, and the relations which their science sustains to the Biblical doctrine of immanent divine efficiency.

The forms under which Dr. Cocker discusses the leading

theories which he opposes are: 1. The hypothesis of natural law. 2. The hypothesis of active force communicated to matter at its creation. 3. The hypothesis of a plastic nature. His own views may be summarized as follows: 1. Matter is not a mere phenomenon of force, but is an entity of a purely passive character, serving as the recipient and vehicle of force. 2. It consists of ultimate continuous atoms or molecules. 3. Force can not be a property of matter. It is an attribute of mind or spirit alone; and spirit force is the only force in the universe. 4. All the forms of energy manifested in the universe are only transformations([1]) of the one omnipresent force issuing from the one fountain-head of power — the *Divine Will*. 5. All the phenomena of molecular life (bioplasmic phenomena) are the result of the immediate presence and direct agency of God.

Thus the final conclusion is, that "God is not simply the *transitive*, but the *immanent*, cause of the universe. * * * His ceaseless energy produces all the phenomena of nature." Is not this identification of the dynamical life of the universe with God, Pantheism? To this question he replies: "The theory which represents the Deity as the transitive cause of the universe — a Δημιουργός mechanically fashioning the materials supplied to his hands, and then leaving it to the working of its own inherent forces — is rank Deism. The hypothesis which regards the Deity as *no more* than the dynamical life of the universe — an informing and organizing soul associated with matter — is naked Hylozoism. The theory that reduces all existence, material and mental, to phenomenal manifestations of one eternal, self-existent substance, which evolves itself according to an inward law of necessity, and which is elusively called

---

([1]) On the theory of immanent divine agency the "different forms of energy" are not "*transformations*" of one divine will-force; they *are* the divine will-force in its varied self-imposed modes of activity.

God, is Pantheism. But the doctrine which embraces the two conceptions of *transcendence* and *immanence*, and while it teaches the immanence of God in matter, proclaims the infinite distinctness in essence between matter and God, and the infinite omnipresence of a personal God above and beyond the limitations of matter, is Christian Theism."

If we recognize the world as created and sustained by divine power, and accept the testimony of revelation that the free and loving impartation of happiness to other conscious beings was the final cause of creation, we reach the inquiry, What has been the method of God in the treatment of his rational creatures? What are the phenomena and laws of the providence of God in human history? The conclusion developed from the discussion of this question sets man as an objective point in the geological transformations of the earth and its successive faunas and floras, and in the final configuration of the terrestrial surface; and establishes a parallelism between the educational development of the race and that of the individual; transferring the work of human education, in each successive stage, to a new theatre, until at length, the stages of Oriental, Hebrew, Greek, and Roman civilization being passed, the Christian civilization seems destined to be fully unfolded and perfected upon a continent presenting, physically and politically, the freest scope for the activity of the appointed agencies of human perfection and happiness.

Descending to a discussion of the question of providence and prayer, the author strikes what he announces as "the most sharply defined issue between Science and Religion — in fact, the only real issue at the present time." We are inclined to think this statement quite correct. The old issues of atheism, materialism, and pantheism have vanished in smoke, since we discover it to be impossible to settle upon any well-accepted doctrine of science from which a simple deductive inference does not usher us into the presence of a personal and adorable

Divinity. We shall continue to hear the old accusations hurled against the citadel of science, but we may rest assured that they proceed from combatants who live in the past. The discussion of prayer considered from the stand-point of science is conducted with characteristic learning and conclusiveness; and we think any clergyman placed under the necessity of vindicating prayer from the aspersions of Professor Tyndall may find here a mine of pertinent suggestions. "In prayer," concludes the author, "the intelligent believer does not invoke a different Power from that which is manifested in all the forms of physical energy which are manifested in nature; he does but invoke the *same* Power, and the *only* Power which is the source of all causation, and produces all the processions of phenomena."

The last two chapters are devoted to a discussion of the moral government of the world—its ground, its nature, conditions, method, and end. The *first* subjective condition of moral government is intelligence. In discussing this condition the author is led to place a definition upon conscience. He does not view it as a distinct faculty of the mind, but rather as the "common field in which is revealed the operation of all our faculties in their especial relation to moral law." It is thus: (1) "The *reason* intuitively apprehending universal moral ideas and laws." * * * (2) The *understanding* apprehending the relations in which we stand to God, to our fellow-beings, and to self as a moral personality endowed with reason and freedom. (3) The *judgment* comparing the acts of a voluntary agent * * * with the immutable ideas and laws of the reason, and affirming this is *right*, and worthy of praise and reward, or that is *wrong*, and deserving of blame and punishment. (4) A particular state of the sensibility—the painful or pleasurable emotions which spontaneously arise in the presence of right or wrong in our actions or in the actions of our fellow-men."

In reference to this analysis, we can not avoid raising the

query, In what do the intelligential elements differ from reason, understanding, and judgment, in their exercise upon non-ethical data? Is there any adequate ground for dissociating the moral intuitions of the reason from intuitions concerning modality or quantity—except with the view to a classification of the intuitions? And does the understanding, in seizing upon relations which may constitute the data of an ethical decision, become a different faculty from that exercised upon relations of utility, efficiency, or congruity? Or does judgment, in rendering its decisions? In every case, we respond negatively. There is only a difference in the *subjects* upon which these faculties are exercised. In the analysis of the author, the sensibility is the only power which is *sui-generis*, and this he does not view as subjectively distinct from the general sensibility. His conception of conscience is neat and intelligible; and we quite agree with him that *such* a conscience is *not* a separate faculty of the soul; it is only a certain co-ordination of activities upon ethical data; it is a dethronement of conscience as an autonomy, and a diluting and weakening of it to a mere complex of functions. In all this the theory is a violation of the universal convictions on this subject. We think, in respectful disagreement with him, that the composite activity which he views as a conventional conscience, *does* involve an element which constitutes the natural conscience, and one for which we have no name unless we call it conscience. There is no sensibility but this ethical element which constitutes the feeling that "I ought," or "ought not;" and this becomes pleasurable or painful according as act agrees or disagrees with that which judgment has pronounced right. Conscience proper, we think, is *not* a discerning faculty, and pronounces no judgments; but when once the discernments have been made and the judgments pronounced by the intellect, conscience, as a feeling([1]) of a pecul-

---

([1]) Religion may be defined as *the feeling of the existence of the All-*

iar kind, prompts to actions conformable to the judgments pronounced, and accompanies the contemplation of an act with pleasure or pain according to its conformity or non-conformity with the prompting.

The *second* subjective condition of moral government leads to a discussion of the freedom of the will, the outcome of which (would that space permitted a complete outline of these two chapters!) is as follows: Will is original, uncaused cause; it is not caused by motive; "motives may be reason *for* action, conditions under which it acts, but they are not causes *of* action;" or, in the language of Dr. Whedon, "for its own effect, will or the willing agent is a complete cause; as complete a cause as any cause whatever; and every complete cause produces its effect *uncausedly.*" These enunciations, it seems to us, cut to the marrow of the subject, and harmonize the fact of universal motivity with the fact of conscious freedom.

One can not complete the thoughtful perusal of this work without a feeling of high admiration and profound satisfaction. There has passed before his mind a vision of heavenly beauty. The grand conclusion shines in upon him like a divine illumination, and he feels absorbed in an atmosphere of supernal radiance and tender love. It is a vision of God, of his own free-

---

Cause, and of his inevitable grasp upon us, and paternal interest in us. The feeling is primarily intuitive knowledge; it is strengthened and sanctioned by ratiocinative knowledge. The grasp felt inspires reverence, awe, fear, desire to please, supplication. The paternal interest prompts to gratitude, love, praise, and prayer. The *fear* of God, in the ethnic religious scale, must necessarily precede the *love* of God. The latter is based on a knowledge of what God has done, and purposes to do *for us*. Hence the lowest savages know only a malevolent deity. All the powers of the soul are made ministers to the demands of the religious feeling. Hence religious systems, rites, creeds, institutions, enterprises—all inspired by the unvarying religious feeling, but all reasoned out and executed by finite and erring intelligence.

will resolving to create a world, and populate it with beings physically adapted to it, but yet in his own spiritual image—beings to be made happy; a vision of God *in* the world, maintaining it, communing with it, admitting himself into the consciousness of his beloved intelligences; speaking to them in the voiceless whisperings of reason, in the radiant beauties of the field and the sky, or in the awful voices of the storm and the earthquake and the collapse of planetary systems; God *with us*—Immanuel—strengthening and cheering, lifting us up and pitying us in our distresses, watching for the whispered prayer, responsive to the hymn of adoration, infolding us with his love through all the journey of mortal life, and then, when the light of the cerulean heaven fades in our glazing eyes, revealing us to ourselves in the midst of a light which mortal eyes can not behold, and which floods with ineffable glories that other world from which we are now shut—not by distance, but by life.

An author who can bequeath his readers an impression like this has earned a title to gratitude, to fame, to an eternal reward.

GLIMPSES OF THE EVIDENCE, À POSTERIORI.

XII.

GOD AND RELIGION IN NATURE.

ILLUSTRATIONS OF INTENTIONALITY AND OF OTHER BIBLICAL TEACHING.

I. *Manifestations of Power in Creation.*

WE propose to look out upon Nature, and see what there is to suggest the idea of God and religion. If there be any thing in the universe to prove or illustrate the being and attributes of God, and to confirm our faith in the authority of the Sacred Scriptures, let us endeavor to ascertain clearly what it is, and what it teaches.

The most impressive and most comprehensible phenomena of the Universe are manifestations of POWER. Those which most readily excite our wonder and astonishment, when we pause to consider them, are manifestations of *physical* power. Among the works of human hands, we gaze with amazement on the ponderous bulk of the Pyramids, and the majesty of St. Peter's at Rome, and that marvel of modern engineering which lifts a massive brick block of Chicago stores and moves it bodily to a new location. But what are Pyramids to the Alps, which have been lifted by some power to an altitude thirty-three times the height of the largest Pyramid? And yet the Alps are little more than half the height of the Andes, and not more than the hundredth part of their mass. These ponderous mountain chains have been upheaved bodily, tearing their way through masses of solid rock miles in thickness, uplifting, crushing, tilting, and dislocating the solid floor of half a continent. We must not forget that this is the work of physical power. These are physical masses, moved by physical agencies, and give expression to the efforts of physical power as really as the conscious labors of human hands.

What, again, is the power of man in upheaving bodily a massive, stone-built structure? No strain that man has ever applied has compressed or stretched to a perceptible extent a block of building-stone above an inch or two in diameter. The builder makes no allowance for compression of the stones which lie at the very base of the most ponderous edifices. Yet such are the strains which nature exerts upon the rocky slabs built into the hill-sides that they yield like india-rubber to the pressure; and when, by quarrying, the strain is relieved, the crushed rocks, with a groan, ease themselves back to their original dimensions. Here is power which may well amaze us. We must not forget, in our habit of thinking that these are the phenomena of nature, that they are none the less the results of power—such power precisely as man exerts in raising a pillar or kneading a lump of clay.

But these, after all, are some of the feeblest of nature's efforts. Look beyond the phenomena of uplifted mountain-masses, deep-scooped ocean basins, forest-laying tempests, and land-consuming waves. Look out into limitless space! There hang worlds of ponderous bulk, fashioned by some plastic hand, upheld by some mighty agency, moved onward in their majestic courses by some mysterious power. If we would know how great the power which handles these spheres, think of the total bulk of our own world, and of the crash of matter which its fall would occasion. There is the sun, the ancient mother of the planets, but still fervid in the heat of youth, whose bulk is so great that if its centre were placed where the earth's centre is, the body of the sun would extend in every direction as far as the moon—nay, would extend beyond the moon a distance equal to eight times the circumference of the earth. And yet, so vast a globe of matter as this has been shaped by the

Power which operates in creation, and rolls the planets in their yearly courses. Do not let the phraseology of science mislead us. Science affirms that the spherical form is "natural" to matter—that its particles, gravitating equally toward the centre of gravity, spontaneously produce the sphere. But think again. Is not the shaping of this tremendous mass a real work? Is not the force there which moves the particles, molds the mass, enspheres the planet and the sun? Is it less a stupendous physical force because displayed in the field of nature? And then, again, what is this force? Is it matter acting for itself?—shaping itself? Or is the origin of force outside of matter? Science says "gravity" does these mighty deeds. If nothing more could be said, its deeds are sufficiently amazing to excite our attention and set us to thinking. But what is "gravity?" Whence proceeds that energy which science calls by this name? Gravity is not a being to manifest the attribute of force; nor is it an attribute of the masses moved. These masses are the objects acted upon by the source of power which imparts a gravitating tendency. There must be some *being* in whom the energy resides. And when we come to think more closely, we find the conviction existing in our minds that the fountain of all power is WILL. In human affairs we witness no result which we do not necessarily assume to have been produced by some human agency, prompted by volition. And so, in the field of nature, every phenomenon and event must rest back, for its ultimate cause, on some Intelligent Will. This is a law of our minds. We recognize in nature the same matter, the same forces, the same modes of activity, the same reflections of intelligence, motive, and will, as are disclosed in the finite field of the human body and human activities. It is this which renders nature comprehensible to any extent, and authorizes us to interpret nature as the expression of thought and volition.

Think, again, of the magnitude of the power exemplified in

nature. Over what an inconceivable sweep of space it stretches! The dimensions of the great sun overpower us; but the attempt to take in his distance is almost paralyzing to the mind. Ninety-two millions of miles! This is a small thing in words; but try to realize its meaning. A railway train moves thirty miles an hour; but yet, if a railroad stretched from the earth to the sun, a train would require three hundred and fifty years to pass over it. Had the pilgrims from the *Mayflower* stepped immediately aboard that train, their descendants this year would not have reached the farther terminus of the road. Nay, the distance remaining would be so vast that the great-great-grandchildren of the children of to-day would be the first to reach that distant sun. As our thoughts stretch along over that line of road, dimmer and dimmer and dimmer in the uncompassable distance, how the idea of its vastness oppresses us! And yet there is a power which stretches from the sun to the earth. It bends the whole mass of the world from its straight course, and compels it to career around the sun like a colt held by a halter. It lifts the ocean into a broad tidal swell, and whips the rocky shores with the stormy lash of the waves, before whose power oaken ships are as straw, and granite cliffs but lumps of chalk. How vast the power which reaches so far and works such tremendous results!

But this, too, is one of the least of the powers which busy themselves in the universe stretched out before us. The whole distance which separates the sun from the earth is so inconsiderable in the field of nature that light travels over it in eight and a half minutes. The light by which the reader peruses these lines started from the sun about the time when he read the title of this article. Think now of a space so vast that the same light must travel a hundred, a thousand, ten thousand years, before it reaches its destination. The attempt to compass with thought an interval like this is literally like the attempt to comprehend God himself. And yet we must assert that light is flying over all these mighty intervals of space. Some of the starlight which falls upon our eyes any night has just arrived from a journey of a thousand years. The same powers, also, which work at mountain-building on our earth, and reach forth from the sun to all the planets, stretch even to the remotest star, shaping it, rolling it, hurling it, as if it were the veriest plaything of a child. Nay, it is a power so vast as to seize the whole frame-work of stars and systems in one infinite embrace and send it whirling and wheeling onward through the depths of boundless space, like a handful of pebbles thrown through the air.

Do we need to carry our imaginations farther to be convinced that the power working in nature has no measure, no limits? It is, indeed, infinite. Here, in nature, is at least a demonstration of *Infinite Power*.

II. *Manifestations of Intelligence in Creation.*

Every person distinguishes between results produced without intention, and results produced for a visible purpose. The wild wind scatters the autumn leaves about the yard, or hurries them along the street with restless haste, till they reach some lodgment in a nook or corner, and there they lie. And what is accomplished by all this? One gust whisks them across the street, and another whirls them back again. Their final resting-place depends entirely on the accident of the wind. It makes no difference where the fitful gust may leave the brown foliage to decay. The place where a particular leaf shall lie, or even a pile of leaves, is all a matter of chance; and it is all a matter of complete indifference to every body. So, at least, do people think.

But I walk out into my friend's garden, and there I see a pile of leaves lying upon his bed of early flowering bulbs. Upon the leaves, also, are a few bits of boards, which keep the wind from blowing them away. Now, it occurs to me that this is a useful covering for the bulbs in the soil. It will keep the frost out of the ground, and the bulbs will remain uninjured, and secure an early start in the spring. *This* arrangement was *not* the result of accident. This covering was probably placed here by my friend, and he did it because he *understood* that it would protect his bulbs. In fact, it was his good sense, his intelligence, which prompted him to do it. I can understand this act, and perceive *why* it was performed. I feel very certain that it illustrates my friend's intelligence.

A man walks along the street in the rain with an umbrella over his head, and I feel sure that somebody contrived that umbrella with an understanding of its use. It is intended for rainy weather. It is adapted or correlated to rainy weather. The key which unlocks my door sustains an intelligible correlation to the lock, and all the countless contrivances which make up the admirable improvements of civilized life are so many manifestations of the intelligence of their contrivers. We can not look upon the simplest invention or coadaptation of one thing to another, without feeling compelled to regard it as the *product of intelligence.*

The *world* is full of contrivances which were not made by human hands nor invented by human brains. My hand, for instance, with which I write these words, is a more admirable machine than human ingenuity has ever devised. What is a "walking doll" compared with the varied movements of which the hand is capable? Think of all the pincers, pliers, forceps, or tongs which man has invented, and answer whether one of them could seize and move a pen as my fingers do it. I say nothing of the mind which guides the fingers; I speak only of the mechanism. If it requires intelligence to fashion the pen, does it not require more intelligence to fashion the hand which wields it? Look at the joints of the fingers, and see how admirably they close down upon an object. See how the thumb stands opposed to the fingers. See the marvelous rapidity with which these fingers may be made to glide over the keys of a piano, and the astonishing accuracy with which they elicit a predetermined succession of sounds. Think of the numberless varieties of activity to which they may be put. Is there any human contrivance more exquisitely fitted for the work intended to be performed? Certainly there is none which can perform such a *variety* of work.

Now, I think every one is ready to admit that the hand is as much a work of intelligence as a pair of tongs. This, at least, is the natural, instinctive admission. True, we have never seen the Author of nature engaged in making hands by any such process as men employ; but does that really make any difference? Is it of any consequence to know by what instruments or means a device is carried into execution? Is it of any consequence to know whether a contrivance is the result of human or divine agency? If we can detect contrivance, do we not irresistibly say, Here is mind?

If mind was really concerned in the formation of the hand, how consummate a mind it was! Look into the internal structure of bone and nourishing marrow, joints, ligaments, sheaths, juices, veins, arteries, lymphatics, nerves, muscular fibres, blood, blood-corpuscles, skin, fat—all, and more, entering into the constitution of this little instrument; all, and more, kept continually at work, each in its own way, to maintain this wonderful hand in a state of perfect repair. Look deeper. This very skin is composed of several layers; the deeper layers, of countless little cells, visible only with the microscope; underneath are innumerable loops of nerve-fibres to give it sensibility, while the whole integument is perforated by hundreds of thousands of minute apertures for the escape of vapor, and for other uses; and every part, to the central bone, possesses a minute structure revealed only to the microscope, which is just as elaborate, just as perfect, just as carefully and complicately finished at the farther limits of our powers of scrutiny as in the larger and more visible parts. Down toward the infinitely small, these structural details may be traced; and we have every reason to believe that far beyond the powers of our vision are parts and coadaptations and activities as wonderful as those witnessed in the larger movements of the fingers. Where is the human contrivance displaying a thousandth part of this elaborateness? Indeed, there is nothing to compare with it. The detail is boundless; and the intelligence that could provide for all so far transcends our human powers that to us it is *infinite*.

This is one way in which intelligence is manifested in nature. The end for which a contrivance is produced we style the "final cause;" and we deem it perfectly legitimate to argue intelligence from final causes in nature, because our minds are so constituted that we are *necessarily impelled* to attribute a useful collocation of parts to intelligent purpose. But intelligence is also manifested in nature in quite another way. All the work of nature is performed according to fixed methods; and the very idea of method implies systematic, thought-elaborated, and intelligible order, according to which events are made to transpire.

We were speaking of hands. Has not the reader remarked the striking resemblance between the human hand and that of the monkey? Each is used nearly in the same way; but what is most decisive, each is composed of exactly the same number of bones and joints, similarly connected together, and all the internal fabric is almost identical in the two. In short, the *plan* of the two hands is the same, and no one can fail to perceive it. They are as much alike as a shovel and a spade.

But place, now, the monkey's hand by the side of the squirrel's. The squirrel is a vastly less knowing animal; but he uses his hand in a similar way, and it is easy to show that its structure is substantially identical. The hands of the squirrel and the monkey are built upon *one plan*.

But how does the hand of the cat differ from that of the

squirrel? True, the squirrel can handle a nut more skillfully than a cat; but examination shows that the bones of the two hands are identical in number, form, and arrangement. No one, again, would feel disposed to allege that the plan of the cat's paw is materially different from that of the dog or the bear. In fact, we feel compelled to admit that the fore-feet of all these quadrupeds are constructed on the same plan as the human hand. Now, extending our comparisons, we even find the alligator and lizard and frog possessed of the same kind of anterior extremity. The seal and the otter, to adapt them to swimming, have the fingers webbed; and the whale exhibits even a further shaping of the hand into the form of a fin, which, lastly, in the fish, exhibits the lowest modification of a plan which, in its highest development, is the admirable human hand. The fin of a fish, the flipper of a whale, the paw of a cat, the hand of a man, are only modifications of one set of bones—varied manifestations of one idea.

This is not all. Though we can not here employ the argument, nor appropriate the space to prove it, we may assert that this identity of plan includes also the hoofed quadrupeds—little as the horse's foot resembles the hand which flits over the keys of a piano-forte. But even this is but the beginning of these wonderful resemblances. The entire arm of man is identical in plan with the anterior extremity of all other vertebrates. The wing of a bird is only a human arm shaped and consolidated to support an array of quills. The hinder extremities, also, of all back-boned animals are similarly related to each other; and every one must have observed how closely they resemble the anterior extremities.

Thus we arrive at this remarkable conclusion, that all the limbs of all quadrupeds, birds, reptiles, and fishes are but *modifications of one plan*, which in man we see adapted to the purpose of seizing a pen, greeting a friend, or enforcing an idea by means of a gesture.

It is impossible that all these limbs should be thus connected together by identity of plan unless intelligence had conceived the connection and employed the means to realize it in these various forms. Now, when we think of the countless tribes and species of vertebrate animals, in all parts of the world, inhabiting land, sea, and air, burrowing in the ground, sauntering along the river-shore, climbing trees, and occupying every imaginable situation, we perceive that the mind which has planned and executed all these adaptations according to one ideal conception, must transcend inconceivably all the powers of human intelligence. And when we know that these numberless adaptations have been perpetuated in existence for hundreds of thousands of years before the creation of man, we feel that the intelligence displayed in nature is practically, if not absolutely, infinite.

These are single examples. Could we speak of all, how would our thoughts swell with the intelligible manifestations of the omnipresence of infinite mind in nature!

III. *Manifestations of Beneficence in Creation.*

Sitting before my bright coal-fire this winter evening, I fell into a kind of reverie, which, since it has a moral, I may be pardoned for repeating. How comfortable is this warmth, I mused with myself, and to what inconveniences we should be subjected were we not provided with this anthracite! Oak and hickory wood, it is true, make admirable fires, but how rapidly is the country undergoing exhaustion! It is only on the frontiers that we can now obtain cord-wood at a cheaper rate than coal; and, in the densely settled districts, the price of wood is far above that of coal, and is rapidly increasing. Beyond all question, the supply of wood is melting away; and, unless we had these stores of coal to draw upon, a pound of fuel would soon command more money than a pound of wheat. And what enormous quantities of this coal are consumed! Look into those coal-yards in any of our great cities; there are mountains of anthracite and bituminous coals piled up for the winter's consumption. It is not alone in domestic fires that this substance is made to yield us such supplies of heat. There are thousands of steam-engines all over the country, sawing lumber, weaving cloth, spinning cotton, making pins and buttons, propelling locomotives and steamboats, and performing countless other kinds of work; and, if the supply of coal should fail, half of these engines must cease from their labors. Yes, indeed, this black and smutty article lies at the very foundation of domestic comfort and modern civilization.

But what is it? I asked myself. And then my thoughts ran over the series of steps by which the man of science has attained to a knowledge of the nature and origin of this product of the rocks. Why, this black, hard substance is, after all, nothing but real wood. It is the vegetable growth of other long-past ages. There was no man upon the earth to fell the trees and utilize the forests, and so they were laid by and petrified, and preserved till there *should be* a man to use them. The forests of the human time, then far in the future, would not suffice to supply the wants of the coming man, and so it seems nature began to store away the material of the forests hundreds of thousands of years *before* the world had reached such a condition that man could subsist upon it. This coal could not have been packed down for any other being than man. The beasts — of what use was coal to them? As to spiritual intelligences which may inhabit the earth — of what use is coal to them?—unless to demonstrate to them, as it does to us, that the Power which made the world had the intelligence to know that man was coming, and the goodness to provide for his wants. Yes, I can not see it otherwise. As we can not conceive of any thing done without an adequate motive, and we can discern no other reason why some of the rocks were made combustible, it must have been so ordained for the comfort and uses of man.

15*

But if this was really so, what an amazing amount of work has been done in nature for no other object than human uses! To grow millions of acres of forests and lay them down in beds of coal was but a single one of the steps by which man has been placed in possession of this fuel. All my reading and study on this subject comes up to mind. I seem to sink back into the twilight of the world's long history. The ocean is here, and the land—or, at least, a large part of it—and the sea is full of fishes and mollusks, and various other creatures. But the land is desolate and tenantless. The work of creation has come to a standstill. To this time the march of improvement has been continuous; but now no higher creature can be summoned into being, *because the air is irrespirable.* It is filled with carbonic acid gas, which is immediately fatal to every animal which respires it. Will Infinite Power annihilate this poison, and then call air-breathers into being? Infinite Power could have done both; but Infinite Beneficence chose to wait. All the Northern States except New England and New York had just been lifted above the level of the sea; and all over this area luxuriant forms of strange vegetation sprung into existence, fed on this atmospheric poison, fixed it in the form of stem and leaf, and fell down at maturity, accumulating enormous beds of peat. Now those regions subsided, and ocean returned, and layers of mud and sand were strewed over the beds of peat. Then another uplift poured off the ocean's waters, another growth of strange forests accumulated other peat-beds, and another subsidence resulted in their burial. These vicissitudes were continued many ages. At length, with one grand throe, the Alleghany Mountains were brought up, and the wide expanse of the Northern States lay spread out, a permanent home for future races of animals. But this was not till the atmosphere had become purified. And now could be ushered into being those advancing forms of animal life which must breathe air. The end was secured, and the work of creation could continue. Yea, a greater end was secured, which looked ages into the future, and provided for the wants of human creatures in the nineteenth century of the Christian era. And while the ages were rolling on, earthquake visitations passed over the land, the deep rocky sheets were tilted, and in places folded together, and the deep-hidden beds of coal were exposed at the surface, lest man should fail to discover his store-house of fuel.

The ages still rolled on, and the lands became wasted for the uses of the many tribes of animals which were marched across the stage of being, before the advent of their master. Then, again, Beneficence put forth its hand, summoned a continent-wide glacier to plane it down, washed it once again in the sea, and here was a bright, new, soil-covered surface for man's exclusive use.

Now the promise of the ages was fulfilled. When man came upon the earth, what more could have been devised to render his home abundant in comforts? Every element ministered to his wants and enjoyments. Here were fruits and grains and game to appease his hunger, and the very activities put forth to secure them were pleasurable and healthful. Every function of his being brought delight. He looked forth upon the green field, and its color pleased his eye. The evening cloud, the tinted rainbow, the swaying bough, the painted violet's cup, awakened responses in his soul which made him happy; while the awful precipice and the thunder-voiced tempest found answering emotions which swelled his soul in the presence of their sublimities. Even his questioning intelligence was rewarded with answers in the revelations of truth which beamed from the objects around him. Was he capable of reason—here were objects to be reasoned upon and to yield him the fruits of thought. Nature had her secrets, but she was ready to reveal them when intelligently and persistently asked. And so man worked out the story of the earth and was delighted. He lost no great fact of its wonderful history by being delayed in his coming till countless ages of revolutions had passed. Curious — with insatiate curiosity, he could gratify it by peering into and through those long, dark ages lapsed, and glimpsing the tremendous march of terrestrial events on a forming world. What beneficence was here! With a yearning thirst for a knowledge of the world and himself, how miserable would have been his situation if no idea could have entered his mind! but how blessed, when the world was found stored with stimuli to curiosity and the materials of thought! Of what avail were suggestions to thought while the world was the home only of brutes ? Of what *need* were they to incorporeal intelligences who read directly the idea symbolized in the material form, and have no relations of dependence upon matter? It was to *human intelligence*, materially embodied, that all these things were accommodated. These sources of enjoyment, these material symbols of thought, these records of the ideas of God, these intelligible relics of the long past, these myriad translatable signs of creative power and beneficence, which render the world all luminous with the halo of divine thought—these all sustain no relations as material forms and objects to any other being than man. They were provided for man countless ages before the birth of our race. They were ordained to augment human happiness, and to lift the thoughts to the unseen realities which underlie phenomena, and to lead them, by no uncertain path, to that Supreme Reality in whom all being finally centres.

Nor was this the end of my reveries; for thought floated on over the circle of social relations as sources of happiness to man—over the religious sentiments and hopes, and the materials in nature for their activity and gratification—the yearning of the soul over the profound problems of the past and future of its existence, and the data in our possession for the solution of these great problems; but everywhere rose up reminders of the Beneficence which has exerted so controlling an influence in the ordinations of the world of which man forms a part.

So the very light which beams from my comfortable fire reveals the record of long-continued preparations for the comfort of man; and this is but the title-page of a *volume* filled with recitals of the Beneficence which shines in nature.

IV. *The Unity of Creation.*

How vast is the empire of gravitation! The acorn falls to the ground in the forest, drawn by the same force which bends the courses of the planets. A drop of water in the air assumes the form of a little sphere, and so does the molten lead descending from the summit of the shot-tower. How few of us have realized that the great planet is only a larger sphere hurled into space to assume its form under the same law as a drop of rain!

The spherical form is natural, we say. Right. It only amounts to the same thing to say that it is the result of gravitation—that force, whatever it may be, which draws all the parts equally toward the centre, and which draws all matter toward all other matter. We say it is a *property of matter* to do this; but really, we can only be certain that it is the *method* according to which matter is *moved*. We do not know whether it is a property of matter to move itself according to this method, or a property of something else to move matter. Now, I think we know nothing about matter as *itself acting;* nor about force as itself acting in matter; and all we can say is, that force is exerted by *living will*. I am inclined to think the only reasonable account we can give of that gravitating force which causes the fall of an acorn is this: that some living will is exerted upon it, and that it is a self-imposed method of this will to act always in the same way under the same circumstances. This uniform method is its *law;* it is what we call a *natural law*.

Now, I would like to direct attention to the vastness of the intervals of *space* and *time* through which this WILL has exerted itself, and is exerting itself. We thought the distance of the sun amazingly vast when we calculated that a train of cars would require three hundred and fifty years to travel across the interval; but the distance of Neptune from the sun is such that more than ten thousand years would be required. And yet Neptune—the farthest planet—is not so remote from the sun but he feels the sun's attraction, and is held, as it were, by a halter, careering around the controlling centre always at about the same distance from it. This central attraction is the same which keeps all the planets from flying off in straight lines; and it is the same force which causes the fall of an apple in the orchard. How vast the *presence* of a Being who can thus exert his will in the orchard, and in the sun, and in the remotest planet! There are a hundred and sixty planets revolving about the sun, all moved forward by a single impulse, and all bent out of right lines and into regular orbits by the sun's attraction. There are little less than twenty satellites or moons revolving similarly about these planets. What further excites our wonder is this: that all these bodies revolve in orbits which are a little longer than broad (ellipses), and all lie nearly in the same plane; that these bodies all move in the same direction, from west to east; that they all rotate on their axes from west to east; that they are all a little flattened at the poles; that such of them as we have been able to examine indicate a succession of seasons like our own; and that they have land and water, and clouds and storms, and sunrise and sunset. In short, this little spot which we call our earth is, as it were, but one nook in a vast farm, while all around is the same system of fields and fences and crops and cultivation as we witness within the bounds of our little nook.

But, after all, this is hardly the beginning of the vastness of the empire over which gravitation exercises dominion. The power of gravitation is felt in the stars. They, also, are in motion. Hundreds of them are also revolving in orbits—in elliptical orbits—such motions as can only be explained as we explain the fall of an acorn on the earth. The same power is there—the same WILL is there. The very nearest of those stars is so remote that if we were to represent the distance of Neptune by *ten inches*, that star would be *one mile* away. And yet other stars are two thousand times as remote as the nearest.

We should be still *at home* could we fly to those remotest stars—still in the house of our God. And could we take the wings of light, we might travel over such intervals as we now travel to San Francisco or Calcutta—with this difference, that while by cars we go but fifty feet a second, by light we should go one hundred and eighty-six thousand miles a second. Still, by light, some of our journeys would be rather prolonged. Even by light we should require three and a half years to reach that *nearest* star.

But then, though we can not go, *light goes*. There is a highway for light even to the stars—the farthest stars—for their light has traveled over it in coming to us. That is not a foreign territory from which they glimmer down on us. Those are *our own* skies in which they are set. One ether bathes all the bodies within the visible universe, and is everywhere tremulous with one kind of vibration, regardless of the luminous cause—whether the fire on the hearth, the great sun, or the most distant star.

There is even a closer union than this. The very dust of our streets is made luminous in the sun. There is the same *iron* which rusts in our garden hoe; the same *hydrogen* which we drink from the well; the same *lime* which makes the crayon with which we work our problems on the blackboard; the same *sodium* which forms the salt upon our tables, and salts the water of the ocean. Indeed, we now know that the sun is made of the same materials as the earth. How marvelous an achievement of science was that, to learn the very substance of the sun! But so it is.

And now, more amazing still, those vastly more distant stars are one in substance with our sun; one in substance with the mold which grows our cabbages in the garden. We are surer of this, by far, than we are of the distance of the moon from the earth. How do these facts impress us with the feeling of the unity of the realm of matter! No foreign territory gloams down upon us from sullen highlands over the border. All, all is the dominion of one Will, one Intelligence, one God.

Our thoughts have been roaming among the worlds existing in our day. Let us send them roaming back through time, among other scenes and other worlds. There is a pathway which leads imagination back to a *beginning*. It is too long a road for us to follow now.([1]) Let us fly back, in thought, to that beginning of the existence of our world and all the other worlds which rotate about our sun. How strange the scene! Instead of separate worlds, we behold one vast sphere of fiery vapor, whose diameter is greater than that of the orbit of Neptune. This is the farthest limit to which science guides us backward. Whence that fiery vapor, and whence the forces of matter which abide in it, science can not inform us; but as our reason declares that even matter and force—being dead, involuntary existences themselves—must be but effects caused by some *living will*, so now we fall back on the utterances of our reason, and assert that God is the author of matter and force, and we feel that that saying is true: "In the beginning God *created* the heavens and the earth."

Now, in such a beginning all the bodies of the solar system were merged in one common mass. All these bodies have therefore come forth from a common mass—have had a com-

---

([1]) See chap. v.; also "Sketches of Creation," by the present writer; also *Methodist Quarterly Review* for April, 1873, and January, 1874.

mon origin and a common history—one method, one will guiding all those wonderful changes which, in the long course of ages, have resulted in separate worlds, with a common sun shining down upon all their surfaces alike, and making *one scene* of all the wide expanse of the solar system.

We have not space to recount the vicissitudes of that long history through which planet after planet sprung into being; and that long history of later times, during which our world was undergoing a special preparation; continents growing; mountains rising; soils preparing; and all with intelligible reference to the wants of *a being* then thousands of years in the future. What we wish especially to impress is this: that hundreds of thousands, and probably millions, of years were consumed in the history over which our minds have glanced; but all the work proceeded according to *one method*. One set of physical forces, under the mandate of the almighty Will, began, continued, and completed the building of the world, and all the worlds.

This firmly jointed fabric of the material universe, therefore, with all its vastness, has foundations reaching back almost through an eternity, which are as much a solid and connected whole as the visible parts which rise above the horizon of time. The power, intelligence, and goodness which we see developed in the economy of nature are attributes of the same Being through all the immensity of *space* and all the immensity of *time*.

V. *The Religious Nature of Man.*

It has sometimes been held that man knows nothing of God except through the written revelation; but who can stand under the canopy of the starry sky and gaze and ponder without devotion? Who can think of the magnitudes, the distances, the complexities, the harmonies, which characterize the visible creation on which he gazes, and not feel that there is a Power infinitely great which upholds and moves; an intelligence infinitely vast which plans and provides? The aspects of nature have in all ages inspired men with awe and reverence. It is not alone the Hebrew Psalmist who exclaims, "The heavens declare the glory of God, and the firmament showeth his handiwork." The sun, moon, and stars have always inspired devotion; and men in their ignorance have mistaken the heavenly bodies for the real divinity apprehended in their inmost souls, and have worshiped them. Deeply impressed with the presence of superior power, savage tribes have worshiped mountains and rivers, thunders and tempests. Other tribes, groveling in deeper ignorance, have prostrated themselves before the crocodile or the serpent, the uncouth idol or the shapeless stock. Alas that human beings should go so far astray from the true God!

But there is a lesson in all this. Man *must* have an object to worship. He *feels* the evidences of a power manifested about him—an invisible power greater than himself—a power whose displeasure he fears; to whom he turns for succor when in distress; to whom he feels himself accountable when he sins. In the lowest stages of human condition, this feeling of the divine is only a vague sentiment. In the next stage, it suggests a personal deity or many deities. But underneath all the polytheisms of the world, the human soul has always recognized a *supreme* Divinity, who is regarded as Creator and Judge. The Greeks and Romans worshiped many deities, but always either as mediatorial between man and Jove supreme, or as subordinates, adequate to ordinary emergencies. The ancient Brahmans worshiped fire, sun, and air, and many other deities, but only as manifestations of the one supreme Deity. The Egyptians, also, while polytheistic in their outward practices, held Kneph to be the King of Gods, the creator of all things. Monotheism seems really to be *the deepest faith of humanity.*

I said that all peoples had, somehow, acknowledged the necessity of some being to worship. Worship, prayer, praise, religious rites, religious symbolism—these are part of the history of every people under the sun. The statement is not made lightly. I have examined all the cases of savages *alleged destitute of a religious nature*, and I have been led to these conclusions: In respect to many tribes, the charges are clearly unfounded; in respect to some, we have not sufficient information to base any opinion upon them; in regard to others, it is only true that their religious notions are debased and shocking, while still they are religious in their meaning, and argue the existence of a real religious nature. Only in regard to *three tribes* do I find the testimony such as to render it necessary to admit that they appear to be without any religious sentiments. These are the inhabitants of the Andaman Islands, the Gran Chacos of South America, and the Arafuras of Vorkay, one of the Aru Islands.[1]

I hold that the united testimony, even of savage tribes—even of the most degraded tribes—is in support of the doctrine of the religious nature of man. But when we consider the history of the rest of mankind, how overwhelming becomes the evidence! Every nation that has attained to any degree of culture has had its system of religion. The religions of Egypt and Phœnicia; Judaism, Christianity (viewed merely as a historical phenomenon), Islamism; Brahmanism, Zoroastrianism, Buddhism, and the Greek and Norse religions; Lao-tseism and Confucianism; and, in America, the religions of the Peruvians and the Aztecs—these fourteen great systems of religion have controlled the thoughts, the hopes, the fears, and the destinies of nine-tenths of all the people that have lived upon the earth.

---

[1] The writer has presented and discussed the facts here referred to in two articles published in the *Methodist Quarterly Review* for January and July, 1875.

And even philosophy, in its speculations, tends toward religious themes. It has been the ambition of all founders of philosophic systems to show that they did not subvert prevailing religious ideas. The very highest problems of all philosophy and all science are about the cause of things—the *first* cause—the origin of matter and force, and the orderly structure of the universe. No one, it seems to me, can contemplate the history of the human race and not be convinced that the religious nature has ever been active, ever uppermost.[1]

Such a long-continued manifestation of religious feeling, religious thought, and religious activity must be regarded as an expression of the nature of man—a demonstration that the religious faculties are as deeply seated in our constitution as the intellectual. And then, if our natures impel us inevitably to lift up the voice to God in prayer, there must be a God to hear, or man is grievously mocked. If all mankind have felt impelled to entertain a belief in the future life, there must be a hereafter to man, or his very nature utters a lie. Now, if there be *not* realities answering to the religious faculties of man, there exists here a sad lack of co-ordination, not witnessed in any other faculty or instinct, either of man or brute.

God thus writes his name on every heart. But if man be too proud to confess the feeling of devotion, or if he deny that God has left a testimony in the heart, he can not exercise his *intelligence* without finding out God. We have already seen how, in tracing back the history of our world, we find a beginning—a sphere of fiery vapor—and have been reminded that science can conduct us back no farther. Still, as reason asserts that whatever exists has been caused to exist, we feel confident that the primordial vapor had a cause; and, as *science* can assign no cause, we feel compelled to fall back on that cause

---

[1] A very considerable exemplification of these positions appears in the second and third chapters of the present work.

which the soul spontaneously and universally assigns as the antecedent of all existence. Thus the principle of causality leads thought up to God.

We have heretofore turned our attention to some of the manifestations of intelligence in creation. We have read intelligence in numberless *contrivances*, as in the mechanism of the hand or eye. We have also read intelligence in the admirable *plans* discovered in the operations of nature. We have seen, for instance, that the very plan of the human frame is only a development and perfection of the structure of the lowest vertebrated animal; and that when the fish was first introduced upon the earth, in remote geologic time, it was a germ which was destined to expand into man; it was, in reality, a prophecy of man. Thought we have found inscribed everywhere upon the pages of nature. At least, we have found everywhere such evidences that, were we concerned with mere human affairs, we should assert positively that they are proofs of intelligence. But reason can not make a discrimination here. There is no datum for discrimination. Mechanical adaptations, order, utility, or other correlations, are *everywhere* and *necessarily* proofs of intelligence. Hence the universe displays intelligence, and intelligence as much above human as the universe exceeds a human work.

Again, man distinguishes between right and wrong. All men do it. They feel that certain deeds are right and deserve approval, and that other deeds are wrong and merit condemnation. They feel that there is a moral law which can not be infringed with impunity. Now, if there is a law, there is a Lawgiver. If punishment waits upon wrong-doing, there is a moral Judge. If man exists under a government of moral law, there sits a moral Governor on the throne.

So, reason from whatever datum we will, the conclusion is God. And this conclusion of reason is only identical with the intuition which animates every human heart. This proof that the idea of God arises spontaneously in the human soul, whether as a direct intuition, a conclusion of a process of abstract reasoning, or an impression conveyed by the phenomena of the universe, creates a presumption in favor of a written revelation claiming to come from God. If man knows beforehand that there is a God, he feels predisposed to listen to his messages. This pre-existent knowledge of God is assumed by all the Scriptural writers. They do not attempt to prove the existence of Deity—they do not even assert it. Christ himself did not introduce a religion foreign to human nature. Such a religion could never have found a foot-hold. Christianity finds a deep response in the soul of man. It is built upon a foundation older than itself—a foundation which can never be overthrown without uprooting the instincts of humanity.

Thus the *voices of the universe*, which utter perpetually the name of God and magnify his power, wisdom, and goodness, are found to be in harmony with the *voices of the soul*, which whisper the name of God perpetually in our ears; and both these voices chime with the Scripture which saith, "The Lord God omnipotent reigneth; let the earth rejoice."

VI. *Genesis and Geology.*

In the first chapter of Genesis we find a brief account of the creation of the world. Until modern times, it was the popular opinion(¹) that this narrative taught that the earth and

---

(¹) It is well known that this has not been the universal opinion of philosophers, or even of orthodox theologians. St. Augustine, to go no farther back, maintained that all created things were created instantaneously, but only *potentially* so, and as far as concerned the *emission of original causal efficiency* ("*potentialiter atque causaliter*"); while following this primordial creative volition, through a period of indefinite length, "*per temporum moras*" (as he styles the "days" of Genesis) the forms of the world rose slowly out of potentiality into actuality. Of this opinion St. Thomas Aquinas says, "*Et hæc opinio plus mihi placet*" (2 Sent. Dist. 12, Quæst. 1, art. 2);

heavens were created during an interval of six literal days, and that the work dates back but a few thousand years. These views were entertained when our Bible was translated into English. Since that date, several sciences have sprung into existence which throw a vast amount of light on the history of creation; and if King James's translators had their work to perform to-day, they would see meanings in Genesis which the world had not dreamed of two hundred years ago; and they would make the translation read a little differently, *in order to make it agree more exactly with the original Hebrew.* These sciences—especially geology and astronomy—demonstrate that this creation, though not eternal, has stood millions of years, and that this world even required millions of years for its formation. We know that the Infinite Being *was able* to create this world in six days, but the evidences are that he *did not;* and if he did not, it would be folly to persuade ourselves otherwise. It is infinitely better to learn how God really did proceed, than to turn our backs upon scientific evidence which no candid mind can resist, and wrench our Bible to make it fit a

---

and St. Bonaventure says, "*Multum rationabilis et valde subtilis;* and in reference to his method calls it a "*via philosophica,*" while the contrary opinion is pronounced "*minus rationabilis quam alia*" (Librum secund., Sent. Dist. xii., Quæst. ii., art. 1, conclusio). Cardinal Noris, in 1673, vindicating these views of Augustine, says he "*subtilem prorsus ac se dignam sententiam excogitavit, nempe dies illos intelligendos esse mystice,*" etc.; and the cardinal then condemns the adverse opinions of Lusitanus and Charles Moreau ("Vindiciæ Augus.," c. iv., § ix.; see Migne, "Patrologia Cursus Completus," tom. xlvii., p. 719). Other similar opinions, recorded before the establishment of modern geological views, may be found in Albertus Magnus, Denis the Carthusian (1470), Cardinal Cajetan (1530), Melchior Canus (1560), Bannes (1580), Vincentius Contenson (1670), Macedo (1673), Tonti (1714), Serry (1720), Berti (1740), and, more explicitly, in reference to the days, St. Hildegard, Bertier, Berchetti, Ghici, Robebacher, and Bossuet. For these references I am indebted to Mivart, *Contemporary Review,* January, 1872, where further particulars may be obtained.

misconception of facts. The author of Genesis has given us an account which, when rightly understood, conforms admirably to the indications of latest science. At the same time, he has not attempted to write a scientific history of creation. It possesses a simple, though sublime, style, and is clothed in the thoughts and molded in the structure of Oriental poetry. While poetical, it is not an aimless reverie; while unscientific, it does not depart from the truth. While we have to interpret it in the light of modern science, we have no occasion to reject it as simply an Eastern myth, of no more significance than the legends of the Ganges or of Yucatan. We can show that it exemplifies a most impressive harmony between the utterances of trusting inspiration and the generalizations of rigorous science.

In proceeding to explain this harmony, we must premise a few things bearing on the import of a few words employed by the author or authors of Genesis, which, for convenience, we may ascribe to Moses: 1. The word translated "created," in the first verse, refers to origination from non-existence. It is of no consequence to assert that such creation is "unthinkable," for not only does the text assert such creation, but human reason demands such a resting-place for the chain of finite events. 2. There is a little particle (eth) in the Hebrew, *not translated in our version*, which (often, at least) means *the substance of*, and, standing before the words translated "heaven" and "earth," expresses "the *substance* of the heaven and the substance of the earth."(¹) 3. Instead of "heaven," our text should read "heavens," and the allusion is apparently to other firmaments of stars which Sir William Herschel discovered lying far beyond the confines of *our* starry firmament. 4. The word translated "day" signifies a period of indefinite length—

(¹) Dr. Strong informs us (privately) that he does not attribute such force to this particle. But see the Appendix to this section of the present paper.

as in Gen. ii., 4; Job xiv., 6; xviii., 20; Isa. xxx., 8; Ezek. xxxi., 25; Prov. vi., 34. 5. The word translated "made" in the sixteenth verse, often signifies "appointed," as in Psa. civ., 19.

Now, let us see what science indicates in reference to the order of creation:

FIRST PERIOD. *A Fiery Mist.*—All the matter of the sun, moon, and planets existed primevally at a temperature so high that it was not only fused, but converted into a luminous vapor, and blended in one mass. Its pre-eminent characteristic was *luminosity*. In this, no chemical affinities found play; but the law of cooling and consequent contraction, and also the laws of gravitation and inertia, held sway. Accordingly, it began to cool, and through a long process, which, however interesting, we have not room to trace, it became divided up into a series of planets and satellites—a vast central mass remaining. The smaller masses cooled rapidly, and attained a somewhat solidified and darkened state, while the central mass was so large that it cooled more slowly, and continued (as it still does) to emit supplies of light and heat for the benefit of planetary bodies.

SECOND PERIOD. *Descent of Rains, and Accumulation of Sediments.*—Confining our view to a single planet—our own world—a time came in the process of cooling when the chill of the upper atmosphere condensed the vapor of water for the first time, and clouds began to form. Now the light of the sun, *which had fallen upon the earth from the beginning of its separate existence*, was by degrees shut out, and total darkness enshrouded the world. As these clouds held all the water belonging to our planet, they poured forth the most abundant rains, which, by beating upon the rocky surface, and by the wear of torrents, produced vast amounts of sediment, which were spread over the bottom of the accumulated ocean. Chemical reactions also took place in these waters which threw down sheets of sediments, which mingled with those of mechanical origin. These sediments were the material from which the oldest beds of rock were formed. By such a precipitation of rains, the clouds were thinned—twilight filtered through them, and a *separation* was effected between the waters which were above the earth and the waters which were upon the earth.

THIRD PERIOD. *Uplift of Continents—Appearance of Marine Plants.*—The continued cooling and shrinking of the earth developed *wrinkles* in the crust (or solid exterior inclosing the still heated interior), and these grew from age to age until they became *lands* rising above the level of the ocean. All the continents and islands of to-day have grown from those beginnings. Continent-building commenced while yet the rainy period continued, and, as soon as sufficient light penetrated the waters of the ocean, sea-weeds appeared.

FOURTH PERIOD. *Dispersion of the Clouds—Appearance of the Sun, Moon, and Stars—Plant-growth.*—At length the cooled world ceased to convert the ocean's waters into steam, to be returned in perpetual rains, and so the clouds were dispersed. Now the sun shone again upon the earth. The scene was changed. When the clouds first gathered, the earth was partially self-luminous, and cast no shadow, and consequently there was no night. Now the darkened world cast its shadow behind, and, on the unveiling of the sun, the phenomena of day and night were, for the first time, possible. Sunrise and sunset now possessed a new significance. This is the *Azoic Period* in geological science.

FIFTH PERIOD. *Marine Animals, Aquatic Reptiles, and Birds.*—The simplest possible forms of animal life next appeared, and these were followed by higher and higher in regular succession for many cycles of ages. For more than half this interval, animals breathed only water; and when at length air-breathers appeared, they were still doomed to inhabit the waters. They were aquatic reptiles—great monsters. Just at the close of this period, winged reptiles and then real birds, made their advent, and a great change passed over the life of the globe. This period is composed of the *Eozoic, Palæozoic,* and *Mesozoic* periods of geology.

SIXTH PERIOD. *The Reign of Mammals, followed by the Advent of Man.*—When the long reign of reptiles had ended, quadrupeds and monkeys appeared on the earth, and held exclusive possession, till at last man arrived and assumed dominion.

SEVENTH PERIOD. *The Period now passing.*—Such is the accepted geological story condensed into a few sentences.

Now, turning to an analysis of the Biblical account, we find it to stand thus:

THE THEME (verses 1, 2).—1. All existence flows from God. 2. A glimpse of the cloud-enveloped world in mid-development. (See *Second Period.*)

FIRST DAY (verses 3–5).—*Creation of light.*

SECOND DAY (verses 6–8).—*Firmament, or separation between the waters.*

THIRD DAY (verses 9–13).—*Formation of dry land and plants.*

FOURTH DAY (verses 14–19).—*Appointment of sun, moon, and stars.*

FIFTH DAY (verses 20–23).—*Creation of aquatic animals and birds.*

SIXTH DAY (verses 24–31).—*Creation of land animals and, lastly, man.*

SEVENTH DAY (Gen. ii., 1–3).—*God rested—his Sabbath.*

Now compare the work of these "days" with the events of the seven "periods" before indicated, and judge whether the correspondence is not *real*, and, indeed, much greater than we could expect of a history written in an age before the birth of science, and (according to popular chronology), 2500 years after the close of the events which it narrates. On the old interpretation, the Biblical account was irreconcilable with even popular information. How could light exist on the first day, and plants vegetate upon the third, while the sun, the source of light and of all organic activity, had no existence before the fourth day? Only a short-sighted faith will stake the credibility of its oracles on views of nature which have been proved untenable and incredible.

[APPENDIX.—To the foregoing article the following addendum was made at a subsequent date.

The excessive brevity of this series of articles, necessitated by the straitened limits of these pages, precludes the introduction of any thing but a meagre outline statement of conclusions. Proofs, arguments, illustrations, citations, reflections, must all be omitted. Many difficulties, apparent to every reader, must be left unexplained; and no space remains to expose the defenses of positions which the writer well knows beforehand will be assailed by misdirected attacks.

For instance, we asserted that the particle אֵת, *eth*, used in the first verse of Gen. i., signifies, in some situations, "the substance of" the thing mentioned. One competent and respected critic rightly asserts that certain authorities, whom he cites, give no sanction to such a use of the word. On the contrary, we might have cited the authority of Aben-Ezra, Kimchi, Ainsworth, Buxtorf, Nordheimer, and others. In addition, the Syriac translation so understands the particle; and St. Ephraëm, the learned apostle of the old Syriac Church, in his commentary on this place, uses the same Syriac word ܝܳܬ, *yoth*, and understands it in the same way. And, finally, the verb בָּרָא, *bara*, used in connection, implies, *in the Kal conjugation* (according to Gesenius), *creation* rather than *formation;* and as creation, in contrast with formation, is an origination of *substance*, the context fully sanctions the meaning which we have attributed to the particle אֵת, *eth*.

Again, another critic thinks that by giving יוֹם, *yom*, the signification of a geological "period," we invalidate the grounds for the enjoined observance of the Sabbath. We reply: 1. Philology allows the meaning; and cite for authorities, Augustine, Josephus, Philo Judæus, Tayler Lewis, M'Causland, besides an array of scientific judges, as Whiston, Descartes, Cuvier, De Luc, Parkinson, Jameson, Silliman, Miller, Dana, etc. 2. The events described could not have transpired in six literal days, according to all we know of the order of nature; and the theory of the *sudden creation of fossils and stratified rocks* has long since been abandoned by intelligent critics. 3. The Chalmerian hypothesis of a "chasm" of time between the events of the first and second verses offers insuperable and needless difficulties. 4. The Christian Sabbath is not invalidated by this means, for the Sabbath of God is now in progress. God is now resting from the works of creation to which Moses refers. So man, upon the seventh of *his* days, is commanded to imitate the example of his Creator.

But, in truth, the adequate defense of very intelligible conclusions seems hardly suited to the pages of the Journal.]

VII. *The Mosaic Deluge.*

The authors of the Pentateuch inform us that in the ninth generation after the introduction of Adam's race upon the earth, the wickedness of man provoked the Lord to destroy " all flesh" by a deluge, save Noah and his family. This deluge is represented as prevailing to such an extent that " all the high hills that were under the whole heaven were covered."

Now, a deluge of this kind—taking the language in its literal signification—was a geological event, and geologists have been called upon to declare what their science has to testify respecting such an occurrence. In the first place, it is one of the fundamental principles of geology that the materials of nearly all the stratified rocks have been laid down as sediments in the bottom of the sea. There are few localities upon the land, therefore, which do not testify to the former presence of the sea; and the time was, when this testimony was regarded as confirming the doctrine of a universal deluge. In the next place, the sea has at least once returned over the land since the great continental areas were completed. After the dissolution of the great glaciers which once prevailed over the temperate regions of America, Europe, and Asia, there occurred a general northern subsidence, which permitted the ocean's waters to bury all the northern portions of the continents — an event which the most eminent geologists of the last generation regarded as constituting the deluge recorded by Moses. This submergence, however, though it must have exterminated whole races of animals, is now generally believed to have occurred before the appearance of man upon the earth; and the Mosaic narrative could have no reference to it.

Vast areas of the land-surface, however, have lain under water during a later period; and the human race has witnessed their drainage, if it did not witness and suffer from the deluge and destruction which followed the disappearance of the continental glaciers. The great prairie region of Illinois is indicated, by a number of evidences, to have been covered by an immense lake until long after the representatives of our species had found their way to America. A similar and corresponding region in the South of Russia, in Europe, was, not many centuries since, the bed of a former extension of the Black Sea. This region is the ancient Lectonia, which, in later times, was the home of the warlike Scythians. It was probably drained by the bursting of the barriers of the Thracian Bosphorus. It has lately been shown that the entire country between the Caspian and Black seas was under water until a period geologically modern;([1]) and even the ancient geographers detected the evidences of the recent submergence of the region now covered by the great Desert of Sahara. The ancestors of our race, we may well believe, were spectators of the retreat of the waters from all these regions. Still, it is scarcely probable that the

---

([1]) "Réunion de la Mer Caspienne et la Mer Noir," par le Docteur Bergsträsser, conseiller d'état et directeur des salines du gouvernement d'Astrakan, Paris.

inundation of any of these districts constituted the phenomenon referred to by the sacred historian. It is safe to assume that the water may have rested over these places before the appearance of man upon the earth.

We have, however, geological, traditionary, and even historical evidences of the occurrence of great inundations during the human period. The gravel-beds of the Seine and Somme, inclosing human remains, prove that enormous floods visited Southern Europe after the advent of man. The Chinese records testify to no less than eight or nine great changes in the bed and outlet of the Hwang-ho River, by which means many thousands of square miles of territory have been several times inundated and devastated. The oldest deluge is fixed at twenty-two hundred years before Christ; and the latest great inundation was during the Taiping rebellion, a few years ago. The bed of the river has shifted from three hundred to four hundred miles, and areas larger than all New England have been buried beneath the water. Never was there a more literal "breaking-up of the fountains of the great deep." An inundation in India, in 1819, overwhelmed two thousand square miles by an inroad of the sea; and a similar flood was experienced, in 1872, upon the Western coast.

The Chaldeans preserved the memory of a great deluge in which Xisuthrus and his friends and relatives were saved by a warning of the Deity, in a vessel which also afforded protection to multitudes of quadrupeds and birds, and which finally rested on a mountain. Many other incidents of the story—as the sending-out of birds once, twice, thrice; the offering of sacrifices after the flood; and the subsequent building of cities and temples upon the plains of Babylon—indicate that the Chaldean narrative relates to the same event as the Mosaic.[1] Oth-

---

[1] See, on this subject, the late researches and publications of Mr. George Smith, of the British Museum.

er Eastern peoples, as the Phœnicians, Phrygians, Syrians, Armenians, and Scythians, had traditions of a similar deluge, which have been perpetuated by various ancient writers. The Chinese preserve the story of a deluge which dates back to four thousand years before Christ, the particulars of which strangely resemble those of the Noachian flood. In the books of the Hindoos, also, are records of a devastating flood, located, in some of the accounts, to the south of the Himalayas, but, in the oldest one, to the north of those mountains, toward the region which we now know was the original home of the Brahmanic people, as well as the region of the Mosaic deluge. The Persians, also, have preserved the recollection of a great deluge, sent to punish mankind for their wickedness. In the traditions of the Greeks two deluges are mentioned—that of Ogyges and that of Deucalion. The story of Deucalion and Pyrrha, as narrated by Ovid, is impressively similar to the story of Noah and his family, as told by Moses. In the mythologies of the Scandinavians and Celts re-appear similar traditions.

Finally, traditions of a deluge are found in the islands of the sea and among the natives of America. The Fijians narrate that their islands were once flooded by a great rain, and only a few of their people were saved, by the aid of two of their deities, upon the island of Mbenga. The tribes of North America and the West Indies had traditions of a deluge. The various nations which inhabited Mexico at the time of the Conquest preserved the memory of a great deluge, in which Coxcox and his wife were saved in a floating vessel, which rested, after the flood, upon the summit of a mountain. One of the traditions approximates the Mosaic history in several particulars. Not only is Coxcox saved, with his wife, but also his children and several animals, and a supply of grain. The waters abated at the orders of the Great Spirit. The first bird sent out was a vulture. Other birds were sent, and, finally, a humming-bird, which returned with a leafy branch in its beak.

It is singular to find such coincidences on opposite sides of the globe.

The geological evidences and the traditions of many nations concur, therefore, in testifying to the occurrence of one or more great deluges since the appearance of our race upon the earth; and the traditions are singularly harmonious in reference to the occasion and principal incidents of the deluge. Thus, they generally agree with each other and with Moses in affirming, 1. That the deluge was intended as a punishment for man's wickedness; 2. That it brought destruction to the ancestors of the nation perpetuating the tradition; 3. That one good man and his immediate relatives were saved in a floating vessel; 4. That certain quadrupeds and birds were also preserved; 5. That the vessel finally rested on a mountain; 6. That birds were sent out at intervals to bring back indications of the progress of the retirement of the waters. We may confidently assert, therefore, that the Mosaic narrative of the deluge, in its essential features, is a correct historical statement.

That the deluge was *universal* we have *not* similar grounds for believing. 1. There are no geological evidences of a general inundation since the advent of man. It must be admitted, however, that a deluge which lasted but three hundred and sixty-four days could not have left very permanent records. 2. If the universal inundation were caused by a general subsidence of the continents to the requisite extent, the evidences of this must still exist; but they have not been discovered. 3. If it were caused by the addition of the requisite amount of water to our globe, without a subsidence of the continents, the earth's mass would be so much increased as to derange the harmonies of the solar system. 4. It was impossible for Noah or any number of men to gather zoölogical couples from all the various continents—still less to do it in the time indicated. It is a work which has not been accomplished to this day by the managers of all the zoölogical gardens of the world. 5. The animals from different zones could not have endured the climatic vicissitudes, especially if the ark rested on the summit of a mountain reaching into the region of perpetual snow. 6. The capacity of the ark was extremely inadequate for the accommodation of so many animals and a year's supply of food. 7. The waters of a universal deluge rising five miles above the ordinary level of the sea could not evaporate in three hundred and twenty-five days; and if they could, the atmosphere would be incapable of supporting them; and hence there would be no way of disposing of such a body of water over the land, except by a change of relative levels, which we have stated to be geologically improbable. 8. The deluge may have been "universal" in respect to the descendants of Adam, and yet have been geographically local. 9. The local character of the deluge has for centuries been maintained by many eminent divines, simply on linguistic and general grounds.

If it be asserted that a universal deluge, and all the other events as formerly understood, could be accomplished by miraculous agency, this must be admitted; but it will be noticed that Moses attributes the inundation to *natural* agencies—great rains and a "breaking-up of the fountains of the great deep."

While, therefore, the credibility of the Mosaic statements is fully authenticated by secular evidences, the historian must be regarded as speaking only of that quarter of the world which had become populated by the descendants of Adam; and such expressions as "all flesh died" and "all the high hills that were under the whole heaven" must be taken in an Oriental sense (Gen. xli., 56; Deut. ii., 25; Luke ii., 1; Acts ii., 5), like so many other passages of the Hebrew writings.

VIII. *Man in the Light of Geology.*

What has geology to testify concerning man?

1. *He belongs to the Last Fauna.*—No new types of animals, so far as we know, have been introduced upon the earth since

his advent. All the remains of man are found in the last geological formation. There has been no great geological revolution since his appearance. In the rocks beneath the surface are abundant records of older revolutions, and of older and extinct types of animal life; but these types were all greatly inferior to man. The testimonies of science, therefore, confirm the statement of Moses, that God made man in the last great period of creative activity.

2. *Man's Advent is comparatively Recent.*—There are no authentic discoveries of human remains in Tertiary deposits, or any others older than the last period of glaciation. The geologic events that have transpired since man's advent are not such, therefore, as demanded many thousands of years for their consummation. Some of the more prominent geological events are the following: (1) The later stages of the dissolution of the continental glaciers, and the floods which resulted from the melting ice; (2) The drainage of a vast region of plains north of the Black Sea, and thence to the Caspian and Aral seas; (3) The drainage of the prairie region of the Mississippi Valley; (4) The wanderings of the Hwang-ho and Yang-tse rivers of China over intervals of hundreds of miles, inundating many thousands of square miles of territory; (5) The encroachment of the Pacific upon the eastern shores of Asia, leaving the Japanese islands and Formosa to mark the real limits of the continental mass; (6) The extinction of the cave-bear, cave-hyena, two-horned rhinoceros, hippopotamus, hairy mammoth, and other quadrupeds; (7) The accumulation of peat-bogs in Denmark and Ireland to the depth of twenty or thirty feet; (8) The transformation of the forest growths of many parts of Europe. Other probable events are the formation of Behring Strait between Asia and America, the excavation of the Straits of Dover and of the gorge of the Niagara River.

But great as are these events, it appears that a few thousand years suffice for their accomplishment. 1. The extinctions of quadrupeds are still in progress. The Irish elk existed till the fourteenth century; the urus lingered till the sixteenth century; the dodo, till the seventeenth; the moa and epiornis—gigantic extinct birds of New Zealand—have lived within the scope of tradition; as also the mammoth of North America. The great auk of Arctic America has not been seen for fifty years. It can not be that the other extinctions witnessed by men stretch back to a very remote antiquity. 2. The stumps of the ancient glaciers are disappearing at such a rate that the entire period of glacier-dissolution can not have been vast. The Mer de Glace of Mont Blanc has lowered one hundred feet in twenty years, and has receded at its lower border a quarter of a mile, while the gravel moraines are burying it along its lateral borders. The Glacier des Bossons has shrunken even more. An ice-peak in the Tyrolese Alps has been observed to lower eighteen and a half feet in a few years; and the Alpine glaciers generally are in process of diminution at their lower extremities. The Siberian glaciers, which inclose the well-preserved carcasses of the hairy mammoth, are continually and rapidly dissolving and releasing those carcasses, which are then sought for their ivory. Stumps of the continental glacier of America are preserved, half buried in dust and mountain débris, in some of the gulches of the Sierra Nevada; and the epoch of the prevalence of the great glacier is not so remote but some detached fragments of it still persist in the "ice-wells" of Vermont, New Hampshire, and Wisconsin. Other evidences of the shortness of the post-glacial period are at hand, but we have not the space for their presentation. The total age of our race, therefore, is not necessarily much greater than is indicated by a correct, or even the *current*, interpretation of the Mosaic history of primeval times.

3. *Man's Birthplace was in the Orient.*—We speak first of purely geological evidences. The faunas, or animal assemblages, existing on the different continents exhibit a gradation in point

of rank. The highest is that in the Orient (Europe, Asia, and Africa), characterized by carnivores (flesh-eaters). Next is that of North America, characterized by herbivores (plant-eaters). The third is that of South America, whose leading types are edentates (quadrupeds deficient in some of the sorts of teeth). The fourth is that of Australia, whose mammals consist almost exclusively of marsupials (pouched quadrupeds, like the kangaroo and opossum). This is a marked gradation of the continents; but it existed in the epoch preceding the advent of man, as the latest fossil remains testify. Indeed, something of the same gradation existed far back in geological time. The highest attainments in organization were always in the Oriental quarter of the world. The high rank of the Orient was a perpetual prophecy that the ultimate culmination of the animal series would be there. It always pointed to the Orient as the destined cradle of the human race; and there is no room for a doubt that man first placed foot upon the earth in that quarter to which our Scriptures assign the Garden of Eden.

But historical evidences and traditions point to the same conclusion. All the migrations of our race have radiated from the Orient — first, eastward into China, and south-eastward across the Himalayas; then, from the same centre, westward, in parallel streams and in successive swells, across the Urals and the Bosphorus. The eastern stream, intercepted by the Pacific, continued its course across the isthmus anciently occupying the place of Behring Strait, and populated America; the western surged, at length, across the Atlantic, and met the eastern on the opposite side of the globe. The streams of languages and dialects have, of course, followed the streams of migration. The Orient, moreover, is the home of most of our domesticated animals and plants. Of the seven hundred and seventy plants used for food, five hundred and sixty-five come from the Old World, and two hundred and four from the New. Of the two hundred and thirty-seven starch-producing plants used by man, one hundred and ninety-eight originated in the Old World, and only forty-five in the New. It is perfectly safe, therefore, in view of the secular evidences, to accept the Biblical statement of the Oriental home of our first parents.

4. *Man's Advent was the Prophecy of the Ages.*—The great work of terrestrial preparation always implied man. The ever-improving series of organic forms pointed always to an ultimate consummation. The advance of a thousand ages was a pledge of all possible advance. The earlier terms of the series expressed a law which involved the highest term. Especially, when vertebrate life began its existence in the fish, were the prophecies of its ultimate fullest unfolding in man most distinctly uttered. When each succeeding type of vertebrates became a farther step toward man, the name of man seemed uttered in countless reptilian, bird-like, mammalian, and quadrumanous forms. There was no mistaking the ultimate of such a series. Thus man is the realization of an idea which was kept resounding through the geologic ages. He is correlated to the whole history of organization, and can not be contemplated except as a link in the chain of being which stretches back through geologic eons.

But the whole course of physical preparations also looks toward man. Every great revolution of the terrestrial crust constituted a forward step in the fashioning and furnishing of an abode for intelligent populations. The useful metals, elaborated and eliminated through ages of geological activity, are suited exclusively to human ends. The vast deposits of mineral coal laid by thousands of ages before the creation of man sustain no relations to any other than human existence. Thus man is a consummation foreshadowed through countless ages of organic and inorganic preparations.

5. *Man is the Last Term of the Organic Series.*—As all geological preparations point toward man, so they all converge in man and reach their finality in him. Man signalizes the con-

summation of a plan—the fulfillment of a prophecy—the realization of a long-foreshadowed ultimate. We can conceive of no succeeding organism or intelligence to which the material world and its history should stand in closer relations of correspondence and fitness. So the foreshadowings of man in organic history point toward him as a finality. In him, the physical structure attains its highest conceivable perfection and variety of adaptations to the external world. To man alone is given the erect attitude, which is itself the last possible term of a series of inclinations exemplified in the horizontal fish, the head-uplifting reptile, the inclined bird, the neck-erecting quadruped, and the half-upright monkey. To man alone is vouchsafed the power to defy all physical conditions in his geographical range; for while all his predecessors had been confined within progressively narrowing limits, he first of all became a cosmopolite, and possessed the whole world. There is no term in the series beyond totality. Then, as if to emphasize the completion of the work of organic improvement, and to mark a grand pause in creative progress, nature superadded to the most perfect organism, to a heavenward-looking mien, and the absolute freedom of the world, an endowment of an intellectual and moral nature not vouchsafed to any other animal. Thus man is presented to all intelligences as the final consummation of the long series of revolutions and advances whose records are written upon the pages of science.

IX. *The Finiteness of the Existing Order of Things.*

We are informed in the Sacred Scriptures that the earth and the entire system of nature had a beginning, and originated in the creative activity of Elohim. We are also assured that the world is destined to come to an end—that the heavens shall be "rolled together as a scroll," and the "elements shall melt with fervent heat," and that ultimately there will be established "a new heaven and a new earth."

Now, science is in possession of data which have a strong bearing upon these doctrines. We see every thing in nature undergoing a succession of changes. These changes are a progress *toward* something and a progress *from* something; and we are prepared to show that in tracing backward the series of geological changes transpiring before our eyes, we reach at last a remotest limit — a beginning, anterior to which we have no means of knowing or ground for believing that any change was possible. Thus, the wastage of ocean beaches, the deposition of ocean sediments, the measured escape of heat from the earth, the increased heat experienced in penetrating toward the earth's interior, the traces of ancient heat in many of the rocks — these all are indications of a long history whose beginning, so far as we can judge, was a fiery vapor. We know nothing of any state of matter more remote than this. Indeed, as we understand the laws of matter, we are led to affirm that there was no condition antecedent to this. The fire-mist, so far as science can testify, was the first condition; and as the fire-mist must have begun to change as soon as it began to exist, it can not be an eternity since the series of material changes began. Science, therefore, affirms that the existing order of the universe has not continued from eternity, but is merely a finite effect; and the principles of reason declare that such effect must have been caused by an efficient agent existing before the present universe existed.

If the series of events transpiring before our eyes is tending *toward* something, we are prepared to show that it is an *end* — a finality, toward which it tends. There is more than one series of changes in progress which will bring the existing terrestrial order to an end, and render it physically impossible that the human race should remain in existence upon the earth.

1. The land is wearing out. Every hill and mountain is undergoing a slow disintegration under the influence of the elements. The oceans and the rivers are also eating up the land.

The materials resulting from these incessant erosions are deposited in lakes and seas. Small lakes have been filled within a generation; larger ones, within the memory of man. The delta of the Mississippi is moving into the Gulf at the rate of three hundred and thirty-eight feet a year. The Green Mountains are sensibly lower than a generation back, and the Sierra Nevada is visibly sinking. Some of the highest summits of the Andes are two hundred and twenty feet lower than when first measured by Humboldt, about seventy years ago. The lowering of mountains may be largely due to a yielding of their deep foundations, but no one can deny, on reflection, that agencies are at work which are destined ultimately to rob the land of its soils—to sink the rivers into deep gorges, and drain the continents to sterility, and, finally, to level their inequalities and fill the ocean till again it envelopes nearly the whole earth.

2. It is an established doctrine of science that the world is cooling, as it has been cooling through all the geologic ages. We know of no cause to arrest its cooling. The crust, therefore, which now incloses an intensely heated nucleus is destined to grow thicker, until refrigeration approaches the earth's centre. Who can affirm that insufferable rigors will not prevail upon the earth when frozen to the core? But, however this may be, another cause will render the earth uninhabitable. The water resting on the earth's surface percolates downward till it reaches a heat which changes it to steam and sends it toward the surface. The internal fires hold all the water belonging to the earth within a few miles of the earth's surface. And yet there is no more water than we need. Suppose the cooled crust were twice as thick; the rocks would demand twice the water to saturate them. Now, it has been demonstrated that when the earth shall have been cooled to the centre, the pores of the rocks will have a capacity sufficient to hold ten times the whole amount of water belonging to our globe. They will then drink up the oceans, and the unfilled

pores will suck in all the atmosphere; and the world, with neither water nor atmosphere, will become utterly uninhabitable. This is a condition already attained by our moon. That satellite has cooled to this condition while yet the world is habitable, because its mass is but one forty-ninth part of the terrestrial mass. Yet the moon presents to-day a picture of desolation and death which, in the natural course of events, will hereafter be exhibited by the earth. Here, then, is a limit to the existing terrestrial order.

3. No one doubts that the sun's mass is intensely heated. No one, on a moment's reflection, can fail to understand that the sun loses an enormous amount of heat daily, and that it must inevitably grow cooler, unless some means exist for replenishment. Physicists have considered the problem of the sun's heat and its future persistence with the most profound interest and attention; and though various suggestions have been made, science is not to-day in possession of any facts which render it improbable that the sun is actually cooling. Indeed, the loftiest conclusions of the latest science present our source of light and warmth as a waning, dying orb. Our world was once a glowing sphere, and has reached its present condition so much sooner than the sun because its mass is a million times less. The sun is as certain as the earth or the moon to attain, at length, a state of total refrigeration. It has been a "white" star and a "yellow" star; it is now a "variable" star, and is destined to shine, in some future age, with the ruddy glow of a "red" star—a dying ember. It will become incrusted. Then there will be disruptions and outflows of glowing molten matter, and from time to time it will pour forth a fitful gleam like the other "temporary" stars. But its ultimate solidification is a conclusion which science knows not how to avoid. It is a fearful condition of nature to contemplate, and fills the imagination with pictures of desolation; but the thought, the impending certainty, reveals the vastness of

the power which works these long-coming results, and re-echoes the testimony of our Scriptures that the sun shall be blotted out and the world shall come to an end.

4. There is a grander disturbing force which is destined to interrupt the existence of the present terrestrial and cosmical harmony. All space is filled with an inconceivably thin fluid called ether, the vibrations of which give rise to the phenomena of light and heat. Wherever light exists, there is ether. This fluid is material. It must, therefore, oppose the movements of all celestial bodies. Indeed, the effect of this resistance has already been recognized in the motions of some of those filmy bodies, the comets. Encke's comet is continually approaching the sun, and it is a simple problem in arithmetic to ascertain when it will be drawn into the central luminary. If the ethereal medium is capable of affecting measurably, in a few months, the motion of cometary bodies, it must necessarily affect, to some extent, the motions of all the planets. The earth, consequently, must be gradually approaching the sun, and must be destined to ultimate precipitation upon that body. Here is another crisis impending over terrestrial affairs.

But if the earth is destined to fall upon the sun, the same destiny awaits every planet; and the time must arrive when all the matter of the solar system will be aggregated in one cold, darkened mass. This is the direction in which events are tending. We say this is one of the results of the distant future, if the forces of nature continue to act as they are acting. Holding to the constancy of these forces, and believing that no new force or mode of action capable of averting, even if it could postpone, such a catastrophe, will ever be discovered, we see no way to avoid it, save by miraculous interference, of which science can take no account.

The course of nature, therefore, is tending toward an end. This final aggregation will be a stage of total equilibrium and stagnation of all the forces of matter. No heat, no light, no motion, no life, no change—but the eternal death of the cosmical organism. Eternal? What prevents the Omnific Hand from being stretched forth to arouse the corpse of matter to a new resurrection—to inaugurate a new creation? This we think probable; and thus may arise "a new heaven and a new earth."

We must therefore contemplate the life-time of the universe as limited by natural causes in both directions, and incapable of sustaining itself indefinitely without the interposition of a Power external to the universe, superior to it, and acting independently of the forces of nature.

Is any one of these remote contingencies the mode of consummation of terrestrial affairs foreshadowed by St. Peter? Perhaps not, but they involve the *fiery* catastrophe of the apostle.

(1.) The end of the world, in the meaning of Peter, is that catastrophe which will end its occupancy by human beings.

(2.) Vast stores of molten material remain imprisoned within the crust of the earth. Geologists understand that the progressive changes of the earth have, time and again, involved such disruptions of the crust as to cause the outflow of vast quantities of this molten matter; and that, though the eruptions become less frequent with the lapse of ages, it may be that occasional outbursts, as the rigid crust thickens, grow necessarily more violent. The highest mountains have been upheaved in the later ages of geological history. A devastating outburst may yet occur which will destroy the present aspects of the world.

(3.) The earth may be precipitated into the sun before the period of its total refrigeration arrives.

(4.) Then, even if the sun be totally refrigerated, the impact of the earth upon it would develop heat sufficient to reignite the matter of the world.

(5.) The earth may reach, in its well-known movement with

the sun through space, a region so intensely heated as to answer to a fulfillment of the prophecy of St. Peter.

Thus, there is no occasion whatever to feel diminished confidence in the words of the apostle, or to hesitate to follow natural causes to their ultimate issue, or to fear, in this connection more than elsewhere, that science or philosophy will attain a valid conclusion which was not in full view of the Author of inspiration when each word of our Sacred Scriptures was penned.

X. *The Bible in the Light of Nature.*

We are not proposing, in a brief article, to detail the coincidences which exist between the teachings of the Bible and the conclusions of science and reason. We propose, in view of those coincidences, to maintain that the *authenticity* and *authority* of the Bible may be rationally admitted, and that its *inspiration* is the only explanation of these coincidences.

In the series of articles of which this is the conclusion, it has been our object to set forth the great features of the harmony between science and revelation. It has, of course, been done very meagrely and unsatisfactorily; but, so far as we have succeeded, it has been shown that the material universe presents forms, adaptations, contrivances, correlations, which, judging it as we do the products of human agency, exemplify various attributes and dispositions existing on the part of its Author. For instance, we involuntarily regard the upbuilding of mountains and the movements of cosmical masses of matter as evidences of the exercise of *power*. We involuntarily declare that the mechanical contrivances witnessed in the eye, or the hand, or the system of the heavens, are proofs of the exercise of *intelligence*. We can not resist the conviction that in a world where almost every thing presents some unmistakable and often elaborate, and even anticipatory, adaptation to promote happiness, and where so many things have no discoverable end, if it be not to promote happiness, the attribute of *benevolence* must have actuated the Planner of existing arrangements. We regard the material world, therefore, as proof of the exercise of power, intelligence, and beneficence; and if we are met by the objection that the works of nature so far transcend our comprehension that we can not be certain of the motives and powers through whose activity they came into existence, we immediately and confidently reply that human reason affirms that any product which can be pronounced a mechanism *must* have had an intelligent contriver, who exercised sufficient power to embody his idea, and must have acted from motives deducible, to some extent, from the results of his activity. Any result interpretable in terms of intellect and motive is the result of intellect and motive. This is a law of reason which we can not evade without self-stultification, and a total abandonment of grounds of inference which are ingrained in human nature and underlie all our actions. The data of science supplemented by the data of reason do, therefore, establish the existence of *such* a Creator as is portrayed in our Scriptures.

We have gone farther, and shown that such a unity of physical conditions and such a system of mutual dependencies exist throughout the limits of the visible universe, that it would be eminently unreasonable to assume that the universe had been the product of more than *one* intelligence; and we have shown that a unity no less intelligible and manifest connects all present existence with the whole history of the past; so that it is impossible that indefinite time, any more than indefinite space, should have witnessed the supremacy of more than *one* intelligent power. And this revelation of an infinite and eternal God in nature is identical with the revelation given in our Scriptures. The God of nature and the God of the Bible (viewed in his relations to the natural world) are portrayed in the same character; and this commits science to an indorsement of every thing said in the Bible regarding those divine attributes whose exercise is reflected in the phenomena of nature.

We have adverted to the religious nature of man under all conditions, and have shown that religious ideas, notions, or sentiments are universal and necessary, and therefore ineradicable and innate. The constitution of human nature is, therefore, a sanction of every thing which is revealed in the material world or the Holy Bible respecting the being and attributes of Deity and man's moral relations to him.

Not contenting ourselves with proving that science and philosophy demand such a God as the Bible reveals, we have shown that science also authenticates the Bible in respect to some important statements which still might accord, or not, with secular data. We have shown, for instance, that the remarkable record of creation, generally ascribed to Moses, harmonizes beautifully with the latest determinations of science, and must have been wholly unintelligible, save in its spirit and general purport, to former generations of men; and we have indicated certain remarkable statements in this connection, which prove that the author of Genesis had information vastly in advance of his nation or age, and which he could not have possessed except through miraculous communication. We have shown that the Biblical account of the deluge violates no physical probabilities, while it is sustained by geological analogies, and by traditions extant among many nations and tribes. We have shown that science testifies that man belongs, as the Bible asserts, to the group of last-created animals; that that creation was comparatively recent; that he made his first appearance in the Orient; that he was, in a certain sense, a long-premeditated consummation; and that his advent and possession of the earth constitute a finality in the geological succession of animals. We have shown, finally, that, contrary to the tenor of ancient philosophy, science declares that a beginning of the present order of things is a necessity, and that a conclusion is equally inevitable; while abundant provision exists for such a fiery consummation as St. Peter foreshadows.

What does all this corroboration imply? Not that the Bible needs the sanction of science and philosophy in the minds of most men; but that, if there be men who withhold their acceptance of the Bible until they know whether science and philosophy assent, they may feel assured that science and philosophy *demand* their acceptance. It implies that if the pervading ideas and so many of the collateral statements of the Bible are in full accord with the data and doctrines of science, the whole body of documents may be accepted as authentic and authoritative. It implies that the authors of these documents were in possession of light, even in secular affairs, which did not belong to their times, and could only have come into their possession through immediate intuition—that is, the sacred writers were inspired men. This proof establishes the Bible as the utterance of God, the Author of all truth, and therefore as an infallible authority even in matters transcending the limits of science and philosophy.

If it still be felt that this is admitting supernatural presence and intervention in an affair where human agency may be made to account for all the phenomena, we would further reply: 1. It is incredible that the sacred writers should have learned, save through inspiration, facts and methods which uninspired science has had to labor three thousand years to acquire. 2. The admission of supernaturalism in inspiration is no greater a strain than to admit it in creation. But the tendency of science is to go even farther, and recognize the daily processes of the organic world as but the result of the immediate activity of divine intelligence and power. We can not escape the supernatural, either as an immediate presence or an ultimate resting-point. 3. If such a God exists as the study of nature proclaims, there is an antecedent probability that he would make such a written revelation as our Scriptures profess to be. A God of infinite goodness could not leave his creatures to grope painfully after a knowledge of their origin, relations, and destiny, but, having implanted in them moral and religious aspirations, would make a revelation of their appropriate object. 4. The supernatural teachings of the Scriptures are suited to the constitution and wants of man. Though he may, from nature, find out the existence of God, and may attain to exalted conceptions of many of his attributes, there is a deep-felt insufficiency in nature. Looking up toward the infinite Beneficence to which man feels that he owes every enjoyment, the spirit of prayer rises to his lips, and he would fain cry, "O Lord, rescue me from this evil!" But how dares he enter into the presence of Omnipotence unbidden? With what expectation can he prefer a request from the King of kings? Does not all nature declare that the purposes of Deity are ripening through the ages, and a poor mortal must vainly interpose a human-born motive to divine activity? Will he not be spurned from the presence of the Almighty? And yet he feels: "Oh, if I could but interpose my petition! Oh, if I could move the divine Power to avert this calamity!" He feels that he *must* approach God, and yet how dares he? And with what prospect of a hearing? Will the Infinite Beneficence leave his creatures in this state of uncertainty, or this state of misery? No; he will speak. And when we read the words, "Cast thy burden upon the Lord," "Come unto me," "Ask and ye shall receive," we recognize these as the very words for which the soul was longing. These are words framed for the unsatisfied heart. They fit the occasion; they bear the stamp of authenticity. They can be none but the word of God.

A revelation respecting man's moral relations and future state must touch upon topics beyond the reach of science and philosophy. The search for verities here leads into the inscrutable thoughts and purposes of the Omniscient. Such a revelation as science itself gives us ground for anticipating must be a revelation involving important statements that transcend the reach of demonstrations, and must be accepted solely on the established authority of the Revelator. Faith is the logical corollary of science and the highest flight of reason.

Thus we are led to believe that the cultivation of science and philosophy is not only harmless, but leads the candid mind to a reverent knowledge of God and an implicit faith in the most mysterious utterances of his Sacred Word.

INDEX.

ABARIS, 91.
Abelard, 75.
Abidharma, 55.
Abiogenesis, opposed to logic, 144; not unscriptural, 225.
Abnormal states of faith, 42; causes of, 42.
Abraham, 185.
Absolute attributes, 276.
Abury, 190.
Academia Telesiana, 80.
Academy, Old, 62; Middle, 93; New, 66.
Activity the law of existence, 128.
Advent of man recent, 223.
Æneas of Gaza, 73.
Ænesidemus, 69, 93.
Ætiological argument, 139, 150, 197, 279; formulated, 284–285; viewed critically, 295.
Affinity, chemical, 261–262.
Agassiz, Louis, attacked by Haeckel, 114; philosopher and scientist, 137; on relation of organism and environment, 141.
Agathological argument, 198, 299.
Ahuramazda, 53.
Air as first principle, 56.
Albertus Magnus, 76, 99, 357.
Albigenses, 74.
Alcuin, 73.
Alembert, d', 82, 218, 312.
Alexander of Aphrodisias, 284, 293.
Alexander of Hales, 76.
Alexander, Stephen, 301.
Alexander the Great, 48, 281.
Alexandria, Hebrew literature in, 67.
Alfarabi, 78, 99.
Algazel, 78.
Alkendi, 78.

Alps, upheaval of, 333.
Amalric, 76.
Amblypoda, 171.
America, discovery of, 79.
Ammonius Saccas, 70.
Amosis, 47.
Amphibian stage of embryo, 171.
Amphioxus stage, 171.
Anaptomorphus (*Antiacodon*), 172.
Anaxagoras of Clazomenæ, 58, 121, 221, 280, 282, 285.
Anaximander, 56.
Anaximenes, 56.
Anchippus, 169.
Anchitherium, 171.
Andaman islanders, 189, 353.
Andes, upheaval of, 333.
Animals become extinct, 370.
Anniceris, 62.
Anselm, 266, 293.
Anselmian argument, 299.
Antagonism, a law of progress, 34, 41; self-regulative, 212, 228; of faith and philosophy, 72.
Anthropomorphic language, uses of, 39; found in Hebrew Scriptures, 204.
Anthropomorphic stage, 38, 282.
Anthropomorphism inevitable, 38, 245, 282.
Anticipation of use of organs, 142.
Anticipatory organs not produced by heredity, 147.
Antinomians, 72.
Antiochus of Ascalon, 67.
Antiquity of human race, 222.
Antisthenes, 61.
Ἄπειρον (τὸ) as first principle, 56.
Apollodorus, 65.
Apollonius of Tyana, 68.

386 INDEX.

Apollonius the Grammarian, 71.
Apostolicism, 83.
Apuleius, 68.
Aquinas, 75, 76, 266, 356.
Arabs and ancient learning, 78; contributing science, 79.
Arago, 277.
Arafuras of Vorkay, 89, 353.
Aratus, 272.
Arbitrary volition not implied by intelligence, 131.
Arbrousset, 229.
Arcesilaus, 63.
Archegenesis, Greek doctrine of, 59; must be assumed, 149, 225.
Archetype, vertebrate, 163, 176; of vegetable, 176.
Arguments, theistic, 197-199; equivalences of, 279, 299; in Greek philosophy, 284-286.
Argyll, Duke of, 109, 315.
Aristæus, 91.
Aristarchus of Samos, 213.
Aristides, 71.
Aristippus, 61.
Aristo, 71.
Aristobulus, 67.
Aristotelian argument, 299.
Aristotelianism, 63, 64; serving the Church, 76.
Aristotle, 58, 59, 63, 64, 76, 90, 108, 137, 233, 276, 279, 283, 285, 286.
Armenian traditions of deluge, 366:
Artemia and *Branchipus*, 253.
Articulates, 156.
Aryan religions, 186.
Asceticism of Antisthenes, 61.
Ascidian stage, 171.
Asoka, 54.
Asteroidal zone, 175.
Atheism not defended by Draper or Tyndall, 132; contributing defenses to theism, 176; rejected by Tyndall, 238, 239.
Athenagoras, 71.
Athenians, religion of, 271.
Athenian school of Neo-Platonism, 70.
Athens and its people, 269.
Atomic universe, motions in, 103.
Atomism, held by Anaxagoras of Clazomenæ, 58; not necessarily atheistic, 102, 103, 234; requires causality, 102; implies creation, 103; tendency to, 232.
Atomists: Leucippus, 59, 102; Democritus, 59, 233, 234; Bruno, 59, 234; Tyndall, 59, 102, 232; Epicurus, 64, 102, 233; Lucretius, 65, 233, 236; Gassendi, 102, 234.
Atoms endowed with life, 236; not explained by chance, 242; ultimate realities of science, 256; ultimate constituents of matter, 324.
Attributes of Deity illustrated in nature, 333-351.
Augustine, Aurelius, 289, 293, 356, 362.
Augustinism, 83.
Aurelius, Marcus, 287.
Ausland, Das, 111.
Authority of primitive beliefs, 193.
Averroës, 78.
Averroism, 78; before Averroës, 64.
Averroists, 76.
Avesta, 52.
Avicenna, 78.
Aztecs, belief of, in a redeemer, 22; religion of, 185, 353.

BACON, FRANCIS, 74, 218, 228, 234, 279, 320.
Bacon, Roger, 78, 79.
Baer, Von, 111, 133, 143, 155, 159.
Bain, Alexander, 225.
Baird, S. F., on hybrid woodpeckers, 172.
Balfour, 158.
Bannes, 357.
Bardessanes, 71.
Barker, George F., 129, 225.
Bar-kochba, 72.
Barrow, 266, 293.
Basil the Great, 73.
Basilides, 71.
Bastian, 224, 322.
Batrachian as a stage in evolution of skeleton, 164.
Battle-fields of faith, 207.
Boyle, 80, 218.
Beauty has a teleological meaning, 156.
Beda, 73.
Behistun, inscription at, 53.

Belief, affected by mental states, 92;
rational and emotional avenues
to, 152; various degrees of validity of, 307.
Bell, 158.
Beneficence illustrated in nature, 342–347.
Berchetti, 357.
Berengarius, 75.
Berghaus, 186.
Bergsträsser, Dr., 364.
Berkeley, 81, 218.
Berti, 357.
Bianconi, 109.
Bible, made the criterion of all truth, 233; in the light of nature, 379–384; antecedently probable, 382; supernatural teachings of, 382–383.
Biblical cosmogony. (*See* Cosmogony.)
Biblical deluge. (*See* Deluge.)
Biran, Maine de, 94.
Bird a stage in evolution of vertebrate skeleton, 164.
Birds, connected with reptiles, 171; variations among, 254.
Boccaccio, 79.
Body in relation to space and time, 318–319.
Boëthius, 73.
Bonaventure, St., 357.
Bonnet, 82.
"Book of the Dead," 47.
"Book of Transmigrations," 47.
Bosphorus, Thracian, 364.
Bossuet, 357.
Boulak, Egyptian antiquities at, 46.
Brahmanas, 51.
Brahmanism, bifurcation of, 46; cycles of, 51; one of the ethnic religions, 186, 353.
Brain secreting thought, 225, 255; conditioning thought, 226, 250–251.
Branchipus and *Artemia*, 253.
Braun, Adolf, 111.
"Bridgewater Treatises," 314.
Bronze Age, 190.
Brown, Thomas, 270.
Bruno, 59, 80, 137, 234.
Büchner, 89, 111, 225.

Buckle, 143.
Buddha, 54, 91.
Buddhism a bifurcation of Brahmanism, 46, 52; one of the ethnic religions, 186, 353; in China, 50; in Persia, 53; in various countries, 54; missionary spirit of, 54; degeneracy of, 54.
Buffon, 82.
Burton, 89, 208, 292.
Butler, Bishop, 151, 179, 234, 266, 293, 301, 314.

CAIRO, Egyptian antiquities at, 47.
Cajetan, Cardinal, 357.
Calderwood, 293.
Calvin, 77.
Cambyses, 53.
Campanella, 80.
Canus, Melchior, 357.
Carneades, 63, 94.
Carpenter, W. B., 145, 225, 293, 315.
Carpenter theory, 128.
Carpocrates, 71.
Cartesian vortices foreshadowed, 59.
Casalis, story told by, 229.
Cassianus, 73.
Catholic, Roman, form of faith appearing, 215.
Caucasian race perhaps the Adamic, 222, 223.
Causal intermediation, 120; the field of scientific inquiry, 134, 241, 245; modified by conditions, 139, 250.
Causal intermediation, or secondary cause implies primary causation, 137; absence of primary cause, congruity of antecedent and consequent, 138; efficiency, 139.
Causality, intuition of, 26, 197, 242; doctrine of, 87; intuition of, leads to Deity, 93, 197; universality of intuition, 93; its origin, 94; derivatives of, 298.
Causal relation, implications of, 95, 101–119.
Causation implies, spontaneity, 98; real cause, 101; relation of antecedence, 104; correlative subjectivity and objectivity, 104, 263; self-consciousness, 105, 263; effect conceived, 106, 263; con-

sciousness of principle of causation, 107, 215; motive, 107, 264; contingency, 115, 250, 264; influence of contingency cognized, 116, 264; desire to effectuate, 116, 264; freedom, 116; intention, 116; will, 117, 260, 264; personality, 119, 263; in finite causation, instrumentalities, 265.
Causation, primordial, recession of, 27, 131, 243-245; always believed real, 245.
Cause, denial of reality of, 93; but one species of, 96; arbitrarily assumed, 148; not attainable by science, 131, 241.
Cause, potential, 95; material, 97; formal, 97; negative, 97; exemplary, 97; modal, 97; physical, 120, 134, 240-241, 249.
Cause physical or secondary not real cause, 98; discriminated from efficient, 121, 247; when idea of, arises, 244; assumed as efficient in scientific language, 247.
Cause, primary, faith in, never abandoned, 245.
Causes of skepticism, 179-184.
Causes, true, recognized in environment by Tyndall, 235.
Celsus, 68.
Centrifugal force in organization, 165.
Centripetal force in organization, 165.
Cesalpinus, 79.
Chadbourne, P., 158.
Chaldean deluge, 365.
Challis, Professor, 315.
Chalmerian hypothesis, 363.
Chalmers, 158, 316.
Chance not causal, 101, 242; what it means, 101, 102, 242-243.
Chaos as first principle, 56.
Chevron bones, 183.
Chinese psychic history, 48; religions, 187; traditions of deluge, 366.
Christ, signifies a culminating religious phase, 69; viewed as a martyr, 214.
Christian defense, proper spirit of, 267.

Christian psychic history, 66.
"Christianity and Greek Philosophy," purpose of, 268; style of, 290.
Christianity, made sponsor for false theories, 183; one of the ethnic religions, 185, 383; to ally itself with all truth, 267; concerned in the discovery of all truth, 268; grounded in human nature, 280.
Cicero, 66, 92, 108, 158, 284, 293.
Clark, H. James, 158, 253.
Clark, Samuel, 158.
Clarke, James Freeman, 292.
Cleanthes, 64, 213, 272.
Clement of Alexandria, 72, 91; on the Sacred Canon, 47; on causes, 98; an evolutionist, 143; on inspiration of Greek philosophy, 202; on relations of faith and knowledge, 266; on office of Greek philosophy, 280; on the shallow-minded, 304; on the necessity of knowledge to sustain faith, 311.
Clerk-Maxwell, 234.
Cloister schools, 74.
Cocker, B. F., 109, 118, 134; "Christianity and Greek Philosophy," by, 266; "Theistic Conception of the World," by, 304.
Cohesive attraction, 261-262.
Coleridge, 94, 138.
Columbus, 79, 216.
Comprehensive types in Eocene, 172.
Comte, 89, 137, 143, 208, 276, 293, 315.
Comtean theory of religion, 270.
Condillac, 81.
Condition, in causality, 115, 250; in secondary causality, 139, 250; subjective and objective, 140; organic, 140; permissive, 146; danger of confounding with cause, 250.
Condition, objective, mistaken for efficiency, 145.
Condition, subjective, mistaken for objective, and then for efficiency, 140; mistaken for efficiency, 142.
Conditioned existence, 197.
Condorcet, 82.
Conflict between religious and intellectual faculties, 18, 31, 34, 77, 208.

INDEX.   389

Conflict, law of, 18, 34; how it arises, 26, 211; what it really is, 33, 215, 218, 233; why permitted to exist, 33; with human passions, 35; in individual mind, 312.
Conflicts historically sketched, 46.
Conflicts of faith, 207.
Confucianism, 187.
Confucius, 49, 187.
Conglomeration of planets, 377.
Congruity, a law of secondary causation, 138; enunciated by Coleridge, 138; opposed to doctrine of organized experiences, 148; opposed to abiogenesis, 148.
Conscience, defined and discriminated, 23, 327; defined by Dr. Cocker, 326; not a cognitive faculty, 23; a constituent of the religious nature, 25.
Consciousness of self implied in causality, 105; of causal relation implied, 107; veracity of, 136.
Consensus gentium, 66, 92, 105.
Conservation of force, 181.
Conservatism of religious faith, 29; an indirect cause of skepticism, 179.
Constants of religious systems, 37, 187.
Contenson, Vincentius, 357.
Continents uplifted, 360.
Continuity of motion, 260.
Contradiction between reason and faith, 80.
Contrivance. (*See* Correlation.)
Conviction, grounds of, 306.
Cooke, Josiah, 158.
Cooling of the earth, 375; of the sun, 376.
Cope, E. D., on fossil vertebrates, 171.
Copernicus, 79, 234.
Correlation implies intelligence, 112, 150–153.
Correlations, mechanical and modal, 153; mechanical, 153; modal, 154; conspicuous in nature, 154, 260; modal may be viewed as teleological, 155; imply intelligence, 260.
Cosmical history, 174–177.
Cosmogony, Biblical, 222, 320; proëmium in, 320–322, 361.

Cosmological argument, 279; formulated, 285; equivalences of, 279–299.
Council of Nice, 72, 73; of Soissons, 75.
Cousin, 94, 270.
Cowardice of believers, 182.
Coxcox, 366.
Cranium viewed homologically, 162.
Creation of the world, 220; Biblical idea of, 358.
Creations, occasional and perpetual, 166.
Creeds, effete constituents of, 30, 31, 216; made to embrace non-essentials, 212, 220; purified by conflict, 37, 228.
Creodonta, 172.
Critias, 60, 90.
Cudworth, 109, 272, 314, 323.
Curry, Daniel, 289.
Cusanus, 79, 91.
Cushite religion, 185.
Cuvier, Georges, 109, 137, 140, 159, 363.
Cycles in the fortunes of religion, 35, 213–221.
Cycles, psychic. (*See* Intellectual Phases; Religious Phases.)
Cyclical movements of faith and intellect, 42, 212.
Cynic school, 61.
Cyprian, 73.
Cyrenaic school, 61, 62.
Cyrus the Persian, 53.

D'ALEMBERT, 82, 218, 312.
Damascenus, 73.
Damascius, last teacher at Athens, 70.
Dana, J. D., 277, 363.
Dante, 79.
Darius, 53.
Darwin, Charles, 110, 140, 144, 172, 208, 235, 236, 292.
Darwinism opposed by certain facts, 141, 142; violates principle of congruity, 145; accepted by Tyndall, 235; to be accepted with qualifications, 166, 253–254, etc. (*See* Derivation.)
Darwinists mistaking heredity for cause, 146.

Dawson, J. W., 140, 277.
Days of Genesis, 320–322, 356–357, 359–362.
Deduction the special logic of philosophy, 134; but legitimate in science, 134, 248; examples of use of, 135; employed by Tyndall, 136.
Deductions from the theistic proposition, 199.
Deductive theistic conclusion, 92, 117, 274.
Deductive theistic belief, 191, 274.
Deism, 324.
Deluge of Noah, 223, 363–368; not universal, 367.
Deluges, post-glacial, 364; in China, 365; in Chaldea, 365; Greece, 366; other regions, 366–367.
Democritus, 59, 233.
Demon of Socrates, 319.
Demonstration of being of God. (*See* Deduction, God, Religion.)
De Morgan, 243.
Denis the Carthusian, 357.
Derivative Theory, philosophical implications of, 166; considerations favorable to, 170–172, 253–254; theism of, 174, 224; depending on the whole range of evidence, 253–254. (*See* Evolution and Darwinism.)
Descartes, 74, 80, 94, 99, 166, 218, 234, 266, 275, 273, 363.
Desert of Sahara, 364.
Designs in nature, use of multiplied instances of, 152; writers illustrating, 158; ignored by Lucretius, 233; illustrations of, 333–342. (*See* Final Cause; and Teleology.)
Desire implied in causality, 116.
Deucalion, deluge of, 366.
Dharma-Pitaka, 54.
D'Holbach, 82, 218, 312.
Diastema, 171.
Diderot, 82, 218.
Dinosaurians, 171.
Diodorus Cronus, 61.
Diogenes of Sinope, 61.
Discernment, of correlating forces, 142; in organization, 166.
Dissipation of energy, 124.

Divinity regarded as of human origin, 60.
Divorce of thought from faith, 83.
Dogmas, unscientific, 216.
Dogmatic theologians, 277.
Döllinger, 183.
Domesticated animals and plants, 371.
Dordrecht, Synod of, 80.
Draper, J. W., 29, 34, 66, 131, 132, 244.
Dualism inevitable, 105.
Dubois-Reymond, 257, 258.
Duns Scotus, 76.
Duty, religious, rationally deduced, 205.
Dynamic theory of matter, 128–129; implies a modified pantheism, 130; consequences, if admitted, 133.
Dynamism, unconscious, opposed by idea of causality, 105.

ECCLESIASTICISM in the ascendant, 74, 76.
Eckart, 78, 91.
Eclecticism, 66.
Eclectic Platonists, 68.
Ecphantus, 57.
Effect, conception of, implied in causality, 106.
Efficiency in secondary causation, 139.
Efficient cause—how the term is used, 96; the scholastic sense, 96; not known in science, 96, 120.
Egyptian psychic history, 46.
Egyptian religion, 185, 353.
Eleatics, 57–58, 283.
Electricity, 261–262.
Elements of thought—phrase criticised, 235.
Embryonic development, 171.
Emotional conviction, 152.
Empedocles, 58, 91, 233, 285.
Empedotimus, 91.
Encke's comet, 377.
End of physical order, 123, 127.
Endogenous origin of idea of causality, 94, 95.
Environment, and organic correlations, 140; viewed as impressing organism, 140; contrary view,

141; not efficient, 141; sometimes an objective condition, 146; no explanation of persistent plan, 168; regarded efficient by Tyndall, 235.
Eocene animals, 168–172.
Eohippus, 135, 170.
Eozoic age, 361.
Epictetus, 64, 287.
Epicureanism, 280.
Epicurus, 64, 233.
Epimenides, 91.
Epicycles in psychic history, 45; in Brahmanic thought, 52; in the Socratic school, 61; in the scholastic period, 75.
Equilibrium, tendency to, in nature, 122.
Equine animals, 166–170, 254.
Equivalence of forces, 261–262.
Equus, 169.
Erigena, 75, 76.
Essenes, 67.
Eternity discussed, 315.
Eternity of matter, 63; of universe, 276.
Eth, a Hebrew particle, 358, 362.
Ether, disturbing influence of, 377.
Ethical argument, 198, 284, 299.
Ethical influence of Greek philosophy, 286.
Ethnic religions, 353; common facts of, 21, 187; respect due to, 205.
Euclid, 61.
Eudemus, 63.
Euhemerus, 62, 82.
Evangelical efforts, 304–305.
Evening and morning in Genesis, 322.
Evolution a method of nature, 142; a subjective condition, not a cause, 143; implies a real cause, 144; a system of correlations, 154; the method of methods, 154; a demonstration of mind, 155; only a method, 155; ideal and material, 170.
Evolution philosophy in Greece, 58.
Evolutionist school, 232.
Exemplary cause, 97.
Ex nihilo nihil fit nót a necessary datum, 60.
Exogenous origin, idea of cause, 94.

Experience not the origin of idea of causality, 95.
Experiences accumulated, 235.
External world deniable, 237, 240; rationally admitted, 240; exists as it seems, 240.
Extinctions of animals, 370.

Faith and intellect in reciprocal action, 42.
Faith in God, origin of, 89.
Faith, religious, afflictions of, 27; conservatism of, 29, 32, 220; sometimes defrauded by science, 29; hallows all its objects, 28, 220; should not embrace scientific opinions, 30, 220; fidelity of, 27, 220; rash stakes of, 30; indestructibility of, 31; aggressiveness of, 33.
False reasoning in science, 139, 140.
Farrar, A. S., 36, 76, 287.
Fathers, force of dicta of, 75; Neo-Platonistic, 91.
Faunas of continents graduated, 371.
Faustus, 73.
Favorinus, 69.
Fetichism, 37, 273.
Fichte, I. H., 141.
Fichte, J. G., 195.
Figuier, 272.
Fijian traditions of deluge, 366.
Final cause, 96; implied in causal relation, 108; in Old Testament, 108; held by Socrates, Aristotle, Stoics, Cicero, Lactantius, Galen, 108; by Gregory of Nyssa, Cudworth, and many others, 109; by Huxley and Hartmann, 110; by Owen and others, 111, 158; illustrations of, 337–342; mistaken for efficient cause, 142.
Final cause, opposition to, 110, 111, 235, 283; treated with levity, 113; opposition to, based on an assumption, 151; question of, philosophical, not scientific, 115.
Finiteness of physical order, 123, 127, 319, 373–379.
Fire as first principle, 56.
Fire-mist and its evolutions, 74–176, 359.
First cause only cause, 99.

Fish as expression of vertebrate idea, 164.
Fiske, John, 314.
Fontenelle, 81.
Force, reduced to will, 118, 127, 260; viewed as delegated, 122, 125; viewed as inherent, 122, 256, 322; tending to equilibrium, 123; inherent, is unthinkable, 124; viewed as acting across space, 125; viewed as transmitted through matter, 126; instantaneously renewed, 126; viewed as identical with divine will, 127, 260-261; implies substance, 129, 260; conceivable relations of, to matter tabulated, 130; not known to science, 256; viewed as exerted by matter, 256-257; viewed as external to matter, 257-259; viewed as initially applied, 258-259; not a mode of motion, 259; viewed as first principle, 314; viewed as a phenomenon of the Unknowable, 323.
Forces, not all mutually convertible, 261-262; polar and non-polar, 261; vital, 262; classification of, 262; molar, 333.
Foreknowledge, divine, unqualified, 107.
Formal cause, 97, 106.
Freedom implied in causality, 116, 328.
French philosophy, 81.
Fu-hi, 48.
Future life and rewards, 22.

GALEN, 68, 293.
Galileo, 80, 109, 137, 151, 158, 181, 213, 216.
Gassendi, 79, 137, 234.
Gastrula stage, 171.
Gathas, 52.
Genealogy, of ships, 173; steam-engines, clocks, etc., 173; Gothic dome, conic sections, crystalline forms, 173.
Genesis and science, 222, 356–363.
Genetic relation of equine animals, 170.
Gennadius, 73.

Geology and Genesis, 222, 320–322, 356–363.
Ghici, 357.
Glaciers, 370.
Glanville, 94.
Gnomic poets, 287.
Gnostics, 71, 215.
God, a fact of the ethnic religions, 21; conceptions of, 37-38; acknowledged by Darius, 53; sought in Greek philosophy, 56–58, 280–288; origin of faith in, 89; viewed as a monad, 121; not attained by natural science, 131; grounds of faith in, 150; revealed in organic life, 166; knowable by natural reason, 266; idea of, universal, 274, 282; idea of, complex, 274; demanded by the universe, 275; cognoscibility of, denied, 276; attributes of, illustrated in nature, 333-351; unity of, 347-351; name of, on every heart, 354. (*See* Religion; Religious nature.)
God in the world, 304.
Gods of Greek mythology, 131; obstructed science, 232; discarded by science and philosophy, 244; origin of, 282.
Goethe, 157, 176.
Goette, 114.
Gorgias, 60.
Gran Chacos, 189, 353.
Gravitation, acting across space, 125; Newton's view of, 125; questions concerning, 134; not an original force, 335.
Gray, Asa, 111.
Greek, philosophy, 57; psychic history, 55; language, spread of, 281; mythology, 186, 353; traditions of deluges, 366.
Gregory of Nazianzen, 73.
Gregory of Nyssa, 73, 109.
Grotius, 284.
Grove, W. R., 119, 315.
Gyżicki, 109, 110.

HABITATS of animals, 159–160.
Haeckel, E., 111, 113, 135, 137, 171, 231.
Hæmal arches, 162.

Hamilton, Sir William, 94, 137, 196, 217, 239, 276, 295, 301.
Hand illustrating design, 338.
Hartley, 81.
Hartmann, E. Von, 109, 110, 111, 173.
Harvey, 323.
Hasty generalizations, 181.
Heat, 261-262.
Heavens in Genesis, 358.
Hebrew literature in Alexandria, 67.
Hedonism, 61.
Hegel, 107, 293.
Hegelian, theory of religion, 270; paradoxes, 270.
Hegelianism before Hegel, 279.
Hellenism blended with Christianity, 71; one of the ethnic religions, 186.
Helmholtz, H. L. F., 111, 257, 277.
Helvetius, 82.
Heraclides of Pontus, 62.
Heraclitus, 56, 121, 279.
Herbart, 109.
Herbert, 218.
Herder, 293.
Heredity, a mode of intelligence, 144; an instrument, not a cause, 146; does not account for homologies, 157, 165; perpetuates identity, 165; transmits, but does not augment, 256.
Heresies in early Christianity, 72; crushed by decrees, 73; among later Christians, 183.
Heresism, 83.
Hermias, 72.
Herschel, Sir John, 118, 315.
Herschel, Sir William, 277, 358.
Hesiod, 56, 58, 187, 286.
Hewn-stone Age, 190.
Hicetas, 57.
Hilarius, 73.
Hildegard, St., 357.
Hindoo traditions of deluge, 366.
Hipparion, 169, 171.
Hippias, 60.
His, 114.
Hobbes, 80, 89, 109, 218.
Holbach, Von, 82, 218, 312.
Homer, 55, 58, 87, 286.
Homeric Age, 282, 288.
Homœomeriæ, 58.

Homological argument, 198; critically viewed, 296.
Homology, 155, 156; opposed by theologians, 156; harmonious with theology, 156; opposed by certain anatomists, 157; writers on, 158; in vertebrate structures, 161-165; in cranium, 162; in *os coccygis*, 163; in limbs, 166-170, 340; in world-life, 174-177; exemplified in the world, 260.
Horse, serial types of, 166-170, 254.
Hottentots, ethical perceptions of, 24.
Huggins, W., 277.
Humboldt, A., 375.
Hume, 82, 94, 218, 275, 276.
Humphreys and Abbot, 181.
Hunt, T. S., 275.
Hunter, 323.
Huxley, T. H., 90, 110, 141, 144, 171, 235, 258, 270, 322.
Hwang-ho, overflows of, 365-369.
Hyacinthe, Father, 183.
Hybridity, 172.
Hylozoism, 56, 121, 324.
Hypatia, 70.

Ice-wells, 370.
Ideas, necessary, 297.
Ideas of Plato, 62.
Ideological argument, 286; equivalences of, 299.
Immanence, divine, 59; held by Theophrastus, 63; by the Stoics, 64.
Immanent relation of God to the world, 107, 127, 258, 324; objections to, grounded in mental impotence, 128; does not conflict with doctrine of law, 132.
Immensity discussed, 315.
Impotency of reason, 300.
Incarnations, ethnic beliefs in, 22.
Incrusted condition of a world, 176.
Index Librorum Prohibitorum, 80.
Indian psychic history, 51.
Indo-European race, 45.
Induction, the logic of science, 134; uses *à priori* data, 135; exaggerated estimate of, 135; progress of, 234.
Inductive logic, 64.

Infinite series no substitute for cause, 99.
Infinity, notion of, 197.
Inherent force, 122; consequences of, 123; unthinkable, 124.
Inheritance a mode of intelligence, 144; law of, 165. (*See* also Heredity.)
Innate origin of idea of causality, 94.
Innate sentiments, significance of, 20.
Inquisition, 80.
Inspiration, Jewish and Christian, 91.
Instrument mistaken for cause, 146.
Instrumentality employed in human causation, 265.
Intellect, office of, 33; finds response in the world, 346; may serve religion, 39, 210–211.
Intellectual phases, 44; in Egypt, 46–48; in China, 48; in India, 51; among the Jews, 55; in Greece, 55, 278–280; in Christian history, 66; existing, 83.
Intelligence, revealed in nature, 111, 112, 150, 332, 355; implied in intelligible correlations, 151, 338.
Intention implied in causality, 116.
Intentionality, doctrine of, 150; implied in causality, 264; revealed in nature, 117, 150, 337; intuition of, valid, 151, 152.
Interactions of the religious and intellectual faculties, 15, 32, 88, 215–220; laws of, 42; beneficent, 36.
Intuition, of causality, 93, 197; of substance, 196; of intelligence, 197, 338; of ethicality, 198, 355.
Intuition of God, 90, 294; believers in, cited, 91, 196; credulous believers in, 92.
Intuitional eye, 309.
Intuitions, defined, 191; necessity of, 192; authority of, 21, 193, 304, 354; analogous to instincts, 194.
Ionic school, 56, 278.
Irenæus, 72.
Irreligion, consequences of, 34.
Isaiah, 280.
Islam, a bifurcation of Christianity, 46; the third Semitic religion, 186; spread of, 186.
Italian school, 278.

JACOBI, 91, 196, 270, 295.
Jamblichus, 70, 91.
Jameson, 363.
Jevons, W. S., 96, 135.
Jewish religion, 185, 353.
Jews in Egypt, 48, 67.
John, St., 280.
Jones, H. Bence, 322.
Jupiter in its stormy stage, 176.
Justin Martyr, 289.
Justinian closes Athenian schools, 70, 215.
Justinus Flavius, 71.

KAFFIRS, 229.
Kant, 94, 109, 110, 115, 192, 218, 233, 234, 276, 285, 295; on theistic arguments, 260, 296; his criticism of theistic proofs examined, 299–302.
Kapila, 52.
Kepler, 79, 158.
Khedive of Egypt, 46, 48.
Kneph, 352.
Krönig, 109.

LACTANTIUS, 72, 108, 157, 178, 202, 289.
Lange, 321.
Lanoye, De, on Nile deposits, 181.
Lao-tse, 49, 187, 353.
Lamarck, 140.
Land first formed, 360.
Laplace, 115, 142, 176.
Lateran Council, 75, 76.
Law the tyrant of men, 60.
Law, does not imply capricious intelligence, 132, 259; not efficient, 133, 249; implies intelligent will, 133; a self-imposed mode of activity, 133, 139; not necessary absolutely, 139; definition of, 249, 256; itself an effect, 249.
Laycock, 315, 320, 323.
Learning, light of, reflected reciprocally, 48.
Lectonia, 364, 369.
Leibnitz, 74, 81, 94, 102, 121, 137, 142, 218, 266, 279, 293.
Leibnitzian argument, 299, 302.
Leidy on fossil vertebrates, 168, 171.
Lemuroid stage, 171.

Lessing, 81.
Leucippus, 59, 221, 234.
Lewis, Tayler, 363.
Liberty, idea of, 297-298.
Life, origin of, 224, 235, 236; in monads, 102, 126; in atoms, 236; an insoluble mystery, 237.
Light, distances passed over by, 336; demonstrating unity of creation, 349.
Links, missing, recovered, 168-172.
Liturgical tendencies. (*See* Ritualism.)
Locke, 74, 81, 109, 191.
Lockyer, J. N., 277.
Longinus, 70.
Love and hate, 58.
Lubbock, Sir John, 89, 208, 292.
Lucan, 64.
Luc, De, 363.
Lucretius, 65, 233, 236.
Lusitanus, 357.
Luther, Martin, 74, 76, 77, 217.
Lyell, Sir Charles, 111, 181.

MACCABEES, 67.
Macchiavelli, 80.
Macedo, 357.
"Made," in Gen. i., 16, 359.
Magianism, 38, 91.
Magnetism, 261-262.
Magus, Simon, 71.
Mahan, Asa, 275, 314, 316.
Maillet, De, 140.
Maine de Biran, 94.
Mammals, variations among, 254; reign of, 361.
Man, preparations for, 344-345; in the light of geology, 368-373; belongs to the last fauna, 368; advent of, recent, 369; birthplace of, 370; the last term, 372.
Manetho, 46.
Mansel, 217, 239, 295.
Mantras of the Rig-Veda Sanhitâ, 51.
Marcus Aurelius, 64.
Mariette, Bey, 46.
Marine animals, period of, 360.
Mars in its habitable stage, 176.
Marsh, G. P., 269.
Marsh, O. C., 135, 170, 171; on equine quadrupeds, 168, 170.

Marsupial stage, 171.
Martineau, James, 270, 316.
Material cause, 97.
Materialism of the Stoics, 64; Epicurus, 65; Tertullian, 72; Hilarius and others, 73; Gassendi, 79; Bruno, 80; Rousseau, 81; Mettrie, de la, 81; Condillac, 81; D'Holbach, 82; Democritus, 233; Tyndall, 236-239. (*See* Atomism; Atomists.)
Materialism, more imaginary than real, 226; limited by Tyndall, 238; unconscious, opposed by idea of causality, 105.
Mathematical truths, 302.
Matter and force, table of conceivable relations of, 130.
Matter, created, 99, 315-319; dead, the kind here considered, 125, 149; conscious, necessitates atheism, 122; theistically held eternal, 102; conceived as animated, 121, 236, 257; not voluntary, 121, 257; viewed as adynamic, 122, 126-127, 324; as the seat of inherent force, 122, 257-258; as the vehicle transmitting primordial force, 126; as a phenomenon of force, 128; as possessed of the potency of life, 236; as first principle, 314; as constituted of atoms, 324; identical in different worlds, 349-350.
Maudsley, 225.
Maupertius, 81.
Maximus, 68.
Mbenga, 366.
M'Causland, Dr., 222, 223, 363.
M'Cosh, James, 109, 158, 243, 289, 293, 314.
Mechanical correlations, 153.
Mechanism implies intelligence, 112.
Medusæ, embryonic stages of, 253.
Megaric school, 61.
Melanchthon, 77.
Melissus of Samos, 58.
Melito, 71.
Mental latency, 145.
Mesohippus, 169.
Mesozoic age, 361.
Methodius, 73.
Mettrie, De la, 81.

Meunier, Stanislas, 277.
Mexican traditions of deluge, 366.
Michaelis, 114.
Middle Academy, 63.
Migrations of man, 371.
Mill, J. S., 94, 96, 120, 138, 191, 243, 270, 276, 277, 320.
Miller Hugh, 363.
Miltiades, 71.
Mimansa, 51.
Mind influenced by physical surroundings, 269.
Miohippus, 168–169.
Missing links recovered, 167–172; effect of non-recovery of, 173.
Mississippi delta, 181.
Mitchel, O. M., 158.
Mivart, St. George, 357.
Modal correlations, 153.
Modes of motion, 259–262.
Moffat, J. C., 292.
Mohammedans, 78.
Mojaves, 22.
Molecular groupings, 238.
Mollusks, 159; variations among, 254.
Monads of Leibnitz, 102, 121.
Monism, 105; favored by Tyndall, 233–238; said to be spreading, 239.
Monotheism, among the Greeks, 58, 61, 62, 63, 64; of Apollonius of Tyana, 68; of Athenagoras, 71; favorable to science, 234, 246; the primitive religion of humanity, 273, 352.
Monotreme stage of embryo, 171.
Montaigne, 80.
Montesquieu, 81, 159.
Moody, methods of, 304.
Moon, condition of, 176.
Moral argument, 279.
Moral excellence, ideal of, in Greece, 287.
Moral government, 326.
Moral judgments, 24, 25.
Morality, standards of, 24.
Moreau, Charles, 357.
Morphological conceptions, 176.
Morris, G. S., 109, 247.
Morula stage of embryo, 171.
Moses, 280.

Motion an effect, not a force, 256.
Motive implied in causality, 107.
Müller, Max, 273, 292.
Murphy, 315, 323.
Mutius Scævola, 90.
Mystics, German, 78, 91.
Mythology, Greek, 186, 273, 353; blended with Christianity, 71, 215.

NATURALISM, of Strato, 64; of Epicurus, 64.
Natural selection a mode of intelligence, 144; suggested by Empedocles, 233.
Navajoes' expectation of a redeemer, 289.
Neander, 71.
Nebular cosmogony foreshadowed, 59; by Democritus, 233; by Lucretius, 233.
Nebular history of the world, 174–177, 350.
Nebular theory, attitude of Church toward, 180; defenders of, 277.
Necessary being, 300.
Necessary ideas, 26, 297; relative and absolute, 300.
Necessity of some religion, 184, 352.
Negative cause, 97.
Neo-Platonism, 62, 69, 91.
Neo-Pythagoreanism, 68, 91.
Nescience opposing teleology, 151.
Nescience school, 239.
Neural arches, 162.
Newcomb, S., 277.
Newman, J. P., 289.
Newton, Sir Isaac, 75, 80, 109, 137, 158, 266.
Newtonian argument, 299.
Nice, First Council of, 72, 73.
Nichol, J. P., 277.
Nigridius, 68.
Nihilism, of Gorgias, 60; of Fichte, 195.
Nile deposits, 181.
Nitzsch, 91.
Noachian deluge, 223.
Non-essentials in the creed, 220.
Non-essentials made essential, a cause of skepticism, 183, 221.
Noris, Cardinal, 357.
Norm of faith and intellect, 42, 43.

Norse religion, 353.
Numbers in Pythagoreanism, 56.
Numenius, 68, 73.

OBJECTIVITY, implied in causation, 104; phenomena of, 297.
Objective datum in creative causality, 104.
Occam, William of, 76.
Ogyges, deluge of, 366.
Oken, 176.
Ontological argument, 279; formulated, 268; critically examined, 297; equivalences of, 299.
Ontological intuition, 260; neglected by Kant, 260.
Ophites, 71.
Opinion, tyranny of unreasoning faith over, 32.
Opinions falsely attributed to scientists, 182.
Orbits of faith and intellect, 45.
Order a product of mind, 133.
Organism the seat of all transforming agency, 142, 251; not modified causally by environment, 141, 251.
Organized experiences, 148.
Organs in anticipation of use, 142.
Oriental birthplace of man, 370.
Origen the Christian, 70, 72, 178, 289.
Origen the Platonist, 70.
Origin of species, 224; of life, 224.
Orohippus, 168-169, 170.
Orpheus, 283.
Orphic Hymns, 56.
Oscillations. (*See* Cycles.)
Os coccygis, 163.
Owen, Richard, 111, 157, 158, 170, 322.

PACKARD, A. S., 171, 253.
Palæotherium, 171.
Palæozoic Age, 361.
Paley, 151, 157, 275, 301, 314.
Pantheism, of Melissus, 58; of Speusippus, 62; implied in dynamism, 130; results from monism, 324.
Parker, Samuel, 109.
Parkinson, 363.
Paris, Synod of, 76; University of, 76, 80.

Parmenides of Elea, 58, 279.
Parseeism, 53, 91, 186, 215.
Passions prompting to tyranny, 36.
Patangali, 52.
Patristic intellectual phase, 71.
Paul, St., 280.
Perates, 71.
Peripatetic argument, 299.
Peripatetics, 63.
Persecutions for opinion's sake, 183, 213.
Persian religion, 52.
Persistence of force, 260.
Personality implied in causation, 119; not destroyed by a form of pantheism, 130; not the alternative of divine immanence, 119.
Peruvian religion, 185, 353.
Petrarch, 79.
Phædrus, 65.
Phases, religious and intellectual, 44; seldom quite consecutive, 46; in Egypt, 46-48; in China, 48; in India, 51; among the Hebrews, 55; in Greece, 55.
Phenomena the data of science, 134.
Pherecydes, 56.
Philolaus, 57.
Philo of Larissa, 66.
Philo the Jew, 68, 91, 363.
Philoponus, 73.
Philosophy, denounced by Tertullian, 72; divorced from faith, 74; opposed by Luther, 76, 217; logic of, 134; inseparable from science, 135, 248; needs the data of science, 137; regarded by Lactantius as inspired, 202; made to serve theology, 216; correcting science, 229; used by Tyndall, 236, 241; province of, 240; relation of, to theology, 240, 241; positive, 248; religious, 266, 269-271; of the unconditioned, 277; founded on primitive beliefs, 303.
Philosophy, French, 81.
Philosophy, Greek, 56; groping for a sensible God, 57; essentially religious, 20; regarded by Clement as inspired, 202; seeking for ultimate cause, 213, 280; reached idea of atoms and molecules, 233, 236;

sketch of, 278–280; theological results of, 280–288; shone upon by the true light, 280; propædeutic to Christianity, 281–288; service of, to Christianity, 281–288; theistic arguments of, formulated, 284–286; moral ideas developed by, 286–287; ideal of moral excellence not attained by, 287; religious sentiments nurtured by, 287; intercessor suggested by, 288.
Phœnician religion, 353; deluge, 366.
Phormion, 91.
Phrygian traditions of deluge, 366.
Phylogeny, 176.
Physical cause. (*See* Cause.)
Physical influences on mind, 269.
Physico-theological argument, 279, 285.
Pictet, Adolf, 293.
Planets, unity exemplified by, 347–348.
Plans, conspicuous in nature, 154; fundamental, in animal structures, 159.
Plant-growth, period of, 360.
Planula stage of embryo, 171.
Plastic nature, 323.
Plato, 62, 91, 92, 97, 156, 158, 213, 233, 276, 279, 280, 283, 285, 286, 287, 288.
Platonic argument, 299.
Pliohippus, 169.
Plotinus, 70, 91.
Plutarch of Athens, 70.
Plutarch of Cheronæa, 68, 143, 158.
Polar forces, 261–262.
Polished-stone Age, 190.
Polycrates, 91.
Polytheism, of Athenians, 272; origin of, 282; undermined, 283; dominated by monotheism, 352; of Egyptians, 352.
Pomponatius, 74, 76, 217.
Porphyry, 70.
Positivism involves transcendental ideas, 275.
Post-Socratic schools, 280.
Pouchet, F. A., 224.
Powell, Baden, 322.
Power manifested in nature, 333.
Prairie regions, 364, 369.

Prayer, a fact of ethnic religions, 22; rationality of, 325, 383.
Pre-established harmony, 121.
Prehistoric religion, 20, 190.
Prescott, 289.
Pre-Socratic schools, 278.
Priesthood in ethnic religions, 22.
Priestley, 81.
Primitive beliefs, 191–196; influence of, 194; analogous to instincts, 184; validity of, 209; involved in every theistic argument, 293–303; authority of, 303; strength of, 307.
Primordial causality, 99, 100.
Principle, first, of all things, 314.
Printing, discovery of, 79.
Procatarctic cause, 98.
Proclus, 70.
Prodicus, 60.
Progress through antagonism, 34.
Progressiveness of science, 29, 32.
"Prometheus Unbound," 288.
Propædeutic office of Greek philosophy, 281–288.
Protagoras, 60, 213, 286.
Protohippus, 169.
Psychic cycles, 44.
Psychic history, of Egypt, 46; China, 48; India and Persia, 51; Hebrews, 55; Greeks, 55; under Christianity, 66.
Psychic teleology, 156.
Ptolemy Euergetes, 67.
Ptolemy Philadelphus, 65, 67.
Pueblos' expectation of redeemer, 22, 289.
Pyrrho of Elis, 65, 90, 221, 309.
Pyrrhonism, 280.
Pythagoras, 56, 97, 285.
Pythagorean school, 56, 91.

QUADRATUS, 71.
Quatrefages, 172, 284, 292.

RACE, human, antiquity of, 222; unity of, 223.
Radiates, 159.
Rahab, 280.
Rash generalizations a cause of skepticism, 181.
Rationalistic religion, 218.
Realists among the Schoolmen, 94.

Reason the sole criterion of truth,179.
Reconciliation of science and religion, 206.
Redeemer, ethnic beliefs in, 22, 288–289.
Red stars, 175.
Reformation, how effected, 43.
Regressus in infinitum, 99.
Reid, 94.
Relativity of truth, 60.
Religion, unchanging, 39; suppositions as to origin of, 60, 270–271; some form of, inevitable, 184; philosophy of, 269–271; definitions of, 271, 327–328; in school, 227–228; without intelligence, 88, 211.
Religious beliefs, universality of, 19, 184–187, 208, 351–356.
Religious constants and variables, 37; constants, 187, 353.
Religious conviction, grounds of, 306–312.
Religious faiths, common facts of, 21, 187, 353.
Religious feelings, great influence of, 26, 308; recognized by Tyndall, 237; variations in intensity of, 308; nurtured by Greek philosophy, 287; by all philosophy, 354.
Religious nature, innate, 19; evidences, 19; contrasted with cognition, 22, 210; defined and explained, 23, 27, 210–211; existing in savages, 188–189, 229, 292, 353; of prehistoric tribes, 190; universal, 190; rights of, vindicated, 227, 238.
Religious phases. (*See* Phases.)
Religious predisposition wanting in some, 310; influences felt by them, 310–311.
Religious progress of mankind, 37.
Religious system, early crudity of, 37; improved by conflict, 36, 37.
Religious teacher, responsibility of, 310.
Religious veneration, origin of, 60, 62, 270.
Renaissance, 83.
Reptile a stage in evolution of skeleton, 164.
Repulsion, force of, 261–262.

Response of world to intellect, 346.
Reticence of scientists, 248.
Revelation, antecedently probable, 201, 382; made to more than one race, 201; tinctured by human medium of transmission, 202, 203; must embrace mysteries, 203, 383–384; theistic argument from, 294; not the origin of idea of God, 90, 203, 271, 294.
Right and wrong, intuition of, 355. (*See* Conscience.)
Rights of religious nature, 238.
Rig-Veda, 51.
Rings in world-making, 175.
Ritter, 293.
Ritschl, 71.
Ritualism, tendency to, 50, 51, 52.
Robebacher, 371.
Robinet, 82.
Rocks, strained by pressure, 334; earliest sedimentary, 359.
Roman Church, services of, to learning, 87, 89.
"Roots of things," 58.
Roscellinus, 75.
Rotation of earth taught by Heraclides, 63.
Rousseau, J. J., 81, 218, 312.

SABBATH, 361, 363.
Saccas, Ammonius, 70.
Sacred Canon of Egypt, 47.
Sacred writings of the Egyptians, 47; Chinese, 48–49.
Sacrum, 163.
Sœmann, 277.
Sahara, desert of, 364.
Saisset, 275.
Sankya, 52.
Savages reputed destitute of religion, 188.
Savages, religious nature of, 188–189, 229–230.
Semitic religions, 185–186.
Sensationalism opposed, 192.
Sens, Synod of, 75.
Sentiment of the supernatural, 23.
Servetus, 218.
Scævola, Mutius, 90.
Scandinavian religion, 353; deluge, 366.

Scapula, 164.
Scheiner, 174.
Schellen, H., 277.
Schleiermacher, 91, 196, 270.
Schmid, Rudolf, 109, 155.
Schmidt, Oscar, 111.
Schneider, F., 129.
Scholasticism, 74, 83, 216.
Schoolmen, Neo-platonistic, 91; on the idea of causality, 94.
Science, origin of, 26, 232; harmless toward central faith, 28; hostile to unreasoning faith, 30; progressiveness of, 29, 32; new and old in conflict, 33, 216; progress of, conditioned by religion, 33; does not lead to Deity, 131; deals with phenomena, 134, 240, 246-250; inseparable from philosophy, 135; progress of, an indirect cause of skepticism, 179; interacting with religion, 213-220; recent progress of, 219; conflict of, with church councils, 233; favored by monotheism, 234; transcended by Tyndall, 236, 241; discriminated from philosophy, 240, 241; of Middle Ages, deductive, 248; now excessively "positive," 248; evidences of, irresistible, 311; implies the creation of matter, 319; harmony of, with Genesis, 356–363.
Scientific progress and religion, 33.
Scientific questions mistakenly made theological, 180, 212.
Scientists, reticence of, 248; demands of, 248.
Scotus, Duns, 75.
Scripture, answers anticipations, 203; supposed to uphold irrational faiths, 31.
Scythians, 364; traditions of deluge among, 366.
Secondary causation unreal, 98.
Secular beliefs embodied in creeds, 30, 31, 212.
"Seeds of things," 58.
Seidlitz, 111.
Seine, gravel-beds of, 365.
Semper, 114.
Seneca, 64, 287.
Sensationalism of Zeno of Elea, 58.

Sensus numinis, 189, 209, 271.
Septuagint, 67.
Sequence not implying causal relation, 95.
Serry, 357.
Servitude of thought to faith, 83.
Seven Wise Men, 286.
Sextians, 66.
Sextus Empiricus, 69.
Sexual selection a mode of intelligence, 144.
Shamanism, 38.
Shark-stage of embryo, 171.
She-king, 49.
Silliman, B., 363.
Simon Magus, 71.
Siredon lichenoides, 253.
Skepticism, causes of, 179-184; in Greek philosophy, 60, 63, 65, 69.
Skeptics, the Latin, 69; Hobbes, 80; Hume, 82.
Smith, George, 306, 365.
Socrates, 61, 91, 151-157, 183, 213-214, 233, 266, 279, 280, 283, 284, 286, 287.
Socratic schools, 279.
Soissons, Council of, 75; Synod of, 75.
Somme, gravel-beds of, 365.
Soothsaying, 91.
Sophists, 60, 65, 279.
Sorbonne, 77, 217, 227.
Soul viewed as a monad, 121.
Space and time discussed, 316-319.
Species, origin of, 224.
Spencer, 90, 94, 137, 143, 237, 239, 258, 293, 314; on organized experiences, 148, 254; on the origin of mind, 235, 255; on connection of intelligence and tactual sense, 254.
Speusippus, 62.
Spinoza, 74, 81, 138, 158, 218.
Splint-bones in horses, 170.
Spontaneous generation. (*See* Archegenesis and Abiogenesis.)
Sutras, 51.
Stages of embryo, 171; of cosmical life, 174–176.
Standards of morality, 24.
Stars in stages of progress, 175, 376; remoteness of, 336.
St. Hilaire, Geoffroy, 140.

Stoicism, 280.
Stoics, 63, 64, 108, 284.
Stonehenge, 190.
Stormy period of the world, 359.
St. Peter and final fires, 378.
Strato of Lampsacus, 63.
Strauss, 111.
Subjectivity in causality, 104.
Subjectivity, phenomena of, 297.
Substance, law of, 100; neglected by Kant, 260.
Substance of the worlds, identity of, 349–350.
Succession of organic forms. (See Derivation, Darwinism, Evolution.)
Sufficient reason, 96, 115, 279, 299.
Sun, moon, and stars revealed, 360.
Sun, remoteness of, 336
Sun-worship, 38.
Supernaturalism in national infancy, 26, 38.
Survival of the fittest, a mode of intelligence, 144; suggested by Empedocles, 233; possesses no efficiency as a law, 249–250.
Sutra-Pitaka, 54.
Synesius, 70, 73.
Synod of, Soissons, 75; Sens, 75; Paris, 76; Dordrecht, 80.
Synthesis of thought and faith, 84.
Syrian schools of Neo-Platonism, 70.
Syrian traditions of deluges, 366.
Syrophenician woman, 280.

TADPOLE acquiring lungs, 146–147.
Tæniodonta, 172.
Tao-ism or Tau-ism, 187, 353.
Tatian, 71, 72.
Taurellus, 80.
Tau-teh-king, 49.
Teleological argument, 150, 198; Kant's objections to, 260; equivalences of, 279, 299; formulated, 285; viewed critically, 296.
Teleological facts recently multiplied, 157.
Teleological idea, highest law of universe, 320.
Teleology, explained, 108; meaning of, restricted, 156; psychic, 156; unavailable without *à priori* data, 274–275.

Teleology among the Greeks, 61, 63, 64; in Old Testament, 108; modern illustrators of, 158; said to be rejected by Darwin, 235; familiar illustrations of, 338–342. (See, also, Final Cause; Design.)
Telesio, 79.
Tertullian, 72; paradoxes of, 308–309.
Tertullianism, 83.
Thales, 56, 121.
Theism, combines immanence and transcendence, 325; deductively reached, 191–199; sanctioned by modern science, 319.
Theistic arguments, in Greek philosophy, 284–286; in Kant's philosophy, 299–302.
"Theistic Conception of the World," characteristics of, 313, 328–329.
Theistic conceptions in Greek philosophy, 282–286.
Theistic faith comforting, 199.
Theodorus, 62.
Theologians in error, 304–305.
Theophrastus, 63.
Theosophy, Judaistic, 67, 215; Neo-Platonistic, 69; Gnostic, 71, 215.
Therapeutes, 68.
Thompson, Sir William, 124, 259, 277, 320.
Thoth, 47.
Thought, conditioned by brain, 226; not a product of brain, 238, 255; viewed as first principle, 314; modern, relentless, 267.
Thrasyllus, 68.
Three Gods of Numenius, 68; of Roscellinus, 75.
Time and space discussed, 316–319.
Timon a Pyrrhonist, 65.
Tomitherium (*Limnotherium*), 172.
Tonti, 357.
Totemism, 37.
Transcendence, divine, held by Aristotle, 63.
Transcendental, ideas, 298; argument, 301.
Transient relation of God to the world, 107, 258.
Trinity, doctrine of Gregory of Nyssa on, 73; of Lessing, 81.

Tripitaka, 53.
Truth, an immediate revelation of God, 40; sacredness and religious value of, 40, 88, 206; to be accepted bravely, 206; two orders of, 75, 76, 216.
Ts'in, dynasty of, 49.
Turanian religion, 185.
Tyndall, 90, 257, 258, 259, 277; on the proper sphere of religious faith, 30; on materialism, 59; on atheism, 132; using deduction, 136, 236; on the cause of evolution, 143; materialism of, not materialism, 144, 149, 236; on relation of matter to thought, 145; synopsis of Belfast address by, 231-238; materialism of, explained, 237; theory of, on inherency of force, 322.
Types fundamental, in animal structures, 150; persistence of, geographically, 161; comprehensive, in Eocene, 172.
Type, vertebrate, 161-166.
Tyranny of ecclesiastical power prompted by passions, 36.

UNCONDITIONED existence, 197.
Unconditioned, the, 217, 277.
Unconscious cerebration, 145, 255.
Unconscious mental states, 145.
Unity, of mankind, 223; of thought and faith, 83, 229.
Unity of the world, 347-351; illustrated in solar system, 347-348.
Universe, influence of contemplation of, 152, 351-352; demands a God, 275; infinite mathematically, 275; eternity of, 276.
University of Paris, 76, 80.
Unknowable, the, 217.
Unthinkable beliefs sometimes valid, 200.

VALENTINUS, 71.
Vanini, 79.
Variable stars, 175.
Variations of species, 253.
Varieties of animals, 253-254.
Varro, 69.
Vastness of the universe, 347-351.

Vedanta, 51.
Vendidad, 53.
Veneration for ancestors, 89.
Venn, John, 243.
Veracity of consciousness, 183-196.
Vertebra, 162.
Vertebrate archetype, 163.
Vertebrates, 159.
Vertebrate skeleton, 162; evolved, 164.
Vertebrate type considered, 161-166; the skeleton in, 162.
"Vestiges of Creation," 83.
Vibrations, molecular, 261-262.
Vicarious expiation in ethnic religions, 22.
Vinaya-pitaka, 54.
Vinci, Leonardo da, 79.
Virgil a Lucretian, 65.
Vispered, 52.
Vives, 79.
Vogt, Carl, 225, 292.
Voices of the universe, 356.
Volney, 82, 218.
Voltaire, 81, 109, 218.
Vorstellung, 249.
Vortices suggested by Democritus, 233.

WALLACE, A. R., 173, 315.
Water as first principle, 56.
Watson, Richard, 276.
Wearing out of land, 374-375.
Wen-ti, a Chinese monarch, 49, 50.
Whedon, D. D., 222, 328.
Whewell, William, 137, 158.
Whipple, Lieutenant, 289.
Whiston, 363.
White, A. D., on warfare of science, 77.
White stars, 175.
Wicked heart prompting to skepticism, 28, 33, 35, 179.
Wiclif, 74.
Wigand, Albert, 109, 155.
Will, implied in causality, 117; implies intelligence and sensibility, 117; the ground of all efficiency, 117; acting in gravitation, 134, 335; human, a picture of the divine, 262-263; viewed as first

principle, 314, 324; manifest throughout the universe, 347–351.
William of Occam, 76.
Wolf, 74, 81, 97.
World, viewed as a mechanism, 126, 132, 258; not self-supporting, 323.
World-life, a process of cooling, 74, 359.
Worlds, identity of substance of, 349–350.
Worship in ethnic religions, 21.
Wyman, Jeffreys, 224.

XENIADES, 60, 312.
Xenocrates, 62.

Xenophanes, 58, 65, 285.
Xenophon, 157, 213.
Xisuthrus, 365.

YASNA, 52.
Yellow stars, 175.
Yi-king, 148.
Yom, meaning of, 362–363.
Young, C. A., 277.

ZELLER, 109, 278.
Zeno of Cittium, 64, 293.
Zeno of Elea, 58, 93, 285.
Zoroaster, 91.
Zoroastrianism, 46, 52, 186, 353.

THE END.

www.ingramcontent.com/pod-product-compliance
Lightning Source LLC
Chambersburg PA
CBHW022121290426
44112CB00008B/757